LOYALTY AND LOSS

THE HISTORICAL SERIES OF THE REFORMED CHURCH IN AMERICA
NO. 77

LOYALTY AND LOSS
The Reformed Church in America, 1945–1994

Lynn Japinga

WILLIAM B. EERDMANS PUBLISHING COMPANY
Grand Rapids, Michigan / Cambridge, UK

Wm. B. Eerdmans Publishing Co.
2140 Oak Industrial Drive SE, Grand Rapids, Michigan 49503
PO Box 163, Cambridge CB3 9PU UK
www.eerdmans.com

Printed in the United States of America

Library of Congress Cataloging-in-Publication Data

Japinga, Lynn, 1960-
  Loyalty and loss : the Reformed Church in America, 1945-1994 /
Lynn Japinga.
     pages cm. -- (The historical series of the Reformed Church in
America ; no. 77)
  Includes bibliographical references and index.
  ISBN 978-0-8028-7068-1 (pbk. : alk. paper) 1. Reformed Church in
America--History--20th century. I. Title.
  BX9565.J37 2013
  285.7'3209--dc23
                    2013002921

To my parents,

Roger and Wilma (Allspach) Winkels,

Models of loyalty and grace.

The Historical Series of the Reformed Church in America

The series was inaugurated in 1968 by the General Synod of the Reformed Church in America acting through the Commission on History to communicate the church's heritage and collective memory and to reflect on our identity and mission, encouraging historical scholarship which informs both church and academy.

www.rca.org/series

Web pages for the book with photographs and other resources is available at:

www.rca.org/series/loyalty

General Editor
      Rev. Donald J. Bruggink, PhD, DD
      Western Theological Seminary
      Van Raalte Institute, Hope College

Associate Editor
      George Brown Jr., PhD
      Western Theological Seminary

Copy Editor
      Laurie Baron

Production Editor
      Russell L. Gasero

Commission on History
      James Hart Brumm, MDiv, Blooming Grove, New York
      Douglas Carlson, PhD, Northwestern College, Orange City, Iowa
      David M. Tripold, PhD, Monmouth University
      Audrey Vermilyea, Bloomington, Minnesota
      Matthew Van Maastricht, MDiv, Milwaukee, Wisconsin
      Linda Walvoord, PhD, University of Cincinnati

Contents

Foreword

"Boys, this is history!" The voice is my father's and we are standing on a battlefield at Gettysburg, on the grounds of Mt. Vernon, next to the Liberty Bell, or in the streets of old Williamsburg. While the exclamation is a bit awkward, it was uttered with the same sense of awe that he would use in the prayers before and after every family meal.

For my father, history was often a sacred place that reminded him of special people and events. But what is history? This volume from the pen and heart of Dr. Lynn Japinga encourages us to stretch our definitions of history. She does so by using not only the usual primary textual sources one would expect, but by interweaving oral history that depends on the memories of those who shared the latter half of the twentieth century. She invites us to listen not only to the minutes of the General Synod or the formal papers of theologians, but to the sometimes irascible letters to the editor of the *Church Herald*. The voices we hear come from the pews as well as the pulpits of the Reformed Church in America. Dr. Japinga wants us not only to think about the conflicts of the church but to feel the anxiety and the anger, the pride and the passion, of those who struggled to speak the truth in love.

For many people, history deals with eras beyond memory, while *this* history struggles to understand the last several decades. In so doing, it presents us with an enormous challenge. The memories of leaders and followers, of preachers and prophets, of quiet folk and those who couldn't seem to stop speaking place Dr. Japinga as well as the readers in a difficult place. If we listen to such a great diversity of voices, whose voice and interpretation of history can we trust? With the skill of a trained historian, Dr. Japinga ushers us into the presence of many leaders we remember well, or who are still with us. She ushers us into places where many of us have stood and into conflicts that some of us helped create or have tried to resolve.

We are also stretched by this history of the Reformed Church in America in the last fifty years of the twentieth century in that the author stands within the circle of conflict, rather than outside of it. This is not where we expect to find historians. We assume that they will stand above the fray, or at least outside the history that they are trying to explore. This reveals our penchant for objectivity in the historical enterprise. We assume that if one can be far enough away from the period and the people who participated in the conflicts that the history will be more objective in nature.

Dr. Japinga dares to write history that is still swirling around us and in so doing she helps define "what history" will inform and guide us. Of course every historian stands and observes from a place. There is no pure objectivity, for everyone brings to the historical enterprise one's own perspectives and values. Dr. Japinga stands inside the circle, rather than beyond it or above it. It is a dangerous place to stand! Can she balance her perspectives and prejudices, her values and visions for the church to which she, too, belongs, while acknowledging those who stand in other places and argue for different dreams concerning our shared future? In other words, can she bring a sense of fairness to the work and finally to history? The method of standing so close to the people and era one is describing presents the author and the reader with an enormous temptation for history to be used as a tract rather than a trustworthy guide to our past. At the same time, the sense of intimacy this method creates can bring insights that can never be surfaced by those who write from places outside the context. We can hear notes within the symphony that disappear with time and distance. Through empathy, we can sense feelings and perspectives that are lost to those who safely write from afar.

And so we hear my father say with awe, "This is history," and we cannot help but wonder if it is. Has our author brought the necessary skills that will walk us into a time many of us inhabited and introduce us to people some of us knew or know? Is the record finally a fair description of the historical conflicts of the latter half of the twentieth century for the Reformed Church in America?

I believe it is, and because I believe so, I am eager for many to read this remarkable record the author has entitled *Loyalty and Loss*. Of course, the stream that runs through the years described still carries us along. It is the same stream, but we are at a different place. By listening closely to the richly diverse voices of the not too distant past, Dr. Japinga has suggested how we have come to this place in our journey. While many of us may find it to be a hard or unsettling place, it should not be a surprising one, with the aid of the people who surround us in this volume. Lynn has offered insightful words, a faithful witness to the voices and values of the past, and a fair recounting of our conflicts. She is not a stranger in a foreign land, but a member of the RCA family wondering out loud about our words and ways. With the writing of this book, she has made herself vulnerable as a historian, but in so doing, all of us have been served. She has not observed us from a high mountain far away but has stood in the valley and heard the sacred words and sentiments of our hearts. For this I am deeply grateful!

Gregg A. Mast

Preface

In 1997 the Reformed Church in America (RCA) held its annual General Synod meeting in Milwaukee, Wisconsin. The major issue that year was a discussion of the proposed formula of agreement between the Evangelical Lutheran Church in America and three Reformed denominations: the United Church of Christ, the Presbyterian Church (USA), and the Reformed Church in America. A group of Lutheran and Reformed theologians had met from 1988 to 1992 and drafted *A Common Calling*, which outlined the reasons why these two theological traditions should enter into full communion, despite the four centuries of separation which kept them from sharing the Eucharist. Subsequently, representatives of the four denominations produced *A Formula of Agreement*, which outlined the specific ways the denominations would work and worship together, while retaining their separate identities.

The Reformed Church in America was the first of the four denominations to vote during the summer of 1997. The *Formula* had already engendered considerable suspicion and debate within the RCA. Ironically, some people welcomed a closer relationship with the Lutherans but opposed the United Church of Christ, primarily because of its openness towards gay and lesbian people. Anxiety levels were high.

I was a corresponding delegate to this synod, because I had served on the committee that drafted *A Common Calling*. I arrived in Milwaukee with my own anxieties. I was irritated and at times angry about the way the debate had proceeded in the previous weeks. I was afraid that the Reformed Church would vote against the *Formula* and single-handedly derail a decade of ecumenical work. I did not want to be embarrassed by my church.

The synod opened with worship and Communion, which I rather grumpily attended. I sat toward the back and watched people go forward to receive the elements. I saw people I cared about. People who had nurtured me when I was a child or a college student. People I had learned from, and people I had taught. People I liked and people I disliked. People who thought as I did and people who strongly disagreed. It was the RCA family gathered around the Table. For better or worse, it was *my* family. I think I became a bit more gracious and patient in the week that followed. The Reformed Church did approve the *Formula*, as did all the partner churches. Lutheran and Reformed could share the same Table.

I was raised in the Second Reformed Church in Grand Haven, Michigan. I attended Wednesday night catechism classes and Sunday evening Reformed Church Youth Fellowship. I went to church twice on Sunday, whether I wanted to or not. I sang "Blest Be the Tie That Binds" at the end of every evening service and sometimes thought that the ties bound much too tightly. I graduated from Hope College, an RCA institution. I attended Princeton Seminary, where I was steeped in Reformed theology and Calvin's *Institutes*.

After my first year of seminary, I was looking for a place to do my required church internship. I noticed in the *Church Herald* that someone named Leonard Kalkwarf had just been elected vice-president of the General Synod, and I discovered on a map that his church in Willow Grove, Pennsylvania, was only forty-five minutes from Princeton. I made a phone call that has had a profound impact on my life. Soon I was working in one of the most gracious and loving congregations I have ever encountered, the Reformed Church of Willow Grove, and I was blessed with a very wise (and very busy) mentor. I learned a great deal about the Reformed Church in the next two years, met interesting denominational leaders, and found that the denomination as a whole was quite different from the portion of it I had encountered in western Michigan.

Following Reformed Church tradition, Leonard Kalkwarf was elected president when his year as vice-president was finished. As president, in June of 1984, during a very hot week in New Brunswick, New Jersey, he posed a question to the synod that has intrigued the Reformed Church in America ever since: "What is the glue that holds us together?" The question also intrigued me, and I have spent most of my professional life trying to answer both this question about glue and broader questions about RCA identity.

What kind of church is the RCA? What is its identity? Scholars who study denominations usually label it "mainline" because of its long history, moderate theology, and record of ecumenism.[1] At various denominational meetings and on RCA blog sites, however, it is not unusual to hear some members assert that the RCA has been and should be far more conservative. Such speakers suggest that if the RCA distanced itself from the mainline churches, returned to its true roots, and affirmed biblical inerrancy, the denomination would again grow and thrive.

A recent analysis of denominational structures suggested that strong denominations usually have a clear sense of identity. Congregations within these denominations affirm common theological beliefs and know what distinguishes them from other churches. Congregations who are part of the Assemblies of God, for example, emphasize the role of the Holy Spirit. Missouri Synod Lutherans generally know how and why they are different from members of the Evangelical Lutheran Church in America. The authors concluded that the RCA, on the other hand, is a denomination with a relatively weak identity. Surveys have shown that Reformed Church members do not have a clearly defined and shared set of theological beliefs.[2] They do not always know how the RCA is distinct from other denominations. One reason for this is that the Reformed Church's identity has been contested throughout much of its history.

The question of identity is related to a disturbing trend in American religion—the slow but steady decline of membership in mainline denominations. Does the lack of clear identity explain the decline? Can these denominations grow again? Sociologists of religion who measure attendance doubt that this trend will be reversed. The declining numbers have caused a great deal of anxiety and a profound

---

[1] Robert Putnam and David Campbell, *American Grace: How Religion Divides and Unites Us* (New York: Simon and Schuster, 2010), 573.

[2] David A. Roozen, "National Denominational Structures' Engagement with Postmodernity: An Integrative Summary from an Organizational Perspective," in *Church, Identity, and Change: Theology and Denominational Structures in Unsettled Times,* ed. David A. Roozen and James R. Nieman (Grand Rapids: Eerdmans, 2005), 606.

sense of loss among denominational leaders, ministers, and church members. What is the church doing wrong? What must it do to improve? Some Reformed Church members think the denomination should adopt wholeheartedly the practices of successful megachurches. Others suggest it should develop and emphasize its Reformed identity, theology, liturgy, and polity. At the same time that denominations are lamenting their losses and wringing their hands in despair over their failures, some sociologists offer the sobering analysis that mainline decline has been caused by demographics and other factors external to congregations. Internal improvements are unlikely to reverse the decline.[3]

These questions about what the Reformed Church in America is and how it will survive are woven throughout both the familial affection and the fierce debates that characterized the denomination in the latter half of the twentieth century and thus frame this book as well. Three broad themes will appear repeatedly. The first is identity. What kind of church is the Reformed Church in America? Is it conservative or liberal? Mainline or evangelical? Will it be ecumenical or avoid such entanglement? Will it try to convert individuals or transform society? At General Synods and other gatherings, on the pages of the *Church Herald* magazine, and more recently on the RCA blog site, people have argued passionately for positions on each end of these spectrums and many places in between.

When people are asked to describe the identity of the Reformed Church, perhaps the most common response is that it is a family. This is the second theme of the book. Reformed Church members historically shared a name, beliefs, history, and occasionally some Dutch DNA. They knew each other through church, college, and seminary connections. The RCA can be a cozy community of like-minded people that provides safety and security to its members. The RCA can also be a family that is closed, stifling, and hurtful. At times it has refused to welcome outsiders. It can be more concerned about its own survival than the fate of the larger world.

The third theme is conflict. Families fight. That is an inevitable but painful reality which can undermine a family's identity and security. Conflict can be a sign of petty territorialism, but it can also be a sign of deep loyalty and commitment as people defend a cause or an idea that means a great deal to them. Throughout its history, but perhaps more

---

[3]   Donald Luidens, "Between Myth and Hard Data: A Denomination Struggles with Its Identity," in *Beyond Establishment: Denominational Cultures in Transition*, ed. Jackson Carroll and Wade Clark Roof (Louisville: Westminster/John Knox, 1993), 248-69.

intensely since 1945, the Reformed Church has experienced conflict over questions like these: How should it read the Bible? How should it relate to other churches? How should it understand the nature of the church? How should it respond to American culture? How should it deal with social issues such as racism, poverty, and homosexuality?

Conflicts often arose within the "family" when it expanded or began new relationships. When a new wave of Dutch immigrants arrived in the nineteenth century; when New Brunswick Seminary hired a Congregationalist professor in 1923 and a Scottish Presbyterian in 1946; when the denomination considered mergers, membership in ecumenical councils, and the *Formula of Agreement*; when some congregations from the United Church of Canada wanted to join; when the RCA emphasized church extension and multiculturalism— each border-expanding episode has caused significant debate. More recently there have been heated discussions of the extent to which gay and lesbian people should be part of the Reformed Church family.

The Reformed Church knows that it needs to grow, welcome new members, and accept new ideas, but to what extent should the denomination change its basic identity in order to appeal to new parishioners? If Reformed congregations want to reach out to former Baptists, for example, does the doctrine of infant baptism become expendable when these potential newcomers prefer to "dedicate" their children? If the denomination receives new congregations who do not believe in women's ordination, what effect will this have on the Reformed Church's commitment to gender equality? How much should the denomination be willing to accommodate or change? To what extent should new members be expected to adopt RCA beliefs and practices? Which beliefs and practices are central to Reformed identity and cannot be changed without threatening that identity? Reformed Church members may not agree on the answers, but thinking about these questions will be essential to the future of the denomination.

The Reformed Church's story is not always an attractive, inspiring one. Its members are flawed, fallible human beings, who are part of a flawed, fallible church. Throughout its history, Reformed Church congregations have caused their share of pain to members and others by being judgmental and exclusive. But they have also been sources of grace. In this book I have chosen to focus on conflict as a significant factor in the denomination's recent history. Other historians might tell the story in other ways. But in my judgment, this is who we are—a denomination shaped by very different opinions which compete for the right to determine the Reformed Church's identity and define the boundaries of the family. In the past, the Reformed Church generally chose to be a large tent with room for diverse opinions under its shelter. At various times some members have tried to make the tent much smaller and exclude certain people and ideas. The denomination has usually resisted these efforts, but the struggle continues.

There have been several occasions when some members grew so angry and frustrated that they thought about leaving. Some did leave. The denomination as a whole, however, has stayed together, despite the presence of significant differences of opinion among its members. There has been enough of a shared identity, a strong sense of family, some willingness to work through conflict, and a high degree of loyalty. Those things have kept the denomination together in the past. Whether they will continue to suffice for the future, or whether there will even be a Reformed Church in America in the future, is an open question.

Acknowledgments

A number of people have read this manuscript at various points and offered helpful suggestions. My thanks to Laurie Baron, Elton Bruins, Don Buteyn, John Coakley, Jane Dickie, Eugene Heideman, Jeff Japinga, Mary Kansfield, Carl Kleis, Gregg Mast, and Phil Van Eyl. Donald Luidens read several drafts and provided much needed editing and encouragement when I was particularly discouraged by the writing process. The Commission on History of the Reformed Church in America and its editor, Donald J. Bruggink, also provided useful comments.

I am grateful to all the people I have interviewed for their generosity, honesty, and insights. They welcomed me into their homes, hearts, and lives. Not all are named in the book, but I was inspired by each of their ministries and by their loyalty to the Reformed Church in America.

I have benefited from many conversations about the Reformed Church. Leonard Kalkwarf, Alvin Poppen, Isaac Rottenberg, Dennis TeBeest, and Arthur Van Eck quickly and graciously answered my questions. I have also appreciated the wisdom of the late Richard Oudersluys and John W. Beardslee, III.

Russell Gasero, the denomination's archivist, provided an exceptional level of support. He found letters, papers, and photos. Geoffrey Reynolds and the Joint Archives of Holland also provided assistance with resources. Pamela Valkema maintained her constant grace and good will as she transcribed interviews and made numerous copies.

I received financial support from the Van Raalte Institute and Hope College Faculty Development Funds. A generous grant from the Louisville Institute made it possible to conduct the interviews.

I have been graced to be part of a number of loving and supportive congregations, either as parishioner or pastor. For the last two decades I have been a member and occasionally a preacher and pastor at Hope Church in Holland, Michigan. This congregation and its pastors embody all the best of what it means to be Reformed. I am deeply grateful to be surrounded and nourished by such courage, compassion, and commitment.

My family members, Jeff, Mark, and Annie, have been generally tolerant of the slow pace of this project. I appreciate their encouragement and the many diversions they provide. My parents, to whom this book is dedicated, have been connected with the Reformed Church for most of their lives. They live out a faith which is thoughtful, gracious, and hospitable. They have demonstrated loyalty and love to each other, their family, and the church.

CHAPTER 1

All in the Family: The Varied Roots of the Reformed Church in America

On the cover of a June 1959 issue of the denominational magazine, the *Church Herald*, there is a photo of a stereotypically perfect family going to church. The father and two sons wear suits and ties. The mother and daughter wear dresses and hats and carry purses. The adults and oldest child carry Bibles. The older boy holds the younger boy's hand. All are smiling. It is the quintessential American image of the 1950s and the early years of the baby boom.

When Reformed Church members speak about the denomination as a family, they often mean a family like the one in the picture, in which everyone is well dressed, well-behaved, and devoted to their church, their Bibles, and one another. More skeptical observers think of the denomination instead as a somewhat dysfunctional family whose members distrust and dislike one another and spend much of their time arguing. An RCA minister once observed that the Presbyterian Church in which he was raised functioned like a business, but the Reformed Church felt like a family. An older colleague replied, "Yes, but someone is always leaving dirty socks on the floor."[1]

[1] Oral history interview with Paul Kranendonk, May 14, 2001, Whiting, New Jersey. Kranendonk was raised in a Presbyterian church in Wisconsin that included many

If the Reformed Church is like a family, then the annual meeting of the General Synod, the denomination's highest governing body, is its annual family reunion. Some delegates have known each other since college or seminary. Others are cousins or siblings or fathers and sons. Yet at many synods, tensions are high, disagreements are sharp, and a visitor might wonder why this denomination stays together when delegates hold such different views on abortion, homosexuality, biblical interpretation, worship, ecumenical relationships, and the ordination of women.

Perhaps the Reformed Church in America is more like a blended family. The Reformed Protestant Dutch Church officially began in 1628 when Dutch immigrants settled in Manhattan. Over the next two centuries, it became an urban and urbane denomination, one of the most city-based churches in the country. In 1850 the Reformed Church welcomed into membership several congregations of recent Dutch immigrants from small towns and rural communities in the Netherlands. These immigrants settled primarily in the Midwest. The different histories of the two immigrant groups made for a complicated relationship. The expanded family experienced considerable conflict and frequent power struggles over who would be in control. Each group brought its own theological emphases, world view, and faith practices. They were at different places in their degree of Americanization, and they related differently to the surrounding culture. However, they were both Dutch and Reformed and, for better or worse, that made them family.

Blended families often find it a challenge to create a new identity that is not defined or dominated by one of its constituent units. A similar dynamic may explain why the Reformed Church has discussed its identity so frequently, especially in the last few decades. When Leonard Kalkwarf, then president of the General Synod, asked in 1984 if there was any glue that held the RCA together, he sparked a multiyear study of denominational identity that, in the end, was inconclusive. Nobody seemed quite sure what was holding the church together, except perhaps the ministers' pension plan.

A decade later, in 1997, the General Synod Council directed the general secretary, Wesley Granberg-Michaelson, to develop a unifying vision for the denomination. He took several people on retreat, and they returned with a *Mission and Vision Statement* that identified outreach,

---

parishioners of Dutch descent. He attended Hope College and Western Seminary and served RCA churches in New York and New Jersey.

creativity, and diversity as the glue which could hold the denomination together. It said: "The Reformed Church in America is a fellowship of congregations called by God and empowered by the Holy Spirit to be the very presence of Jesus Christ in the world. Our shared task is to equip congregations for ministry—a thousand churches in a million ways doing one thing—following Christ in mission, in a lost and broken world so loved by God."[2]

The 2003 General Synod expanded the role of outreach as a source of denominational unity and identity when it adopted a program entitled, "Our Call." The statement proclaimed that the Reformed Church would "follow Christ in mission together, led by the Holy Spirit, and [work] with all the partners God provides." Moreover, it asserted, "We believe that God is calling the Reformed Church in America over the next ten years to focus its efforts and resources on starting new congregations and revitalizing existing congregations, thereby empowering fruitful and faithful ministries for the glory of God."[3]

"Our Call" provided a unifying purpose but also intensified the debate about identity, purpose, and structure. Some members believed that the Reformed tradition had long stifled their creativity and that the new statement freed them from outdated language and policies and freed the Reformed Church to grow. Others saw "Our Call" as evidence that the church had given up the basic beliefs and commitments of Reformed theology and had adopted instead a generic American evangelicalism. Still others said "Our Call" was necessary because the Reformed Church had lost its identity when it began to act like all the other mainline denominations.

The discussion and analysis of denominational identity is not a frivolous effort, as some critics have suggested, but essential to the vitality and future of the Reformed Church in America. Throughout most of its history, but especially during the last sixty-five years, most of the conflict within the denomination can be traced to uncertainty about identity. In part, this uncertainty is the result of a deep sense of loss. Religion in general does not have the same influence either in the broader American society or in small communities as it once did.

---

[2]   Available on the RCA website at http://www.rca.org/Page.aspx?pid=1459. For a thoughtful analysis of the statement see Steve Mathonnet-Vander Well, "No Longer Business as Usual: The Reformed Church in America Seen through Its Mission Statement," in *Church, Identity, and Change*, ed. Roozen and Nieman, 436-57.

[3]   *Acts and Proceedings of the General Synod of the Reformed Church in America*, 2003, 66. The text of "Our Call" is also available at http://www.rca.org/Page.aspx?pid=1457.

Denominations have lost members and eliminated staff positions. The "good old days" (if they ever existed) are mostly gone.[4]

The Reformed Church is not alone in its uncertainty about identity. Most mainline denominations have discussed this topic during the past few decades, in part because religious life has changed so dramatically since World War II. In the 1950s church attendance was socially acceptable and often expected. In 1958, church membership and attendance reached an all-time high, with 49 percent of the population claiming to attend church weekly.[5] Protestant theologians such as Reinhold Niebuhr preached in pulpits around the country and occasionally appeared on the covers of major news magazines. With a generous donation from John Rockefeller Jr., the National Council of Churches and a number of denominations (including the RCA) built the Interchurch Center at 475 Riverside Drive in upper Manhattan. Variously known as the "God-Box," "Vatican on the Hudson," or simply "475," the building provided office space for a score of denominations and interdenominational agencies. Mainline Protestantism was dominant and influential.

Fifty years later, many denominations have left the Interchurch Center and moved to headquarters scattered throughout the heartland. Mainline churches have experienced significant declines in membership since the 1970s and varying degrees of budget crises and resulting staff cuts. Many books have described this decline, pointing to demographic, geographic, and cultural shifts in the religious landscape. Some studies have suggested that mainline denominations are boring, irrelevant, and out of touch with contemporary reality, while the new mega/evangelical/nondenominational churches now possess the power and influence that the mainline has lost. The "mainline" has been moved to the "sideline."[6]

These internal denominational shifts are paralleled by the extraordinary cultural transformations the American people have

---

[4]   For a discussion of changes in denominational life, see Robert Putnam and David Campbell, *American Grace: How Religion Divides and Unites Us* (New York: Simon and Schuster, 2010) 70-133.

[5]   Putnam and Campbell, *American Grace*, 98.

[6]   For overviews of postwar religion in America, see Patrick Allitt, *Religion in America Since 1945: A History* (New York: Columbia Univ. Press, 2003) and Robert Wuthnow, *The Restructuring of American Religion: Society and Faith Since World War II* (Princeton: Princeton Univ. Press, 1988). For a discussion of the shift from mainline to sideline, see Dean R. Hoge and David A. Roozen, eds., *Understanding Church Growth and Decline, 1950-1978* (New York: Pilgrim, 1979); Wade Clark Roof, *American Mainline Religion: Its Changing Shape and Future* (New Brunswick: Rutgers Univ. Press, 1987); David A. Roozen and C. Kirk Hadaway, *Church and Denominational Growth* (Nashville: Abingdon, 1993).

experienced in the six decades since the end of World War II. The GI Bill gave servicemen the opportunity to attend college and move from working class to middle class. People bought homes in the suburbs and filled them with the consumer goods that replaced guns and grenades in factory production lines. They also filled their homes with the children who would be known as the "baby boomers." In 1945 people received information from the radio and the newspaper. By the 1950s, television made it possible for people to see human tragedy, not simply to read or hear about it. The assassinations of John and Robert Kennedy and Martin Luther King Jr. in the 1960s, the Vietnam War, the student protests, and the civil rights actions in the South all became more immediate and dramatic because of television. In recent years, the development of the Internet, cable television, and smart phones have contributed to the expectation of constant information and communication.

Religious life and worship styles also have changed substantially in the last sixty years. In 1945 most congregations sang traditional hymns accompanied by organ music. Worship was more formal, parishioners dressed up, and ministers often wore robes. A congregation of six hundred members could be staffed by one pastor who relied on numerous volunteers.

In 1945 many church members identified strongly with the denomination in which they had been raised. They had been taught that the Reformed or Lutheran or Roman Catholic faith was the best, if not the only, way to worship God. Sixty years later many people looking for a church care little about denominational affiliation and generally believe that every denomination is equally Christian. Today's church-shoppers (a term unimaginable in the 1940s and 1950s) are more interested in finding a church where they feel comfortable.

After the ecclesial euphoria following WWII, differences became more heated in the 1960s and beyond, when denominational meetings included vigorous discussions of the Vietnam War, civil rights, women's ordination, gay rights, abortion, and a host of other issues that were also being debated in American culture and politics. A few schisms occurred, but in most denominations people who disagreed about these issues managed to live and work together despite the internal conflicts.[7]

Partly in an attempt to neutralize some of this conflict, religion in the 1970s tended to become more individualized than institutional,

---

[7]   See Wuthnow, *Restructuring*, 12, 132-214. The Presbyterian Church (USA), the United Methodist Church, and the Episcopal Church, for example, all have very active and influential conservative groups.

more emotional than doctrinal, more relational than hierarchical. People felt freer to choose the parts of religious life that appealed to them and to discard the rest. They said more often that they were "spiritual but not religious," which likely meant they believed in God or engaged in a spiritual practice but had little or no institutional connection or commitment. At the same time, the formation of the Moral Majority in 1979 and the election of Ronald Reagan in 1980 signaled the new power and influence of religious conservatives in moral and political issues. This link between religion and politics contributed to a resurgence of denominational turbulence, which would simmer and occasionally explode over the next three decades.

Because of these challenges and changes, the half century following World War II is one of the most interesting periods in American religious history. Denominational life was shaped and reshaped by church growth and decline, the development of denominational bureaucracies, the emergence of difficult social problems, the expansion of technology, and the baby boom and the baby bust. Churches at various times resisted the culture and then acquiesced to it, opposed secular values and then imitated them, kept their distance from the world and yet tried to fit in. Whether they resisted change or welcomed it, at the end of the twentieth century churches ministered to a world and a culture that was very different from that of 1950.

This book tells the story of the Reformed Church in America during these tumultuous years from 1945 to 1994. A number of books have been written about the colonial period and the early history of the denomination, and even more about the mid-nineteenth century immigration.[8] However, there is much less scholarship dedicated to

8   For the colonial period, see Gerald F. De Jong, *The Dutch Reformed Church in the American Colonies*, Historical Series of the Reformed Church in America (hereinafter, HSRCA), no. 5 (Grand Rapids: Eerdmans, 1978) and Randall Balmer, *A Perfect Babel of Confusion: Dutch Religion and English Culture in the Middle Colonies* (New York: Oxford Univ. Press, 1989). For the early nineteenth century, see Firth Haring Fabend, *Zion on the Hudson: Dutch New York and New Jersey in the Age of Revivals* (New Brunswick: Rutgers Univ. Press, 2000). For overviews of almost four centuries of RCA history, see Donald J. Bruggink and Kim N. Baker, *By Grace Alone: Stories of the Reformed Church in America*, HSRCA, no. 44 (Grand Rapids: Eerdmans, 2004); James Van Hoeven, ed., *Piety and Patriotism: Bicentennial Studies of the Reformed Church in America, 1776-1976*, HSRCA, no. 4 (Grand Rapids: Eerdmans, 1976); James Van Hoeven, ed., *Word and World: Reformed Theology in America*, HSRCA, no. 16 (Grand Rapids: Eerdmans, 1986); Howard Hageman, *Lily Among the Thorns* (New York: Half Moon, 1953); Renee House and John Coakley, eds., *Patterns and Portraits: Women in the History of the Reformed Church in America*, HSRCA, no. 31 (Grand Rapids: Eerdmans, 1999). For the nineteenth-century immigration to the Midwest, see Gerrit J. Ten

the period since 1945. Several authors have studied particular mission fields or liturgical practices.[9] Hope College sociologists Donald Luidens and Roger Nemeth have surveyed RCA members and written articles about their characteristics and beliefs and giving patterns at particular times.[10] But no broad overview of the late twentieth century—a tumultuous and definitive period in the life of the Reformed Church—has been published.

The half century between 1945 and 1995 was a crucial and transformative period within the Reformed Church. The achievements, conflicts, and decisions of those years have shaped the RCA into its current form. And yet, it is evident at General Synod and classis meetings and on the denominational blog site that many members do not know what the Reformed Church has said in the past about such issues as homosexuality, biblical interpretation, abortion, or infant baptism. As a result, advocates of various positions occasionally make inaccurate pronouncements. Others assume that the identity of the denomination ought to match their particular beliefs, but they are not aware of the range of opinions that has been part of the church's theological and cultural heritage.[11]

The purpose of this book is to describe and analyze the major events, issues, and conflicts that occurred in the Reformed Church in America between 1945 and 1994.[12] Before beginning that story, however, it will be helpful to take a longer look back.

Zythoff, *Sources of Secession: The Netherlands Hervormde Kerk on the Eve of the Dutch Immigration to the Midwest*, HSRCA, no. 17 (Grand Rapids: Eerdmans, 1987); James D. Bratt, *Dutch Calvinism in Modern America* (Grand Rapids: Eerdmans, 1984); Elton J. Bruins, *The Americanization of a Congregation*, 2nd ed., HSRCA, no. 26 (Grand Rapids: Eerdmans, 1995); Elton J. Bruins and Robert P. Swierenga, *Family Quarrels in the Dutch Reformed Churches in the Nineteenth Century*, HSRCA, no. 32 (Grand Rapids: Eerdmans, 1999); Robert P. Swierenga, *Dutch Chicago: A History of the Hollanders in the Windy City*, HSRCA, no. 42 (Grand Rapids: Eerdmans, 2002).

[9]   Lewis R. Scudder III, *The Arabian Mission's Story: In Search of Abraham's Other Son*, HSRCA, no. 30 (Grand Rapids: Eerdmans, 1998); Morrell F. Swart, *The Call of Africa: The Reformed Church in America Mission in the Sub-Sahara, 1948-1998*, HSRCA, no. 29 (Grand Rapids: Eerdmans, 1998); Eugene P. Heideman, *From Mission to Church: The Reformed Church in America Mission to India*, HSRCA, no. 38 (Grand Rapids: Eerdmans, 2001).

[10]   See Corwin Smidt, Donald Luidens, James Pennings, and Roger Nemeth, *Divided By A Common Heritage: The Christian Reformed Church and the Reformed Church in America at the Beginning of the New Millennium*, HSRCA, no. 54 (Grand Rapids: Eerdmans, 2006), for an analysis of survey research conducted in both denominations.

[11]   For examples of this range of opinion, see James Cook, ed., *The Church Speaks: Papers of the Commission on Theology, Reformed Church in America*, Vols. I and II, HSRCA, nos. 15, 40 (Grand Rapids: Eerdmans, 1985, 2002).

[12]   The year 1994 is the end point for this study because a new general secretary began his work in that year.

Colonial Beginnings and Midwest Immigrants

The Reformed Church traces its roots in America to the 1620s, when Dutch settlers arrived to explore the New World and to make money. They were not searching for religious freedom or trying to establish a "city set on a hill" like the Puritans in Massachusetts. The Dutch Reformed Church in the Netherlands took an interest in the settlement, however, and sent two deacons to provide spiritual nurture and read sermons on Sunday and, in 1628, a pastor who presided over the first official Dutch Reformed worship service.[13] Dutch was the language of worship for many years, so the congregations did not attract many non-Dutch settlers, though the culture of New Amsterdam itself was very open. New Amsterdam was taken over by the British in 1664 and renamed New York. Relatively few Dutch people immigrated after that, so the Reformed Church grew primarily by natural increase. During the colonial years, Dutch settlers moved up the Hudson and west along the Mohawk Rivers, east into Long Island, and south and west into New Jersey. By 1776 they had established about one hundred churches in the towns and cities of the Mid-Atlantic region.[14]

For most of a century, these churches provided a comfortable spiritual home for Dutch farmers and businessmen. In 1720, however, a new pastor was sent from Amsterdam to central New Jersey. The Reverend Theodorus Frelinghuysen brought an emotional, rigorous, pietistic emphasis to his work and caused a great deal of controversy.[15]

---

[13]   The Anglicans settled in Jamestown, Virginia, in 1607. The Pilgrims came to Plymouth in 1620. The Puritans arrived in Boston in 1630. Dutch Reformed religious services began in 1624, but the denomination did not officially begin until an ordained minister arrived and served Communion. The Dutch Reformed Church has been known by several different names. By the nineteenth century it was generally referred to as the Reformed Protestant Dutch Church. In 1867 the name was changed to the Reformed Church in America. See Bruggink and Baker, *By Grace Alone*, 31.

[14]   See De Jong, *Dutch Reformed Church*. For an overview of Dutch life in the colonies in the seventeenth century, see Russell Shorto, *Island at the Center of the World: The Epic Story of Dutch Manhattan and the Forgotten Colony That Shaped America* (New York: Doubleday, 2004). Shorto emphasizes that the diversity present in New Amsterdam occurred in part because the financial backers of the colony were more interested in making money than they were in protecting religious purity. Non-Reformed and Jewish people were encouraged to settle and promised religious freedom.

[15]   For a collection of Frelinghuysen's sermons, see Joel R. Beeke, ed., *Forerunner of the Great Awakening: Sermons by Theodorus Jacobus Frelinghuysen*, HSRCA, no. 36 (Grand Rapids: Eerdmans, 2000). James Tanis, *Dutch Calvinistic Pietism in the Middle Colonies: A Study in the Life and Theology of Theodorus Jacobus Frelinghuysen* (The Hague: Martinus Nijhoff, 1968). For a more critical appraisal see Herman Harmelink, III, "Another Look at Frelinghuysen and His 'Awakening,'" *Church History* 37 (December 1968): 423-38.

He considered some of his parishioners to be unconverted, and he accused the Reformed Church pastors in New York City of arrogance and vanity. Supporters claimed he brought true, experiential religion to the staid Dutch people who previously had only head knowledge of their faith. Critics said he discredited Reformed theology and practice with his rigor and emotionalism. Frelinghuysen attempted to redefine the Reformed Church as a pietistic church. Some of his emphasis on emotion, conversion, and experiential religion did become part of church life, but his demand for rigor and exclusion did not become institutionalized as a defining factor in denominational identity.

As the Reformed Church grew, it needed more formalized structures to do its work. After several decades of conflict between those who wanted more independence for the American church and those who wanted to keep close ties with Amsterdam, the Reformed Church approved the Articles of Union in 1772, which provided independence but continued communication with the "mother church." The American church also established two institutions of higher education, Queen's College in 1766 (now Rutgers University) and New Brunswick Theological Seminary in 1784. The church demonstrated its commitment to missions by establishing a Board of Domestic Missions in 1831 and a Board of Foreign Missions in 1857. It also worked with other denominations in various ecumenical efforts, such as the American Bible Society and other missionary and benevolent societies. The denominational staff consisted of one paid agent.[16] By 1847 the church was thoroughly Americanized. Its congregations took pride in their ethnic heritage, but they knew that emphasizing "Dutchness" would not ensure their future survival. They had to become inclusive in order to grow.

The Dutch immigrants to the Midwest had a much more conflicted history. During the 1820s and 1830s, the Reformed churches in the Netherlands experienced a revival, and a number of ministers and members became more intensely pietistic.[17] This led to tensions with the state church (*Hervormde Kerk*) and eventually to a separation known as

---

[16] For further reference, see Arie Brouwer, *Reformed Church Roots* (New York: Reformed Church Press, 1977); Marvin D. Hoff, *Structures for Mission*, HSRCA, no. 14 (Grand Rapids: Eerdmans, 1985); Bruggink and Baker, *By Grace Alone*.

[17] Pietism is difficult to define. Generally it means a more emotional and behavioral emphasis in Christian faith and life. Pietists often stress a certain kind of religious experience, often a dramatic conversion, and they usually set high moral standards that they expect people to follow. At times a pietist emphasis has led to an attitude of superiority over other Christians who do not share the same kind of religious experience or language.

the *Afscheiding*. In the late 1840s, several of these separatist Dutch clergy led groups of church members to the United States. Albertus Van Raalte brought a contingent to Holland, Michigan, as did Hendrik Scholte to Pella, Iowa, and Cornelius Vander Meulen to Zeeland, Michigan. Some members of these groups eventually settled in other parts of western Michigan, as well as Chicago, Wisconsin, and northwest Iowa.[18]

The newcomers were not wealthy and the places they chose to settle did not provide easy living; Holland, Michigan, for instance, consisted of a forest that needed to be cleared. The immigrants had very little money to purchase land or to build churches, so Albertus Van Raalte appealed to the established Dutch churches in the East. They responded with financial aid and an invitation for the immigrant churches to join the Reformed Protestant Dutch Church.[19] Some of the newcomers hesitated, uncertain about the orthodoxy and purity of the eastern churches, but Van Raalte encouraged the immigrant churches to join their Dutch brothers and sisters in the faith, and they did.

Conflict emerged almost immediately. Several churches in western Michigan objected to practices in the eastern church—such as singing hymns rather than only psalms—and worried that the union was dangerous because the eastern churches were so Americanized. These congregations left the Reformed Church in 1857 and formed the Christian Reformed Church in North America. Three decades later, Reformed Church members debated the place of Freemasons within the church. Eastern congregations had always allowed Masons to be members, but many of the new immigrants thought that Masons were anti-Christian and should be denied membership. The Dutch church, by this time named the Reformed Church in America, allowed individual congregations to prohibit Masons from membership but refused to legislate for the entire denomination. This decision caused an additional group of congregations—including the Pillar Church in Holland where Van Raalte had been pastor—to join the Christian Reformed Church in 1884.[20]

18   There is a vast literature on this *Afscheiding* (separation) in the Netherlands and the emigration which followed. See Bruins, Swierenga, Swierenga and Bruins, Bratt, and Ten Zythoff, cited above.

19   For background on one significant relationship between Van Raalte and and an eastern pastor see Elton J. Bruins and Karen G. Schakel, eds., *Envisioning Hope College: Letters Written by Albertus C. Van Raalte to Philip Phelps, Jr., 1857 to 1875* (Grand Rapids: Eerdmans, 2011).

20   Despite coming from similar roots, the two denominations have developed very different patterns and cultures. Some of these have changed, but, historically, the RCA supported public schools while the CRC developed separate Christian schools. The RCA sang hymns; the CRC sang only psalms. The RCA encouraged its members to participate in organizations that were not specifically Christian

A few years after this schism, the RCA considered a merger with the Reformed Church in the United States (RCUS). This denomination was largely composed of German congregations with similar beliefs and practices. The proposal was approved by the General Synod in 1892 and by the requisite number of classes, but, after a great deal of discussion, synod delegates in 1893 voted down the declarative action.[21]

In the 1920s, Reformed Church members disagreed over the hiring of a Congregational minister, Edward Strong Worcester, who had been invited to teach theology at New Brunswick Seminary. Some conservatives thought he was too liberal and did not endorse the doctrinal standards with sufficient enthusiasm. Multiple votes had to be taken at the synod of 1923. At a late night meeting after many of his opponents had given up and gone to bed, Worcester received the required three-quarters of the votes.

In general, however, the two branches of the church functioned reasonably well together. The eastern churches had more influence in the denominational program, and denominational leaders tended to come from the East. Between 1850 and 1945 only twelve presidents of the General Synod came from the Midwest. Synod meetings were almost always held in the East. Denominational boards and committees usually met in New York City and drew most of their members from the East in order to avoid extensive travel time and costs.

There were few arguments about controversial social issues in the first half of the twentieth century because the church made few substantive statements. The Committee on Public Morals advocated temperance and Sabbath observance, and synod delegates usually approved their recommendations, even if they did not practice them personally.[22] During the Great Depression, the committee changed

---

such as labor unions, scientific societies, and Boy/Girl Scouts; the CRC did not wish its members to cooperate with non-Christian groups and encouraged the development of separate societies. Accurately or not, RCA churches often believed CRC churches considered them too liberal and too Americanized. Some families had such strong feelings about the other group that if an RCA member wanted to marry a CRC member, it was considered a mixed marriage and nearly as dangerous as marrying a Roman Catholic. Currently the two denominations engage in joint projects but merger is not considered a viable option. See Smidt, et. al., *Divided By a Common Heritage*.

[21]   See Eugene P. Heideman, *The Practice of Piety: The Theology of the Midwestern Reformed Church in America, 1866-1966*, HSRCA, no. 64 (Grand Rapids: Eerdmans, 2009), 67-78, and Herman Harmelink III, *Ecumenism and the Reformed Church*, HSRCA, no. 1 (Grand Rapids: Eerdmans, 1968), for a discussion of this merger proposal.

[22]   The committee lamented in 1925 that, despite all of its encouragement to RCA members to obey the Prohibition laws, a number of them had stills in their back yards! *Acts and Proceedings*, 1925, 957.

its name to the Committee on Social Welfare and observed in its report that poverty was not simply a matter of individual laziness and incompetence but the result of unchecked capitalism.[23] On the whole, though, the denomination supported the country and the status quo and rarely criticized national policy. Most members agreed that the church should encourage religious belief and practice, not meddle in the work of the government.

Still, the seeds of difference and eventual conflict had been planted. Shifting population patterns contributed to an increasing gap in the social environment of eastern and midwestern churches. White Protestants in the East moved out of city neighborhoods where Reformed Church congregations had been located, and Jews, Catholics, Hispanics, and African-Americans moved in. Urban Reformed congregations did not prove to be very effective at reaching out to their new neighbors. Some churches simply closed down. Others followed their people to new neighborhoods, but some of these eventually closed as well. Church growth and fund-raising became far greater challenges in eastern churches. Meanwhile, in the Midwest, many Reformed Church members continued to live in small towns or neighborhoods where most of their neighbors shared not only skin color but religion and ethnicity.[24]

Most members of the Reformed Church participated in the prosperity of the 1920s, the hardship of the Great Depression, and the anxiety of World War II. These experiences held the disparate elements of the denomination together for several decades. But trouble was brewing. The eastern churches were losing members and giving less money to the denomination. The Midwestern churches were gaining members and giving more. Some members in the Midwest began to wonder why they were still treated as the church's poor and powerless younger sibling.[25]

---

23   *Acts and Proceedings*, 1932, 149-50.

24   Daniel Verwey served as pastor of the Union of Highbridge Church in the Bronx from 1916 to 1946. Twelve hundred new members joined the church during those years, yet the net growth was 190, from 285 members in 1916 to 475 in 1946. At the beginning of his ministry he could walk to all his parishoners' homes. Thirty years later he had to drive, and some had moved into New Jersey or Staten Island. These parishioners would find it increasingly difficult to justify a long drive on Sunday morning, especially during the gas rationing of the war years. Daniel Verwey, "My Thirty Years in a Metropolitan Church," *Church Herald* (hereinafter, *CH*), Jan. 3, 1947, 12-13.

25   Richard Oudersluys, professor of New Testament at Western Theological Seminary from 1942 to 1977, made this observation in conversation with the author. In 1944, the two midwestern particular synods (Chicago and Iowa) gave $277,000 to the Board of Foreign Missions and $252,000 to the Board of Domestic Missions. The

On the eve of the Second World War, the Reformed Church in America was a thoroughly established denomination, balanced between the largely urban and suburban congregations of the East and the more Dutch and rural congregations of the Midwest. It was a solid and significant member of the larger Protestant ecumenical community.

The Structure of the Reformed Church in 1945

In 1945 the Reformed Church operated with minimal staff and structure. The stated clerk, James Hoffman, managed the details of the General Synod and the day-to-day business. The assessment[26] was a mere eighteen cents per member. Much of the denomination's work was done within six boards: the Board of Foreign Missions (BFM), The Woman's [sic] Board of Foreign Missions (WBFM), the Board of Domestic Missions (BDM), the Women's Board of Domestic Missions (WBDM), the Board of Education (BE), and the Board of Pensions (BP).[27] In 1946 the two foreign boards merged, as did the two domestic boards in 1951. The boards reported to the General Synod every year, and technically the synod elected the executives and board members, but in practice the boards possessed a great deal of autonomy. The fact that they had to raise all their funding, however, meant that the boards did not stray far from Reformed Church members' dominant beliefs and practices.

The denomination was divided into five regional judicatories (the Particular Synods of Albany, New York, New Jersey, Chicago, and Iowa). The particular synods did not wield a great deal of power in 1945. Most employed a field secretary responsible for church extension. Particular synods supervised the classes, submitted overtures, and dealt with judicial matters, but they did not engage in programming or offer services to congregations.

---

three eastern synods gave $135,000 to the BFM and $116,000 to the BDM. *Acts and Proceedings*, 1945, (BFM report) 29, (BDM report) 28.

[26] Each congregation paid a certain amount per member to support the work of the denomination.

[27] Each board had at least one paid executive, along with bookkeepers and secretaries, but the volunteer board members, particularly the executive committees, did a good deal of detailed work and decision making. Members often developed a deep commitment to "their" board and to a particular field within the board. Some traveled at their own expense to visit missionaries. Many gave generously to the boards and enlisted support from other churches and individuals. The executives were often former missionaries and were highly regarded both by RCA members and ecumenical partners. Luman Shafer, secretary of the BFM, was one of the first civilian Americans to enter Japan at the end of World War II. See Gordon Laman, *Pioneers to Partners: The Reformed Church in America and Christian Mission with the Japanese*, HSRCA no. 75 (Grand Rapids: Eerdmans, 2012), 532-35.

The regions were further divided into forty-two classes,[28] each with a stated clerk but no paid staff. Classes functioned as vehicles for communication and venues for fund-raising. Board and agency representatives appeared at classis meetings to share information and solicit financial support. Another task of the classis was starting new churches. The most influential role of the classes was bringing overtures, or requests for action, to the General Synod. These provided much of the agenda for synod meetings. Each year the classes submitted between twenty and fifty overtures asking the denomination to start or stop doing something or to take a position on an issue.

In 1945, as now, General Synod meetings dealt with the business of the denomination. Most delegates were assigned to standing committees, which discussed foreign and domestic missions, interchurch relations, and the president's "Report on the State of Religion."[29] The Standing Committee on Overtures possessed the most power because it discussed and made a recommendation on every overture, regardless of topic. Some recommendations from the church's committees and agencies were filtered through a standing committee, which advised the synod whether to approve, deny, or take no action. Other recommendations went directly to the floor of synod, where they were often discussed at great length. In the processes of debating and voting there were few constraints on individuals regarding the length and number of speeches they made. Delegates were not seated in any particular order, and they generally sat with people from their region of the church, which occasionally led to bloc voting.

Denominational Communication in 1945: The *Church Herald*

The most significant communication tool for the denomination during the second half of the twentieth century was the *Church Herald*.[30] The magazine operated independently of the denomination and was managed by an editorial council. Bernard Mulder, an ordained minister

---

28 *Classis* is the singular; *classes* is the plural. *Classis* is a Latin word meaning "fleet of ships." A classis consists of clergy and elders from a varying number of churches, often twenty to thirty, who meet several times a year to engage in tasks that churches could do not alone, such the supervision of candidates for the ministry.

29 Some delegates were assigned to committees that dealt with travel expenses or excused absences. Some delegates were assigned to serve Communion or to act as tellers. This meant that committee work was very unevenly divided.

30 The first RCA publication was the *Magazine of the Reformed Dutch Church*, which appeared monthly from 1826-1830. The *Christian Intelligencer* was published weekly in New York City from 1830 to 1934. Hope College published the *Leader* in English from 1906 to 1934. The *Christian Intelligencer* and the *Leader* combined in 1934 to form the *Intelligencer-Leader*. The name was changed in 1944 to the *Church Herald*.

who grew up and pastored churches in the Midwest, served as editor from 1937 to 1945. Mulder was a theological moderate yet was accepted by both wings of the denomination. Under his leadership, subscriptions increased from six thousand to thirty thousand, with about 20 percent of the readership located in eastern churches. His tenure as editor ended when he was elected secretary of the Reformed Church's Board of Education in 1945.

Louis H. Benes Jr. became editor of the *Church Herald* in September 1945 when he was just thirty-nine. After graduating from Central College and Western Seminary, Benes was ordained and served the Fifth Reformed Church in Albany for six years, Fifth Reformed in Grand Rapids for eight years, and Hope Reformed in Los Angeles for two years. He brought a more conservative voice to the magazine.

The *Church Herald* was published weekly (except for a few weeks in the summer), and each issue contained twenty-four pages of dense type. Benes had a small staff to assist with production and distribution, but he wrote two full pages (about two thousand words) of editorials each week. No one else in the denomination had this much voice and, therefore, influence. However, Benes was extremely careful not to claim a great deal of personal editorial authority; he almost never said "I" but always used "we" in his editorials. While it may have been standard editorial practice, the tone suggested that he was expressing not just his opinions but those of God and conservative Christianity. This language augmented his already very authoritarian style and implied that there was little room for disagreement.

The *Church Herald* contained several different types of literature. The bulk of the magazine consisted of articles written by Reformed Church authors and invited guest writers. It also included news stories about other churches in the nation and the world, reports of judicatory meetings (classes and regional synods), news from congregations, and lists of calls to ministers which had been extended, accepted, and declined. Finally, letters to the editor allowed space for anyone in the denomination to express an opinion. Many did voice their perspectives, but the letters page was disproportionately filled by unhappy conservatives from the Midwest. Under the editorship of Benes, most easterners and other moderates were unlikely to read the magazine and even less likely to expend the time and energy to write a letter. This makes the *Church Herald* somewhat skewed as a source of information, but it is still an extremely valuable means of understanding the Reformed Church during these decades.

The Limits of Labels

Most discussions of religious identity in the twentieth century use the terms *liberal* and *conservative*. For the first seventy-five years of the nineteenth century, the most popular and/or culturally influential denominations[31] experienced relative consensus about theology and used the word *evangelical* to describe themselves.[32] Mainline denominations disagreed about revivalism and slavery and social reform, but they generally agreed about doctrine. That changed in the last quarter of the century when Darwinism and critical methods in biblical studies challenged a literal reading of Genesis. Religion scholars, pastors, and parishioners began to ask questions about the Creation, the miracles, the Virgin Birth, the divinity of Jesus, and the Mosaic authorship of the Pentateuch.

Two tendencies became evident in mainline denominations.[33] One side of the spectrum, usually labeled "left" or "liberal," saw few conflicts between faith and science. For this group, the great value of Christianity was in its fruit: kindness, generosity, compassion. God was a Father who loved his children and wanted the best for them. The left was not overly concerned about doctrinal precision; deeds were more important than creeds. Christianity did not have to be irrational. Intelligent moderns could be serious Christians without sacrificing their intellects.

The other end of the spectrum, usually labeled "right" or "conservative," saw more of a conflict between faith and science. The essence of Christianity was its orthodox beliefs. God was a Father who judged his children, found them wanting, and sent his Son Jesus to atone for their sins on the cross. The doctrines of Christianity might appear irrational to the human mind but had to be accepted. If science or reason conflicted with Christian faith, then science or reason was wrong.

Liberals tended to be relatively optimistic about human nature and believed that the world was improving. Conservatives tended to be

---

[31]   These included the Presbyterians, Congregationalists, Episcopalians, Northern Baptists, Methodists, and the RCA.

[32]   The word *euangelion* in Greek means "gospel." In the nineteenth century it was applied to churches that proclaimed the gospel of Jesus Christ.

[33]   These descriptions are rather broad generalizations and do not describe every liberal or conservative, but they illustrate the basic mindset and approach of each side. For a more detailed discussion of these movements see Kenneth Cauthen, *The Impact of American Religious Liberalism* (Washington, D.C.: Univ. Press of America, 1983); William R. Hutchison, *The Modernist Impulse in American Protestantism* (Cambridge: Harvard Univ. Press, 1976); George Marsden, *Fundamentalism and American Culture: The Shaping of Twentieth Century Evangelicalism, 1870-1925* (New York: Oxford Univ. Press, 1980).

relatively pessimistic about the persistent nature of human sinfulness. Liberals tended to be inclusive and open to a range of positions. Conservatives tended to emphasize purity and the need to preserve correct beliefs and protect themselves from those with dangerous ideas. The term *modernist* came to be used either synonymously with liberal or for those on the far end of the spectrum. The word *fundamentalist* was used after the publication of *The Fundamentals*, a set of essays defending particular elements of Christian doctrine, such as the Virgin Birth, the divinity and resurrection of Jesus, the veracity of the miracles, and the inerrancy of the Bible.[34] Fundamentalists came to be viewed as somewhat rigid and angry defenders of orthodoxy.

The word *liberal* or *modernist* was often used inaccurately to describe anyone slightly to the left of a speaker or writer. Similarly, the term *fundamentalist* was often applied disparagingly to anyone slightly to the right. Despite the easy popularity of the terms, there were many Christians who did not fit neatly into either group. These Christians were faithful church members who valued the Bible without reading it literally. They saw truth in both the theories of evolution and the stories of creation. They believed in Jesus as their Savior but did not expect all other Christians to believe exactly as they did. They wanted the church to be a place that welcomed all Christians and not just the like-minded.

Similarly, the Reformed tradition, at its best, is neither fundamentalist nor liberal but an alternative way to think about religious belief and experience.[35] For example, liberals (especially before World War I) believed in the progress and perfectibility of human nature. Fundamentalists have tended to view the world as hopelessly corrupt. The Reformed perspective sees truth and limitation in both views. In contrast to liberal optimism, the Reformed tradition articulates a belief in total depravity that recognizes the effect of sin on

---

[34]   *The Fundamentals; A Testimony to the Truth* (Chicago: Testimony Publishing, 1910-1915). There were twelve volumes in the series. Tensions between the two perspectives peaked in American society during the Scopes trial in Dayton, Tennessee, in 1925. State law prohibited the teaching of evolution, and high school biology teacher John Scopes deliberately challenged the law. Two high-profile lawyers participated in the trial: the former secretary of state, William Jennings Bryan, for the prosecution, and the renowned Chicago attorney, Clarence Darrow, for the defense. Scopes was found guilty, but fundamentalism was mocked by the media, and the law was eventually changed.

[35]   Eugene Heideman, letter to the editor, *CH*, Feb. 25/March 3, 1972, 25. For a discussion of Reformed theology see John Hesselink, *On Being Reformed* (Ann Arbor: Servant Books, 1983); M. Eugene Osterhaven, *The Spirit of the Reformed Tradition* (Grand Rapids: Eerdmans, 1971); Hendrikus Berkhof, *Christian Faith: An Introduction to the Study of the Faith* (Grand Rapids: Eerdmans, 1979).

all aspects of human life—the will, the reason, and the emotions. Still, the Reformed tradition is not hopeless about human nature but insists that redeemed human beings have the capacity to transform the world because God works through people to bring about the realm of God. Fundamentalists and most evangelicals have emphasized the saving of souls. Liberals have emphasized the saving of the world. The Reformed tradition has always cared about both the redemption of persons and the transformation of society.

The Reformed tradition recognizes the limits of human knowledge, the sovereignty of God, and the need always to be reforming. It understands its Standards[36] as particular historical expressions of the faith, not equal in authority to scripture. It has not adopted a rigidly literalist view of scripture and has accepted critical methods and scholarship and acknowledged a human element to the writing of the Bible.

The most divisive conflicts in the Reformed Church did not arise between fundamentalists and modernists, because the denomination had very few modernists. Instead, the debate over identity was fought among theological moderates shaped by Reformed principles and a group I will call "purists," who insisted they alone were truly Reformed. The purists were actually shaped more by fundamentalist perspectives on the Bible and the church than by the Reformed tradition. Between these contending parties is a group of generally conservative Christians who, depending on the issue, sided with either the moderates or the purists. As the Reformed Church debated its identity in response to various conflicts, opportunities, and social changes, the moderates and the purists were the most outspoken. Each group tried to win the cooperation of the conservatives in the middle, who would determine the outcome of most debates.[37]

The use of the term *purist* is unusual and has not been a part of the RCA lexicon, but it can be a helpful way to describe a particular

---

[36] In addition to the three ecumenical creeds shared by most churches (Apostles, Nicene, and Athanasian), the RCA has identified three confessions, or Standards, which have shaped its history and beliefs: the Belgic Confession, the Heidelberg Catechism, and the Canons of the Synod of Dort.

[37] In the RCA, the purist/conservative/moderate categories were further complicated by regional differences. Most Eastern members were moderates, with the exception of the Passaic (NJ) Classis and a few other areas where Dutch immigrants had settled in the nineteenth century. Most Midwestern members were conservative, but there were exceptions. Holland, MI; Pella, IA; and Orange City, IA, all had at least one congregation that had historically been more progressive or Americanized. Central Reformed in Grand Rapids was moderate. There were purists from both regions, but most were from the Midwest. Generally, in this book, Eastern is synonymous with moderate, and Midwestern is synonymous with conservative.

perspective within the denomination. At several points during these five decades (1945-1994), a relatively small group of people exerted a rather large influence over denominational actions. That they were conservative was not unusual, but they were conservative in a different way from many of their fellow members. They insisted that the Reformed Church must preserve its purity (as they defined it) and Dutch Reformed identity. They feared the dangerous influence of other denominations and strongly opposed mergers and membership in ecumenical bodies. Although they could be loving and gracious in personal interaction, in print and in public they could be abrasive and highly critical. They were quick to use the label "modernist" to dismiss fellow Reformed Church members and other Christians with different perspectives. Purists cared deeply about what they saw as the integrity of the gospel and the identity of the RCA, and they frequently tried to reshape the denomination into an institution they found more appropriate and faithful. The desire for purity frequently led them to exclude or criticize individuals, beliefs, and ecumenical connections that did not completely agree with their commitment to biblical literalism, the uniqueness and superiority of Reformed theology, and the need for a high level of personal morality and religious commitment.

On the other hand, Reformed Church moderates were profoundly shaped by Reformed theology, polity, and liturgy. They valued the Bible but were not literalist in their reading of it. They were ecumenical, because they believed that God had not entrusted the whole of the gospel to the Reformed Church in America. They trusted that God brought the church into being and that God would protect it, so Christians did not need to be so anxious about its purity.[38]

Occupying the middle ground between these two poles were many people who were theologically conservative but lacked the angry, dismissive edge of the purists. Conservatives were likely to agree with the purists that the Bible should be read literally, but they were not likely to label and dismiss as modernists those RCA members who did not think in a similar way. Conservatives might have been convinced about the superiority of Reformed theology, but they were more open to ecumenical relationships and less likely to demand full agreement. Conservatives might faithfully attend Sunday evening services without

---

[38]   M. Verne Oggel, a pastor in New Jersey, expressed this view when he wrote that RCA membership in the World Council of Churches fostered connections to churches throughout the world. "Orthodoxy is not so frail and shaky a thing that it cannot endure occasional exposure to a degree of heterodoxy." "Is the World Council of Churches Orthodox?" *CH*, Aug. 22, 1952, 8.

condemning as unChristian those churches that decided not to hold them. This group had an extremely influential role in the Reformed Church because they usually determined the outcome of difficult issues. Would the RCA merge with another denomination as the moderates wanted? No, the conservatives voted with the purists against that. Would the RCA end its relationship with the National Council of Churches as the purists wanted? No, on this issue the conservatives voted with the moderates.

These categories are notoriously slippery, and church members at times moved from one group to another depending on the issue. Some were purists on one issue but not on another. Some purists became more open and flexible later in their lives. At many points there was little to differentiate the purists and the conservatives. When the denomination was less conflicted, and when there was no particular issue to be opposed, the purists acted more like conservatives. But when an issue such as merger or women's ordination challenged the identity of the Reformed Church, then the purists became vocal and critical.

Isaac Rottenberg, a pastor and denominational executive, said that he saw the greatest differences in the church not between liberals and conservatives but between lovers and haters. "Lovers" valued relationships and worked at preserving them. They had strong beliefs and expressed them honestly, but they did not impugn the Christianity or commitment of those with whom they disagreed. They often had a sense of humor. As an example he cited Jerome DeJong, a prominent spokesman for the most conservative element of the denomination. He and Isaac had been friends for decades despite their disagreements on a variety of social and theological issues. "Haters," on the other hand, valued rightness more than relationships. They were quick not only to disagree but to question the motives and faith of others. Those who might be labeled this way probably would protest that they did not hate anybody, but rather they loved the truth and would defend it at all costs, even if that meant denouncing fellow church members.[39]

---

[39] Oral history interview with Isaac Rottenberg, May 8, 2000, Holland, MI. As part of the research for this project, I conducted more than seventy-five interviews with retired clergy, missionaries, and laypeople. Almost all of the people with whom I talked demonstrated extraordinary affection for and commitment to the RCA. They told powerful stories of their childhoods, college and seminary, and the places they served throughout their careers. The tapes and transcripts are in the possession of the author. For a further discussion of the interviews see Lynn Japinga, "'No One Has Ever Asked Me This Before': The Use of Oral History in Denominational History," in A Goodly Heritage: Essays in Honor of the Reverend Dr. Elton J. Bruins at Eighty, ed. Jacob Nyenhuis, HSRCA, no. 56 (Grand Rapids: Eerdmans, 2007).

These categories and the analysis may seem a bit abstract and vague, but the people who hold these beliefs are fascinating. They are also infinitely complex and defy easy attempts to label them. They engaged in arguments which may appear irrelevant or parochial, but their arguments arose at least in part from their deep loyalty to the Reformed Church. In the chapters that follow, I will explore the roles that purists, conservatives, and moderates have played in the struggles to define the identity of the Reformed Church in America during the latter half of the twentieth century.[40]

---

[40]   I am painfully aware of how much has been left out of this story, although this might come as a surprise to a reader holding a lengthy book. It is my hope that this book will encourage future historians to explore the many other stories that can be told about the RCA and its people.

CHAPTER 2

1945-1950: Evangelical or Ecumenical?

At the end of the Second World War, the Reformed Church in America saw itself as a New York-based, mainline, ecumenical denomination that was slightly more theologically conservative than other mainline churches. It had survived the difficult years of the Great Depression and the war and appeared ready to move forward along with the rest of the country. Instead, the Reformed Church experienced a set of conflicts between 1946 and 1950 that divided its members and called its identity into question. The conflicts arose because members disagreed about church policy, biblical interpretation, and ecumenism. Underlying the conflicts was a power struggle over which faction would control the denomination, determine its identity, and decide its future. The Reformed Church's identity had long been defined by the eastern churches, but in the late 1940s the Midwestern churches demanded greater representation and authority.

In the year immediately following the end of World War II, however, Reformed Church members had more pressing concerns than their church's identity. It was an anxious time in American history. The Allies had defeated Germany in May of 1945, and Japan in August of that year, and the American people felt euphoric about the victory, the homecoming of the soldiers, and the end of shortages and ration cards. But they were also uneasy. The war had lifted the country out of a severe economic depression, and people wondered if hard times would return with the end of the war. There were not enough homes or jobs for all the returning veterans.

The condition of the world provided many other reasons for anxiety. European countries needed major reconstruction but lacked building materials as well as sufficient food for their people. The death and destruction of combat had been horrific, but it had been even more agonizing to discover the Holocaust and the raw human evil evident in the concentration camps. The atomic bomb raised questions about warfare and morality that struck at the heart of national and religious identity. The bomb had ended the war and spared the lives of many American soldiers, but at a cost of 200,000 Japanese civilians. Finally, the Soviet Union threatened the world's already tenuous sense of peace and security when it drew an Iron Curtain around Eastern Europe. The former ally quickly became viewed as an enemy.

Some Americans turned to religion as a way to deal with their anxiety and interpret the profound evil of the war. Membership in churches and synagogues reached an all-time high of about 72 million people, but few of the new worshipers joined RCA churches. Between 1927 and 1947 the Reformed Church grew by about 10 percent while the Assemblies of God grew by 374 percent, the Southern Baptists by 60 percent, the Lutherans and the Christian Reformed Church by 30 percent.[1]

Some Reformed Church members questioned the quality of religious commitment underlying this growth. Louis Benes, the editor of the *Church Herald,* frequently lamented that modernism had seeped into American religion. By this he meant a more relaxed, accepting style of church life rather than a strict one that emphasized doctrinal precision. If an otherwise theologically orthodox congregation discussed race and economic issues, held social events rather than prayer meetings, discontinued its Sunday evening worship service, or engaged in any other activity that did not aim to convert people, Benes

---

[1]   Then General Synod president Harry Hager reported these statistics in his "State of Religion" address in 1947. *Acts and Proceedings,* 1947, 230-37. Robert Wuthnow, *The Re-structuring of American Religion* (Princeton: Princeton Univ. Press, 1988), and Robert Ellwood, *1950, Crossroads of American Religious Life* (Louisville: Westminster/ John Knox, 2000), argue that after the chaos of the Depression and WWII, American people wanted to return to traditional beliefs and ideas.

frequently labeled the congregation "modernist."[2] He did not identify particular congregations but implied that many American churches were suspect. Eastern RCA congregations also came under this cloud of suspicion, as many of them had not held Sunday evening services for decades. Were they modernists? Benes never said so explicitly, but his implicit judgment contributed to a midwestern distrust and suspicion of eastern churches.

This fear of modernism far exceeded the actual presence of liberal religious ideas in American religion, and certainly in the Reformed Church. But modernism appeared to threaten not only religious purity, but national security as well. Benes believed that only a pure and uncompromised Christian faith could prevent a Third World War, nuclear destruction, or a Communist takeover. The world was in grave danger, and only God, acting through orthodox Christianity, could save it.[3]

Despite these undercurrents of uncertainty in both the church and American society, the mood at the General Synod of 1946 was positive. Harold Leestma, a young pastor at the Laketon Bethel Church in Muskegon, Michigan, reported that the synod meeting was hard-working, inspiring, and devotional. The Reformed Church had adopted the United Advance Fund Drive[4] and demonstrated "unity in attitude

---

[2]   Louis Benes, editorial, "The Secularization of the Church," *CH*, Dec. 13, 1946, 5. In the introduction to this volume modernism was described as a form of liberalism that questioned the divinity of Christ and the truth of the miracles. Benes used the word much more broadly to include not only beliefs but also practices and tendencies. Benes thought it was essential for Christians to have a conversion experience and demonstrate complete intellectual assent to particular doctrines. He believed that a congregation that lacked these high standards would stop teaching doctrine and emphasize social events and political issues instead. There were many churches, however, including many in the RCA, who took the Christian faith seriously and yet wanted to make it more relevant and engaging to those who were not already members. They were hardly modernists simply because they offered social activities and discussed current events.

[3]   Benes identified a number of parallels between modernism and communism. Both tried to gain influence by stealthily infiltrating either Christianity or American democracy. Both began with small, innocuous practices or beliefs that led to dangerous changes. Both shared a high regard for human ability but failed to recognize human sinfulness and the need for divine intervention to restore the world.

[4]   The United Advance provided emergency relief for Europe and capital improvements for the boards and the three RCA colleges. It raised two million of its $2.3 million goal. Two years later, in the midst of denominational conflict, some congregations threatened to withhold support from the United Advance if the denomination took an action of which they did not approve. The drive was administered by Marion de Velder, pastor of Hope Church, Holland, MI. It was the first of many

and aspiration, unity in faith and fellowship, unity in doctrine and decisions."[5] This unity did not last long. In the next few years, four controversies would test the identity and unity of the Reformed Church in America.

Henry Bast and the Board of Foreign Missions

The first controversy erupted late in 1946 when a purist Midwestern pastor questioned Reformed Church policies and accused several of its institutions of liberalism. In February 1946, Henry Bast,[6] pastor of the Bethany Reformed Church in Grand Rapids, Michigan, attended his first meeting of the Board of Foreign Missions.[7] He later thanked Francis ("Duke") Potter, executive secretary, for a "profitable and enjoyable" experience and a "very fine program." He attended the May meeting, but not those in June or October. In November 1946 Bast abruptly resigned from the board because he did not agree with its policies.[8] Potter and Milton Stauffer, the board's president, begged him to reconsider his resignation, and the Executive Committee refused to accept his resignation when it met in December. A small group of board members met with him in March. Each time he insisted that he could do nothing from within to repair the problems of policy and structure.

In the fall of 1946, Bast published a pamphlet entitled, "An Appeal to the Ministers and Laymen of the Chicago and Iowa Synods," and two letters to the editor of the *Church Herald*. He identified two reasons for his resignation. First, he believed that the board's structure did not give equal voice to all members. Each particular synod had one member

---

denominational projects that eventually brought him into the roles of stated clerk and general secretary.

[5]   Harold Leestma, "Onward! The Church! My Impressions of the General Synod Meeting," *CH*, June 14, 1946, 12.

[6]   Bast was born in the Netherlands in 1906. He graduated from Hope College in 1930 and Western Theological Seminary in 1933. He served the Richmond Reformed Church in Grand Rapids from 1933-1939, taught Bible at Hope College from 1939-1944, and served the Bethany Reformed Church in Grand Rapids from 1944-1956.

[7]   Bast was elected to the Board of Foreign Missions in June 1945 but did not attend the meeting in October 1945. The full board usually met four times a year, generally once in the Midwest, but none of the midwestern members attended more than two meetings. Train travel was difficult during the war, and board members often chose not to spend the time and money to travel east to conduct routine business.

[8]   Henry Bast to Francis Potter, Feb. 23, 1946. Henry Bast to Milton Stauffer, Nov. 21, 1946. These letters and extensive additional correspondence are in the Board of Foreign Missions papers, General Synod Archives, located in the Gardner Sage Library, New Brunswick Theologlical Seminary, New Brunswick, New Jersey (hereinafter, GS Archives).

on the board, but the full board met only four times a year and board members from the Midwest generally attended no more than twice. The Executive Committee, composed of eastern representatives who lived near New York City, conducted business at other times. Several of these easterners were related to each other or to New Brunswick Seminary, and Bast complained that power was concentrated in a few families.[9] These nonrepresentative boards also wielded too much power, he alleged. Board executives answered only to their individual boards rather than to the whole church.[10] Subcommittees of the boards that selected staff members or missionaries were even less representative of the entire church.[11]

Bast's second criticism was far more damaging and divisive. He charged that the Reformed Church, particularly New Brunswick Seminary and the Board of Foreign Missions, had been infected by liberalism. Cooperation with ecumenical organizations had caused a "noticeable drift in the boards away from the evangelical Christianity which is the faith of the Reformed Church."[12] Bast implied that the secretary who was responsible for overseeing new appointments at the Board of Foreign Missions (unnamed, but Ruth Ransom) was

---

[9] The board included 42 members, 26 from the three eastern synods and 16 from the two western synods. There were 18 ministers, 9 laymen, and 15 women. Nineteen people (12 men and 7 women) served on the Executive Committee. After the 1946 merger of the Board of Foreign Missions and the Woman's Board of Foreign Missions, the new board included several couples who had served on the previous boards: John and Frances Beardslee, David and Lillian Van Strien, and Anthony and Christina Van Westenberg. In 1946 the Executive Committee included the Van Striens and Beardslees (John was president of New Brunswick Theological Seminary [NBTS]), Marjorie James (whose husband taught pastoral theology at NBTS), Joseph Sizoo (named president of NBTS in 1947), and Mrs. John Van Strien, sister-in-law to David Van Strien. For a discussion of board structure after the merger, see Mary Kansfield, *Letters to Hazel: Ministry within the Woman's Board of Foreign Missions of the Reformed Church in America*, HSRCA, no. 46 (Grand Rapids: Eerdmans, 2004), 130-38.

[10] The method of board appointment was ambiguous. Officially, the General Synod elected members of the boards, but it often elected people that the boards or secretaries had recommended. When accused of being self-perpetuating, the boards always insisted that the synod elected their members. Technically they were correct.

[11] Bast was also a member of a subcommittee of the Board of Education, and he reported that a different subcommittee had appointed a staff person of whom the Midwest did not approve. The board's action did not require confirmation by the General Synod, so those who opposed it had no recourse. The person in question was probably Calvin Meury, who became secretary for young people's work in 1947.

[12] Henry Bast, letters to the editor, *CH*, Nov. 29, 1946, 7; Dec. 27, 1946, 10. Bast, "An Appeal to the Ministers and Laymen of the Chicago and Iowa Synods," priv. pub. pamphlet, n.d., Bast papers, Joint Archives of Holland, located at Hope College, Holland, Michigan (hereinafter, Joint Archives).

a modernist who favored liberals over conservatives.[13] Bast also claimed that Reformed Church's participation in ecumenical groups demonstrated its lack of concern for doctrinal purity.[14] Bast implied that acknowledging the validity of other Christian perspectives called into question the uniqueness and superiority of Reformed theology.

Bast concluded the pamphlet with a scathing critique of the inequities between the two sections of the denomination. Although the midwestern part of the church gave most of the money to missions, eastern members determined how it was spent. Bast asked pointedly, "Are we going to allow the policies and the direction of the church to continue to be formulated by an area of the church [the East] that does not have enough spiritual vitality to give adequate support for the work?...Rise up now and reclaim the Reformed Church for the historic and living Christian faith."[15]

Bast drew a great deal of criticism for the tone and content of his letters and pamphlet, but he did not back down. Barnerd Luben, field secretary for the Board of Foreign Missions, asked Bast to return to the board and try to change things from within. Many years later Luben recalled that Bast "was as stubborn as an ox and wouldn't listen."[16] In part, Bast was motivated by fear of what "the neighbors" would think. In the midwestern enclaves of Holland, Grand Rapids, and Chicago, he reported, Christian Reformed critics "watch over everything we do with the closest scrutiny. Everything that we do that is a departure from the Reformed tradition is thrown up at us continuously." Bast also felt the

---

[13]   Ruth Ransom was a Methodist who headed the Women's Board of Foreign Missions. After the boards merged she was named candidate secretary, who not only recruited new missionaries but held considerable power in the board's process of candidate selection. The BFM appointed Jay Kapenga in 1944 and Blaise Levai in 1946, before Ransom was responsible for candidates. Both graduated from New Brunswick and may have been more moderate theologically but were hardly modernists/liberals. Harvey Hoekstra, a WTS graduate, was initially turned down by the board but later accepted.

[14]   As examples of ecumenical groups, Bast named the Federal Council of Churches and the International Council for Religious Education. He also saw a lack of denominational purity in the Board of Education's willingness to use materials from liberal churches, and in the fact that several board executives and New Brunswick Seminary professors were from other denominations.

[15]   Bast, "An Appeal."

[16]   Luben worked out of an office in Kalamazoo, Michigan. He grew up in Coopersville, Michigan, and served for a decade as a missionary in Japan. He described train trips to board meetings in New York with a number of other board members from western Michigan. His wife, Edith, made a big box supper for everyone, and he recalled high morale and loving relationships. Oral history interview with Barnerd Luben, May 4, 2000, Ridgewood, NJ.

scorn of fundamentalist churches that portrayed themselves as more conservative and spiritual than the Reformed Church, especially in their use of faith missions.[17]

Bast's resignation was finally accepted with regret at the May 15, 1947, meeting of the Board of Foreign Missions. The board responded to Bast's structural critique by appointing a Special Committee on Board Organization and Procedure, which recommended several changes that made the board more representative.[18]

Bast's other comments sparked a great deal of anger and resentment among those he had labeled as liberals. Milton Hoffman, professor of church history at New Brunswick Theological Seminary, asked how Bast could accuse him of deliberately betraying the doctrine of the Reformed Church when Bast had never been to New Brunswick Seminary? How could Bast condemn people he did not know based on such minimal evidence?[19] The New Brunswick Board of Superintendents reported to the General Synod in 1947 that the criticisms threatened "the peace and harmony of the Reformed Church," and added,

> We wish to record our concern over the methods used, and our regret about the unsubstantiated attacks made upon the integrity and character of the Faculty and the unsound doctrinal beliefs of the graduates and student body. These allegations are detrimental to the Seminary, the ministry and the peace of the Church. We strongly express our complete confidence in the integrity and teaching of the Faculty and in the Christian convictions of the

[17] Henry Bast to F. M. Potter, Dec. 23, 1946, GS Archives. Faith missionaries had to raise their own support (rely on faith) rather than receive funding from denominations.

[18] BFM Minutes, May 15, 1947. The special committee recommended that all members attend the October meeting in a western location and the May meeting in the East, and that major policy issues be decided at these meetings. Election of officers should be done by mail. The Executive Committee would retain its considerable authority (as stipulated in the by-laws) but should consult more extensively with the board. Three members of the Executive Committee should be from the Midwest, one board member should represent Western Seminary, and all committees should have both eastern and western members. The board as a whole recognized the wisdom of having fewer married couples but decided to reduce the number gradually, and so refused to accept the resignations of Christina Van Westenburg and Lillian Van Strien. Some of these actions contributed to the loss of power and influence by women on the BFM. The special committee decided to ask an ordained minister to chair the Candidates' Committee. The board debated this at length, because the chair conducted extensive and time-consuming correspondence. Marjorie James had served effectively in the position, but she was thanked for her efforts and replaced. See Kansfield, *Letters to Hazel*, 131-38.

[19] Milton Hoffman to Henry Bast, March 13, 1947, Benes file, FCC Correspondence, Joint Archives.

students. These are in keeping with the Doctrinal standards of the church. We therefore recommend to the General Synod that hereafter those making charges against individuals or Institutions of the church use the Constitutional channels.[20]

The Classis of South Long Island and the Particular Synod of New Jersey submitted overtures in 1947 that asked whether a person who unfairly criticized RCA boards and institutions should serve on the editorial board of the *Church Herald*. The overtures did not identify him by name, but they clearly referred to Henry Bast. The synod's Committee on Overtures responded that it regretted the "unhappy developments but it feels nothing positive and valuable can be gained by any specific action. We feel that sheer Christianity and church policy demand that the church take the shock of the experience and that we all 'go forward.' We therefore recommend no action."[21]

Some midwestern ministers also took issue with Bast's harsh approach. Gerrit De Motts[22] pointed out that Bast's anger was particularly inappropriate in the time of grief and loss following the war, in which De Motts and many others had lost sons. Grief could be better healed with peace than with anger.

> This is no time for suspicion and distrust in the Church. This is a time to work and pray for peace, for the comfort of sorrowing hearts, for the healing of the wounds of a whole nation, and of the whole world....Who are these young men of ministerial cloth, who can so quickly forget, and whose itching for a denominational purge, apparently, blinds their vision to greater needs of to-day? Is it not far better in such a time as this to mind the business of the Lord, and boldly proclaim Him, Who is our Peace?

De Motts noted that name calling and criticism of boards and institutions did not simply attack those institutions but defamed the character of the individuals in them and tarnished their reputations. It was unfair to make allegations without proof, and the church must

---

[20] *Acts and Proceedings*, 1947, 70-71.
[21] *Acts and Proceedings*, 1947, 123, 125. The 1947 Overtures Committee was composed of six ministers from the Midwest and four from the East, which may have made it more forgiving and polite toward Bast than the NBTS Board of Superintendents. The committee did ask that the new General Synod president send a pastoral letter to all RCA ministers to create confidence and settle unrest.
[22] Gerrit De Motts was born in Waupun, Wisconsin, in 1886; graduated from Hope and New Brunswick; served several pastorates in the East, Midwest, and West; and at the time of this controversy was serving a church in Wisconsin Rapids, WI.

defend those who were attacked until they were proven guilty. He concluded, "Maybe our Reformed Church needs a purge of slandering ministers rather than of highly exaggerated evils." Better to be kind and concerned about the peace of the church, he said, than to engage in these sorts of debates.[23]

In response to the debate about board structure, eight classes and two particular synods submitted overtures requesting that the General Synod either move the boards to the Midwest or study the matter. These groups thought moving the boards would be more economical and efficient and would link staff members more closely to the more financially generous and spiritually committed section of the church. The General Synod appointed a study committee composed of five laymen (one from each particular synod) and Dr. John Beardslee Jr., president of the General Synod and former president of New Brunswick Seminary.[24]

The committee reported to the General Synod in 1948 that it was actually more economical and efficient to stay in New York than to move to the Midwest. The Reformed Church leased space from the Presbyterian Church offices in New York City, and the rent was considerably less than it would be for comparable space in Chicago. Board executives preferred to stay in New York City because it was easier to manage banking and other missionary details, and because they valued the presence of other denominations and interdenominational agencies.

The committee also explored the underlying issues of representation and fairness and concluded that the regions were adequately represented on the boards. Admittedly, the executive committees were not balanced, but it was not feasible for an Iowan to travel to New York six times a year. Board members often *chose* not to attend regular meetings because they felt the expense was not justified for routine business. The committee concluded that the attendance patterns did not result from an eastern attempt to seize power but from the members' desire to use the board's money for missions rather than travel. The committee did see room for improvement. To assure fair and balanced representation, it recommended (and synod agreed) that a permanent Committee on Nominations should make board

---

23   "Limping Logic," priv. pub. pamphlet, circa 1947, Joint Archives. Two decades later, Henry Bast lost a son in Vietnam.

24   *Acts and Proceedings*, 1947, 123. The five laymen were Eugene Alhart (Rochester, NY), James Kavanagh (Bronxville, NY), Henry Kloese (Chicago, IL), Frederick Bauer (Union City, NJ), and Herbert Mentink (Pella, IA).

appointments, the executive committees should represent the whole church, and board members should attend all meetings regardless of expense. The committee concluded that the boards should stay in New York for at least five years.[25]

The varied responses to Bast's complaints demonstrated very different views of the church. The purists argued that the Christian faith in general and the Reformed Church in particular needed to be protected from the dangerous influences of modernism that had infiltrated RCA boards and institutions. If there were modernists who held positions of power and authority, they must be identified and removed, even if they claimed to be orthodox. The purists were afraid that the church would be damaged or destroyed. They had a deep sense of loyalty to orthodoxy and purity. They were not as concerned about preserving relationships and being generous toward other Reformed Church members.

The moderate view of the church tended to be more positive and optimistic. The moderates believed that Reformed Church members were honest and strongly committed to the church, and that board members were sincere and trustworthy Christian people. If people claimed to be orthodox, they should be treated as such. Moderates did not believe that church members and classes should use overtures or pamphlets to attack other members of the church. People and institutions should not be labeled as liberals or modernists without substantive evidence. Such attacks were impolite and un-Christian and bypassed the appropriate channels for discernment. The Reformed Church had a system of checks and balances that could handle dangerous ideas; therefore, its members did not need to be so fearful.

Between the purists and the moderates were a large group of conservatives who may have agreed with the purists about biblical literalism and doctrinal purity, but they agreed with the moderates about the values of kindness and high regard for others. Like Gerrit De Motts, they were less likely to call for a purge of modernist elements, most likely because they did not see modernism as particularly threatening to the Reformed Church.

---

[25] *Acts and Proceedings*, 1948, 146-52. The committee also examined board expenditures, in response to Bast's claim that the Midwest gave 71 percent of the denominational benevolence budget but received little in return. The committee noted that a large percentage of the money raised by the Board of Domestic Missions was used by the synods of Chicago and Iowa for salary supplements and new buildings. Much of the money available in the Church Building Fund had been raised in the three Eastern synods but was used by the two Western synods. The Board of Education supported five educational institutions and four were located in the Midwest.

The "blast from Bast," as it was called, raised important questions about how the denomination should deal with disagreement within its ranks. The boards recognized that Bast had made some valid points about structure, and they made a concerted effort to include more midwestern members in their decision-making processes. But the denomination would not concede to all of his demands. The denominational offices would not be moved to the Midwest. Rigid biblical literalism would not be instituted at the seminaries.[26] Not every charge of heterodoxy needed to be investigated. The conservatives voted with the moderates on these issues.

Bast's criticism set some unfortunate precedents, however. The accusations of liberalism and spiritual laxity continued to shape the Midwest's perception of the East for several decades. Bast's uncivil tone was relatively rare in the Reformed Church, but it received attention and results. He introduced a rather mean-spirited style that would profoundly affect the church during the next few decades. For those who sought to create a pure church, it became acceptable not only to criticize other church members but to question their faith and integrity.[27]

The Federal Council of Churches

The second major conflict of the late 1940s involved a debate about the Reformed Church's membership in the Federal Council of

---

[26] In 1948 the Classis and Particular Synod of Chicago overtured the General Synod to determine the RCA's position on higher criticism of the Bible "in order to insure that the same position shall be taught to and maintained before our future ministers in both our Seminaries." The Committee on Overtures responded that higher criticism developed in the nineteenth century, long after the Standards and Constitution were written. Ministers and professors affirmed the inspiration of scripture when they signed the formula at ordination and subsequent installations. The committee expressed confidence in the seminary boards and faculties and recommended no action. The moderate voice in the RCA was strong enough to dismiss overtures like this that appeared unduly critical and suspicious. *Acts and Proceedings*, 1948, 122.

[27] A parallel debate occurred in the late 1940s at Hope College, an RCA school in Holland, MI. The college more than doubled in size after the war and desperately needed faculty. Purists criticized the president, Irwin Lubbers, for hiring academically qualified faculty with a broader view of Christian faith than the purists considered appropriate. Purists also tried to limit enrollment in order to preserve a majority of RCA students. They also tried to prohibit dancing, not only on campus, but in off-campus locations with faculty supervision. Lubbers received a great deal of criticism but refused to allow purists to dictate the identity of the college. See minutes of the Hope College Board of Trustees, Joint Archives, and James Kennedy and Caroline Simon, *Can Hope Endure? A Historical Case Study in Christian Higher Education*, HSRCA, no. 48 (Grand Rapids: Eerdmans, 2005), 104-13.

Churches (FCC). In 1908, more than thirty Protestant denominations formed the council to address social, political, and religious issues and to formalize their long history of cooperative work in missions and social reform. Eastern congregations generally valued the council as a tangible sign of the Reformed Church's ecumenical commitments. Some midwestern members became increasingly suspicious of the council, however, because they feared it harbored modernists, and—in 1931, 1934, 1936, and 1944—several classes submitted overtures protesting the RCA's membership. Each time, the General Synod's Committee on Overtures recommended remaining in the Federal Council, and each time the synod agreed.

When Louis Benes became editor of the *Church Herald* in 1945, he initially responded positively to the Federal Council and praised the "well planned program" of the meeting he attended early in 1946.[28] After the Bast pamphlet was published, his attitude changed dramatically. Benes said nothing positive about the council meeting he attended in December 1946. He claimed that most of the leaders were liberals who were "unable to represent or express the evangelical and historic principles of the faith." He criticized a proposal to merge the council with other ecumenical groups because he feared that the resulting National Council of Churches (NCC) would eventually become like Rome, with too much power and control. "A super-organization planning for the denominations in matters of religious education and the missionary program, which deal with the heart of the Christian faith, would jeopardize the evangelical emphases of those groups remaining within its orbit of influence."[29]

Bast and Benes did not use the term *evangelical* in the broad sense of the term that described most mainstream Protestant churches in the nineteenth century. Their definition was much narrower and included a literal reading of an inerrant Bible and an emphasis on personal piety over against social action.[30] This form of evangelicalism encouraged

---

28 Editorial, "The Federal Council Meets," *CH*, March 22, 1946, 5.

29 Editorial, "The Federal Council Meets," *CH*, Jan. 17, 1947, 6-7. Benes questioned the orthodoxy of FCC churches in part because he believed that if one minister in a denomination was a liberal, the whole denomination must be liberal, because a truly orthodox denomination would not allow a liberal to remain within it. The groups contemplating merger with the FCC included the Foreign Mission Conference, Home Missions Council, United Council of Church Women, and the International Council of Religious Education.

30 Bast, Benes, and others were heavily influenced by the rise of evangelicalism in the 1940s. It was a kinder, gentler, more intellectual version of 1920s fundamentalism but continued to emphasize personal piety and separation from the world. Influential evangelical individuals and institutions at the time were Billy Graham, Wheaton College, Fuller Seminary, and the National Association of Evangelicals.

strict Sunday observance and opposed dancing, drinking, and attending movies. It wanted to preserve the "faith once delivered to the saints" without any alteration to church practices or doctrinal formulations. It feared that religion was in danger and must be protected.

Many eastern Reformed churches would have described themselves as evangelical in the broad sense of emphasizing the gospel, but not in the way Bast and Benes meant. Eastern Reformed Church members were more likely to be moderates who were open to change and development in their understanding of the faith. They had a more flexible view of personal piety and Sunday practices. They firmly believed that interdenominational cooperation was an essential part of the evangelical identity of the Reformed Church.

In March 1947 Benes wrote a lengthy editorial, entitled "Infiltration," that described the subtle dangers of the Federal Council of Churches. He criticized an FCC devotional booklet, called "The Fellowship of Prayer," because its Easter material did not emphasize sufficiently the bodily resurrection of Jesus. He wrote, "We understand that the pamphlet is prepared for use in the Congregational-Christian Church (quite pinkish theologically), and is taken over by the Federal Council without changes." He did not say what "pinkish" meant, or provide any evidence as to why he used the label, but the phrase would have planted the suspicion in many readers' minds that a Communist taint existed in both the Congregational-Christian Church and in the Federal Council.

Benes next criticized a liturgy produced by the United Council of Church Women because it failed to mention individual guilt, the sin of the world, or an atoning Savior. Instead of dismissing this as an unfortunate example of liturgy written by committee, Benes diagnosed something far more ominous. Since becoming editor, he wrote, "we witness the continual seeping down of poisonous ideas inimical to the Christian faith from various interdenominational organizations." The literature, committees, and conventions of these groups "present a very diluted and unscriptural Christianity. These become sounding boards from which ultra-liberal professional groups can propagandize the churches of America with their theology." He encouraged Reformed Church members to defend their faith against these liberal groups and ideas.[31]

---

[31] *CH*, March 14, 1947, 6-7. The Congregational-Christian Church merged with the Evangelical and Reformed Church in the 1950s and took the name, United Church of Christ.

In the same issue of the *Church Herald*, three ministers reported on the annual meeting of the International Council of Religious Education. They were dismayed that some of the council's literature implied that children were inherently good and failed to emphasize the sacrificial death of Jesus. The ministers pronounced that the council had dangerous leadership, was not true to the Bible or evangelical Christianity, and was at heart fundamentally unlike the Reformed Church. The authors felt intimidated and feared the direction this group was taking the denomination.[32]

These anxious critiques of ecumenical organizations sparked several responses. Supporters of the Federal Council noted that it was a functional organization that helped churches do their work more effectively but did not control them.[33] A number of Benes's friends wrote personal letters encouraging him to be more moderate. Richard C. Oudersluys, a professor of New Testament at Western Theological Seminary, asked him to write wise, positive editorials that spoke for the whole church and not just the Midwest. Edwin Jones reminded Benes that when they served neighboring churches in Albany, they had very different opinions, but they loved each other and worked together for the denomination and the Albany Council of Churches.[34]

The debate continued at the General Synod of 1947. Nine classes overtured against membership in the FCC, seven called for continued membership, three asked that the council become more evangelical, and two asked for further study. The Committee on Overtures responded to this sharp difference of opinion by recommending that a committee be formed to study both the Federal Council and the National Association of Evangelicals. The synod approved.[35]

Some Federal Council supporters sought more definitive action. The Classis of Ulster (New York) submitted an overture protesting the *Church Herald*'s criticism of the council and related organizations. The

---

32   Gary DeWitt, William Swets, Russell VandeBunte, "A Report on the Council of Religious Education," *CH*, March 14, 1947, 11, 21. The ICRE was an organization of staff members from the educational offices of the mainline churches.

33   Theodore Thielpape, letter to the editor, *CH*, Feb. 28, 1947, 10. See also David Van Strien, "Concerning Our Membership in the Federal Council," *CH*, March 28, 1947, 8-9, and Winfield Burggraaff, letter to the editor, *CH*, May 16, 1947, 14.

34   Richard Oudersluys to Louis Benes, March 15, 1947. Luman Shafer to Louis Benes, March 19, 1947. Edwin Jones to Louis Benes, March 18, 1947. Benes file, FCC Correspondence, Joint Archives.

35   *Acts and Proceedings*, 1947, 124. The synod also approved a recommendation from the committee that the RCA continue membership in the FCC for another year "with the avowed purpose of getting the Council to take positions doctrinally more consonant with Biblical Christianity."

classis claimed that the magazine's opinions did not represent those of the whole denomination and that its divisive spirit damaged the cause of Christ in the world. It asked that the editor be directed to refrain from attacking these organizations and give space to a range of opinions.

Benes responded with a vigorous defense of his editorial freedom. He had evaluated literature which endangered the evangelical faith and the doctrinal standards of the Reformed Church in America. He had not discussed personalities, attacked organizations, or advocated withdrawal, and he resented the fact that "some, at least, want us to smother our own evangelical convictions, and acquiesce silently in the distribution of literature which directly or indirectly denies the fundamentals of our evangelical faith." The overture "raises the question as to whether the *Church Herald* is to become controlled and censored, and silence [*sic*] from calling attention to the supreme importance of faithfulness to the Gospel of our Lord and Savior Jesus Christ as over against the perilous unbelief of our time."[36] Benes believed the overture represented only a minority view and that most Reformed Church members supported his effort to preserve the faith.

Benes further insisted that he gave a similar number of column inches to differing opinions, and that the Federal Council in particular received a considerable amount of space for news releases. Letters to the editor also expressed both sides of the issues. He quoted the editorial policy of the *Church Herald*, which required the magazine both to proclaim the gospel and defend the faith from error. He concluded:

> When that faith is endangered or imperiled, either by open attacks, or superficial substitutes, it becomes our bounden duty to point out that evil. In such an age as ours, facing unbelief in many forms and places, it is our task to call attention to where this evangelical faith is in jeopardy, and to the supreme importance of faithfulness to the Gospel of the Grace of God revealed in the Holy Scriptures that is needed in our day of moral anarchy, religious confusion, and denial of that Gospel, and to that high calling the Church Herald stands committed."[37]

---

[36] *Acts and Proceedings*, 1947, 108-13.

[37] Ibid. Benes also noted that the magazine's circulation was about 36,000, and fewer than 20 percent of subscribers lived in the three eastern synods. There were 212 midwestern congregations that purchased subscriptions for all members, but only 30 eastern congregations did. He argued that the magazine would be more efficient and effective if everybody read it. The subtext was that if eastern members did not read the magazine, they had no right to complain about it.

Benes believed that he acted fairly and allowed both sides the space to speak. What his critics had perceived, however, was that the editor of a magazine (particularly one as certain of himself as Benes) possessed a higher degree of authority and influence than did authors of news articles or letters. Some critics argued that although he claimed to speak for the whole denomination, Benes actually represented only a few purist midwesterners who disliked the denomination's longstanding ecumenical commitments.

Benes's editorials conveyed a somewhat arrogant tone, which suggested that he knew what was best for the church. He wanted the Reformed Church to be conservative and evangelical in precisely the way he and Bast defined those words. He insisted upon ecclesiastical purity, while other Reformed Church members valued inclusivity and cooperation.[38]

The controversy about the Federal Council of Churches abated after the synod met in the summer of 1947, but in January 1948 Benes revived the discussion. He lamented that the proposed National Council of Churches would be a Protestant totalitarian bureaucracy. "What such a super-bureaucracy with liberalism in control would mean for the Evangelical faith, we leave to our readers to imagine. All of the several functions of the several denominations, such as missions, education, youth work, etc., would be determined by the plans and programs sent out from this super-Council."[39] David Van Strien replied that the FCC did not wish and indeed lacked the power to control churches or usurp their authority. This would also be true for the new NCC. He ended with a barbed comment about the magazine: "Trusting that the Church Herald [sic] may continue to be the organ of the entire denomination, through which the unity of the Spirit may ever be made manifest."[40]

Opposition to the Federal Council continued to grow. The Evangelical Brotherhood, a group of more than a hundred Reformed Church ministers and laymen, gathered in Chicago in January 1948 to pray for new spiritual life and growth in the denomination. They believed that growth could best be achieved by leaving the Federal Council and eliminating liberalism from the church. The Evangelical Brotherhood asked participants to sign a pledge that affirmed their faith in the inspired and inerrant Bible and their loyalty to the Standards. It said: "We will promote and support only such interdenominational

[38]   The Committee on Overtures recommended no action on the Ulster overture because Benes's report had addressed the issues. *Acts and Proceedings*, 1947, 123.

[39]   Editorial, "A Protestant Super-Church," *CH*, Jan. 23, 1948, 6-7.

[40]   David Van Strien, letter to the editor, *CH*, March 19, 1948, 13.

fellowship and cooperation as is evangelical and in harmony with our Standards of Faith. We hold that any council or conference of Christians or churches, to be in harmony with our Standards of Faith, must publicly affirm the authority of the Bible as the infallible Word of God and the only rule of faith and practice."[41] This purist perspective insisted that the Reformed Church could only cooperate with other Christians who accepted the Reformed Standards as true doctrine and the Bible as infallible. This was a very narrow definition of identity that would have ruled out most ecumenical endeavors and some RCA congregations.

Barnerd Luben attended the gathering of the Evangelical Brotherhood in his capacity as a field secretary of the Board of Foreign Missions. He wrote rather poignantly of the session:

> One thing pleased me so much. When all the trouble erupted a year ago, I was made to feel like a heretic. It nearly broke my heart to be outside the circle of former friends. Gradually I was reestablished, but I thot [*sic*] that after this meeting I would be forever outside the pale. However, to great relief, to say the least, those with whom I had differed made it plain we were still friends. I feel this is a gain. I differ with their conclusions, strongly disapprove of their tactics, but rejoice that we have reached a point where we can differ and be friendly.[42]

Luben was generally conservative, but not a purist. As a former missionary and board secretary he knew the importance of ecumenical cooperation, but he also valued his connections to purist friends.

The Western Seminary professor Richard Oudersluys took issue with the Evangelical Brotherhood's assumption that the Reformed Standards expressed the truth of the Christian faith more accurately than any other confession. Oudersluys noted that creeds and confessions helped a tradition to define itself and its beliefs, but they should never be seen as the only correct interpretation of the faith nor be used to separate Christians from one another. They were not a test of true Christianity. Christian unity did not demand full agreement on every theological point but a shared commitment to the gospel of Jesus Christ. Oudersluys believed that Christian unity was more endangered

---

[41] From a report written by Barnerd Luben, "Meeting of the Evangelical Brotherhood," Jan. 26, 1948, RCA Controversies file, General Synod Archives.

[42] Barnerd Luben, "Meeting of the Evangelical Brotherhood," Jan. 26, 1948, RCA Controversies file, General Synod Archives.

by exaggerated individualism and institutionalism than by theological disagreement.[43]

In April 1948 the faculty of the two seminaries published a joint statement supporting the Reformed Church's membership in the Federal Council. They noted that the RCA had both contributed to the FCC and benefited from membership.[44] Although they said nothing particularly new, the document was noteworthy because it was so rare. The professors' cooperation signaled that they could speak jointly even if the eastern and western sections of the church were at odds. The statement also distanced the Western Seminary faculty from the purists who were so opposed to ecumenism and modernism.[45]

The committee appointed in 1947 to study membership in the Federal Council of Churches and the National Association of Evangelicals gave a lengthy report to the General Synod in 1948.[46] The committee identified the following objections to the Federal Council:

- Some prominent ministers with close connections to the FCC had made statements about the Virgin Birth and the atonement which seemed to deny basic Christian beliefs.
- The council affirmed only a minimal creed. It asked members simply to affirm Jesus Christ as Divine Lord and Savior.
- The council criticized the American government.
- Membership in the FCC disturbed the unity of the RCA.

---

43   Richard C. Oudersluys, "The Unity of the Church," *Western Theological Seminary Bulletin*, March 1948, 3-7. Daniel Y. Brink, a pastor at the Trinity Reformed Church in West New York, New Jersey, thanked him for the article, noting that when easterners expressed similar opinions they were suspected of heresy. Daniel Y. Brink to Richard Oudersluys, April 6, 1948, Oudersluys correspondence, Joint Archives.

44   RCA History of Controversies—FCC, General Synod Archives. All the faculty members signed the statement except William Goulooze from Western.

45   George Heneveld, an eastern pastor, praised the statement as a gift that would bring peace to the church. Gerrit Vander Lugt, the president of Central College, thanked the faculty for taking a "statesmanlike stand" amid a "sea of negation." He hoped it would convince people that a "vociferous and negative minority doesn't necessarily speak for the church." But a pastor in Minnesota told the president of New Brunswick Seminary that he would not read the statement to his consistory because he thought the faculty had overstepped its role. George Heneveld to John W. Beardslee, Jr., April 28, 1948; Gerrit VanderLugt to Joseph Sizoo, April 23, 1948; William Wolbrink to Joseph Sizoo, April 27, 1948; all in History of Controversies file, General Synod Archives.

46   Members included Lawrence Borst, Pella, IA; Charles Campbell, Flushing, NY; F. Raymond Clee, Albany, NY; Martin A. Punt, Hasbrouck Heights, NJ; John S. Ter Louw, Brandon, WI; and John W. Beardslee, Jr., New Brunswick Theological Seminary, *ex-officio*. Critics might have protested that the group did not represent the RCA accurately because it contained four eastern and two midwestern clergy.

- The council might become a super-church in which all denominations merge into one.
- The RCA should not be in fellowship with Eastern Orthodox churches.

The committee responded that the council encouraged cooperation but not organizational unity. The committee acknowledged the possibility of error and disagreement within the council, but argued that the Reformed Church should give people the benefit of the doubt rather than assume dishonesty. The committee insisted that when council members affirmed their belief in Jesus Christ as Divine Lord and Savior, they were not modernists trying to infiltrate orthodox Christianity but faithful Christians who believed that Jesus was God. The committee had little patience with some of the criticism: "We are not inclined to sympathize with those who are ready to accuse their brother ministers of trifling with words, or of hypocritically covering their own heterodoxy by the use of standard phrases. We have too high an opinion of the honesty of the ministry to accept these insinuations."[47]

The committee also offered a number of positive reasons for the Reformed Church to retain its membership in the FCC. The council provided concrete help in the work of missions and evangelism. It produced informative papers about labor, race, peace, and other social issues, which could assist churches in determining their beliefs and actions. Most importantly, it offered an antidote to purist isolationism. "Our Reformed church cannot withdraw from American Protestantism. There are tasks that no Christian denomination can perform alone.... If the Reformed Church is to make her voice heard she must speak with others." The committee observed that currently throughout all of American and world Protestantism, "there is [a] noticeable...moving towards the acceptance of a deeper, more profound, conservative, and evangelical interpretation of the Christian faith."[48] It argued that, contrary to the purists' belief, the RCA was not the faithful remnant preserving the only true church. The Reformed Church needed to appreciate the Federal Council rather than fear it. This significant ecumenical relationship should be continued.[49]

The report also considered whether the National Association of Evangelicals (NAE) could serve as an alternative to the FCC. Those who

[47] *Acts and Proceedings*, 1948, 153-65.
[48] The new World Council of Churches, developed largely out of missionary movements, met for the first time in 1948.
[49] *Acts and Proceedings*, 1948, 153-65.

wanted the Reformed Church to join the National Association praised its detailed doctrinal statement, evangelical leadership, and enthusiastic and spiritual meetings. The committee was more skeptical, in part because of the NAE's purist and judgmental attitudes, and concluded that the NAE was not a viable ecumenical partner for the RCA.[50]

Committee member Lawrence Borst (a pastor in Pella, Iowa) did not agree with the committee's conclusions and issued a minority report, which was a relatively rare practice in the Reformed Church. He wrote, "It is with sadness that we are forced to dissent from the views of the other members of the committee. I am using the plural pronoun 'we' because I am speaking not only for myself but for a large section of our church which I represent." Borst reminded the church that the Federal Council had been asked to change in 1934 but continued its modernist ways. He did not believe the Reformed Church should "remain in an organization which not only appears to have no concern for the Evangelical faith, but seems to be insistent in its refusal to take a stand for the historic Christianity" [sic]. He asked the RCA to withdraw from the council until it repudiated its modernism. The synod defeated the minority report 151-65. It then approved the majority report, but it also approved an amendment expressing the hope that the council would "take positions which are more consonant with Biblical Christianity."[51]

The decision to stay in the Federal Council demonstrated that the Reformed Church had chosen a moderate, inclusive identity. While the synod acknowledged the desire for a more evangelical emphasis in the FCC, it did not succumb to the suspicion of the purists. The Reformed Church as a whole would be polite rather than divisive and would assume the best of others rather than the worst. It would trust that people meant what they said. It was hopeful about the state of the Christian faith and did not feel compelled to defend it from error or infiltration. It valued ecumenism and cooperation. By staying in the Federal Council, the Reformed Church maintained its mainline ecumenical identity and refused to adopt a more rigidly evangelical or purist approach that denigrated other Christians.

---

50   The committee noted that the NAE had been extremely critical of the FCC, thus fostering division among Christian churches when they needed unity. The NAE also claimed the right to decide which denominations were truly Christian and worthy of NAE membership, which ironically made it into the kind of superchurch that RCA purists opposed. Finally, the NAE supported Christian day schools and criticized public schools, which was not the historic position of the RCA.

51   *Acts and Proceedings*, 1948, 165-74. When the synod voted on the minority report, each delegate's name and vote were recorded in the minutes, another rare practice. If it was intended to encourage conservative delegates to vote with the purists, it was not successful.

Hugh Baillie MacLean and the Interpretation of Scripture

While Henry Bast, Louis Benes, and other purists were criticizing structural and ecumenical arrangements in the Reformed Church, another controversial issue was developing more quietly. It centered on biblical interpretation, which had been debated in several American denominations. In Europe in the late eighteenth century, biblical scholars developed a form of biblical analysis and interpretation known as "higher criticism." By the late nineteenth century, it was being taught in many American universities. Scholars asked who had written the various books of the Bible and when, and some Christians found their answers troubling. For example, textual inconsistencies in the first five books of the Bible led many Old Testament scholars to conclude that the books had not all been written by Moses but were instead a product of four different strands or sources edited much later into a single narrative.[52]

Charles Darwin's work on evolution raised more troubling questions about the interpretation of the book of Genesis. Were the creation accounts intended to be read literally, as a factual description of the events they described? Or did they function more as mythical stories which affirmed the Creator's role in the origins of the world and humanity? Fundamentalists insisted that God created the world in six twenty-four-hour days, and that any other belief denied the Bible's truth and authority. In response to questions about authorship, they said that because Jesus referred to Moses as the author, then Moses must have written every word of the first five books of the Bible. Fundamentalists claimed that any view of the Bible other than complete inerrancy demonstrated doubt, unbelief, and modernism.

At first, the Reformed Church proceeded relatively unscathed by the debates about biblical interpretation.[53] That changed in 1946, when New Brunswick Seminary hired a new lecturer in Old Testament. Hugh Baillie MacLean was a Scottish Presbyterian, educated at St. Andrews University in Scotland and Union Theological Seminary in New York.

---

[52] One such inconsistency is that Genesis 1 presents a very different account of creation from Genesis 2. The vocabulary, the name of God, and especially the order of the creation events are significantly different and cannot be explained fully by arguing that Genesis 2 is an expansion of Genesis 1.

[53] For various perspectives on the RCA's views of scripture see John De Witt, "What is Inspiration?" in *Vision From the Hill*, ed. John W. Beardslee III, HSRCA, no. 12 (Grand Rapids: Eerdmans, 1984), 60-71, and Eugene P. Heideman, *The Practice Of Piety: The Theology of the Midwestern Reformed Church in America, 1866-1966*, HSRCA, no. 64 (Grand Rapids: Eerdmans, 2009), 163-209.

He served as a military chaplain in Britain during World War II. At his inauguration as a General Synod professor of theology in September 1948, he gave an address entitled, "The Relevance of the Old Testament."

MacLean began the lecture by observing that some biblical scholars argued that the Old Testament had been superseded by the New Testament and was out of date and irrelevant. They claimed that the Old Testament portrayed God as cruel and angry and quite unlike the merciful God of the New Testament. MacLean wholeheartedly disagreed and affirmed instead the lasting value of the Old Testament. His role as a professor, he said, was to help seminary students understand the circumstances that gave rise to the books, so that their sermons could "make the Old Testament live so that men and women today can see themselves portrayed in its pages." It was clear that he loved the Bible and wanted his students to love it too, so that they could speak meaningfully about it to their parishioners.

MacLean used biblical scholarship and criticism to aid in the interpretation of scripture. He believed that the Bible was both God's Word *and* the words of human beings reflecting on their experience with God. Human beings were fallible, and their understanding of God's ways evolved over time. MacLean suggested, for example, that when the Bible reported that God commanded the Israelites to exterminate the Canaanites (a rather troubling ethical problem), it may not have been God's will so much as the Israelites' later reflection about what they *should* have done to preserve their nation and its purity.[54]

Midwestern minister Bert Van Malsen was disturbed by this last example and insisted that it was not Reformed to deny the truth of scripture. If Deuteronomy was false history, then the Bible was not a reliable source of spiritual guidance. If the writers attributed anything to God that was not literally true, the Bible was not ultimately authoritative.[55] Harlan Steele, a pastor in Hopkins, Michigan, wondered what the Reformed Church believed about the inspiration of the Bible. He wrote, "If these two widely divergent views can exist within our denomination side by side [those held by MacLean and Van Malsen], then it means that our doctrinal standards are just a sham—they don't mean a thing."[56]

The controversy appeared to end after these two letters, but during the spring of 1949, thirteen classes submitted overtures to the General

---

[54]   Hugh Baille MacLean, "The Relevance of the Old Testament," *CH*, Oct. 22, 1948, 16-17, 22. The lecture is also reprinted in Beardslee, *Vision from the Hill*, 138-50.

[55]   Bert Van Malsen, letter to the editor, *CH*, Dec. 3, 1948, 9.

[56]   Harland Steele, letter to the editor, *CH*, Jan. 21, 1949, 10.

Synod criticizing MacLean. One classis lamented that "the minds of many in the church have been disturbed by certain expressions" in the inaugural address and asked that MacLean explain his views on the authority and historical credibility of the Old Testament. Seventeen other overtures expressed confidence in MacLean and the seminary, and several of these protested the way MacLean had been treated.[57]

At the 1949 General Synod, MacLean was asked to meet with the synod's Committee on Overtures to discuss the charges. He shared with the members of the committee a letter he had written to the Board of Superintendents of New Brunswick Seminary:

> These discussions in the church press have been a source of great regret and grief to me personally, casting aspersions, as they do, not only on my integrity, but on the institution in which I am privileged to teach. May I say that no query or question regarding any point made in my address has been made to me personally. Certain people have given expression in the press to interpretations of my remarks without first approaching me to find out whether these interpretations were correct or not. I know that some of them were advised to write directly to me if they were disturbed by what I said, but this advice they chose to disregard completely, despite my willingness and readiness to discuss any issue that had been raised. A friendly approach of this kind would have been more in keeping with the spirit of Jesus Christ, and the New Testament.[58]

The Committee on Overtures affirmed MacLean's lecture and beliefs and commended both seminaries, but the damage had been done. His letter demonstrated how painful it was to receive this kind of criticism. Overtures cost little or nothing to the sending bodies, but they could do a great deal of damage to the person who was criticized so publicly. The critics had taken a couple of sentences of the speech and assumed, since MacLean used critical methods and recognized a human element of authorship, that he did not believe the Bible was inspired and authoritative. In fact, MacLean's commitment was to the larger truth of scripture—God's love for humanity and desire for justice.[59]

---

57   *Acts and Proceedings*, 1949, 69-74. The critical overtures all came from the Western RCA, while the supportive overtures came from New York and New Jersey.
58   Hugh Baillie MacLean file, General Synod Archives.
59   After this controversial beginning, MacLean served the seminary and his students with dignity and grace. Students recalled his ability to make the Bible come alive.

Some Reformed Church members raised questions about the way this conflict had been handled. They objected particularly to the use of overtures to express opinions rather than to propose a course of action for the denomination.[60] The Overtures Committee discouraged this practice and also suggested that, in the future, disagreements should first be dealt with in person rather than through overtures.[61] Later in the summer of 1949, the members of the *Church Herald* Editorial Council discussed both the value of editorial freedom and the danger of criticizing institutions and individuals. The council decided that controversial articles should deal with general problems and principles rather than specific institutions.[62]

The purists who advocated a literal interpretation of scripture had adopted some very rigid, defensive, and angry practices in their attempt to reshape the denomination. At heart, however, the Reformed Church was not fundamentalist, and the moderate and conservative sections of the church resisted these tactics. The denomination as a whole did not require strict biblical literalism and did not believe that a completely pure church was an achievable goal. Nor did most Reformed Church members wish to see faithful colleagues attacked in public. Most importantly, they believed there could be space for multiple perspectives within the denomination.

Some found his course difficult because it challenged what they had learned at home or in college. Robert Hoeksema recalled feeling as if the Bible had been torn out from under him. He considered leaving NBTS, but he stayed, listened, and asked questions. Hoeksema said he always knew that MacLean loved him, wanted the best for him, and prayed for him. "And I have spent the rest of my life thanking the good Lord that I sat under Hugh Baillie MacLean who gave me a Bible that I can now live with. He was a very key person in my theological orientation. I am forever grateful to him and for him." Forty-five years later, Hoeksema had tears in his eyes when he spoke about MacLean. Robert Bedingfield also struggled with his vocation in his first year of seminary. He did not feel called to the parish but did not know what else he should do. MacLean suggested military chaplaincy. Bedingfield spent twenty years in the Navy and said that what he learned from MacLean about the prophets proved to be a great help as he worked on race relations and other challenging issues. "MacLean left his fingerprint on my soul," Bedingfield said. MacLean died of a heart attack in 1959 at the age of forty-nine. He spent only a dozen years in the RCA, but he had a tremendous impact on a group of students who went on to provide significant leadership in the denomination. Robert Hoeksema said of him, "He embodied, for me, what it was to be a prophet. He changed my life." Oral history interviews with Robert Hoeksema, May 16, 2001, Hatboro, PA, and Robert Bedingfield, July 17, 2002, Holland, MI. See also my article about MacLean: "Critical Questions," *CH*, April, 2003, 8-10.

60   The Classis of West Sioux and the Particular Synod of Iowa had both used overtures in 1949 to express their confidence in the editor and policies of the *CH*.

61   *Acts and Proceedings*, 1949, 133.

62   Louis Benes, editorial, "*CH* Council," *CH*, Oct. 21, 1949, 6-7.

Merger with the United Presbyterian Church in North America

The final source of conflict during this period involved a proposed merger between the Reformed Church in America and the United Presbyterian Church in North America (UPCNA). The two denominations had much in common. The UPCNA was a small denomination with origins in the Scottish Covenanter tradition, a separatist Calvinist body. It had maintained a separate Presbyterian identity rather than join the larger Presbyterian Church.[63] Most of its congregations were located in Ohio and Pennsylvania, between the Reformed Church's centers in the East and Midwest. Its polity and theology were similar to that of the Reformed Church in America.

The merger proposal raised a number of difficult questions. Could the Reformed Church carry out its ministry more effectively by joining forces with a similar denomination? Would merger undermine its unique identity and heritage? Should it press its ecumenical commitments to their logical conclusion and unite with another denomination? Or did church union endanger the Reformed Church's purity and evangelical character?[64] The answers revealed widespread disagreement, with the eastern section of the church showing greater willingness to merge and the Midwest showing greater resistance.

The eastern churches and clergy feared that the denomination would not be viable much longer without a merger. They wanted to be part of something bigger, with a more recognizable name, and perhaps they wanted, too, to regain some of the status and recognition the Reformed Church had enjoyed in the nineteenth century. Eastern churches viewed merger as an antidote to the loss of influence and recognition that they had already experienced. They feared the losses would continue, and probably increase, if they did not take this step.

Midwestern churches feared that merger would take away their conservative identity and infect them with liberalism. Many wanted to preserve their Dutch heritage. The Reformed Church still played a

---

[63] The larger Presbyterian Church had divided before the Civil War because of disagreement over slavery. The northern section was known as the Presbyterian Church in the United States of America (PCUSA), and the southern section was the Presbyterian Church in the United States (PCUS). The PCUSA united with the UPCNA in the 1950s and took the name United Presbyterian Church/USA (UPC/USA). When the northern and southern branches reunited in 1983, the new church took the name Presbyterian Church U.S.A. [PC(USA)].

[64] Harmelink, *Ecumenism*, 79-85. Lynn Japinga, "On Second Thought: A Hesitant History of Ecumenism in the Reformed Church in America," in *Concord Makes Strength: Essays in Reformed Ecumenism*, ed. John Coakley, HSRCA, no. 41 (Grand Rapids: Eerdmans, 2002), 10-34.

significant role in numerous Dutch communities,[65] and members in these towns thought they had little to gain by giving up their name. Reformed churches in the Midwest were still growing. Merger offered little to them except new ideas and new people who did not share the same history, ethnicity, and values. They saw nothing but potential loss.

Despite these very different attitudes, merger talks began in earnest. In November 1944, committees from the Reformed Church and the United Presbyterian Church held an exploratory meeting and discovered they had much in common. The Joint Committee began formal discussions in 1945 and established a very optimistic timetable. The committee expected to complete a "Plan of Union" by the fall of 1946 and engage in fellowship and a process of discernment during 1947.[66]

In the spring of 1946 Louis Benes wrote positively about a merger with the UPCNA, in part because of its similarity to the RCA. He believed the proposed merger offered a middle ground between indiscriminate ecumenism (joining with everybody) and antiecumenism (joining with nobody). He encouraged Reformed Church members not to be sentimental about the past and their comfortable friendship circles. If the two denominations were one in Christ, how could they stay apart? He encouraged congregations to get to know one another and offered the *Church Herald* as a clearinghouse for pulpit exchanges.[67]

Criticism began almost immediately. A number of Reformed Church members expressed their opposition to merger via letters to the *Church Herald*. Paul Wezeman, an elder from the First Reformed Church in Chicago, wrote that there was a more logical and necessary candidate for merger. Although he did not name it, he probably meant the Christian Reformed Church.[68] Herman DeVries, an elder from Corsica, South Dakota, made a threat that would become commonplace in the next few years. "The way our church feels, many members will leave the church. I'm sure it will create more hot heads than warm hearts....We have belonged to the Reformed Church all our lives. The Reformed Church has gotten along very well, and we have peace in our fellowship, while union might bring strife."[69] Gerrit Hospers, a retired minister in East Williamson, New York, feared that union would give liberalism "a

---

65 For example, Holland and Zeeland, Michigan; South Holland, Illinois; Pella and Orange City, Iowa.
66 *Acts and Proceedings*, 1945, 108, 142-52; 1946, 159-62. The first meeting was initiated by a letter to the RCA from the UPCNA in July 1944.
67 Editorial, "Church Union," CH, April 26, 1946, 5.
68 Oct. 25, 1946, 6.
69 Ibid.

larger field of mischief."[70] Despite these criticisms, late in 1946 Benes still supported union and expected that it would occur if given enough time.[71]

During the next several years, a number of articles and even more letters to the editor appeared in the *Church Herald* reflecting both positive and negative opinions on the merger. Those in favor of union argued that a single denomination would be more efficient, because it would have one educational curriculum and one administrative structure. A larger church could have more influence within American Protestantism and engage in more missionary work. Geographic coverage would be better in a merged church. Reformed Church members who moved to Pennsylvania or Ohio could join a United Presbyterian congregation and not be lost to the denomination. Ministers would be less likely to leave the denomination if there were more opportunities for service.

Some members, especially those from the East, believed that a merged church offered better name recognition. Alvin Neevel, field secretary in the Particular Synod of New York, pointed out that eastern churches no longer had a significant Dutch population from which to draw members, so being known as the Dutch church was not an asset. The population of many cities in New York and New Jersey was shifting rapidly, and newcomers were arriving from many parts of the country. They had rarely heard of the Reformed Church in America and were unlikely to join. Union would definitely help the East, Neevel believed, because people would be more likely to join a church named Presbyterian.[72]

Supporters of merger also appealed to biblical and theological arguments. They cited John 17 and Jesus' prayer that "they may all be one." They argued that denominations were a sign of sin and brokenness and that whenever a breach among Christians could be healed, it was God's will to do so. There was no reason for two similar Calvinist denominations to remain separated.

Those opposed to merger made their case even more frequently in the *Church Herald*. They argued that a denomination with such a long history should not give up its distinctive identity, heritage, and

---

70 Nov. 8, 1946, 6.
71 Editorial, "The Plan of Union," *CH*, Nov. 29, 1946, 5.
72 Alvin Neevel, "Do We Understand?" *CH*, Jan. 6, 1950, 8-9. Another eastern pastor, Martin Punt, noted that eastern RCA churches constantly dealt with competition from the Roman Catholic Church. Protestant division and discord provided a reason for Catholics to think of themselves as the one true church. Punt argued that Protestants needed to be unified in order to meet the challenges of Rome and secularism. Martin Punt to Louis Benes, Nov. 3, 1947, Benes file, FCC Correspondence, Joint Archives.

tradition. Midwesterners in particular were unwilling to give up the Reformed identity and sense of family. Opponents of merger did not believe that the UPCNA was theologically similar enough for union, because it affirmed different Standards and used them in a more flexible way that might allow space for liberalism. This Presbyterian denomination was also a close relative to the northern Presbyterian Church, which had many liberal members. Merger in general, and with the UPCNA in particular, seemed theologically dangerous. The RCA would be better enlivened by a revival than a merger.

Albertus Pieters, a retired Western Seminary professor, did not believe that merger posed a threat to orthodoxy or Reformed identity, as the purists claimed. Instead, he believed that merger was simply a fad. If organizational unity was essential for the church, Pieters claimed, Christ would have established and preserved it. Since Christ did not, that meant denominations were human organizations for administrative purposes, not sinful structures. Finally, Pieters opposed merger simply because he thought that most people were not very interested. "As things stand now, even if a formal union is brought about, it will be too much like marriage without love."[73]

Some opponents of the merger emphasized practical problems rather than theological issues. Critics questioned the proposed arrangements for colleges, seminaries, boards, and investments. Harry Hager, a pastor in Chicago, complained that some of the Presbyterian colleges allowed dancing and one had a smoking lounge for women students. The Presbyterians also permitted membership in secret societies such as the Masons, which many Reformed Church consistories prohibited. The two churches had different liturgical styles.[74]

The merger discussion raised many questions about trust. Could Reformed folks be certain that Presbyterian members were appropriately conservative? Did the two denominations interpret the Bible and the Standards in the same way?

Critics were especially skeptical about the possibility of other mergers in the future. Harri Zegerius, a pastor in Grand Rapids, read the UPCNA magazine and found many people writing about potential mergers with the Northern and Southern Presbyterians. He concluded, "When you marry a girl, you may not necessarily want to marry the relatives."[75]

---

[73]   Albertus Pieters, "Church Union...Why Shouldn't We? Why Should We?" *CH*, Jan. 28, 1949, 12-13.

[74]   Harry Hager, "Shall We Be Reformed or Presbyterian?" *CH*, Dec. 2, 1949, 12-13, 23.

[75]   Harri Zegerius, "Union with the United Presbyterians—What Next?" *CH*, May 13, 1949, 8.

Reformed Church members also expressed different levels of trust in the work of the Joint Committee. John VanWyk, a pastor in Alto, Wisconsin, was appointed to the committee in January 1948. He later reported that he had been ambivalent about merger, but when he attended the meetings he felt the presence of the Spirit and decided that union must be within the will of God. The Spirit would not have created such unity within the Joint Committee if it was not God's will. In view of that, he said, God forbid he should be opposed or even lukewarm.[76] Reformed members of the Joint Committee respected the deep Christian faith of the Presbyterian representatives and experienced their meetings as cordial, cooperative, and productive. They believed the Holy Spirit had brought the two denominations together.

Opponents of merger, however, were absolutely certain that the Holy Spirit was *not* leading the RCA toward merger, and that the Joint Committee must be wrong in its claims. The fact that two small committees got along well did not necessarily mean the two denominations should merge.

Harry Hager served on the Joint Committee but refused to agree to the merger. He believed that churches in the particular synods of Chicago and Iowa were psychologically unprepared for merger because they were relatively recent immigrants. He also feared that the Presbyterian churches would not adopt Reformed practices such as Sunday evening services and the Heidelberg Catechism, and thus merger would weaken rather than strengthen the Reformed Church. He concluded that the Reformed Church was not ready and that merger would divide the denomination.[77]

As the time for voting approached, the debate intensified. Some members wanted to preserve the feeling that the Reformed Church was an extended Dutch family, while others preferred that the church be broadened by blending with another denomination. M. Verne Oggel, a pastor in Glen Rock, New Jersey, argued that there were no substantive differences in doctrine and that opponents of merger simply had an emotional preference for keeping the denomination as it was—a big family. This should not take precedence over the value of unity.[78] Jay Van Sweden responded that opponents of merger did not simply want to maintain the Reformed Church as it was but to make it more faithful

---

[76] J.C. Van Wyk, letter to the editor, *CH*, April 23, 1948, 14.

[77] Hager, "Shall We Be Reformed?"

[78] Melvin Verne Oggel, "A Plea for Union with the United Presbyterians," *CH*, Feb. 18, 1949, 18-19. Oggel had recently returned to the RCA after serving Northern Presbyterian churches for twenty years.

to the Standards. He believed that a merged church would be a fertile breeding ground for increased modernism and rejection of scripture. Van Sweden also feared that the joint structure would not lead to more efficiency but to more board control.[79]

The most fearful Reformed Church members saw a modernist conspiracy behind the UPCNA merger. Jacob Blaauw, a pastor in Grand Rapids, served on the Joint Committee but, like Hager, refused to sign the final document. He insisted that modernists realized the church had lost power and influence but refused to admit that they were at fault for failing to preach sound doctrine. They tried to keep the church afloat by merger and machinery with the goal of creating "a great pan-Presbyterian super denomination here in America." Blaauw concluded: "My beloved brethren of the Reformed Church, I am not ready to vote for the dissolution or absorption of our beloved Reformed Church into such a merger."[80]

The most vigorous critics of merger (the purists) often insisted that they were loyal to the Reformed Church, and that supporters of merger were disloyal because they were willing to give up their RCA identity. Ironically, these loyal purists also threatened to leave the denomination if the merger was approved. They wanted to preserve the "true" or "historic" Reformed Church and refused to be swallowed up in a merger.[81] Eastern members (usually moderates) believed that loyalty to the Reformed Church meant keeping it alive, and the best way to do that was through a merger. Eastern churches did not threaten to leave the denomination if the merger failed; at least, they did not threaten such action in the pages of the *Church Herald*.

The merger proposal sparked a great deal of debate about the process of decision making. According to the *Book of Church Order*, if the General Synod approved the merger proposal, a majority vote in two-thirds of the classes was required for final approval. A number of letters to the editor asked that the requirement be increased to a three-quarters vote in three-quarters of classes. Some letters also requested that each congregation be allowed to vote, so that the decision would be made by all members and not simply a few representatives.[82] The

---

[79]   Jay Van Sweden, letter to the editor, *CH*, March 18, 1949, 14.

[80]   Jacob Blaauw, "Is Church Union the Answer?" *CH*, Jan. 20, 1950, 10-11, 22.

[81]   *Acts and Proceedings*, 1949, 131. The classes of Holland and Grand Rapids submitted overtures in 1949 asking that congregations that did not want to be part of the merged church be allowed to leave the RCA but keep their property. The *Book of Church Order* specified that the classis, not the congregation, owned the church building and property.

[82]   C. Bussema, letter to the editor, *CH*, March 4, 1949, 8.

final proposal of the Joint Committee in 1949 increased the voting requirement as requested (to a 75 percent vote in 75 percent of the classes) and included an "escape clause" for a congregation in which 75 percent of the members chose not to align with the merged church.[83] Both were significant departures from Reformed Church precedent and polity.

The General Synod approved the merger in 1949, but only nineteen classes approved it with a three-fourths majority, far short of the thirty-four votes required.[84] The vote was clearly divided along regional lines. Eastern classes approved merger and midwestern classes opposed it. The purists had persuaded the conservative middle that the Reformed Church would lose its unique identity. Merger provided too few benefits and too much uncertainty and anxiety. Moderates were very disappointed by the vote because they believed the Reformed Church had lost an opportunity for a larger witness and a greater influence in American society. They were unquestionably loyal to the denomination, but they wanted to see its presence expanded.

The 1940s closed with mixed results for the purists and moderates. The conservatives had agreed with the moderates on the matters of denominational structure, Federal Council of Churches affiliation, and the role of higher criticism, but they had voted with the purists against the merger with the UPCNA. The Reformed Church chose to continue being ecumenical in its relationships. There was a limit to ecumenicity, however, and the church chose to preserve its identity and heritage rather than merge with another denomination. The identity being preserved was not a purist one, but one that was relatively open and flexible and confident that God would preserve the church.

---

[83]   *Acts and Proceedings*, 1949, 166.
[84]   Two additional classes received support from two-thirds of the delegates, and three classes from more than half. The twenty-four classes who had a majority in favor of merger still fell short of the thirty-four required.

CHAPTER 3

1950–1963: Purity or Participation?

Early in 1950 the Reformed Church in America had resolved the conflicts of the 1940s by deciding that the denomination would not be as pure and separate as some members wanted, nor as ecumenical as others preferred. It would stay in the Federal Council, but it would not merge with the United Presbyterians. The compromise left both sides disappointed. Underlying these conversations were very different views of the role of the church in the world. The purists wanted congregations to demand a high level of commitment and refuse to compromise their values for the sake of popularity. They did not want the Reformed Church to fraternize with denominations that did not share its beliefs and practices. At the other end of the spectrum, moderates hoped that the denomination would become much more engaged in and with the broader American culture. They wanted to participate more fully in ecumenical life and present the gospel in ways that nonchurched, non-Dutch people might find appealing.

The social contexts of midwestern and eastern Reformed congregations continued to be quite different. Many midwestern churches were located in small towns founded by nineteenth-century

Dutch immigrants. These towns were ethnic enclaves[1] in which large numbers of residents shared a common Dutch heritage and attended Reformed or Christian Reformed churches. The school teachers, mayors, and doctors would likely be Dutch Reformed. The communities closed down on Sundays, teachers led prayer in schools, and many residents shared a moral code that frowned upon drinking, dancing, and going to movies. The Reformed faith dominated these communities, and Christian values shaped behaviors. Ethnic and religious "outsiders" were present (in varying numbers and with varying degrees of acceptance), but clearly they were not free to reshape the town ethos.

Meanwhile, in New York and New Jersey, towns that had once been distinctively Dutch were now filled with people from many different ethnic groups. In Newark and Brooklyn, many of the neighborhoods were Catholic or Jewish. A number of Dutch immigrants settled in Paterson, New Jersey, in the nineteenth century, but by the 1950s the community was religiously and racially mixed. Most Eastern Reformed churches knew that they could not dominate or shape the moral code of their communities as they might have done two centuries before. Reformed church members were a minority, and they knew that if Christianity was to have an impact in society, Christians of various denominations would have to work together. Religion had to earn the right to be heard and respected.

These geographical and cultural differences were exacerbated by the lingering effects of the disagreements of the late 1940s. In 1950 Reformed Church members were fragmented and angry with each other. Moderates who had supported merger believed that the purists had misrepresented the United Presbyterian Church and exaggerated the dangers of union. Purists who had opposed merger believed they were being unfairly criticized for preserving the denomination's identity. The Reformed Church did not know what kind of church it should be. It needed to develop an identity that could be shared by church members with very different views.

To begin a conversation and hopefully to facilitate some reconciliation, Howard Hageman was invited to address the General

---

[1]   Sociologists use the term, *enclave*, to describe a community that is relatively closed off and isolated. Its members may work in a broader context, but much of daily life, education, shopping, worship, and socializing occur in an area where people are remarkably similar in ethnicity and beliefs. Examples of enclaves in the 1950s include Pella and Orange City, Iowa, and a number of small towns surrounding them; Oostburg and Cedar Grove, Wisconsin; South Holland, Illinois; Holland and Zeeland, Michigan; and some neighborhoods in Grand Rapids and Kalamazoo, Michigan.

Synod in June 1950 on the topic, "Where Do We Go from Here?" He was thirty years old at the time and had been pastor of the North Reformed Church in Newark for five years. He had published articles on Reformed Church history and was considered a gifted theologian who could speak to the whole church. Hageman began the speech by putting a positive spin on the vote against merger. "We have decided that the kingdom of our God and of His Christ can best be served by us if we cling to our particular denominational life and remain the Reformed Church in America." Hageman pointed out that neither side had actually provided much service to the kingdom. Each side blamed the other for the conflict, but the real cause of tension, Hageman said, was that the denomination lacked a clear sense of identity and mission.

Hageman made three specific suggestions that he hoped would shape a common identity for all Reformed Church members, regardless of theological stance. First, he encouraged the RCA to explore how its creeds and confessions spoke to contemporary concerns. The Reformed Church claimed to value John Calvin and the Canons of Dort but failed to translate sixteenth-century statements into language that spoke to twentieth-century issues. It had used Reformed theology as a fortress in which to hide rather than as a means to make a difference in the world. Like the man in the parable with one talent, Hageman said, "We have taken our heritage, wrapped it carefully in a napkin, and buried it, when we should have been out trading it freely in the marketplace of the world."

Next, Hageman suggested that the denomination needed a new sense of what it meant to be a church in the Reformed tradition. For example, John Calvin had valued the use of the mind, and Calvinist churches had always emphasized education for children and adults. Still, some Reformed churches provided only minimal Sunday school education and confirmation classes and appeared to be waiting for revivalists to convert their children. Hageman considered this profoundly un-Reformed. "How can we prosper," he asked, "until we are willing to become what we are?"

Finally, he encouraged Reformed Church members to recognize that ecumenism was an essential part of their history and identity. During the time of John Calvin, Hageman said, the Reformed church was "not afraid to meet even those with whom it did not agree, because it had great confidence that the truth was mighty and would prevail. This catholicism is implicit in our inheritance and the fact that today we are fearful, insecure, and aloof simply indicates that we do not really possess with a strong grasp the essentials of our church life." Hageman insisted that ecumenism, theological relevance, and the intellectual aspect of the faith were not modernist tendencies, as some purist critics charged, but crucial to Reformed identity.

Hageman concluded that the Reformed Church could not easily determine its direction for the future because the church could go only where the Lord led. If God was leading the church, then its members should be less anxious and more confident. "What have we to lose? What have we to defend? What have we to fear? Our smallness, our limitations, our handicaps—these are not the things that matter....Our faithfulness, our obedience, our loyalty—these are things that matter, these are the source of our might." If the church worried less about its own purity and preservation, it would have more resources available to do God's work and make a difference in the world. Hageman encouraged the Reformed Church to get out of its snail's shell, discover who it was, and then become that, without apology. A clear sense of identity and purpose would help the denomination share its love of theology, be more attractive to non-Dutch people, and engage with the world.[2]

The "world" of America that needed to be engaged was, at least on the surface, a pleasant and optimistic place. The decade of the 1950s was a time of growth and prosperity. An unprecedented number of babies were born. New suburbs sprang up almost overnight, filled with families of war veterans who were rising in the ranks of corporate America. Many of the women raised the children, maintained beautiful homes, and volunteered in churches.[3]

And yet people were anxious, especially about communism in both its obvious and more insidious forms. The Soviet Union developed a nuclear weapon, China invaded Korea, and the Communists seemed

---

[2]   Howard Hageman, "Becoming What We Are," *CH*, Sept. 29, 1950, 11-14, 23. Hageman's wife, Carol, reported that early in his career he was invited to Central College in Pella, Iowa, to preach at its religious emphasis week. The local pastors were suspicious and sat in the front row for every sermon. They did not know quite what to make of Hageman and finally referred to him as "that conservative liberal." Oral history interview with Carol Hageman, Feb. 26, 2000, Guilderland, NY. Hageman was the quintessential example of an RCA moderate. His sermons were deeply biblical because he thought that scripture continued to speak to human beings in the present, but he was not a fundamentalist. He was also shaped by and conversant about Reformed theology, especially John Calvin. See Gregg A. Mast, *In Remembrance and Hope: The Ministry and Vision of Howard G. Hageman*, HSRCA, no. 27 (Grand Rapids: Eerdmans, 1998).

[3]   Betty Friedan later observed that the suburban housewife may not have been as happy as she seemed. Friedan described the frequent use of alcohol and tranquilizers to dull "the problem that had no name." Women were not as fulfilled by domesticity and children as they were supposed to be. See Betty Friedan, *The Feminine Mystique* (New York: Norton, 1963).

poised to take over the free world. The president of Western Seminary, John R. Mulder, flew into New York City one night in the fall of 1950 and later wrote that he was impressed by its beauty but struck by the city's vulnerability to attack. "I hope the enemy will never come, and that the disaster that lies inherent in the structure of New York City will never become an actuality. Let us hope that the circumstances that are now obtaining in Korea will promise us some days of peace."[4] Peace was slow to arrive.

Organized religion was eager to provide spiritual solace and practical techniques to achieve the peace and prosperity Americans were seeking. Some of the most popular religious books during this period included Norman Vincent Peale's *The Power of Positive Thinking* (1952), Rabbi Joshua Liebman's *Peace of Mind* (1946), Bishop Fulton Sheen's *Peace of Soul* (1948), and Billy Graham's *Peace with God* (1953). Perhaps as a result of the answers it offered, religion regained a great deal of popularity and influence in the 1950s. People lined up outside the Marble Collegiate Church in New York City to hear Norman Vincent Peale preach. Congregations served as social centers in their communities, particularly in the suburbs, where young families lived far from grandparents. President Eisenhower joined a Presbyterian church in Washington, D.C. and extolled the virtues of religion. The church seemed to be more socially significant than it had been for several decades.

The most successful American congregations in the 1950s, such as Marble Collegiate in New York City and New York Avenue Presbyterian in Washington, D.C., were generally welcoming and hospitable. They wanted to attract new members, not discourage them by demanding a high level of commitment or theological literacy. American culture and many of its churches valued patriotism, family, personal well-being, upward mobility, and the acquisition of material goods. Churches often supported the status quo, and, in turn, American culture appreciated religion as a social institution—as long as it did not criticize American society.[5]

The purists in the Reformed Church did not approve of this low-demand approach and regularly criticized the shallow state of American religion. Louis Benes observed that, although church membership had increased from 35 percent of the population in 1900 to 54 percent in 1950,

---

[4]   John R. Mulder to Otto Grundler, Oct. 11, 1950. Mulder Correspondence, Joint Archives, Box 9, Sept. 1950-Sept. 1951, E, F, G.

[5]   See James Hudnut-Beumler, *Looking for God in the Suburbs: The Religion of the American Dream and Its Critics, 1945-1965* (New Brunswick: Rutgers Univ. Press, 1994).

crime, divorce, and liquor consumption had also increased dramatically. As he saw it, church membership had not improved morality.[6] In 1953 he noted that membership had increased to 59 percent of the population, but he lamented that 41 percent of the population (68 million people) still did *not* belong to a church, and many who did belong were Roman Catholic.[7] Benes also complained that Protestants did not attend weekly services as faithfully as Catholics did.[8]

In another editorial, Benes identified three major failings in contemporary religious life. First, churches too easily gave up old ideas and traditional language because young adults in particular did not understand such phrases as "washed in the blood," "died for our sins," and the "throne of mercy." Benes insisted that religion was entitled to a distinctive vocabulary just as science and medicine were. Truly converted people would understand and love the old language, whereas changing the words could result in a loss of meaning and, eventually, loss of the core of the gospel.[9]

Second, Benes believed that American churches wasted too much time on nonessential matters like social work, rituals, and ecumenism. "And all the while we diddle and dawdle on the periphery of religion, the world hastens to ruin morally and spiritually for want of what lies at the heart of the gospel."[10] Benes was convinced that because of the atomic bomb and the threat of communism, the world was living on the edge of an abyss and desperately needed to hear the hope of the gospel. "The Church asleep must become the Church revived. The Church complacent must become the Church conquering. The Church formally religious must become the Church spiritually alive and mighty. But all our help is in God. Our strength is in His Word alone, and our power in His Holy Spirit. Only with God can we live safely on the edge of the abyss."[11]

Finally, Benes thought that most churches expected too little of their members. Although he offered little evidence to support his claim, he averred that laypeople preferred to attend churches with strong preaching, high expectations, and definitive beliefs. In a typical

---

6   Editorial, "Church Membership in America," *CH,* July 7, 1950, 4.
7   Editorial, "America for Christ," *CH,* Nov. 13, 1953, 6.
8   A survey of adult Protestants found that 25 percent attended weekly, 43 percent occasionally, and 32 percent never. Among Catholics, 62 percent attended weekly, 20 percent occasionally, and 18 percent never. Editorial, "Church Attendance in the United States," *CH,* Feb. 9, 1953, 6.
9   Editorial, "The Language of the Gospel," *CH,* March 21, 1952, 6.
10   Editorial, "Moral Decay or Christian Faith—II," *CH,* March 7, 1952, 6-7.
11   Editorial, "Religion as Usual?" *CH,* Dec. 26, 1952, 6.

rhetorical flourish he wrote: "Let us indoctrinate. Let us indoctrinate in our preaching, let us indoctrinate in our Sunday School and Catechism classes, let us indoctrinate in every meeting and activity of our churches. Only when people know the Truth will they believe it, and love it, and live it, and proclaim it to others."[12] Benes had no sympathy for critical thinking or for the notion that Christians could choose the beliefs they found appealing and acceptable. He insisted that American religion was infected with "spiritual sterility" and it could only be redeemed by returning to the "clearcut certainties of the Word of God."[13] Congregations that preached and taught this way would never be popular, but a church that pleased God did not need human approval.[14]

Moderates considered this view of the church too inflexible and narrow. They were far less concerned about the purity of the church and the danger of corruption from the world. They were more confident and less fearful. They acknowledged the problems of communism and rapid social change, but they did not fear imminent moral decay or Communist takeover. They recognized the tension inherent between secular and Christian values, but they insisted that the world belonged to God and the church should not fear, hide from, or abandon it.[15]

One example of the contrasting attitudes in the Reformed Church can be seen in the different ways the same phrase was used. When Benes referred to "the faith once delivered to the saints," he implied that the old faith was true and needed to be protected from alteration or threat.[16] David Van Strien, a General Synod president and pastor in North Bergen, New Jersey, expressed more confidence when he used the phrase:

> As we present this report, uncertainty is written large across the world but certainty is indelibly engraved upon the heart of the

---

12 Editorial, "Have We Failed Our Laymen?" *CH*, Oct. 9, 1953, 6-7. It is interesting that as much as he criticized communism for using indoctrination, he was willing to use the word and the strategy to teach Christianity.

13 Editorial, "The Secret of Church Growth," *CH*, May 23, 1952, 6.

14 Editorial, "Peaceful Coexistence," *CH*, Oct. 7, 1955, 6.

15 This perspective is particularly evident in the "State of Religion" speeches given by eastern clergy who served as presidents of the General Synod: David Van Strien (1952), Frederick Zimmerman (1954), and Daniel Y. Brink (1956). Most seminary professors from both schools would have agreed, along with some clergy from the Midwest, particularly Gerrit Vander Lugt, a theologian who served as president of Central College and as president of the General Synod in 1955.

16 Similarly, Harry Hager insisted that old-time religious practices such as family devotions, Sunday evening services, and prayer meetings should be preserved because, "While there may be modern advancement in other phases of life, that does not hold with respect to the matter of that most holy faith that was once for all delivered to the saints." "A Plea for the Old-Time Religion," *CH*, July 21, 1950, 10-11.

church, for wherever we look without we see a question mark, but wherever we look within we perceive an exclamation point—"the faith once delivered to the saints," proclaimed with boldness to a cringing world; yea, preached in love to a world that is afraid.[17]

Van Strien believed that God guided and protected both the church and the world, and that the world was not so much evil as fearful. He also believed that "the faith once delivered" was not a fragile thing in need of protection but something that could grow and change.

The purists frequently dismissed social transformation as a distraction from the real work of saving souls, but moderates considered it an essential part of Reformed identity.[18] In his president's report to the General Synod in 1955, Gerrit Vander Lugt criticized the Reformed Church for failing to address social and international issues. Instead, he said, the Reformed Church treated people as disembodied souls in need of salvation but paid no attention to their broken environments. Vander Lugt reminded the synod that "the Gospel has not only personal but social and political significance....All of life must be transformed by the power of God's Word." The gospel had something to say about questions of race and economics.[19]

The discussion illustrated the different attitudes that purists and moderates held toward secular culture outside the church, or "the world," as they called it. Benes and other purists saw the world as an evil and immoral entity that needed to be conquered by Christianity and replaced with a Christian society. Vander Lugt and other moderates saw the world as an entity created by God but now broken and in need of God's transforming grace. He said, "The power of the Gospel in persons of faith can and will release for the good of our society and the world the infinite resources of God's grace for the transformation of the world. The Church has a faith not *in* but *for* the world—faith in the transcendent power and love of God as revealed in Christ to accomplish what is impossible to us by ourselves." Vander Lugt insisted that God created the world, sent Christ to redeem it, and called Christians to be "centers of His redeeming grace for the reclaiming of the world."[20] In

[17] *Acts and Proceedings*, 1952, 210-21.
[18] For an analysis of some of the various ways Christians have understood the connection between the church and society, see H. Richard Niebuhr, *Christ and Culture* (New York: Harper, 1951), particularly "Christ Transforming Culture," 190-229.
[19] *Acts and Proceedings*, 1955, 255.
[20] *Acts and Proceedings*, 1955, 258. This distinction between the world as evil and the world as broken is subtle but important. Fundamentalists and evangelicals usually described the world as hopelessly evil. They believed that God would eventually take

his view, Christians should trust the power of God rather than fear the power of the world.

The moderates argued that the world could only be reclaimed if the church spoke in a language that could be understood. Daniel Y. Brink, president of General Synod and a pastor in Scotia, New York, observed in his State of Religion address in 1956 that although American society had been changed radically by financial security, racial integration, and suburbanization, the church was still telling the old, old story of God's love using nineteenth-century thought forms. When contemporary people heard the gospel in out-dated language, they dismissed it as irrelevant, not because they were unconverted or hostile, but because it meant nothing to them. Even the Apostle Paul adjusted his message so that it could be heard by different audiences. Brink said to the synod, "All of us who speak for Christ must constantly ask ourselves whether we are using a language that is meaningful to the folk of our new generation, or merely employing time-honored phrases and thought patterns dear to the hearts of the fathers but confusing and meaningless to their children."[21]

Moderates believed that the church did not exist or survive because of human effort but by the grace of God. The church and its members were strong and solid and would not easily crumble or lose faith. The church did not have to defend itself or conquer the world. The church should present the gospel in an attractive and meaningful way because it had something to offer that the world needed. The church would not be endangered by new ideas or practices or by members who were less than completely faithful. God would preserve God's church.

These differing views of the church amplified the suspicion and distrust that existed after the conflicts of the late 1940s. When Joseph Sizoo resigned from the presidency of New Brunswick Seminary in 1952, he alluded to a long-standing assumption within the denomination that New Brunswick Seminary produced liberals and Western Seminary produced evangelicals. Sizoo observed that many young ministers were frustrated by these over-simplified stereotypes and disappointed with the denomination.[22]

---

the Christians out of the world and give them a glorious life in heaven. Moderates more often described the world as a good entity, created by God, but now broken by human sinfulness. Instead of abandoning the world, however, they believed that God would transform it. The Bible demonstrates a similar ambiguity and includes texts that support both perspectives.

[21]   *Acts and Proceedings*, 1956, 219-31.
[22]   Joseph Sizoo, "To the Fellowship of the Reformed Church," *CH*, Aug. 15, 1952, 8.

Justin Vander Kolk, a professor of theology at New Brunswick Seminary, also discussed the recurring tensions within the Reformed Church when he addressed the Synod of New Jersey in the spring of 1953. He acknowledged the denominational divisions and lack of trust but tried to see them in a positive light. He appreciated the Reformed Church in part because it included people from Newark, New Jersey, and Orange City, Iowa, who were very different. "It is as though the Lord of the Church had called us together just in order that we might learn to live together and trust one another and love one another so that He may point to us as a group of the most stubborn people on earth whom His grace has subdued and whom His love has welded into oneness." If God can reconcile Jews and Gentiles, God can reconcile the different sections of the Reformed Church, he said. But Vander Kolk admitted that this required a great deal of patience.

> I will, for myself, confess that it is painful to know that one is regarded with suspicion by fellow Christians because he labors in an institution of the Reformed Church where it is supposed that heresy abounds and sound doctrine is unknown. But this pain can be accepted and carried as a light burden if we believe that out of this pattern of distrust—based upon misinformation and sometimes also upon plain "cussedness"—there will emerge and is even now emerging a new pattern of understanding and good will. We have a unique opportunity as a denomination to demonstrate the fact that the Gospel of Jesus Christ can produce unity in diversity and that true Christian fellowship can exist despite real differences.

He acknowledged the difficulties inherent in being in the moderate wing of the Reformed Church, but he encouraged the Synod of New Jersey to trust God and move into the future.[23]

Despite these lingering suspicions, there were fewer angry debates on particular issues at General Synod meetings during these years. For a time, Reformed Church identity was expansive enough to include multiple perspectives without constant conflict. Moderates and conservatives[24] expressed opposite viewpoints on a range of issues from

---

[23] Justin Vander Kolk, "Ought the Reformed Church Preserve Its Historic Identity?" *CH*, May 29, 1953, 12-13, 21.

[24] In what follows I will generally not distinguish between conservatives and purists. They took similar positions on most of the issues. At times the purists took a more separatist stance. However, because most of these issues did not come to a vote or threaten to change the RCA in significant ways, purists felt less need to criticize, condemn, or separate from those who did not agree with them.

ecumenism to racism to the role of women. These views often arose out of very different theological perspectives. The following overview illustrates some of the reasons that conservatives and moderates came to such different conclusions on these issues. Many of the underlying attitudes and beliefs were still apparent three decades later.

Family Disagreements: Ecumenism

Ecumenism caused far less debate and division in the 1950s than it did in the previous decade. The large assembly of the National Council of Churches met every two or three years instead of annually and made fewer controversial statements. Louis Benes wrote positively about these meetings, but some purist members remained suspicious of ecumenical efforts. When the World Council of Churches met in Chicago, a laywoman asked how the Reformed Church could cooperate with Christians who adored Mary or did not believe in the Virgin Birth. "Surely we who know these doctrines to be false and anti-Biblical, cannot wholeheartedly bid them welcome. How can we be such hypocrites? No wonder we're not growing in grace." She insisted the Reformed Church should be busy winning souls, not wasting time with worldly associations.[25] Ronald Brown, pastor of the Beverly Reformed Church in Wyoming, Michigan, complained that a photograph related to the Week of Prayer for Christian Unity showed two Reformed Church ministers with a Roman Catholic and an Orthodox priest. The photograph implied that these traditions were Christian, Brown said, but he refused to pray for unity with false churches or seek fellowship between light and darkness.[26]

The moderate wing of the denomination viewed ecumenism more positively and occasionally chided the purists for their criticism of other traditions. Gerrit Vander Lugt suggested that the Reformed Church's narrow focus on itself as a family was not virtuous but self-centered. "We are apt to be an introverted community. Sometimes it appears to me that as a church we suffer from an 'inferiority complex.' We are afraid of ourselves—afraid we will lose our identity as a church if we become serious about cultivating fraternal relations."[27] Similarly, M. Verne Oggel, a pastor in Glen Rock, New Jersey, valued the church's membership in the World Council of Churches because it provided connections to Christians throughout the world. Oggel believed that

[25] Lois Peterson, letter to the editor, *CH*, June 11, 1954, 2.
[26] Letter to the editor, *CH*, March 8, 1963, 17.
[27] *Acts and Proceedings*, 1955, 243-44.

the faith was not easily damaged or destroyed and the church did not need to work so hard to protect it. "Orthodoxy is not so frail and shaky a thing that it cannot endure occasional exposure to a degree of heterodoxy."[28]

Conservative and moderate Reformed Church members found common ground when they participated in the ecumenical Billy Graham crusade in New York City in 1957. They served as ushers, choir members, and counselors. A number of eastern churches received new members from among those converted in the crusade.[29] Conservative Reformed Church members found this practical, task-oriented ecumenism more appealing than the larger, more diverse councils.

The conservative middle of the Reformed Church may have grown slightly more tolerant of other Protestants, but these members were still dubious about Roman Catholics. They were not alone in this, as even the mainline Protestant journal *Christian Century* criticized the Catholic Church during this decade. Roman Catholics had become more of a presence in American culture as they acquired more education and middle-class status. They felt freer to criticize examples of Protestant domination in schools and other institutions. Some Protestants found this new confidence intimidating.

Louis Benes was far more critical of the papacy than of individual Roman Catholics. He frequently argued that Rome was trying to break down the separation of church and state by demanding public tax money to support Catholic schools and hospitals.[30] He also criticized Catholic attempts to insert religious symbols onto public property. When the Vanguard rocket was launched in March 1958, it carried a medal of St. Christopher, the patron saint of travelers. The infantry school in Fort Benning, Georgia, attempted to display a statue of St. Maurice, patron saint of the foot soldier. Benes considered these efforts

---

[28]   M. Verne Oggel, "Is the World Council of Churches Orthodox?" *CH*, Aug. 22, 1952, 8.

[29]   *CH*: Editorials, "Billy Graham in New York," March 15, 1957, 6-7; "Miracles in New York," June 28, 1957, 6. Winfield Burggraaff, "Let Me Commend the Crusade," July 19, 1957, 4, 15. Editorial, "New Converts in the Churches," Sept. 6, 1957, 6-7. Religious News Service, "Graham Says New York Crusade Broke All Records," Sept. 13, 1957, 2. "Paterson Area News," Nov. 8, 1957, 20-21. "Queens Church Celebrates Centennial," May 9, 1958, 20. Edwin Mulder, who became general secretary of the RCA in 1983, attended an event where Graham spoke to eight hundred ministers and encouraged them to "preach for a verdict." By this he meant a relationship with Jesus Christ. Mulder said this emphasis on personal faith (rather than a more propositional view of faith as things to be believed) profoundly shaped the rest of his ministry. Oral history interview with Edwin Mulder, Feb. 23, 2000, New York, NY.

[30]   Editorial, "Separation of Church and State," *CH*, Sept. 14, 1951, 6-7, 9.

a "sinister method for the propagation of the Roman Catholic faith."[31] Ironically, Benes constantly lamented that faith was not recognized in public life, yet when Catholics acknowledged their faith, he dismissed them as superstitious and manipulative.

Benes believed that the Roman Catholic Church was inherently authoritarian and opposed to democracy. He cited examples of Catholic tyranny in Spain and Colombia and concluded, "We ought not to forget that Rome, like Communism, is by its very nature intolerant, and according to its own words essentially opposed to freedom of religion." In an editorial about the growth of Roman Catholicism in cities he wrote, "Rome, organized to control rather than to serve, to dictate rather than to develop democracy, is gaining in influence in many areas of our national life."[32] Benes believed that democracy and the freedom of the individual developed out of the Protestant tradition and that "Rome always has, and still does, oppose these freedoms. Herself totalitarian, she is inevitably opposed to democracy."[33] Benes frequently linked Catholicism and communism because he assumed both demanded obedience, denied individual freedoms, and persecuted dissenters.[34] Such statements seemed so obvious to Benes and many of his readers that they needed no evidence or justification.

In 1959 Pope John XXIII announced the formation of a council which would be known as Vatican II. Leroy Nixon, a pastor in Flushing, New York, immediately dismissed the idea: "This is one of the tricks that the bishop of Rome has often used to bolster his false claim that he is the vicar of Christ on earth and therefore the right head and ruler of all Christians." Benes was intrigued, but skeptical. What Catholics mean by ecumenism, he said, is for other churches to acknowledge the validity of the Roman Catholic Church.[35]

In the Reformed Church, dislike of Catholics could be intertwined with regional tension. Eastern pastors traditionally wore clerical collars, while midwestern ministers usually did not. Mrs. Garrit Sytsma wrote from Denver, "I have noticed recently in the *Church Herald* pictures of ministers dressed like Roman Catholic priests. Why do some of our Reformed ministers dress different from the laymen? Why bring such a custom into the Reformed Church?"[36]

---

31 Editorial, "Missiles and Foot Soldiers," *CH*, May 30, 1958, 6.
32 Editorials, *CH*: "Religion and Irreligion in the U.S.A.," Dec. 5, 1952, 6; "What Makes Churches Grow?" Sept. 25, 1953, 6-7.
33 Editorial, "Reformation and Revival," *CH*, Oct. 16, 1953, 6.
34 Editorial, "Captives to the Word of God," *CH*, Oct. 30, 1953, 6-7.
35 Leroy Nixon, "John Calvin's Answer to the Bishop of Rome," *CH*, March 10, 1959, 4; Editorial, "Pope John's Proposal," April 17, 1959, 6-7.
36 Letter to the editor, Aug. 15, 1952, 8.

Suspicion of Roman Catholics peaked in 1960, when Benes and many others expressed uncertainty about the prospect of John F. Kennedy as president of the United States. Kennedy insisted that he supported the separation of church and state, but Benes wondered if he would have the freedom to implement his belief while the Vatican claimed the right to guide all aspects of a Catholic's life.[37]

To his credit, Benes came to appreciate Pope John XXIII. When the pope died in 1963, Benes praised him as a simple and humble man who challenged the ecclesiastical system, began a process of renewal, and welcomed Protestants. "This one man, by the gracious largeness of his kindly heart, has defrosted the religious climate of four centuries, and changed the whole religious atmosphere of Christendom."[38] Not all Reformed Church members were so gracious. When the General Synod voted to extend condolences to the Roman Catholic Church on the death of John XXIII, John R. DeWitt, a pastor in Paterson, New Jersey, insisted that his negative vote be recorded in the minutes.[39]

Eastern members generally had more contact with Roman Catholics because of the demographics of New York and New Jersey. They did not generally label Catholicism as a false church, although they certainly disagreed with many Catholic beliefs. Moderates did not see the Reformed Church as the only true church or as possessing all the answers. They viewed ecumenism as a way to work with and learn from other Christians. Conservatives were more likely to claim that the Reformed tradition represented the true faith and that others were wrong. In their eyes ecumenism was nonessential and a possible danger to the church's purity. They believed the Reformed Church did not need any other Christian perspectives for its faith to be complete.

Family Disagreements: Church and State

Church and state issues, particularly the role of religion in public schools, caused a great deal of national debate between 1950 and 1963. Many public schools had considered it their responsibility to teach generic religion and morality using prayer and Bible readings. In the nineteenth century, Roman Catholics protested that this was in fact

---

[37] Editorial, "Vatican Affirms Political Role," *CH*, Aug. 5, 1960, 6-7.

[38] This statement illustrates how much Benes had mellowed in nearly two decades as editor. It also shows the power of the late pope to influence people. Editorial, "The New Religious Climate," *CH*, July 12, 1963, 6-7.

[39] *Acts and Proceedings*, 1963, 447-48. A number of nineteenth-century Dutch immigrants settled in Paterson, NJ, and the RCA churches in this area were much more conservative than most others in New York and New Jersey.

Protestant religious training, and they began to develop their own parish schools. By the early 1960s the complaints about religion in public schools had increased dramatically. Some parents (of various religious traditions or none) simply did not want their children to be taught religion in school or stigmatized for choosing not to participate.

Conservative Reformed Church members believed that religious instruction in schools prevented moral deterioration and secularism and that America would fail if children were not taught to be Christian. Louis Benes conceded that public schools should not teach specific doctrines, but he insisted that they teach religion in order that children might be saved and become witnesses for Jesus Christ. Benes considered this a legitimate task for tax-funded public institutions, and yet he opposed public aid for parochial schools because "no parent has the right to expect a taxpayer to help pay for indoctrinating his child with his particular religion."[40]

Benes showed little sympathy for dissenters. He insisted that a few secular Americans should not be permitted to ban the Bible from the public schools. He even went so far as to insist that no one should be permitted to express hostility or indifference to religion, and that schools should teach reverence for and dependence upon God.[41]

Some Reformed Church members recognized the ambiguities involved in the public schools' required religious practices but refused to give them up. George Heneveld, a pastor in Hawthorne, New Jersey, noted that the United Secularists of America had challenged the daily reading of five verses from the Old Testament. He admitted that the exercise provided minimal religious value because a student read the verses in a perfunctory manner and the other students paid little attention. Nevertheless, he insisted, "it is a symbol and one that we do not want to surrender."[42]

Moderate Reformed Church members expressed more caution about religion taught in schools. In 1957, an amendment proposed to the Michigan Constitution would have required ten verses of the Bible to be read daily in all schools, and all students to memorize the Ten Commandments and the Lord's Prayer. Harold Englund, a pastor at the Second Reformed Church in Zeeland, warned that the amendment was unwise because it would probably be challenged and schools might be further restricted. He also noted that reading Bible verses did not

---

40 Editorials, "Religion in Public Schools," *CH*, July 25, 1952, 6; "Public Aid for Parochial Schools?" Sept. 12, 1952, 6.
41 Editorial, "The Bible in Public Schools," *CH*, Jan. 11, 1952, 6-7.
42 George Heneveld, "Battling Atheism," *CH*, Dec. 16, 1949, 10.

Christianize students, and that neither teachers nor the state should be coerced into teaching religion.[43] He did not believe that forced religious training would increase morality or ensure the future of America.

The controversy increased during the next decade, when the U. S. Supreme Court entered the fray. In 1962 the Supreme Court ruled that the New York Board of Regents could not write and require a school prayer even if students were allowed to opt out. The First Amendment did not permit the government to establish religion in a public institution, and school boards should not be in the business of writing prayers. Benes accused the court of trying to eliminate God from public life. He acknowledged that no one should be forced to participate in religious practice, but he did not think the "aggressive minority" should be allowed to impose their will on the majority.[44]

Benes was equally troubled in 1963 when the court ruled it unconstitutional for public schools to use the Lord's Prayer or devotional Bible reading. He admitted that most Protestants would not want the Koran read or the "Hail, Mary" prayed, but he believed schools should provide religious exercises for those who wanted them. He feared that the court's ruling established the religion of secularism and permitted the minority to restrict the rights of the majority.[45]

Reformed moderates did not believe that public school devotions were very effective, so they were not particularly troubled by their loss. Marinus Swets, an English professor and a member of the Garfield Park Reformed Church in Grand Rapids, wrote that children developed their basic temperaments and values at home before they started school. Required devotions were unlikely to make them religious if they were not so already. Swets suggested that faith would be more effectively taught by family devotions than by a school prayer that had been carefully crafted not to offend anyone.[46]

Purist and some conservative Reformed Church members believed that white Protestant Christians ought to continue to have a place of influence and dominance in American society. They believed it was legitimate for Christians to encourage, even require, all members of American society to live by Christian values. The court decisions

---

[43]   Harold Englund, "Don't Rock the Boat," *CH*, Oct. 4, 1957, 8.

[44]   Editorial, "Prayer in the Public Schools," *CH*, July 13, 1962, 6-7.

[45]   Editorial, "The Supreme Court Decision," *CH*, July 26, 1963, 6-7. The court decision did permit the academic study of religion in public schools.

[46]   Marinus Swets, "As the Twig is Bent," *CH*, Oct. 11, 1963, 11, 30. Howard Hageman pointed out that Protestants had used the separation of church and state against other religious groups but disliked the fact that the court had applied it to Protestants as well. "We'd Better Start Thinking!" *CH*, July 27, 1962, 8.

threatened this privileged position. Moderate members, on the other hand, argued that they lived in a diverse society with multiple races and religious beliefs. They did not believe Protestants were entitled to a place of privilege. The Protestant community was free to offer its opinions, and ought to do so in a winsome way, but it had no right to impose religious beliefs and action.

Family Disagreements: Civil Rights

If Roman Catholics and agnostics were treated as outsiders in America in the 1950s, African Americans fared even worse. In the South, Jim Crow laws mandated separate drinking fountains, bathrooms, and seats on buses, and in many areas African Americans were permitted to hold only the most menial jobs. In the years leading up to and following World War II, tens of thousands of African Americans moved north to find work. Segregation was a bit less harsh in northern cities, but many Northern whites refused to share their schools, neighborhoods, and churches with people of other races.[47]

Reformed Church members experienced racial issues quite differently depending on where they lived. Few members of racial/ ethnic minorities lived in the midwestern small towns where Reformed churches proliferated, but New York, New Jersey, Detroit, Chicago, and Los Angeles became increasingly diverse. As city neighborhoods changed, white people often moved out to the suburbs and their churches followed them.[48] For these congregations, the issue of race relations was not an abstraction. It affected their property values and the number of members in their congregations.

The conversation about racial issues in the Reformed Church was marked by a few bright spots and many examples of fear, ignorance, and insensitivity. One of the bright spots was Louis Benes. Despite his generally conservative and at times purist beliefs about theology and social issues, he was quite progressive about race. He encouraged Reformed churches to welcome people of other races and to stay in a community when the neighborhood changed rather than follow the exodus to the suburbs. He criticized church members for racist

---

[47] See Swierenga, *Dutch Chicago*.

[48] Harold Korver was pastor of the Calvary Reformed in Chicago from 1962-1967. In an interview he recalled his desire to stay in the church's neighborhood as it changed and help the church become multiracial, but he was told by an African-American pastor in the area that African-Americans would never attend a white church and that it would be better if Korver left. Oral history interview with Harold Korver, July 22, 2004, Paramount, CA.

attitudes and white flight. He praised the efforts of Martin Luther King Jr. at a time when many people thought King was a Communist. Benes wondered why so much progress in race relations came grudgingly and why people had to be forced by the courts to do what was right. He adopted a paternalistic tone at times, as when he asked whether some "colored people" would make good church members "if we loved them and took them in, and helped them?" But he posed the difficult questions and encouraged fair treatment.[49]

There were a number of other positive examples of racial sensitivity throughout the Reformed Church. A direct encounter with racism often led to greater awareness. Several students from New Brunswick Seminary traveled to Richmond, Virginia, early in the 1950s to attend an interseminary conference. One of the students was Wilbur Washington, an African-American. The students drove all night and stopped for breakfast, but Wilbur said he wasn't hungry and stayed in the car. It took the others a while to catch on, but eventually they realized he wasn't hungry because he knew he would not be served. They asked the owner if their friend could join them in the restaurant. When he refused, the students left. They all chose to be hungry for a bit longer.[50]

The Reformed Church's Christian Action Commission wrote a remarkably progressive "Credo on Race Relations," which the General Synod adopted in 1957. The credo consisted of ten statements that called the church to confess the sins of racism and to take concrete actions in support of racial justice. For example, the credo said:

> We believe that the racially inclusive and culturally integrated church represents the highest demonstration of the transforming fellowship of reconciliation which characterizes the Christian fellowship at its best. We believe that Christians should actively support those groups or agencies which are striving to achieve social justice. We believe that each generation inherits from the past problems for which it cannot be held directly accountable, but for whose solutions it is held responsible.

The two most controversial statements dealt with intermarriage and housing. The credo noted that the issue of intermarriage was emotionally charged and often used to excuse injustice, but there was

---

[49] Editorials, "Apartheid in South Africa—and Here," *CH*, Dec. 4, 1953, 6-7; "Progress in Race Relations," Feb. 12, 1954, 6.

[50] Oral history interview with Leonard Kalkwarf, March 19, 2002, Willow Grove, PA. He was one of the students.

no biblical reason to prohibit interracial marriage. The credo also opposed racially restrictive housing covenants, agreements in which home buyers promised not to sell their homes to African Americans.[51]

Benes heartily approved of the statement,[52] but others vigorously opposed it, particularly the section on intermarriage. August Nydam, a layperson from Chicago wrote,

> We who have our church on the fringe hold a very different opinion than do the churches of the east, the majority of whom do not have this problem....The downfall of Israel was the sin of intermarriage, with the Canaanites, and their idolatry. Since we believe we are the adopted children of our God, this rule also applies to us. We could also worship with the colored folks, and have good communion with them spiritually, but to intermarry is wrong. For if God wanted us to be all one, He would have made it so from the beginning. We have no animosity toward any. But to intermarry is beyond our comprehension, and our best judgment, and our church as Reformed should not sanction such things.

F. Hetherington, a layperson from Huntington Park, California, wrote, "It is beyond my comprehension that any group of Christians can get so worked up over this racial problem that they condone such marriages, which are offensive to man's better nature and against all natural laws from the beginning of time." He suggested that members of the Christian Action Commission prove their sincerity by moving to a predominantly Negro neighborhood and sending their children to Negro schools. He doubted they would do this. He concluded with a threat that if the credo had become the stated policy of the Reformed Church, it was time for him to change his church affiliation.[53]

Some examples of racism were more subtle. Earle Winters, executive of the Particular Synod of New Jersey, described the effect of changing neighborhoods on Reformed churches in Newark. The First Reformed Church once filled its twelve-hundred-seat sanctuary twice on Sunday mornings, he said, but a different class of people now lived around the church and new methods had to be adopted. "The people are Spanish-speaking and colored. They are slow in school so the church has set up a remedial reading clinic...to help these people keep up with the rest of their class in their schools."[54] This example demonstrates

51 *CH*, July 5, 1957, 4-5.
52 Editorial, "Our 'Race Relations Credo,'" *CH*, July 19, 1957, 6.
53 August Nydam, F. Hetherington, letters to the editor, *CH*, Aug. 30, 1957, 11, 15.
54 L. Earle Winters, "I'm a Back-Yard Missionary," *CH*, May 4, 1962, 4-5.

both a genuine effort to minister to the community and the persistent presence of racism and paternalism.

Reformed Church members opposed racism in a variety of ways. The theologically conservative Classis of Passaic (New Jersey) expressed its disapproval of racial restrictions in summer recreation areas and asked its churches not to hold picnics in restricted areas.[55] Ruth Pals of Belmond, Iowa, worked in a settlement house in Chicago and wrote an article that challenged stereotypical assumptions about racial characteristics. Black people were not lazy or immoral, she said, but they had been economically and spiritually depressed for generations, and their family life had frequently been violated. She believed that the best way to counteract these powerful stereotypes was to pray for right attitudes and get acquainted with people of other races.[56]

Howard Hageman wrote sympathetically about young African Americans who turned to drugs and crime out of frustration with racism in the ghettos. "Instead of clucking piously about the wickedness of these things [drugs and crime], the time has come for the Church of Jesus Christ to stand up and testify to their real source—the sinful smugness of people like you and me."[57]

The tension over race issues was particularly evident at the 1962 General Synod, when the synod's president, Norman Thomas, asked each congregation to ensure that housing in its town was open and available to all. The General Synod Committee on the President's Report affirmed a belief in equal rights but recommended no action. The committee thought that congregations should not force integration in their communities because it was a "vexing problem" with "emotional overtones." General Synod delegates were more courageous. The synod defeated the committee's recommendation and instead approved a motion asking each congregation to study the Open Housing Covenant and implement its recommendations.[58]

Reformed Church members also differed on the validity of the protests that had become so essential to the Civil Rights movement. Beginning in 1955 with the bus boycott in Montgomery, Alabama, African Americans took a number of actions to call attention to segregation in the South. Well-dressed young black men sat at lunch

---

[55] "Church News," *CH*, May 12, 1961, 18.
[56] "Erroneous Ideas about Negroes," *CH*, Dec. 6, 1963, 12, 22-23. Although it is no longer used, *Negro* was a term of respect in the 1950s, and I have chosen to use the term when an author does.
[57] "I Tremble," *CH*, Jan. 4, 1963, 10.
[58] *Acts and Proceedings*, 1962, 287-89, 343-44.

counters waiting to be served and were frequently pulled off their stools and beaten. White and black students known as Freedom Riders rode interstate buses, and on one ride students were beaten and the bus was set on fire. In Mississippi in 1964, three college men (two white, one black) were killed because they helped African-Americans register to vote. African-Americans marched peacefully in Birmingham, Alabama, in 1963, and for this dangerous activity the marchers were sprayed with fire hoses, bitten by police dogs, beaten, and jailed. The March on Washington in August 1963 culminated with Martin Luther King Jr.'s famous "I Have a Dream" speech.

Benes supported these demonstrations of civil disobedience because of the rampant discrimination African Americans experienced when they tried to vote, get a job, travel, or attend school. He believed it was appropriate to protest unjust laws. Benes published reports from those who attended the March on Washington, and he praised the dignity and discipline demonstrated there.[59] In 1963 the General Synod commended those involved in nonviolent protests for their courage and self-discipline and took an offering for the Southern Christian Leadership Conference.

On the other hand, Wyoming pastor Ronald Brown argued that sit-ins were illegal even in response to unjust laws. He insisted that scripture provided no example of civil disobedience and that Christians must obey all laws.[60] Robert Nyhoff of Hamilton, Michigan, agreed that it was sinful to break laws. He wrote, "I pray that the Negro may be free someday. There is enough crime and lawbreaking today without churches adding to it. Let us rather preach Jesus Christ and Him crucified, risen, and coming again. The love of God will solve the racial problem."[61]

These varied responses illustrate the significant disagreements about racial issues that existed both in the Reformed Church and across America. Some people thought racial discrimination was perfectly appropriate in a Christian society because God had made different races and wanted to keep them separate. Some Christians thought racism was wrong but could only be cured by proclaiming the gospel. If racist

[59] Editorials: "In Brief," *CH*, May 10, 1963, 7; "Moving Too Fast?" June 14, 1963, 7; "The March on Washington," Sept. 20, 1963, 6. Also articles: Louis Pojman, "The March on Washington," Sept. 20, 1963, 12-13; Donald De Young, "Elmendorf in the March," Sept. 20, 1963, 13, 21; Joseph Blacknow, "My Impressions of the March," Sept. 20, 1963, 21.

[60] Ronald Brown, "Does the end justify the means?" *CH*, Aug. 23, 1963, 10, 30-31. Several letters critical of Brown appeared, *CH*, Sept. 20, 1963, 22.

[61] Robert Nyhoff, letter to the editor, *CH*, Oct. 4, 1963, 16.

people were converted, this model maintained, God's love would change their hearts and make them more accepting. Reformed conservatives generally took this position, with the exception of Louis Benes and a few others. A third view argued that many supposedly Christian people were racist and showed no inclination to change, but if they were forced by law to treat people equally whether they wanted to or not, eventually their attitudes might change as well. Love and personal piety were not enough. The structures of society had been infected by the sin of racism, and only structural changes such as laws and court orders would ultimately heal racism and bring about justice.[62] Reformed moderates often adopted this strategy. They believed that the church needed to take an active role in combating racism, not only by preaching against it but by working to make social and economic structures more equitable for all.

Family Disagreement: Communism

Communism, especially the expansionism espoused by the Soviet Union and the People's Republic of China, was one of the most frightening and divisive issues in American society during the 1950s. The Korean Conflict and the Iron Curtain in Eastern Europe demonstrated the vulnerability of small nations to Communist expansion. The United States and the Soviet Union continued to develop atomic weapons, which escalated the Cold War. Communities set up bomb shelters in public libraries and city halls. Some people built backyard shelters, hoping to preserve family privacy during a nuclear attack. School children practiced hiding under their desks. Despite the happiness, confidence, and economic success of the decade, the looming presence of communism did not make life feel very safe or secure.

Frightened people sought scapegoats. Senator Joseph McCarthy and the House Un-American Activities Committee (HUAC) searched for Communists who might pose a threat to American security. They accused people with merely a tangential tie to a Communist or Socialist group of being Communist sympathizers. The accused could clear their names if they identified others who had been involved.

Many church members, including some in the Reformed Church, fully supported McCarthy and the HUAC because they believed that unchecked communism would take over the world and destroy religious

---

62   This model was used by Martin Luther King Jr., and the Southern Christian Leadership Conference as they worked for legislative change such as the Civil Rights Act of 1964 and the repeal of Jim Crow laws.

freedom, capitalism, and the American way of life. The first step in that grim process would be the infiltration of American institutions so they could be destroyed from within. HUAC and the American public must remain vigilant.[63]

Two Reformed Church committees advocated a calmer approach. In 1953, the Committee on Social Welfare encouraged Christians to be courageous rather than fearful, because God guided the events of the world. Communism would ultimately fail because of its own shortcomings, the committee said, and did not need to be so aggressively opposed.[64] In 1954, the Committee on International Justice and Goodwill cautioned against the national obsession with communism, the hysterical and reckless methods of investigating it, and the deep anxiety about nuclear weapons. The committee urged that all Christians "recover and preach anew a faith in God as the ruler of history, a faith which may be an effective antidote to the growth of a hysteria which may lead to rashness on the part of peoples or their leaders."[65] Trust in God should make people confident rather than fearful, the committee affirmed.

Louis Benes also tried to discourage an overreaction to the perceived threat of communism in 1954 when the World Council of Churches met in Evanston, Illinois. Zealous anti-Communists wanted to deny visas to Czech and Hungarian delegates, but Benes pointed out that many Christians behind the Iron Curtain were simply trying to make the best of a difficult situation.[66] Benes frequently criticized communism as a system, but he was not willing to condemn everyone who lived in a Communist country.

By the 1960s some of the furor over communism had abated, but the HUAC continued its work.[67] Howard Hageman offered a more

---

[63] Social justice agencies were particularly suspect. At the 1960 General Synod, delegates refused to support the National Urban League and the National Association for the Advancement of Colored People because they might be Communist. *Acts and Proceedings*, 1960, 180, 186-87.

[64] *Acts and Proceedings*, 1953, 165.

[65] *Acts and Proceedings*, 1954, 131. The Committee on Social Welfare was formed in 1932 when the Committee on Public Morals merged with the Committee on Social Service and Industrial Relations. It changed its name to the Christian Action Commission in 1955. The Committee on International Justice and Good Will was formed in 1922 in connection with a similar committee of the Federal Council of Churches. It merged with the Christian Action Commission in 1959.

[66] Editorial, "Welcome the World Council," *CH*, May 21, 1954, 6.

[67] Divergent opinions continued. In 1961 the Classis of Philadelphia asked the synod to condemn the actions of the HUAC, while the Classis of California asked the same synod to commend it. *Acts and Proceedings*, 1961, 132.

nuanced analysis of communism in response to a member of the John Birch Society who claimed that seven thousand Protestant ministers were Communists. Hageman said he knew a number of ministers but never met one who was a Communist. He thought it was more likely that Protestant laymen and clergy would be tempted to trust in the stock market rather than God, or read financial reports more regularly than the Bible, or value social expediency rather than social justice. Hageman believed that uncritical acceptance of capitalism posed a greater threat to the nation than communism.[68]

John Beardslee III, a professor at Central College and a member of the Christian Action Commission, also pointed out that not all those opposed to communism had Christian motives. "Communism is satanic, but 'anti-communism' may also be satanic. Not everyone who 'opposes communism' is serving Christ." The most avid opponents of communism may actually be eager for financial gain or election to office.[69] Robert Schuller, a pastor in California, protested Beardslee's article and defended the virtue of the HUAC. Schuller hoped that future articles from the Christian Action Commission would be more positive.[70]

The debate over communism suggests how difficult it was to discern a Reformed approach to national security. Reformed theology strongly affirms God's providential oversight of the world, but finding a way to live out this faith without being too passive or too controlling has been a constant challenge for the Reformed Church. Conservatives emphasized the need to fight against the danger of Communist "infection," while moderates emphasized the power of God to preserve the world from danger.

Family Disagreements: Liturgy

In addition to these broader, external issues, the Reformed Church demonstrated some disagreement about two ecclesiastical issues. The first was liturgy. At mid-century, the church was using a collection of liturgical forms most recently revised in 1906, and they were showing their age. The form for the Lord's Supper, for example, was lengthy and rather didactic. In 1950, the General Synod appointed a Committee for the Revision of the Liturgy. Its members included Howard G. Hageman, M. Stephen James, Richard C. Oudersluys, and

---

[68] Howard Hageman, "7,000 Knees to Baal," *CH*, May 19, 1961, 8.
[69] John Beardslee III, "Who's Against Communism?" *CH*, April 20, 1962, 15.
[70] Letter to the editor, *CH*, May 25, 1962, 20. Schuller noted that one of the members of the HUAC attended his church.

Gerrit T.Vander Lugt.[71] The committee studied the liturgies of early, Reformation, and contemporary churches; wrote several articles about liturgy for the *Church Herald*; and offered provisional liturgies in 1952. Congregations used these forms for three years, and the General Synod approved them in 1955.

There had been very little debate about the new forms, and yet they were not approved by the requisite two-thirds of the classes in the spring of 1956. Some critics said the process needed more time or the language needed to be more artistic or the forms seemed too "Romanist." Some conservatives were concerned that the baptismal liturgy might imply "baptismal regeneration," the idea that the act of baptism is what saves a person rather than conversion. Supporters of the liturgy argued that this was not the case because the sacraments signified God's actions of grace. They also reminded Reformed Church members that the new liturgy reflected a return to Reformation practices.[72]

The committee produced new provisional forms in 1958 and suggested that each particular synod form a committee to study the liturgy during the five years the forms would be used. In 1963 the committee produced another liturgy, this time with a significant revision of the Communion prayer. This set of forms was approved by the General Synod in 1965 and by the classes in 1966 and published in book form as *The Liturgy and Psalms* in 1968.[73]

Family Disagreements: The Role of Women in the Church

The movement toward women's ordination has often been dismissed as an outgrowth of the secular feminist movement. Critics

---

[71] Hageman was pastor of the North Reformed Church in Newark, NJ; James was a professor and later president of New Brunswick Theological Seminary; Oudersluys was professor of New Testament at Western Theological Seminary; and Vander Lugt was president of Central College.

[72] James Eelman, "Our Liturgical Heritage: Some Comments on the Revised Liturgy," *CH*, Feb. 24, 1956, 8. Bert Van Soest, Morris Folkert, Arthur Johnson, "Shall We Approve the Revised Liturgy?" *CH*, March 2, 1956, 11, 20. Gordon Girod, "Straining Out a Gnat: More Thoughts on the Revised Liturgy," *CH*, April 20, 1956, 10, 22. James Eelman, letters to the editor, *CH*, March 23, 1956, 17, 22; May 11, 1956, 17, 23.

[73] The new Communion liturgy brought out the joyful, celebrative, hopeful elements of the Lord's Supper in addition to the traditional emphasis on memorial and sacrifice. For an extended discussion of the changes in the liturgy, see Christopher Dorn, *The Lord's Supper in the Reformed Church in America* (New York: Peter Lang, 2007), 107-21; James Hart Brumm, ed., *Liturgy among the Thorns*, HSRCA, no. 57 (Grand Rapids: Eerdmans, 2007).

have claimed that women were perfectly content in their roles as housewives and mothers until the 1970s feminist movement created dissatisfaction in society that spilled over into the church, where women began to demand a voice and a role. The reality is actually quite different. The first request to ordain women came to the General Synod in 1918.[74] Since women were not permitted to be delegates to classes, only men wrote and voted on this overture. Men continued to work for the ordination of women for more than half a century because they thought it was the just, wise, and biblical course of action. Women may have encouraged them to do so from behind the scenes, but men took the actions.

In 1951 the Classis of Westchester in New York overtured the General Synod to delete the word "male" from the qualifications for ordination to the office of elder and deacon. The Overtures Committee recommended no action for three reasons: the need was not apparent, the Reformed Church was not ready, and opening the offices to women might diminish men's sense of responsibility. In 1952 Westchester Classis resubmitted the overture and provided additional reasons why the change was necessary. All but three congregations in the classis supported the overture, and many had already developed alternative governing structures that included women. A number of Reformed Church women served in leadership roles on denominational mission boards.[75]

Donald Blackie, a pastor at the Hope Reformed Church in Los Angeles,[76] encouraged the Classis of Westchester to review 1 Timothy 3, which clearly stated that elders and deacons should be men. If congregations lacked sufficient men to do their work, Blackie wrote, they should make new converts rather than change the Bible. Albertus Pieters, a Western Seminary professor, responded that the Bible was authoritative for faith and ethics but not necessarily for church order. Scripture did not mandate, or even mention, the structures of General Synod and classes. The Reformed Church permitted women to teach on the mission field, and, while it existed, the Women's Board of Domestic Mission exercised authority over male ministers. Pieters concluded that

---

[74] *Acts and Proceedings*, 1918, 477-78.
[75] "Report of the General Synod," *CH*, June 22, 1951, 4-9; "Classis Westchester Overture," Dec. 29, 1951, 24-25.
[76] Blackie graduated from Westminster Theological Seminary in 1934. The seminary had been formed in 1929 when J. Gresham Machen left his position at Princeton Seminary and started both Westminster and a new denomination, the Orthodox Presbyterian Church. Westminster emphasized doctrinal purity and a fundamentalist approach to scripture. A number of purist/conservative RCA clergy attended Westminster.

women should be eligible for church office, and congregations should be free to ordain them. Peter Ammeraal, a layperson from Zeeland, Michigan, retorted, "Certainly God has ordained men to be above women," and insisted that scripture clearly said that women should only teach other women and children.[77]

In 1952 the General Synod received thirteen overtures concerning women's ordination, six asking to delete the word "male" and seven asking to retain it. This time the Committee on Overtures recommended sending the *Book of Church Order* amendment (to delete the word "male") to the classes. Four members of the Overtures Committee disagreed and issued a minority report arguing that the change was unbiblical and unlikely to be approved by two-thirds of the classes, and that the discussion would strain the peace of the church. The synod voted in favor of the amendment, but it was defeated by the classes.[78]

Frederick Zimmerman, a pastor at the First Church in Albany, addressed the issue when he was president of the General Synod in 1954.

> I hope to see the day when we shall take them [women] in as working partners rather than as the silent ones we insist upon their being today, in the Consistories, Classes and Synods of the church....It's about time we exercised Christian grace rather than legalistic quotations to keep us in our places and put them in their supposed place. What's good enough for the country in giving the franchise to women ought to be a spur to us to do likewise.[79]

James Eelman, a professor at New Brunswick Seminary, said he had no practical problem with women as leaders, and he thought the Bible could be used to support either side of the argument. But he believed that ordained people represented God and Christ and that God related to humanity through the ordained offices. Eelman did not believe women could represent God because "in the Bible God is always masculine and His people are always symbolized as feminine." A female minister could not represent the male God.[80]

---

[77] Donald Blackie, letter to the editor, *CH*, Jan. 25, 1952, 13; Albertus Pieters, "Shall We Allow Women to Be Elected as Elders and Deacons?" March 7, 1952, 8; Peter Ammeraal, letter to the editor, March 28, 1952, 10.

[78] *Acts and Proceedings*, 1952, 110-12. Changing the *Book of Church Order* required three steps. First, the General Synod had to approve the change by a simple majority. Then, two-thirds of the classes had to approve by a simple majority. Finally the amendment went to the synod for a declarative action.

[79] *Acts and Proceedings*, 1954, 218.

[80] James Eelman, "Shall Women Be Admitted to the Offices of the Church?" *CH*, April 27, 1956, 8, 20. At one point in the article, Eelman referred to the "scared office"—a typographical error that spoke volumes.

In 1955, the synod adopted a proposal to study the ordination of women. A committee was appointed consisting of Gerrit Vander Lugt (president of Central College), Lambert Ponstein (religion professor at Hope College), Vernon Kooy (NBTS), Richard Oudersluys (WTS), and Andrew Meyer (elder at North Park, Kalamazoo). In 1957 the committee published a series of articles in the *Church Herald*. One article reviewed the previous actions of the General Synod, beginning in 1918. A second essay reviewed the practices of other churches in the United States and the world. Many had already ordained women, while others continued to debate the question. Two extensive essays on the role of women in the Old and New Testaments concluded that there was nothing in the Bible to prevent women from holding office. The committee recommended that the synod make a declarative statement that scripture did not exclude women from the offices of the church but actually emphasized their inclusion. The synod approved this. It also approved a recommendation to open the offices to women in 1962, but this was not approved by the classes.[81]

The fact that the denomination's most respected scholars encouraged the ordination of women carried little weight with many Reformed Church members. George Hazekamp, an elder from Clifton, New Jersey, wondered why the Reformed Church would spend $1,000 to study this question when the Bible said clearly that Jesus received the ministry of women but never ordained them, and the apostles chose seven men to be deacons. Hazekamp concluded, "Are any of those who are so anxious to please their own desires able to point to one instance in either Old or New Testament where a woman was ordained or anointed? Please let us continue in the old ways wherein we and our forefathers have been blessed in our Reformed Church."[82]

Some classes and consistories found alternative ways to give women a voice. In 1957 the Bronxville consistory invited the president of the women's society to attend monthly consistory meetings as a guest.[83]

---

[81]   Gerrit Vander Lugt, "Ordination of Women in the Reformed Church," Jan. 4, 1957, 10-11; Andrew Meyer and Lambert Ponstein, "The Practice of Other Churches in the Ordination of Women," Jan. 11, 1957, 10; Vernon Kooy, "Ordination of Women and the Old Testament," Jan. 18, 1957, 7, 21; Richard Oudersluys, "The Ordination of Women and the Teaching of the New Testament," March 15, 1957, 8-9. *Acts and Proceedings*, 1958, 321-31. The committee recommended a two-part process in which classes would first vote simply on a proposal to open the offices to women in 1962 and then vote again on the constitutional changes. *Acts and Proceedings*, 1959, 236.

[82]   Letter to the editor, *CH*, May 31, 1957, 17.

[83]   "Church and School News," *CH*, Dec. 27, 1957, 16.

In 1958 the Classis of California unanimously disapproved of women's ordination but advised churches to "seek the counsel of their women more often than they have." Leroy Swim from Midland, Michigan, said that women could use their gifts in teaching and counseling without being ordained, but they should not be permitted to organize or direct official church business.[84]

Missionaries on the field saw the value of women's leadership more clearly than the church at home. Ruth Broekema and Jean Walvoord were ordained elders by the Presbyterian Church of Taiwan where they served as missionaries.[85] Suzanne Brink preached regularly in Japan. The women's mission boards, both foreign and domestic, made numerous decisions about missionary work and supervised male missionaries.[86]

At this point the debate over the ordination of women was relatively restrained, in part because the moderates who advocated women's ordination were a small group and did not garner significant support. But the lines were being drawn for later debates. The moderates' desire to engage the issue would soon clash with those who wanted to preserve the old ways of thinking and a literal reading of the Bible. The issue would become extremely divisive during the 1970s.

Unifying Forces: Church Extension

In 1950, Howard Hageman suggested that a focus on church extension might provide the denomination with a shared sense of mission that could transcend some of its conflicts. Most Reformed Church members, regardless of theological position, supported growth because it brought people into the church, boosted the denomination's self-esteem, and helped it focus outside of itself. Growth was not a panacea, however, and it did not resolve the church's theological differences.

The Reformed Church sponsored a few very successful church starts, which renewed members' pride and energy. In the new housing development of Levittown, New York, a new RCA congregation grew rapidly, its pews filled with veterans and their families. The church was

---

84 John H. Muller, "Classis California News," *CH*, April 18, 1958, 19, 21. Leroy Swim, letter to the editor, April 18, 1958, 17.

85 *Acts and Proceedings*, 1958, 87-88. Missionaries were commissioned at a ceremony held during a General Synod meeting. They were not ordained, because "missionary" was not an office like that of elder, deacon, or minister, although many male missionaries had been ordained as either ministers or elders.

86 See Kansfield, *Letters to Hazel*; House and Coakley, *Patterns and Portraits*.

started in 1949 and, by the fall of 1951, it had 363 members and 500 children in Sunday school. By May 1953, it had grown to 500 members and 750 children. In the first four years of the church's life there had been 12 funerals and 291 baptisms.[87] This was not the norm for Reformed Church congregations. The number of children under ten in the United States had increased 39 percent in the previous ten years, but RCA Sunday school enrollment had declined.[88]

A new church in Midland, Michigan, provided another encouraging example. The Reformed Church previously had no churches in Midland, but the new congregation grew quickly because of the growth of Dow Chemical Company. The pastor, Donald Buteyn, reported that many people who joined the church knew very little about the Christian faith, so he developed a home study program and provided people with a set of books.[89]

A number of new churches were started in Dutch enclaves using the method of "swarming" or "daughtering." A church grew until it was considered too large, and then some of its members started a new church in the community. The Christ Memorial Church in Holland, Michigan, was formed when the Trinity and Maplewood Reformed churches sent members to start a church in a different part of town.

The Reformed Church also planted churches in new suburban housing developments. Harold Lenters started a church in Portage, Michigan, during the height of its growth as a suburb of Kalamazoo. He said it was relatively easy to attract people to a new church in their neighborhood. While some of the members were new to church life, many had left an older part of town and wanted to leave their old church behind as well.[90]

The most famous church planter of the decade was Robert Schuller. He grew up on a farm in northwest Iowa, attended Hope College during World War II, and then attended Western Seminary. He had served a church near Chicago for five years when he received a call from the Classis of California to start a new church in Orange County. When Schuller and his wife, Arvella, arrived in southern California, the only place available for Sunday church services was a drive-in movie theater. Arvella played the organ (towed in weekly on a trailer), and

---

[87] "Growth at Levittown," *CH*, Sept. 28, 1951, 23; "Growth at Levittown," Jan. 30, 1953, 24; "Advancements at Levittown," May 15, 1953, 23.

[88] Bernard Mulder, "Facts and Figures from the Board of Education," *CH*, May 29, 1953, 10.

[89] Donald Buteyn, "*Reach* Them and *Teach* Them," *CH*, March 18, 1955, 10, 22-23.

[90] Oral history interview with Harold Lenters, May 14, 2004, Sioux Center, Iowa.

Robert preached from the roof of the refreshment stand. The church drew a number of people previously unconnected with any church. Within a decade, the Garden Grove Community Church had more than 2,600 baptized members and had built a combination walk-in/drive-in church. Schuller opened the Institute for Successful Christian Leadership, where pastors could learn the secrets of his success. He eventually began a television ministry, wrote more than thirty books, and built the Crystal Cathedral.[91]

While Reformed Church members agreed in principle about the value of church growth, they continued to debate the details. For example, what should new churches be called? When a church started in a new area, some leaders were reluctant to label it "Reformed" because the unfamiliar term did not feel inviting and welcoming. Many new churches preferred the name "Community" as a way to show engagement and concern for the neighborhood. Louis Benes encouraged churches to use the name Reformed to identify their theological perspective. He thought the word was nothing to be ashamed of and did not need to be hidden. "When we preach the Reformed Faith, we do not preach anything else than the New Testament faith, or anything else than the Word of God." Benes dismissed "Community" churches as spiritually powerless, theologically colorless, and more interested in social gatherings than mission work.[92]

What practices should new churches adopt? Most midwestern Reformed churches still held Sunday evening services, while most eastern Reformed and mainline congregations had dropped them. In new churches located outside of Reformed enclaves, an evening service was not seen as "seeker-friendly." It seemed to discourage potential members who feared they might be criticized if they did not attend.[93] Reformed Church leaders inclined to accommodation said that if the evening service discouraged potential members, it should be eliminated,

[91]   *Acts and Proceedings*, 1965, 363. See his autobiography, *My Journey: From an Iowa Farm to a Cathedral of Dreams* (San Francisco: HarperSanFrancisco, 2001). He wrote a very popular book espousing church growth, *Your Church Has Real Possibilities* (Glendale: G/L Regal Books, 1974). His most controversial book was *Self-Esteem: The New Reformation* (Waco: Word, 1982). For a critical analysis of Schuller see Dennis Voskuil, *Mountains into Goldmines: Robert Schuller and the Gospel of Success* (Grand Rapids: Eerdmans, 1983). Oral history interview with Schuller, July 20, 2004, Garden Grove, CA.

[92]   Editorial, "Community or Reformed Churches," *CH*, Nov. 10, 1950, 6.

[93]   Fred Buseman, "The Reformed Church in America's Ministry in the Suburbs from 1940-1965," S.T.M Thesis, University of Dubuque Theological Seminary, 1967, 42, Joint Archives.

especially since a second sermon required extensive pastoral preparation for the few people who attended. Those who valued purity said that the evening service was part of Reformed identity and history, and it should not be sacrificed for the sake of popular appeal. Those who did not like Reformed practices need not join.

What were the best strategies to reach the unchurched? Louis Benes insisted on rigorous standards and criticized any attempt to make church membership less demanding. "True Christianity is zealous, enthusiastic, even fanatical....The future belongs to the fanatical, to those who will give their all to the cause."[94] On the other hand, pastors who started new churches thought that unchurched people were likely to be put off by a high-demand church with definitive theological beliefs. People would not want to join a church that thought of itself as fanatical. Pastors of new churches attempted to develop congregations that had integrity but did not demand complete agreement and "fanatical" devotion to the Standards and Reformed traditions. These pastors began with new members where they were and tried to provide some substance for their faith. This approach seemed to be most effective in attracting the unchurched during the 1950s.

For much of its history, the Reformed Church had grown by following its members to new communities. Starting churches outside the shelter of an enclave required a different approach. Howard Hageman observed in 1960 that new churches were more successful when Reformed Church members did *not* form the core. He encouraged the denomination to develop a more intentional and coordinated plan for church extension in other parts of the United States.[95]

The Reformed Church lacked such a plan for growth in part because it lacked clarity about who was responsible for church extension. Classes, particular synods, and the Board of Domestic Mission all started churches, but this led to overlap and competition. The rationales for starting new churches varied significantly. Some viewed church extension as a way to fight immorality and secularism.[96] Others maintained that unsaved people needed to hear the gospel, be converted,

---

[94] Editorial, "Too Religious?" *CH*, April 29, 1955, 6.

[95] *Acts and Proceedings*, 1960, 226-28. When he served as General Synod president, Hageman reported in his "State of Religion" address that he had been told frequently that when a number of RCA people were part of a new church start it was less appealing to unchurched people.

[96] The Board of Domestic Missions said of itself: "The story of Domestic Missions is the story of the spiritual purpose of the Church contending against those factors, forces and conditions which would prevent or limit its fullest expression in the life of our time." Board of Domestic Missions report, 4, bound with *Acts and Proceedings*, 1957.

and encouraged to join a church. Howard Hageman and others insisted that it was the very nature of the church to be in mission, and that the Reformed Church had a great deal to offer to American society. All agreed that church growth would help the denomination support its colleges, seminaries, and missionaries. Church extension "paid off" because new churches often gave generously to the denomination's mission program.[97] Reformed Church leaders wanted the church to grow in order to bring people to Christ and make a difference in the world, but they also feared that if the denomination did not grow, it would not survive.

After World War II an influx of Dutch immigrants to Canada appeared to offer potential new members for the Reformed Church. Many of the immigrants were very poor and spoke little English. In response, the Board of Domestic Missions developed immigrant care centers in Toronto and Edmonton and started churches in areas where the immigrants settled. Some members asked whether it was wise to develop RCA churches in Canada or if it would be better for the immigrants to join the Presbyterian Church in Canada, the United Church in Canada (the dominant mainline church), or the Christian Reformed Church. They thought it was poor stewardship to build Dutch-Canadian RCA churches.

Supporters argued that Dutch immigrants to Canada were a natural fit for the Reformed Church because they were part of the family. Louis Benes noted:

> If we think of building the Reformed church on this continent, there is probably no other place where we can at present invest our funds with as quick and sure and real returns. These brethren of the Reformed Faith are people of conviction, of character, and of devotion. We sometimes complain that in many areas of our land people do not know what the Reformed church is, or stands for. Our friends in Canada do not need to have the word "Reformed" explained to them. They are one with us in faith and devotion to God and His Word.[98]

---

[97] In 1958 an Iowa pastor compiled statistics about the results of church extension. He found that 128 churches organized between 1932 and 1958 had 18,656 members, an average of 146 per church. In the past year they had received 1,411 members by confession of faith and 1,857 transfers. They had 13,941 baptized children. They gave $370,000 to RCA benevolences, $61,000 to other, and $1.9 million to congregational purposes. Henry VanDyke, "See How They Grow," *CH*, Dec. 5, 1958, 10.

[98] Editorial, "Advance in Canada," *CH*, April 27, 1951, 7, 14. Compare this much more negative assessment by BDM secretary Richard Vanden Berg about the Puerto Ricans and Caribbeans moving to Harlem, NY: "Many of these people do not

Despite their faith and devotion, even the Dutch immigrants might fall away if they did not receive enough attention and funding. Two years later Benes wrote, "They love the Lord, and they believe His Word. But it is also true that if we do not answer their urgent call to come and help them, many of them will in time wander away from the Church, and their children will be lost to the Kingdom of God."[99] Perhaps this was a rhetorical strategy to attract financial support, but it demonstrated little confidence in the faith of the immigrants.

The successes and failures of church extension raised a number of broad questions about denominational life. How would the Reformed Church find the financial resources to start churches and pay for land and buildings? Should the denomination continue its extensive support for missionaries around the world or should it spend more money on church extension? Who would decide the denomination's priorities?

Unifying Forces: Internal Structure and Funding

During the 1950s, Reformed Church members began to think more intentionally about how the denomination made decisions and established priorities.[100] Some people believed that the denomination did not have enough bureaucracy to function well. The General Synod met only five days a year, and there was no ongoing body to make decisions between meetings or provide leadership for the denomination as a whole. The stated clerk, James Hoffman, worked for the General Synod about half time. His role was not to supervise staff or "cast a vision" but to manage denominational details. A "staff conference" composed of representatives from each board met regularly at denominational headquarters. Theoretically this group might have set policy, but instead it handled trivial matters, such as when to replace the mimeograph machine, who would clean the kitchen, and how much to spend on gifts for departing staff members. It had no official power or authority.

Those who wanted the denomination to be more structured disliked the fact that the boards (Foreign Mission, Domestic Mission,

---

have the Christian faith to steady and sustain them in this period of transition. They become a fruitful ground for the spread of atheism and communism. Either through Christianization they will become valuable citizens of our country, or through the neglect of the Christian Church they may become a serious menace." "Domestic Missions Today," *CH*, Nov. 25, 1949, 16.

99   Editorial, "Opportunity in Canada," *CH*, Nov. 16, 1951, 6.

100   For a detailed overview of the development of bureaucratic structures in the RCA see Hoff, *Structures for Mission*.

Education, and Pensions) set their own budgets, established their own fund-raising goals, and raised their own money. No one questioned whether the interests of the denomination might be better served by putting more money into church extension than foreign missions. No one set priorities or strategized for the denomination as a whole. The General Synod reviewed the work of the boards and approved their budgets, but in general the boards operated as they pleased. This model worked well enough when the Reformed Church was relatively small and familial. But as the church grew larger, as the denomination was expected to provide more services, and as other denominations became increasingly complex in their structures, the pressure grew to adopt a more sophisticated governmental structure. Someone needed to be in charge.[101]

Over the years, several General Synod presidents attempted to create an executive committee to oversee the ongoing activities of the denomination, but each time some members objected to the cost and the danger of centralized authority. Meanwhile, the role of president had expanded beyond simply presiding over the annual meeting and making a speech on the state of religion. Presidents began to travel more extensively to survey the church and meet with the boards and attend the staff conference.

The most problematic aspect of the denominational structure was fund-raising. Each board conducted separate fund-raising campaigns, and pastors and congregations felt increasingly overwhelmed by the multiple appeals they received from these competing agencies. For example, the stated clerk of Muskegon Classis reported that at the spring meeting of the classis in 1951, "Many interests received consideration." The classis heard from *Temple Time* (radio work) and the Ministers' Fund (pensions). In addition, all churches were asked to raise their quota for the Nickel-a-Meal Fund (church extension). The work of the Extension Committee in the classis, the Expansion Committee in the particular synod, and the work in Canada were commended. Foreign

[101]   In 1953 several classes asked that denominational headquarters be moved to the Midwest in order to be closer to the most thriving areas of the RCA. The committee that studied the matter presented a list of pros and cons for staying and moving but concluded that the major issue was not the location of headquarters but the independence of the boards. The General Synod gave the committee another year but insisted it deal only with the location question. When the committee reported in 1955, the National Council of Churches had decided to build an ecumenical headquarters at 475 Riverside Drive in New York City, and the committee recommended that the RCA invest in that building and remain in New York. *Acts and Proceedings*, 1954, 289-93; 1955, 328-32.

mission work was considered prayerfully and the needs of Japan, India, and China were presented. The Committee on Education described the needs of the colleges, and the classis urged all churches to give an extra dollar per member to Camp Geneva. Once this parade of pitchmen had passed by, the Classis of Muskegon had little time for any other work. The clerk reported, "Evangelism, important as it is, did not receive its due because of lack of time, but will be given more time in the fall."[102]

Edward Tanis, a pastor at the Second Reformed Church in Pella, Iowa, described a similar experience of overload in 1950. The congregation was paying off a $20,000 loan for remodeling. A church start in a nearby town asked ten dollars per family. Central College was conducting two fund drives. The Board of Domestic Missions had distributed Nickel-a-Meal boxes. The Board of Foreign Missions wanted money for a Japanese Christian University, and also for three projects focused on women and girls. A hospital in Iowa City sought a contribution for a chaplain. Institutions like Pine Rest and Bethesda asked for money as well. The problem, he said, is "How to present all this and keep folks smiling and giving!"[103]At the very least, the Reformed Church needed a more coordinated approach to fund-raising.

The Board of Foreign Missions usually raised its full budget, but the Board of Domestic Missions found it more difficult to raise money for building loans, salary support, and the purchase of property for new church starts. Meanwhile, many congregations were burdened by sizeable mortgages for expansive new buildings.[104] Giving for congregational purposes increased more rapidly than denominational benevolences. Congregations increased their giving to regional, local, and non-RCA benevolences and gave less to the denomination.[105]

In 1949 the General Synod appointed the Commission on a United Approach to determine an effective strategy for denominational

---

[102]   A.T. Laman, "Muskegon Classis," *CH*, May 11, 1951, 20.

[103]   Edward Tanis to Marion de Velder, Oct. 6, 1950, United Approach Correspondence, General Synod Archives.

[104]   Some churches had deferred building programs for almost two decades. They lacked money during the Depression and materials during the war. During the 1950s the *Church Herald* regularly featured photos of new church buildings on its cover.

[105]   This has been a source of debate for sixty years. Should congregations give all their benevolent money to the denomination? Or to local projects? How could a church determine which agencies were most reliable? Was the ecumenical American Bible Society more deserving of support than the evangelical American Home Bible League? Should churches and individuals support the sad-faced orphans regularly pictured in *Church Herald* advertisements? Or donate only to established denominational agencies? Should the denominational magazine accept advertising from groups that diverted donations from RCA projects?

fund-raising.[106] The commission met for several years and presented multiple reports to the synod. It recommended the formation of a Stewardship Council, staffed by an executive, to coordinate and promote the denominational program directly to congregations. The synod balked at the expense, and board executives feared they might lose some of their autonomy. The commission eventually removed the recommendation for an executive officer, and the synod approved the formation of the Stewardship Council in 1952.[107]

The formation of the Stewardship Council was one piece of a larger discussion of denominational identity and priorities. The Reformed Church had long thought of itself as a church that was committed to foreign missions. It had produced many excellent missionaries and exerted influence in the Middle East, India, Japan, and China. Some congregations, most notably in two adjacent small towns in northwest Iowa (First, Orange City, and First, Sioux Center) gave large gifts to foreign missions every year. The deep commitment to foreign missions, the large number of powerful and charismatic missionaries that the denomination loved and supported, and the independence of the Foreign and Domestic Mission Boards made it very difficult to raise questions about whether money should be spent on church extension rather than mission.

Other Reformed Church institutions also needed money and found it difficult to compete with the boards. Joseph Sizoo, president of New Brunswick Seminary, wrote to the Board of Domestic Missions secretary, Richard Vanden Berg, that the Stewardship Council would advance the interests of the boards but leave the seminaries "pretty well out in the cold." Sizoo noted that the synod expected the seminaries to teach a certain curriculum but provided only 1.5 percent of undesignated gifts as financial support.

If we go out in the Church to raise money, the various Boards are always resentful because we are interfering with a program

---

[106] Marion de Velder served as chair and other members included ministers Howard Schade, Frederick Zimmerman, Edward Tanis, and Daniel Brink and elders James VerMeulen, W. Lloyd VanKeuren, Stanley Crocker, Maurice TePaske, and Raymond Freeman.

[107] *Acts and Proceedings*, 1950, 175-85; 1951, 173-82; 1952, 153-57; 1953, 190-98. The letters and papers collected in the Stewardship Council file in the General Synod Archives document a lengthy and often frustrating process for the members of the Commission on a United Approach. Some board members and executives resisted any measures that seemed to take away some of their freedom and independence. Some RCA members did not want to spend money on an executive, even if it appeared he would be able to raise money for the RCA program. Some RCA members valued efficiency, while others preferred independence.

or technique or publicity which they have already arranged. The result is that the Seminary becomes sort of an outcast or step-child. Too often the policy has prevailed in General Synod that those who are most vocal and talk loudest get the approval for their several projects. I am more deeply convinced the longer I am here that the Reformed church must establish some new over-all strategy and I *have* hoped your Commission would do that sort of thing.[108]

The Stewardship Council did not have the authority to establish priorities for allocating funds. Instead, it reviewed budgets, oversaw special projects and promotional materials, set up a schedule for fund-raising, and developed stewardship training programs for use in congregations. The council had very high expectations for the denomination, which could be both affirming and guilt-inducing. In 1954 Reformed Church members gave 12 percent more to denominational benevolences than in 1953, and yet the council chastised the church for not giving enough. In 1955 church members gave $75,000 more than they had been asked to give. The council concluded that the goal had been too low and that denomination should ask for more money lest it appear to lack faith and courage.[109]

Despite this level of generosity, in 1953 the colleges and the Board of Domestic Missions desperately needed money for buildings and church extension. The Board of Foreign Missions also sought to raise money for missionary homes and a library at the Japanese Christian University, Meiji Gakuin. The Stewardship Council allowed them to conduct a denominational fund drive, which would be called *Eendracht*,[110] the Dutch word for unity. The council set a goal of $1.5 million, with 40 percent divided among the three colleges and 30 percent allocated to each board.[111]

---

[108] Joseph Sizoo to Richard Vanden Berg, Jan. 19, 1951, United Approach Correspondence, General Synod Archives.

[109] *Acts and Proceedings*, 1955, 214-15.

[110] In the fall of 1955, John Harvey, a layperson from Battle Creek, asked why the RCA chose a name that was so difficult to spell, pronounce, and define. He wondered when the RCA would become Americanized in its thinking, membership, representation, and slogans. John Harvey, letter to the editor, *CH*, Aug. 26, 1955, 17.

[111] Promotional material for the fund drive included pictures of the colleges' ugly dormitories and inadequate library and music spaces. See photos, *CH*, Jan. 21, 1955. No one asked whether a library at Central College was more or less important than a library at Meiji Gakuin, a Christian university the RCA supported in Japan. Perhaps the answer was simply that they were equally important, and that some members chose to support the colleges and others preferred foreign mission projects.

Eendracht was not just a fund drive, however. Gerrit Vander Lugt, president of the General Synod, wrote that it provided a way to repent of sin that had divided the church and find renewed faith in Jesus Christ, who could unify and strengthen the church. It was a call to deeper spirituality and devotion.[112] The drawback to spiritualizing a fund drive, however, was that a lack of complete success was perceived to be a failure of piety and commitment as well as of fund-raising.

Eendracht did not meet expectations. At the end of 1956, only $973,000 of the $1.5 million goal had been raised, while the Board of Foreign Missions budget received more than it had asked for.[113] Congregations had the resources but chose not to donate to the fund drive.

In 1956 the Stewardship Council convinced the General Synod that the denomination needed an executive for stewardship. As the Commission for a United Approach had realized in 1950, the work of the council required more leadership than could be had from occasional committee meetings. Giving had increased significantly during recent years, but the council believed that it would have increased much more under the leadership of a full-time executive. Howard Teusink was appointed to the position.[114]

In 1958 the Stewardship Council proposed a major change in the way the Reformed Church managed undesignated benevolences (the gifts congregations sent to the denomination that did not specify a particular board or project). In the past the undesignated money had been divided based on the total benevolence budget. If the Board of Foreign Missions' part of the budget was 37 percent, it received 37 percent of the undesignated money. The BFM could easily take in more than it had asked for the year, while other boards received less than they needed. In the new equalization process, once a board received what it had asked for in a given year, it received no more undesignated funds until all boards had met their budgets. The Board of Education heartily approved the plan, in part because it had the most to gain.

---

[112] "An Open Letter to the Members of the Reformed Church," *CH*, Jan. 21, 1955, 10.

[113] *Acts and Proceedings*, 1956, 229. Richard Decker, letter to the editor, *CH*, May 25, 1956, 19; editorial, "When Up Seems Down," Sept. 28, 1956, 6; David Laman, "The Board of Foreign Missions Meets," March 8, 1957, 10, 23.

[114] *Acts and Proceedings*, 1955, 227-29; 1956, 188-99. Teusink was a pastor who had served several midwestern churches before becoming director of the Youth Department of the Board of Education in 1953. In the previous decade, denominational benevolences had almost doubled, from 1.8 to 3.5 million. Giving for congregational purposes had increased from 5.7 to 12.1 million, and giving for other benevolences from $312,000 to $576,000.

Irwin Lubbers, president of Hope College, wrote that everybody would get what they needed without competition.[115] The Board of Foreign Missions, on the other hand, had the most to lose and protested that the Stewardship Council lacked the authority to make this decision. Despite that objection, the equalization plan was approved.

The frequent discussions about funding suggested that the Reformed Church still lacked a way to make decisions about what was best for the whole church. Several General Synod presidents expressed a desire for structural improvements. Frederick Zimmerman hoped that the Stewardship Council might be a venue for discussions about policy, but the Stewardship Council did not wish to be diverted into matters that were not part of its portfolio.[116] In 1956 General Synod president Daniel Brink observed,

> There is not too much provision in our organizational structure for giving attention to strategy rather than to tactics. While there are many individuals, committees, agencies and institutions constantly busy with the administrative details of our denominational functioning, there is relatively little emphasis upon the broader matters of our welfare. There are many persons competently busy oiling the ecclesiastical machinery and adjusting its gears, but too few of us taking the time to consider whether there are not better ways of producing what we want.[117]

In 1955 the General Synod had asked the Committee on Revision of the Constitution (which usually dealt with small changes) to make a substantive revision. The committee brought the revision back to the synod in 1957 and identified a list of topics that needed further study.[118] In 1958, the committee returned with several additions to the constitution. The most significant was a proposal for an Executive Council, which would exercise leadership for the denominational program. The committee explained the need for the council as follows:

> In the absence of a central continuing policy-formulating body, the denomination is being committed to policies in missionary work, education, church extension and otherwise by individual

115 *Acts and Proceedings*, 1958, 232-33. Irwin Lubbers to Howard Teusink, April 30, 1958, Stewardship Council Papers, RCA Archives. For a discussion of the equalization process, see Hoff, *Structures for Mission*, 103-06.
116 *Acts and Proceedings*, 1954, 217; 1955, 213-21.
117 *Acts and Proceedings*, 1956, 220-21.
118 *Acts and Proceedings*, 1955, 108-10; 1957, 121.

boards, Classes, and unofficial bodies of individuals. In its short sessions the General Synod can do little more than rubberstamp what is brought to it for approval.

The Revision Committee hoped that an Executive Council would be able to look at the big picture of the denomination and make decisions according to the needs of the whole and not special interests.[119] The synod approved these amendments and they were sent to the classes.

In the spring of 1959, the classes approved changes in the *Book of Church Order* necessary to create an Executive Council. At the synod that year the president, Marion de Velder, asked delegates to withhold final approval because there were too many unresolved problems. He and the next three presidents, Howard Hageman, Henry Bast, and Norman Thomas, developed a new proposal for a General Synod Executive Committee, which Bast presented and the synod approved in 1961.[120] The General Synod Executive Committee was given a three-year trial period before it was added to the Constitution. The executive committee functioned very well and quickly proved to be a significant addition to the denomination, in part due to the presence of some very gifted elders and ministers.[121]

As part of the discussion about policies, priorities, and implementation, a committee was formed to examine the role of the stated clerk of the General Synod. James Hoffman, who held the position, was about to retire. The committee proposed an expansion

[119] *Acts and Proceedings*, 1958, 139. At this synod, the president, Howard Schade, asked in his "State of Religion" report why synods had always resisted recommendations for an Executive Committee. "Can it be that the Church prefers a stumbling and fumbling administration to one of order and defined procedure?" *Acts and Proceedings*, 1958, 250-51.

[120] *Acts and Proceedings*, 1959, 244-46. For an extended discussion of the formation of the GSEC, see Hoff, *Structures for Mission*, 111-47. The GSEC was composed of the president, vice-president, and three past presidents of the General Synod, the stated clerk, four pastors, and six elders. The official task of the GSEC was to implement decisions and policies of the synod through the proper agencies and channels, and to strengthen and coordinate the work of the boards, institutions, and agencies. *Acts and Proceedings*, 1961, 330-31.

[121] The GSEC kept very detailed minutes of its meetings, and they demonstrate the substance of the conversations and the commitment of the members to the well-being of the denomination. GSEC members were less interested in debating purist versus moderate theological positions than they were in developing an efficient and productive organization. The clergy members were Norman Thomas, Bernard Brunsting, Marion de Velder, Henry Bast, Howard Hageman, Daniel Y. Brink, Harvey Hoffman, Raymond Van Heukelom, and Bert Van Soest. Elders were Ekdal Buys, Carl Cleaver, Max de Pree, Adrian Heerschap, Arad Riggs, and Maurice Te Paske. *Acts and Proceedings*, 1962, 345-46.

of the clerk's role to give it more responsibility for representing the General Synod in ecumenical and other contexts.[122] Marion de Velder was named full-time stated clerk in 1961 and became the nucleus of a much more integrated denominational program.[123] These two changes, the development of the General Synod Executive Committee and the shift to a full-time stated clerk, would change the denomination's style significantly over the next decades.

Conflict Resurfaces: The Coventry Case

Toward the end of the 1950s, another controversy erupted that once again involved competing interpretations of the Bible. In May 1958, the Classis of Passaic[124] examined New Brunswick Seminary senior William Coventry. During the exam on the Standards, Coventry stated that he did not believe the Bible was inerrant and that he was not certain Adam was a real person.[125] The classis did not approve his answers and refused to grant him a license to preach. Four churches appealed the decision to the Particular Synod of New Jersey. The particular synod sustained the appeal and recommended that the classis grant Coventry the license. When the classis met to consider the case, it again defeated a motion to grant the license. This action created a storm of controversy, and some churches asked to be transferred out of the classis. Ray Pontier, a pastor in Clifton, New Jersey, wrote that the dogmatism, inflexibility, and demand for conformity within the classis made membership impossible for those who believed there was some freedom in the faith.[126]

The Classis of Passaic appealed the decision of the particular synod to the General Synod. The Particular Synod of New Jersey then refused either to force the classis to grant the license or to grant it directly. Meanwhile, Coventry had accepted a call to a church in the adjacent Classis of Paramus, and he had begun ministry there. He

---

122   *Acts and Proceedings*, 1960, 333-34. Committee members included the Revs. Theodore Brinckerhoff, Marion de Velder, Howard Schade, and James Hoffman, and elders Arad Riggs, Maurice Te Paske, and Carl Cleaver.

123   De Velder was born in Boyden, Iowa, in 1912. He graduated from Central College and New Brunswick Seminary. He served the North and Southhampton Reformed Church, Churchville, PA; Hope Church, Holland, MI; First Church, Albany, NY; and Central Reformed Church, Grand Rapids, MI. He served as president of the General Synod in 1959, as well as on numerous denominational committees.

124   A number of ministers in the classis graduated from Westminster Theological Seminary, which was known for its very conservative, even fundamentalist, beliefs.

125   Coventry's Old Testament professor at NBTS was Hugh Baillie MacLean, who had been the subject of scrutiny a decade earlier.

126   Letter in Coventry file, General Synod Archives.

could not celebrate baptism or Communion, however, because he had not been ordained. The Classis of Paramus tried unsuccessfully to have both Coventry and his home congregation moved into its jurisdiction, so that Paramus could grant his license. After extensive discussion with clergy from both classes, Coventry asked to be re-examined in January 1959. The examiner gave him a list of very specific questions about biblical interpretation, and this time Coventry wrote and read more orthodox answers. At this point the classis granted him the license.[127]

As in the late 1940s, the debate over the literal interpretation of scripture frequently turned from ideology to personal character—especially when the purists questioned the faith and orthodoxy of New Brunswick Seminary's professors and students. Justin Vander Kolk, professor of theology at New Brunswick, wrote after the Coventry case had been resolved,

> As one moves about among our churches, as one hears and overhears expressions of distrust and suspicion directed against institutions, boards and church courts, what is most disturbing is not the fact that questions are raised, for no aspect of church life is beyond criticism, but rather the spirit in which the criticism is spoken. It often takes the form of sharp anathemas hurled down from above as though the critics occupy a position unassailably correct....It is a strange turn of affairs when those who are most relentlessly destructive in their criticism place themselves before the church as champions of orthodoxy and are by some regarded as such.[128]

The purists demonstrated deep loyalty to orthodox belief and defended it vigorously, even if it meant voicing harsh criticism of other Reformed Church members. Moderates like Vander Kolk thought that the purists' view of orthodoxy was shaped more by fundamentalism than by Reformed theology. Moderates generally demonstrated their

---

[127] This case raised difficult questions about the authority of scripture. Was Adam a real person? Was it necessary for an RCA minister to believe that he was? If Adam was a mythical figure rather than a real person, did that call into question the truth of Genesis? Did the Book of Genesis provide scientific facts about human origins, or was it a poetic attempt to show that God had been intimately involved in creation? Did individual classes have the authority to set standards that were more conservative than the denomination's? Purists argued that the Bible had to be read literally because it was all true. Moderates insisted that RCA members could be faithful to the Bible without believing in a literal Adam or six, twenty-four-hour days of creation.

[128] "The Call to Service," *CH*, March 27, 1959, 10, 22-23.

loyalty to other Reformed Church members and the denomination as a whole, but they were willing to allow some differences in theological formulation.

In 1959, two classes, one representing each side of the debate, asked the General Synod to offer a definitive statement about biblical interpretation. The Theological Commission[129] studied the issues and in 1960 offered a statement on the historical character of Genesis. The commission said that the Book of Genesis described God's role in the origins of the world and of humanity. Genesis affirmed God's presence and power using symbolic language, but it did not provide a literal, eye-witness account of creation. The statement acknowledged that commission members disagreed about some of the details of interpretation, but these diverse opinions existed in both the denomination and in Protestantism as a whole and should not cause concern. The members of the Theological Commission had discussed their differences and recognized that each side had a high regard for scripture. They concluded that the Reformed Church should allow some latitude in the interpretation of details.[130]

The commission also encouraged pastors to trust laypeople's ability to deal with challenging issues.

> We fear that sometimes undue tensions and conflicts have arisen within the hearts of our people, because we, as ministers of the Word, have failed to enter into frank conversation on issues that might be of a somewhat controversial nature. Honest and open discussion of matters pertaining to biblical interpretation and

[129] The Theological Commission was formed in 1959 and immediately given two overtures to discuss. The Classis of South Grand Rapids asked the synod to discuss biblical criticism. The Classis of Paramus asked for a study of the inspiration of scripture and, in particular, whether candidates had to demonstrate a belief in the Bible's verbal inspiration, *Acts and Proceedings*, 1959, 122, 124-25, 365-67. At this synod, the RCA's Commission on Judicial Business issued a report that identified a number of more effective ways Passaic could have dealt with the Coventry case, *Acts and Proceedings*, 1959, 130-42. The commission was not particularly sympathetic to the purists in the Classis of Passaic.

[130] About this time, Lester Kuyper, professor of Old Testament at Western Seminary, also received some criticism for failing to read the Bible as literally as some purists preferred. He had published an essay about the interpretation of Genesis 2-3 in the *Reformed Review* in Dec. 1959 and March 1960. John Ludlum (pastor in Passaic Classis, NJ and a member of the WTS Board) and Gordon Girod (pastor at Seventh, Grand Rapids) raised some questions about Kuyper's view of the Bible, specifically about Adam. Girod said in a letter that he wanted clear lines to be drawn in the debate and wanted to know which side Kuyper was on. The WTS Board affirmed Kuyper's work and the issue was not widely publicized. See Lester Kuyper, Papers re Controversy Genesis 2-3, 1960, Joint Archives.

doctrine, rather than causing dissent and division within the Body of Christ, have frequently enriched and strengthened the faith of the Church and her witness to the world.[131]

A year later the Theological Commission produced a paper explaining in more detail how scripture ought to be understood and interpreted. The paper said that scripture was inspired by the Holy Spirit and made use of the language and thought forms of the authors. It had both a divine and a human aspect. One of the key passages in the paper said, "Scripture as the Word of the faithful God is infallible and inerrant in all that it intends to teach and accomplish concerning faith and life." This phrase honored the inspiration of scripture but avoided rigid literalism and inerrancy.[132]

A small pamphlet war ensued. The first was written by John Ludlum, a pastor in Englewood, New Jersey, and John R. DeWitt, a pastor in Paterson, New Jersey. They reflected an extremely conservative, literalist perspective on scripture, shaped more by Westminster Seminary and fundamentalism than by Reformed theology. The pamphlet insisted that to deny any part of Genesis was to deny all of God's revelation. It criticized anyone who took a position even slightly more moderate than the one it advocated. This pamphlet was widely circulated in the Reformed Church. Isaac Rottenberg, a member of the Theological Commission, responded with a pamphlet explaining in more detail the commission's Reformed view of scripture.[133] Despite the controversy, the Theological Commission's statement was accepted provisionally in 1961, slightly rewritten in response to feedback, and approved by the General Synod in 1963.[134]

The controversies over Coventry and biblical interpretation show that some of the sharp differences present in the late 1940s persisted into

---

[131] *Acts and Proceedings*, 1960, 325-27. Holland native Carl Kleis attended New Brunswick Seminary from 1956 to 1959. His father, Clarence, a physics professor at Hope College, visited Carl and accompanied him to his Bible course. Clarence was so intrigued by what he learned that he bought a number of books and went back to Third Reformed Church to teach an adult Bible class using the insights of contemporary scholarship. Carl said the students at Third responded very positively. Oral history interview with Carl Kleis, May 15, 2001, Southampton, PA.

[132] *Acts and Proceedings*, 1961, 383-88.

[133] The pamphlets and extensive correspondence are available in the papers of the Theological Commission, General Synod Archives.

[134] *Acts and Proceedings*, 1962, 124-25; 1963, 264-67. The commission removed a phrase to which many people objected, which referred to scripture as "fully human and fully divine," but it retained the "all it intends to teach" phrase despite some criticism of it. See Cook, *The Church Speaks*, xv- xviii and 1-10.

the early 1960s. Purists argued for a literalist interpretation of scripture and the creeds and wanted to exclude those who disagreed with them. In the end, though, the moderate position prevailed. The Reformed Church was a confessional church, but it was not fundamentalist. It took the Bible seriously as God's Word, but it was not willing to say that everything in the Bible was literally true. The Reformed Church was willing to tolerate some differences of opinion and would not punish people for thinking differently.

By 1963, these tensions had cooled enough that the General Synod president, Bernard R. Brunsting, offered a very positive assessment of the denomination in his "State of Religion" report. In the past, he said, denominational conflict had led to hair-splitting, sulking, and sabotage, but the Reformed Church had entered a new phase of its life in which different viewpoints (within the bounds of the constitution and confessions) were permitted. There was mutual respect, friendship, and love. The strongly conservative view was respected and influential. "The raised voice of anger and sarcasm is dying in our church. In its place is the voice of conviction within the framework of good churchmanship." Brunsting predicted that harmony would continue to increase if people spoke frankly and yet valued the views of others. He compared the Reformed Church to a mosaic containing many pieces of different colors and sizes which formed a coherent whole.[135]

Brunsting was optimistic, but he was almost completely wrong in his prediction. In the next six years there would be a great deal of hair-splitting, sulking, and sabotage, along with plenty of anger and sarcasm. In 1969 the Reformed Church in America would consider division.

Why were peace and good-will so fleeting? The denominational congeniality of the 1950s and early 1960s occurred at a time of social and cultural harmony. There were few major social issues that demanded an official response, so the church did not have to formulate one. There were no new ecumenical possibilities. In general, Americans were getting along. But when the social and cultural crises of the later 1960s occurred, it was as if the entire denomination was picked up and shaken. The Reformed Church may have been a mosaic of many different stones, but it found that the glue was not strong enough to hold the pieces in place when the mosaic was turned upside down. The denomination would move from congeniality to chaos in just six years.

---

[135] *Acts and Proceedings*, 1963, 380. He also suggested a second metaphor. The denomination was like a large cable made up of many individual strands of wire, which together were strong enough to support bridges.

During the decade of the 1960s there were still some Reformed Church members who wanted the church to emphasize the denomination's purity and remain aloof from American culture. They began to realize, however, that a denomination that constantly criticized the culture and tried to preserve its own purity would find it very difficult to survive. The Reformed Church as a whole had decided that it would try to participate in the broader world in a thoughtful and meaningful way.[136]

---

[136] Many of the clergy I have interviewed describe the 1950s and early 1960s as some of the best of their ministry. The church was a significant presence in their lives and in the lives of their parishioners. The church offered a sense of community that people appreciated. People seemed to value the church and their pastors. Many churches were growing. The pastors worked hard but believed that their work was appreciated.

CHAPTER 4

1963–1968: One Church or Two?

In the introduction I described a perfect church-going family who graced the cover of a 1959 issue of the *Church Herald*. The children of this family would probably look quite different by the end of the 1960s. As young adults, they might be wearing pony tails, bell-bottom jeans, tie-dyed shirts, and sandals or bare feet instead of shiny shoes. Their internal changes would be far greater. They may have read *The Death of God* in a college religion class. They may have protested at the Democratic National Convention in Chicago in 1968 or participated in an anti-war rally or a civil rights demonstration. The older boy might be considering a move to Canada to avoid the draft. The girl might be taking birth control pills. The parents might be wondering what happened to their well-dressed, well-behaved children.

In the Reformed Church as well, the decade of the 1960s was a time of change and conflict. In 1963, the president of the General Synod believed that the denomination's conflicts were behind it, and that the church faced a pleasant future in which differences were respected. In 1969, the Reformed Church considered a proposal to dissolve the denomination because its members seemed hopelessly at odds. This chapter will explore the rapid polarization of the Reformed Church in America during the 1960s. How did the church move so quickly from harmony to discord?

The decade began with the election of John F. Kennedy as president of the United States in 1960. He brought youth, vigor, children, hope, and optimism to the White House and to the nation. But a constellation of events late in 1962 and 1963 left the nation anxious, unsettled, and conflicted. The Cuban Missile Crisis in late 1962 underscored dramatically the threat from the Soviet Union. The publication of Betty Friedan's book, *The Feminine Mystique*, raised difficult questions about the role of women in society. During the spring of 1963, the racial crisis in Birmingham, Alabama, pitted nonviolent protesters against police dogs, fire hoses, and an ardently segregationist government, all replayed on the evening news. The March on Washington in August 1963 was peaceful, but the massive protest and Martin Luther King Jr.'s "I Have a Dream" speech showed the extent of African-American frustration and hope. Finally, the assassination of President Kennedy in November 1963 stunned the nation and ended the period of hopefulness that had characterized his "Camelot" presidency. In a *Church Herald* editorial, Benes commented only briefly on the assassination, but he was remarkably prescient. "A whole nation has been stricken and wounded— it may even be in ways which we do not perceive."[1]

Conflict increased as the decade continued. Violence became the "new normal," with four assassinations,[2] the war in Vietnam, and urban riots. Some young adults considered law enforcement officers, the government, academia, the church, and their parents to be hopelessly out of touch, irrelevant, and entrenched in the status quo. On the other side of the "generation gap," some older people saw young adults as irresponsible, idealistic hippies addicted to drugs and free love. They thought that these baby boom children should cut their hair, get married, get a real job, and stop whining. These are the stereotypes of the 1960s, but there was some truth to them.

The Reformed Church entered the 1960s with a less fractious identity. The eastern and midwestern sections of the church were living together in relative calm and shared a concern for church extension. Even the most conservative Dutch members realized that the denomination could not survive as a narrow enclave, and many congregations were being reshaped by new residents and new ideas. Some communities

---

[1]   "Lest We Forget," *CH*, Dec. 6, 1963, 6.
[2]   President John F. Kennedy in 1963, Malcolm X in 1965, Martin Luther King, Jr. and Robert Kennedy in 1968.

would be homogeneous for another decade or two, but the Reformed Church was trying to engage the world and draw in new members. It viewed itself as a relatively inclusive church with tolerance for both moderate and conservative ideas.

By the mid 1960s, a major shift had occurred in membership. The three eastern synods had 122,172 members in 1960 and 115,151 in 1966. This decline occurred for a variety of reasons, including the move from an urban to a suburban-centered environment, the impact of lower birth rates (in part due to the governmental approval of the birth control pill in 1960), and the growing mobility of middle- and upper-middle-class easterners. The three midwestern synods had 103,755 members in 1960 and 117,869 in 1966, continuing a century-long pattern of steady and gradual growth.[3] These synods had not yet experienced the demographic upheaval that the East did.

In part as a result of these very different cultural contexts, theological diversity continued.[4] When asked to identity the most important issue facing the Reformed Church in 1961, the purist voices said it was lack of agreement on the authority of scripture. The moderates said it was denominational identity.[5] The two groups also differed on the role and authority of the Reformed Standards (Belgic Confession, Heidelberg Catechism, Canons of Dort). Purists wanted the Reformed Church to insist that members believe exactly what the confessions said. Moderates said that the church should value the sixteenth-century confessions but was not bound to articulate its faith in the same way.[6] The purists emphasized authority and uniformity, while the moderates emphasized the need for the church to speak meaningfully in a changing social context. Could the groups remain in the same denomination? Purists wanted the church to discourage or even discipline those who held moderate views. Moderates were willing to respect conservative perspectives, but they did not want the purists to determine denominational identity.

[3] Howard Hageman, "New Directions," *CH*, March 1, 1968, 9.

[4] A number of eastern members complained that the *Church Herald* represented only the Midwest and particularly the most conservative RCA members. In response to this complaint, Louis Benes loosened his control of the editorial page during the 1960s and established a group of guest editors who represented a range of regions and perspectives. He also published a number of forum articles in which two to four people expressed contrasting opinions on a question or topic.

[5] Henry Bast, Gary DeWitt, Howard Hageman, Norman Thomas, "The Greatest Issue Facing the Reformed Church in America," *CH*, April 21, 1961, 12-13, 23.

[6] Gordon Girod, Isaac Rottenberg, "Confessing Church or Credal Church?" *CH*, May 19, 1961, 12-13, 29-31. The multiple perspectives offered in these types of articles may have fostered more suspicion than mutual understanding. The expression of moderate views occasionally provoked angry letters to the editor.

The purists and the moderates grew increasingly polarized during the 1960s. Purists had exerted less influence in the 1950s, when there were no major issues that required a General Synod vote. Some purists had been angered and energized by the debate about the Bible, sparked by the Coventry case in 1959. They would be further angered and energized in the 1960s by a proposal to merge the Reformed Church with another denomination, as well as by other social and ecumenical issues. As the two ends of the spectrum moved further apart, a number of people wondered whether the Reformed Church in America could continue to be one church.

Merger with the Presbyterian Church in the United States (Southern Presbyterians)

In the late 1950s and early 1960s, ecumenism reached the height of its popularity in American Protestantism. In 1957 the Congregational Christian Churches merged with the Evangelical and Reformed Church to form the United Church of Christ. In 1968 the Methodist Church and the Evangelical United Brethren merged to form the United Methodist Church. A variety of ethnic Lutheran denominations combined to form the American Lutheran Church in 1960 and the Lutheran Church in America in 1962.

In December 1960, Eugene Carson Blake, stated clerk of the United Presbyterian Church,[7] preached a sermon at the Grace Episcopal Church in San Francisco that challenged mainline Protestant denominations to consider merger. The sermon sparked an ecumenical effort called Consultation on Church Union (COCU). The United Presbyterian Church (UPC/USA or the "Northern" Presbyterian Church), the United Methodist Church, the United Church of Christ, and other denominations joined in a laborious endeavor to discern whether churches with very different polities (episcopal, presbyterian, and congregational) might be united.[8]

The Reformed Church shared the burst of ecumenical interest in the early 1960s. Ironically, instead of leading to greater harmony and cooperation with other denominations, this ecumenical enthusiasm led the Reformed Church to the brink of division.

---

[7]   Blake had also served as president of the National Council of Churches and would soon become general secretary of the World Council of Churches. He was featured on the cover of *Time* magazine May 26, 1961.

[8]   Robert Ellwood, *The 60s Spiritual Awakening* (New Brunswick: Rutgers Univ. Press, 1994), 52-57.

In 1961 several classes submitted overtures to the General Synod asking the Reformed Church to begin merger discussions with the two Presbyterian denominations.[9] The synod instructed the General Synod Executive Committee (GSEC) to hold exploratory conversations with the PCUS and UPC/USA.[10] GSEC representatives reported to the synod in 1962 that the talks with the Northern Presbyterian Church were cordial but had not led to further action. However, the conversation with the PCUS representatives—the "Southern" church—produced such good rapport that the GSEC arranged to meet with the PCUS Permanent Committee on Inter-Church Relations. This meeting was equally positive, and the two groups affirmed their "readiness to be led into whatever forms of church life and work are revealed as God's will for us." They proposed a Joint Committee (twelve members from each denomination) to discuss their future.[11]

Judge John Fulton, chair of the PCUS Inter-Church Committee, was invited to address the General Synod in 1962, and he gave a humorous and engaging description of the recent PCUS General Assembly. Like the church in Acts 19, he said, the Presbyterians had found themselves a bit confused about their purpose and tasks. When they reached the part of their agenda which proposed a conversation with the Reformed Church in America, however, they experienced a strong sense of unity and divine guidance. After hearing this winsome speech, the synod adopted the proposal for a Joint Committee without dissent.[12]

A great deal of ecumenical interest was expressed at the Synod of 1962. Eighteen classes submitted overtures about union. Eight sought union with the PCUS, eight with the UPC, one with the United Church of Christ, and one with the Christian Reformed Church. The Overtures Committee concluded that the PCUS was the obvious

---

9   The Particular Synod of New York asked for merger talks with the Southern Presbyterians (PCUS). The Classes of Westchester, Philadelphia, and Paramus asked for merger talks with the Northern Presbyterians (UPC/USA), *Acts and Proceedings,* 1961, 133-38.

10 The small United Presbyterian Church, which had discussed merger with the RCA in the late 1940s, had since merged with the larger Northern Presbyterian Church to form the United Presbyterian Church/USA.

11 The Presbyterian Church had split in 1837 over slavery and never reunited. The PCUS (Southern branch) was generally considered to be more conservative theologically than its northern counterpart. The PCUS and the RCA had already engaged in common mission work in Iraq, Taiwan, and Mexico, and they were working jointly on a new education curriculum.

12 *Acts and Proceedings,* 1962, 348-51, 354-56. Fulton's speech was so well received that delegates voted to include it in the minutes, which was quite unusual.

choice because it was theologically conservative, Calvinist, smaller, and located in a different region of the United States from the RCA. The Overtures Committee believed it would be unwise for the Reformed Church to converse with several different churches simultaneously and recommended "that the Executive Committee be encouraged to take steps looking toward merger with the Presbyterian Church in the U.S. and to hold other union possibilities in abeyance."[13] The synod approved this.

Initially the Joint Committee from the two denominations discussed cooperative strategies to strengthen their Reformed witness in the United States, but when the groups realized how much they had in common, they quickly shifted their focus toward merger.[14] Hindsight suggests it might have been wiser to continue the emphasis on shared witness, at least for a time.[15]

Criticism began almost immediately. Clarence P. Dame wrote that church mergers were costly, time-consuming, and painful, and they did not increase mission work, membership, or spiritual vitality. Abraham Rynbrandt argued that church merger would threaten pure doctrine and RCA identity without solving the denomination's problems.[16] In 1963, only a year after talks began, two classes and a particular synod insisted that dissenting congregations should be allowed to retain their property and pension rights if there was a merger. The synod dismissed their overtures because they were untimely, an action which did not reassure critics.[17]

A group of ministers in Florida argued that the Reformed Church must protect its unique and distinctive witness which is "according to the Word of God." They feared that many Christians, including some in the Reformed Church, want to "enter into the great ocean of ecumenical unification" in one large Protestant structure, which would not preserve

13   Ibid., 122-24. The overtures were probably written before classes knew about the GSEC's talks with the PCUS.

14   Howard Hageman, "Unity for the Sake of Mission," *CH*, May 4, 1962, 8. Members of the Joint Committee included Norman Thomas (chair), Chester Meengs, Ruth Peale, Arad Riggs, Henry Te Paske, Gerrit Vander Lugt, Raymond Van Heukelom, Marion de Velder, Bernard Brunsting, Ekdal Buys, Howard Hageman, and Arend (Don) Lubbers. The RCA delegates were at times referred to as the Committee of Twelve, and the whole group as the Committee of Twenty-Four.

15   Robert Ellwood wrote that by 1962 ecumenical fervor had peaked and begun to decline. *Sixties Spiritual Awakening*, 52-57.

16   Clarence P. Dame, "Have Church Mergers Been a Spiritual Success?" *CH*, Nov. 15, 1963, 10-11; Abraham Rynbrandt, "Is Church Merger Wise?" *CH*, April 10, 1964, 10, 23. Dame had supported the merger in the 1940s.

17   *Acts and Proceedings*, 1963, 104-05.

Reformed doctrine. The ministers urged that conversations with the Presbyterian Church be halted,

> so that the confession which we consider unique may not be impaired by compromise or by identification with groups whose size so dwarfs us that we would lose all future self-determining ability to protect our Reformed doctrines. We believe that the Holy Spirit is prompting us to this action in the best interests of all concerned in the Church of Jesus Christ.[18]

These three arguments—denominational uniqueness (or superiority), the fear of being swallowed up, and the need to protect Reformed doctrine—would recur constantly during the next five years of discussion.

Tensions increased in 1964, when seventeen overtures were submitted to the synod. The Joint Committee had barely begun its work on a Plan of Union, but classes were already asking that each congregation be allowed to vote, or that a higher margin of classis approval be required.[19] The Classis of South Grand Rapids overtured, "in the interest of peace," that dissident congregations be allowed to retain pension and property rights. It asked that the synod stop all merger conversation because the PCUS ordained women and its seminary professors did not necessarily believe in an infallible Bible.

The synod referred the overtures about pensions to the Joint Committee and took no action about property rights or voting percentages because it was too early in the process. Five overtures remained, two asking the synod to proceed with merger talks and three asking the synod to stop them. Clearly the church was divided, and there was no obvious compromise position. Donner Atwood, chair of the Overtures Committee, spoke frankly to the synod about mutual distrust, which he considered the root of the conflict.[20]

---

[18]   Raymond Rewerts (for Florida Conference of Reformed Churches), letter to the editor, *CH*, May 29, 1964, 12. The Florida churches had not yet been organized into their own classis.

[19]   The ordinary procedure required to make a change in the *Book of Church Order* is based on a representative system—a majority vote at the General Synod, a majority in a classis, two-thirds of the classes, and a majority at the second General Synod—not votes within congregations. The classes of Zeeland and South Grand Rapids asked for a three-quarters vote in each congregation and classis, three-quarters of the total number of classes, and three-quarters of the final ratifying vote at the second synod.

[20]   As mentioned above, it was very unusual for the minutes of a General Synod to record a speech in addition to the usual reports and actions. It was equally rare to offer such an honest analysis of the synod's actions, particularly of conflict.

Fathers and Brethren, the time has come for us to think the unthinkable, to admit the unadmitable, and to speak, in love, the unspeakable; namely, we must openly admit that some of us, on this subject, take positions at opposite poles from each other. If it were only a matter of being divided on church union, serious as that would be, we would not be as deeply concerned as we are. But, we must confess to each other and before Almighty God that which is of far graver consequence—we of the Household of Faith, who individually and corporately call Jesus Christ Lord and Savior, do not trust each other in this matter (as well as in other areas of concern) and therefore are acting and re-acting out of fear of each other, rather than out of love for each other.

The Overtures Committee recommended that no action be taken on the overtures, because, it said, no solution would please both sides. Instead the committee encouraged the synod to confess its distrust and fear and to allow the Joint Committee to decide whether to move forward. The synod adopted the recommendations, and delegate Donald Wing led a prayer of confession.[21]

Joint confession did not eliminate or even reduce the conflict. Later in the summer of 1964, Rodger Dalman, a pastor from Wyoming, Michigan, complained that those who supported merger frequently accused opponents of being divisive. He argued instead that the real divisiveness came from those who would

give away our denomination and all its institutions without the honest approval of the grass-roots folk who have labored for them, loved them, and paid for them. Are folks who simply desire to keep what God has given them, and what they treasure as a precious heritage, the real cause of division among us?

Dalman did not understand how Reformed Church members could hold their heritage and doctrines so lightly. The PCUS may be orthodox enough, he said, but because of its size and its interest in further union with the UPC/USA, merger would place the RCA on a dangerous path toward COCU and the sacrifice of Reformed doctrine for the sake of unity, which he considered an apostasy.[22]

Dalman's views reflected a purist perspective. He viewed the denomination as a possession, paid for and owned by its "grass roots"

---

[21] *Acts and Proceedings*, 1964, 115-53.
[22] Letter to the editor, *CH*, Aug. 21, 1964, 18.

members. The highest authorities (after scripture and the Standards) were congregational and individual opinion. He demeaned the faith and practice of others who "hold their faith lightly." His use of the word "apostasy" suggests that the debate about merger was not simply a discussion of the best way to organize denominational work. The integrity of the Christian faith was at risk.

Certainly merger posed a risk, but supporters believed the benefits outweighed the risks. Winfield Burggraaff, a pastor in Staten Island, suggested that merger could offer something invigorating and dynamic to a static denomination which was "caught in the doldrums."[23] Jacob Blaauw, a pastor in Zeeland, quickly dismissed this "pathetic argument" because he thought merger required churches to compromise their doctrines. "Church mergers, no matter how great, have not and cannot heal what ails us, and once the Reformed Church has joined in, remember, this is the end, for there is no point of return."[24]

Purists often warned that these mergers that seemed small would lead eventually to Protestant churches being swallowed up by Roman Catholicism. Edward Poortvliet, a layman from Raymond, Minnesota, wrote that he had belonged to the Reformed Church for forty years and cherished its creeds, confessions, and catechism.

> Now comes church union and a proposed march into oblivion, as far as the Reformed Church is concerned. Brother, it really gives me high blood pressure. Why in the world is it that the proponents of this one-world church just don't come out and tell us plainly that it isn't just union with the Southern Presbyterian Church that is in the air? This is just the first link in an ecumenical chain that includes even the Roman Catholics.[25]

Gordon Girod, a pastor in Grand Rapids, wrote that if the Reformed Church joined with the PCUS it would soon become Roman Catholic and lose its historical faith and emphasis on scripture alone. Ronald Brown from Wyoming, Michigan, wrote that "merger is an utter abandonment of the Reformed faith and the first giant step toward Rome."[26]

---

23 "The New Testament and Church Union," *CH,* Nov. 12, 1965, 10, 22-23; "Church Union Is in the Air," Jan. 7, 1966, 10, 22-23. Burggraaff quoted John Foster Dulles, who said that in international relations, "the dynamic usually prevails over the static."
24 Letter to the editor, *CH,* Jan. 28, 1966, 24.
25 Letter to the editor, *CH,* April 22, 1966, 23.
26 Letters to the editor, *CH,* July 15, 1966, 22-23.

Many opponents feared that merger meant loss. The Classis of Wisconsin asked that congregations be allowed to vote for merger because "those who would be most deeply affected by the proposed merger with the Presbyterian US [*sic*] would be the people in the congregations themselves, since from them would be taken, and from their children, the heritage which is rightfully theirs of the identity and traditions of the Reformed Church in America."[27] Eastern churches also spoke of loss, but they feared the loss of influence and relevance more than the loss of identity. Many easterners believed that merger would strengthen the appeal of Reformed churches by linking them with a better known denomination. Merger would strengthen their ministry and mission by providing more resources and more opportunities. Those who supported merger exhibited loyalty to the Reformed Church, but they thought it would only survive if it merged with a larger body.

Classes sent fewer overtures in 1966, which suggested that people may have warmed to the idea of merger, or at least were willing to read the Plan of Union before making a decision. The synod also approved a very strong statement about ecumenism that year.

> ...trusting in the Holy Spirit for guidance, we shall be open to His counsel, willing to converse with any church, ready to cooperate with all Christians, committed to participate in councils of churches on all levels, prepared to merge with any church when it is clearly the will of God, eager to heal the brokenness of the Body of Christ in all ways made known to us, until all are one, so that the world may know that the Father has sent the Son as Saviour and Lord.[28]

However, the church found it far easier to vote for ecumenism in this abstract way than to vote in favor of an actual merger proposal.

The commitment to conversation expressed in this statement was immediately tested. The General Assembly of the Presbyterian Church in the U.S. voted in the spring of 1966 to join the Consultation on Church Union (COCU). The Presbyterians insisted that they simply wanted to keep moving on the ecumenical path while continuing merger talks with the Reformed Church. Some delegates to the General Synod were furious and demanded an explanation from the PCUS. Other delegates

---

[27]   *Acts and Proceedings*, 1966, 132. Twenty years later, many of those who were children in the 1960s would no longer be connected with the RCA. Some would join mainline denominations like the Presbyterian Church.

[28]   Ibid., 294-95. This policy statement, "The Unity We Seek to Manifest," was recommended by the Committee on Interchurch Relations.

suggested that the RCA join COCU also, but the president, Donner Atwood, ruled the motion out of order because of the 1962 vote to hold all other merger possibilities in abeyance. The Presbyterians later said they viewed joining COCU as part of a larger conversation, and they did not think it was inconsistent with or antithetical to the PCUS-RCA conversation.[29]

Whether that statement was true or not, opponents of merger within the Reformed Church had acquired a new target and new energy. A number of clergy and laymen formed "The Fellowship of the Concerned." The group published several advertisements and letters insisting that the purpose of COCU was to form one large denomination. The ads claimed that the Bible would no longer be the authority in faith and practice and, further, that every denomination joining COCU would have to compromise its faith. The group asked the RCA to stop merger talks and to declare a moratorium on church union discussions so that the peace and order of the Reformed Church would be restored.[30]

Some Reformed Church members argued that the main role of the denomination was to keep the peace. The Classis of Chicago sent an overture to the General Synod in both 1967 and 1968 asking that it table all merger actions. "Priority should be given in General Synod decisions to maintaining the primary responsibility of the Reformed Church in America, above all other responsibilities, of preserving undisruptiveness within our denominational fellowship." The classis believed that stopping the merger process would reduce unrest and disruption within the denomination.[31] The very action that one group sought to keep the peace, however, would have created a firestorm of controversy for other

---

[29] *Acts and Proceedings*, 1966, 301-07; 1967, 258-71. PCUS members were nearly as divided over merger as those in the RCA. Some PCUS members hoped that merger with the RCA would prevent a merger with the UPC. Others did not want to waste time with the RCA but preferred to move directly to a reunion of the Northern and Southern Presbyterian churches. Some PCUS members thought that joining COCU was a means to derail the conversations with the RCA and allow the PCUS to refocus on merger with the UPC. Others insisted this was not the case.

[30] Fellowship of the Concerned, letter to the editor, *CH*, June 3, 1966, 16. The group was originally formed to oppose merger with the PCUS. In the fall of 1965 it published an advertisement in the *Church Herald* that read, "Laymen! Are you concerned about the implications of church merger? Be informed, be Reformed. If you write to Jacob Blaauw he will send information," Oct. 22, 1965, 20. Signers included C.P. Dame, Adrian Newhouse, Cecil Martens, Lloyd Arnoldink, Jacob Blaauw, Jerome DeJong, Gary DeWitt, and Jacob Prins.

[31] *Acts and Proceedings*, 1968, 107. A similar overture appears in *Acts and Proceedings*, 1967, 120.

Reformed Church members. An action (like merger) that disrupted some people was seen as energizing and motivating by others. There was also significant disagreement within the denomination over the premise that "undisruptiveness" was indeed the primary responsibility of the denomination, or if it simply functioned as a code word for maintaining the status quo.

In 1967 the PCUS and RCA held parallel meetings in Bristol, Tennessee. The two groups met separately for business meetings but shared meals and some "inspirational" sessions. Delegates reported enjoying one another's company, but friendship would not be enough to change the minds of the most vigorous opponents of merger.

Prior to the 1968 General Synod, the sides had clearly solidified. In May 1968 the Fellowship of the Concerned published an advertisement in the *Church Herald*, signed by eighty-eight ministers and sixty-six consistories, supporting the continuation of the Reformed Church, unchanged by merger. A second advertisement appeared in June, signed by an additional thirty-seven ministers and forty-six consistories.[32] Those supporting merger said that the insistence on being "unchanged" was precisely the problem. In a *Church Herald* article, Arvin Roos, a pastor in Denver, complained that opponents of merger often demonstrated a very narrow and static vision of faith. Instead of trust in God, faith had become "a set of crystallized documents safely sealed from inquiry, locked in the treasure-vault of the past! The 'faith once delivered to the saints,' a favorite cliché, is apparently confined to precious parchments written in the sixteenth century, and apparently not an iota of light has broken loose from the Word of God since." Merger with the Presbyterian Church, he wrote, would enable the Reformed Church to move beyond this narrow view, become a national church, and respond to the needs of the world.[33]

Sixteen overtures opposed to merger were submitted to the synod in 1968. Several asked for higher voting requirements and/or congregational votes. The synod took no action on most of them because the Plan of Union could no longer be changed. Despite all the criticism and debate, the synod voted 183-103 to approve the proposed merger.[34] Some delegates who were initially unsure of their position may have voted in favor of merger after hearing the discussion at the synod. Some delegates appeared willing to give the classes an opportunity to vote, while remaining fully convinced that merger would not be approved.

---

[32]   "For a Continuing Reformed Church," *CH*, May 3, 1968, 16; June 7, 1968, 14.
[33]   "Go Forward with Faith," *CH*, April 26, 1968, 21, 30. Roos became a Presbyterian in 1971.
[34]   *Acts and Proceedings*, 1968, 273-97.

Although the critics of merger had spoken loudly, dramatically, and frequently prior to the vote, at the synod they remained a minority.

More than six months remained before the classes would vote on the issue.[35] Tension increased considerably during this time. The moderates thought that the purists had exaggerated the dangers of merger and misrepresented the Presbyterian Church, while the purists thought the moderates were willing to compromise Reformed identity, theology, and family. The moderates hoped the denomination would move into a more ecumenical future with greater potential for influence, and they resented purist attempts to stifle discussion by citing a need to keep the peace or preserve "undisruptiveness." The purists thought that the moderates were willing to sell the denomination's birthright in order to gain respect and influence.

As the denomination moved toward the votes of the classes on merger, both sides grew increasingly angry and defensive. The harmony and mutual respect that Bernard Brunsting had observed in 1963 seemed light years removed. The hair-splitting, sulking, and sabotage that he thought had disappeared had in fact returned. There was precious little trust or good will in this family.

Membership in the World Council and the National Council of Churches

The debate about merger, which created such negative energy in the Reformed Church, spilled over into other ecumenical relationships. Between 1950 and 1965 there had been no overtures and relatively few complaints about the Reformed Church's membership in the ecumenical councils. In 1965 the Classis of Central California and the Particular Synod of Michigan sent the first of many overtures that asked the General Synod to withdraw from the National Council of Churches (NCC). These overtures offered what had by this time become standard arguments: the National Council wanted to be a super-church, it emphasized social action more than evangelism, it spoke *to* rather than *for* its constituents, and it had been corrupted by Communists. The synod took no action on these overtures.[36]

That hardly ended the criticism, however; attacks on the NCC and the RCA's membership in it only intensified. Anthony Moolenaar from De Motte, Indiana, wrote in a *Church Herald* letter, "If we stay in the NCC much longer many of our Reformed Church people will rebel.

---

[35] The results of this vote are discussed in the following chapter.
[36] *Acts and Proceedings*, 1965, 106-07, 113-14.

The NCC will soon dictate to our General Synod what we must believe and print in our paper."[37] After Louis Benes wrote positively about the NCC's General Assembly in 1966, J.E. Bilyeu from Anaheim answered with a succinct and personal message to the council: "Get lost! Who needs you?"[38]

In August 1967, the Family Reformed Church in San Diego, California, asked the Reformed Church, through a letter to the *Church Herald*, to leave the National and World Councils because they focused more on politics and social issues than on evangelism. The congregation refused to be bound by anything the councils said and affirmed its loyalty to the Reformed Church in America.[39] This pronouncement raised a significant question about the meaning of loyalty. Did a congregation demonstrate loyalty to the denomination when it advocated the elimination of an ecumenical relationship that had been part of the Reformed Church's identity since 1908? The San Diego congregation surely thought so; moderate members of the denomination would have disagreed.

Critics of the councils also claimed that membership threatened their loyalty to the nation. In a remarkable conflation of Christianity and nationalism, the Classis of South Grand Rapids petitioned the synod in 1967 to withdraw from the NCC because "its many pronouncements on international political issues and related matters are inconsistent with our patriotic and national feelings. They do, as a matter of fact, destroy confidence in our elected federal officials. Further, they give aid and comfort to the enemy purporting to speak for a large segment of Protestant people in the United States."[40]

In the same year, the Classis of California overtured the synod asking that each congregation be allowed to vote on the question of continuing denominational membership in the National Council of Churches and the World Council of Churches.[41] As with similar requests regarding merger with the Southern Presbyterians, this motion suggested a fundamental confusion about the representative nature of the Reformed Church's polity. The synod took no action.

Some critics feared that the relationship with the councils would contaminate them. At times, suspicion of the councils led people to

---

[37]   March 25, 1966, 16.
[38]   Editorial, "The General Assembly of the National Council of Churches: An Editorial Report," *CH*, Dec. 23, 1966, 6-7, 31-33; J.E. Bilyeu, letter to the editor, Jan. 20, 1967, 25.
[39]   Daniel Fylstra (pastor) and Leo Wears (clerk), letter to the editor, *CH*, Aug. 26, 1966, 21.
[40]   *Acts and Proceedings*, 1967, 114-15.
[41]   Ibid., 116.

blame them for the actions of other groups. In December 1967 the *Church Herald* published a news story about a U.S. Conference on Church and Society worship service. The story included a photo and the phrase, "slim, young dancer in an electric blue leotard." The Ruth Circle of the First Reformed Church in Lynden, Washington, quoted the line and asked whether this was what the gospel was about.

> Our Christian witness is disqualified when we subscribe to the standards of the NCC. The gospel has, instead of being glorified, been brought into abasement by its notorious pronouncements. We are deeply concerned about the association of our Reformed Church in an organization that emphasizes much that Christianity does not stand for, and we protest![42]

In 1968 four overtures requested withdrawal from, or at least a study of, the Reformed Church's participation in the National Council. The Classis of Minnesota insisted that the NCC "has taken a radical, leftist position in the areas of politics, economics, and ethics." It was no longer the conservative, evangelical organization that the Reformed Church had joined, and evangelical Christians could not remain members. In response to these overtures, the synod agreed to appoint a committee to study the National Council and report its findings in 1969.[43]

Considering how deeply purist Reformed Church members distrusted other Protestants, it is not surprising that they were even more suspicious of Roman Catholics. George Hazenkamp of Clifton, New Jersey, said he was shocked to read in a local newspaper that the Catholic Church in Pequannock, New Jersey, held an interfaith prayer service that included three Catholic priests and two Reformed Church ministers. "How far are we turning away from the faith of our fathers?... Are we slowly moving to the day of one universal church with one head?"[44] Two laywomen were surprised by his response. Wanda Neff of Schenectady pointed out that the Reformed Church professed to believe in the "one Holy Catholic Church." Erna Kamphuis of Sheboygan, Wisconsin, said she belonged to an interfaith dialogue group in which she had realized that Reformed Church members were not God's only chosen people.[45]

---

[42] "Unconventional Worship Service at Church-Society Conference," *CH*, Dec. 1, 1967, 2; letter to the editor, *CH*, Jan. 12, 1968, 17.

[43] *Acts and Proceedings*, 1968, 104-06, 120, 124.

[44] Letter to the editor, *CH*, Feb. 23, 1968, 16.

[45] Letters to the editor, *CH*, March 8, 1968, 17.

Howard Hageman encouraged Reformed Church members to appreciate other Christian traditions. He described an incident in which John Calvin received a copy of the Episcopal Prayer Book from an English Puritan who thought it was too Catholic. Calvin responded that it contained *multas ineptas tolerabiles*, which Hageman translated to mean, "many foolish things which you can live with." Calvin's words were important to remember in the current ecumenical discussion, Hageman said. Some say that the Reformed Church should have no fellowship with a church that does not have evening services, but those are customs, not the heart of the gospel.[46] Hageman had little sympathy with the purist view that the church needed protection.

Moderates like Hageman valued ecumenical relationships as a sign that the Reformed Church was part of the larger Christian community. The most ardent purists distrusted ecumenical relationships (at least with mainline denominations) because they feared contamination and loss of identity. The two views would collide dramatically at the synod in 1969.

Denominational Identity

During the decade of the 1960s the Reformed Church debated a wide range of issues that at heart dealt with denominational identity. What kind of church would it be? Did all congregations, members, and ministers need to think and act alike? If not, could those who differed genuinely respect one another, or would there always be a sense of judgment on those who disagreed?

The issue of biblical interpretation continued to cause controversy. In 1963 the Reformed Church introduced a new education program, entitled the Covenant Life Curriculum, published in cooperation with the PCUS and other denominations. The adult program included courses in Bible, church history, and theology that were intellectually challenging and informed by contemporary scholarship in religion. Some teachers complained that it took too much time to prepare and was too difficult for them and their students. More strident critics charged that the curriculum was too liberal because it had been shaped by a neo-Orthodox perspective on scripture. Bert Van Malsen, a pastor in Grant, Michigan, criticized the curriculum because one textbook said the Bible *became* the living Word when people read and studied it. He insisted that the Bible was always the Word of God, but readers were spiritually dead and needed to be made alive in order to understand it.

---

[46]   "Calvinist Forbearance," *CH*, March 11, 1966, 9.

Any weakness had to be in the readers, not the text. John Nordstrom, a pastor in Harlingen, New Jersey, responded that his church appreciated the curriculum because it had sparked serious study and conversation about the Bible. It encouraged people to wrestle honestly with the faith and learn together.[47]

In 1965, two overtures requested action against the Covenant Life Curriculum. The Particular Synod of Michigan overtured the General Synod to refer the curriculum to the Theological Commission on the grounds that it contained objectionable material. The synod chose instead to affirm the Board of Education, which had produced the curriculum.[48] A similar overture from the Particular Synod of Chicago expressed concern about "the direction of Theological Orientation in the R.C.A. as it relates to views on Inspiration, Revelation and Scripture." The overture disapproved of neo-orthodoxy, which it saw as inconsistent with Reformed theology, and asked boards, institutions, and committees to "assure that the content of any publication is in harmony with RCA Standards of Unity." The Committee on Overtures again recommended no action because the overture was unclear and impossible to implement, and because the petitioners' lack of confidence was not justified.[49]

A year later the Particular Synod of Chicago tried a different tactic: it asked the General Synod to study the doctrinal positions taught by the Bible and philosophy departments in the three Reformed Church colleges. The particular synod reported that some students entering the ministry lacked conviction about the authority of scripture, due to the influence of their college professors. The synod's Standing Committee on Higher Education discussed the overture but recommended no action because the overture failed to specify or document charges.[50]

These overtures reflect a purist understanding of orthodoxy. The overtures were quickly dismissed by the General Synod, but they fostered a mood of distrust within the denomination and helped discourage

---

[47]   Bert Van Malsen, "A Disturbing Definition," *CH*, Oct. 4, 1963, 10, 21 (Van Malsen had been the first to criticize Hugh Baillie MacLean in 1948); John Nordstrom, letter to the editor, Nov. 22, 1963, 30.

[48]   *Acts and Proceedings*, 1965, 112, 122.

[49]   Ibid., 111, 122.

[50]   *Acts and Proceedings*, 1966, 140, 83. Elton Bruins and Robert Palma began teaching in the Hope College Religion Department a few months after this overture was discussed. They knew nothing about it. About this time the Covenant of Mutual Responsibilities between the colleges and the denomination was being drafted. It said clearly that the church should not serve as a watchdog over the orthodoxy of college courses and ideas.

creative thinking. They insinuated that the colleges, the seminaries, and the Board of Education were not adequately orthodox in the way the purists defined orthodoxy. The recipients of such criticism resented what appeared to them as hyperorthodoxy and rigidity.

The underlying issue was that the Reformed Church could not agree on how to express its faith or what it meant to be a confessional denomination. In 1959, the synod had asked the Theological Commission to write a new confession of faith. When a first draft was published in 1966, it received significant criticism from both ends of the theological spectrum.[51] Some purists criticized the commission for daring to write a new confession, while some moderates considered creeds and confessions irrelevant. The commission explained patiently that its goal in writing a new confession was to help the Reformed Church think through its beliefs in the context of the twentieth century. "The hope is to get our churches off the dead center of always thinking that our Reformed witness is forever frozen in the confessional documents of the sixteenth and seventeenth centuries."[52] However, Reformed Church members could not agree on the need for a new confession, let alone its content, and the document was not approved.

Purist members expressed considerable anxiety and defensiveness about the status of the confessions if the PCUS merger was approved. Winfield Burggraaff, a member of the Theological Commission, offered a sharp criticism of this fearfulness.

> Many of our pastors and people live in a creedal ghetto, in creedal segregation. We take the Belgic Confession, the Heidelberg Catechism, and the Canons of Dort, construct them into a circular wall around our Reformed Church, and believe that the health and security of our church are to be found only within the segregated areas inside these walls. We denounce as traitors those who occasionally inspect the walls, discovering weak spots; we scream in fear at the suggestion of adding a buttress here and there, or putting some new building blocks into the ancient walls. We adorn these creedal walls with a mystique, an aura of divinity, ascribing to them attributes which belong only to God—holiness, perfection, freedom from obsolescence, immortality. Out of all

---

[51]   Richard J. Mouw, letter to the editor, *CH*, Feb. 3, 1967, 23; Eugene Heideman, "A New Confession of What?" Feb. 24, 1967, 12, 21. The confession appeared March 24, 1967, 17-20.

[52]   Winfield Burggraaff, "The Theological Commission Reports," *CH*, April 12, 1968, 23, 33.

this there develops a creedal separatist mind-set which rejects the freedom we have in Christ.

Burggraaff asked the Reformed Church to seek security in God's grace and the living Word. The fear of change, he concluded, was in fact a fear that God would not remain faithful.[53]

Purists showed a similar resistance to change in the realm of liturgy. Although the Committee on Revision of the Liturgy had been working for nearly a decade on a new liturgy, some congregations insisted they would use the old liturgy after the new one was approved. The committee noted with some irritation the presence of "a growing congregationalism that refused to recognize, in keeping with Reformed Church Polity, an authority higher than that of the Consistory or the Classis." Again, the purists who demanded conformity in biblical interpretation felt free to disregard denominational decisions on liturgical matters.[54] Despite the criticisms, however, the new liturgy provided substantive and significant guidance for Reformed worship. The committee had integrated insights and practices from the early church, the Reformation, the Roman Catholic Church, and other European and American churches.

Along with these debates about belief and worship, Reformed Church members demonstrated sharp disagreements over matters of morality and behavior. Some members insisted that dancing and attending movies were evil, worldly practices, and that the church simply could not relax its moral standards to permit them. Other members argued that, in the face of such significant challenges to contemporary Christianity as secularism and the Death of God theology, it was foolish to worry whether dancing was a sin.

Underlying these questions were deep concerns about the nature of the faith and its transmission to the next generation. Did the Christian life require living in a cocoon of piety sheltered from everything worldly and sinful? To what extent could a Christian participate in "worldly" activities? And what activities qualified as "worldly?" Some older members had been raised in a relatively protected, morally "pure" environment, but their children engaged the larger culture more directly, rejecting their parents' moralism and often the faith behind it.

---

[53] "Why Live in a Creedal Ghetto?" *CH*, Aug. 23, 1968, 14, 30.

[54] *Acts and Proceedings*, 1966, 213. Some moderates criticized the new liturgy because its language already felt dated. It contained prayers for the harvest but no prayers regarding the use of nuclear weapons. See the discussion of the committee's work above, pp. 78-79.

Robert DeHaan, a psychology professor at Hope College, dealt with many of these issues in an advice column he wrote for the *Church Herald* in the mid 1960s. Some advice seekers lamented their inability to pray "well" in public or genuinely to like a mean-spirited neighbor. Others asked for guidance about dancing or the use of alcohol. Many of the letters came from parents whose children would rather attend dances and movies than church. DeHaan rarely condemned questionable activities outright, but he encouraged parents to talk with their children about their options. When a church member was appalled that girls wore jeans and shorts to catechism class, DeHaan observed that they were probably frustrated with church and rebelling against being forced to go.

Some readers preferred clear answers to their moral dilemmas. One woman asked DeHaan whether Christians who approved of social drinking or penny-ante card playing were right or wrong. "Please give a definite answer. I have heard it said that you frequently don't do this." Another woman questioned not only his wisdom but also his salvation when he did not give a thirteen-year-old girl the right answer about dancing. He replied that it was far better for young people to think through a question and find their own answer. An absolute yes or no offered only a temporary and often legalistic solution. DeHaan also chided the writer for questioning his faith and attempting to discredit him.[55]

Louis Benes continued to encourage strict morality, as he had for two decades. He praised the president of Baylor College for canceling a school production of Eugene O'Neill's *Long Day's Journey into Night* because of its vulgar language. Benes admitted that he hadn't read the play, but he believed that literature could not be great if it used vulgar language that dishonored God.[56] Kenneth Vos from Hawthorne, New Jersey, asked how Benes could condemn a play without reading it. Vos described the theme and plot of the play and pointed out that one function of drama was to show that the world was often painful and ugly. If Christians refused to deal with these difficult issues, Vos said, they would quickly lose credibility.[57]

During the summer of 1966, Joyce Kuipers of Jenison complained about a reference to John Steinbeck's novel, *The Grapes of Wrath*, which

---

[55] "Sir, I Have a Problem," *CH*, Jan. 24, 1964, 7; Jan. 8, 1965, 11.

[56] Editorial, "Journey into Night," *CH*, April 19, 1963, 6-7. Benes also noted that the chair of the Theater Department at Baylor resigned after this incident and was immediately hired by a United Presbyterian college to head its Theater Department, which said little for the moral and spiritual tone of that school.

[57] Letter to the editor, *CH*, June 6, 1963, 30-31.

had appeared in the *Church Herald*. She called the book filth and trash and nothing more than a source of new swear words. Two people complained about a picture of teens dancing in the aisles of the Old South Church in Boston. This was not spiritual, one writer maintained. The other asked, "Are we pleasing Father [*sic*] or do we demand that He will please us?" Another letter writer criticized the magazine for advertising Thomas Altizer's book on the death of God. The writer compared this to a temperance magazine selling ads to a liquor company. Christians need to separate themselves from evil, not listen to these ideas.[58]

During the decade of the 1960s there were so many cultural shifts, new religious ideas, and changes in expectations about dress and morality that people often felt threatened and overwhelmed. Herman Luben, a moderate pastor in Utica, New York, observed in 1967 that too many sentences within Reformed circles began, "I'm afraid that...."

Reformed Church members were anxious about ecumenism and liturgical change and merger and changes in moral standards, but anxiety was a national problem. In 1968 Luben lamented the depressing presidential campaign in which the candidates emphasized law and order and appealed to people's fear. Luben wrote, "Many American church men are deeply infected with fear; the fear climate has seeped into their spirits and reversed the miracle: fear has driven out love. Unless we all let God constantly reshape us, we shall be making our decisions by fear rather than faith (which is what is meant, brother, by living in sin)."[59]

But there was more than fear at work. Behind it was a deep sense of loss. Purists thought that too many rules had changed. They had lost stability, certainty, and order. Moderates believed that the denomination was no longer the kind of open, welcoming place it had once been. It was dominated by petty moral issues rather than the larger issues of love and justice.

These disagreements produced a tense General Synod meeting in 1967 in Bristol, Tennessee. The denomination was already showing some signs of splintering from the stress. President Ray Beckering gently chastised church members in his speech to the General Synod:

---

[58] Joyce Kuipers, letter to the editor, *CH*, June 3, 1966, 17; Mrs. F. Dalman, Mrs. M.O. Dilworth, Elmer Van Drunen, letters to the editor, June 17, 1966, 21. The picture of the dancing teens appeared in the May 20, 1966, issue.

[59] Guest editorials, "Tonic for the Anxious Heart," *CH*, Nov. 3, 1967, 6; "Whose Law and What Kind of Order?" *CH*, Oct. 11, 1968, 10.

"To threaten secession before issues have been resolved, to withhold funds from the support of approved programs, to feed fear, are things sad to witness and hurtful to the common cause." He called instead for humility, openness, and mutual trust as more helpful ways to deal with anxiety and disagreement. He encouraged people not to think the worst of each other.[60]

The Committee on Overtures usually possessed the most difficult and controversial agenda. But in 1967 it provided an example of good will, despite dealing with a number of overtures about merger. Robert Schuller chaired the committee and offered this unusual report.

> We would bear witness to this synod of our experience with the Holy Spirit. Though deep and potentially divisive differences of intense disagreement on issues existed in this committee at no time was there the hint of hostility to despoil the mental climate of our meetings. We testify that this is not necessarily a mark of the spiritual stature of your committee but it is in truth a mark of the presence and power of the Holy Spirit whose gifts are "Love, Joy, Peace." In a period of sincere conscientious dissension we recommend that General Synod remind the church that the Holy Spirit calls us to an unconditional love for all people as persons even when their views are to us most disagreeable.[61]

This level of good will was extremely rare during those years. At the end of the 1960s, the Reformed Church lacked a common understanding of denominational identity. There was sharp disagreement on issues of theology and morality and denominational culture. Some people insisted that everyone within the Reformed Church had to think alike; others believed there was room for disagreement. There was little respect for difference and a great deal of judgment of those who differed.

Civil Rights

The social upheaval of the 1960s provided even more reasons for disagreement within the Reformed Church. One of the crucial questions of the decade in both religious life and broader American society was the issue of racial inequity. Conservatives tended to view racism as a sin of

---

[60]   *Acts and Proceedings*, 1967, 306. Beckering was a pastor at the Second Reformed Church in Zeeland, Michigan.

[61]   *Acts and Proceedings*, 1967, 127-28. An amendment to delete "even when their views are most disagreeable" and replace it with "including conscientious objectors to the war in Vietnam" was ruled out of order. Comments about process in a committee were almost never included in the minutes.

individuals that could be "fixed" by conversion (despite the number of professed Christians guilty of racism). Moderates tended to understand racism as a systemic problem that required structural change. New laws might not be able to change racist attitudes, but they could restrain racist behavior.[62]

During the mid to late 1960s, discussion about race centered around two issues. The first was the Civil Rights Act, which would guarantee access to public places and prohibit discrimination on the basis of race. Howard Hageman urged Reformed Church members to flood Washington with letters supporting the bill because all Americans needed to share the responsibility for racial justice. He wrote that when the church in Birmingham was bombed and four girls died, "We were all there—those who still harbor polite prejudice, who think the Negro's demands for citizenship are immoderate and ill-timed, who think private property must be protected at the expense of human dignity."[63] John Beardslee III, a professor of religion at Central College in Pella, Iowa, encouraged Reformed Church members to support the Civil Rights Act because "Christians can no longer allow their neighbors to lie at the mercy of the unregenerate elements in our culture." The bill would not take rights away from anyone, he wrote, but would ensure that the rights that white people expect and demand—education, use of public facilities, and property—be shared by all, regardless of race.[64]

Some conservative Reformed Church members opposed the Civil Rights Act because they thought it would increase government control and deprive people of their "right" to segregate. Ronald Brown argued that no restaurant owner should be forced to serve Negroes. It was morally wrong, Brown wrote, to secure the rights of the minority by undermining the liberty, property, and self-respect of men of all races.

---

[62] These labels have their limits, as discussed in the introduction. The purist category is somewhat less useful when referring to social issues. There was a large spectrum of opinion within both church and American society about social issues. I will describe moderate and conservative approaches, while recognizing that the labels are imprecise. As noted in the previous chapter, Louis Benes was a theological conservative/purist but a moderate on racial issues. Not all conservatives agreed with the views of Ronald Brown. Some conservatives did not think it was appropriate for the church to lobby for civil rights, yet they may have challenged racism in their personal lives. Some moderates who advocated the most open racial policies might not have encountered people of other races regularly. Despite all these caveats, it is still accurate to identify relatively conservative and relatively moderate attitudes about racial issues.

[63] "Were You There?" and "The Continuing March," *CH*, Oct. 4, 1963, 9.

[64] Letter to the editor, *CH*, May 29, 1964, 12-13. Louis Benes also argued that individuals had no right to deprive others of their rights. "Civil Rights for All," *CH*, April 24, 1964, 6.

The real moral issue, he contended, was not civil rights for a few, but the rights of free choice, association, and the marketplace.[65]

Brown also insisted that churches should not lobby for legislation. Social problems such as racism could only be solved by the regenerating work of the Holy Spirit, which could transform sinners' hearts and make them act differently.[66] Similarly, layperson J.H. Shoemaker insisted that new laws could not produce self-respect or economic security. If African-Americans wanted social acceptance and economic abundance, he said, they should work hard, study, save, and build character. He cited J. Edgar Hoover, who insisted that the "Negro movement" was actually a Communist plot to restrict private property.[67]

Moderates and conservatives did not agree about the role of the church in society. Moderates, following John Calvin, believed that the church was called to transform society. Conservatives, influenced more by fundamentalism and evangelicalism, insisted that the church concern itself only with spiritual matters.[68] John H. Muller, a pastor in Orlando, Florida, argued that Jesus chose to be a redeemer, not a reformer, because society could only be transformed by converted individuals. Legislation and picketing would not change the human heart, and therefore ministers should preach the gospel rather than participate in civil disobedience. Only conversion could heal racism.[69]

John Beardslee pointed out that Muller's view was more Anabaptist (which saw the world as unredeemable) than Reformed (which held that the world could be transformed). Beardslee added that Christians could not simply allow their neighbors to be victimized by an unregenerate world but should encourage the world to be more just. Donald DeYoung, a pastor in Harlem, New York, criticized Muller for supporting the status quo. The Civil Rights bill was not liberal social legislation; rather, it guaranteed to all American citizens the rights white men already had. Justice could not be delayed until racist people

---

[65]   Letter to the editor, *CH*, May 29, 1964, 12-13. When he wrote this, Brown was pastor of the Beverly Reformed Church in Wyoming, outside of Grand Rapids. In 1966 he became pastor of the Calvary Reformed Church in South Holland, Illinois.

[66]   Letter to the editor, *CH*, May 15, 1964, 21.

[67]   Letter to the editor, *CH*, May 29, 1964, 12-13.

[68]   This debate affected almost all denominations in varying degrees. See H. Richard Niebuhr, *Christ and Culture* (New York: Harper, 1951). In the last three decades, since the formation of the Moral Majority in 1979, evangelicals and fundamentalists (the "religious right") have been actively involved in politics and social issues, particularly abortion and homosexuality. In the 1960s, however, they generally did not think it was the church's role to get involved in social issues.

[69]   John H. Muller, "Is It the Church's Business?" *CH*, Oct. 23, 1964, 14-15. Prior to serving in Orlando, Muller was pastor of the Hope Reformed Church in Chicago.

became Christian and developed loving feelings. Civil rights laws might not change hearts, DeYoung said, but they could change behavior and perhaps the heart would follow.[70] Christians had an obligation to seek justice for all people.

During the summer of 1965, racial tensions exploded in the Watts area of Los Angeles and in other cities in the following years. Conservatives quickly insisted on the need for law and order and punishment, just as they had in response to demonstrations and sit-ins in the 1950s. Moderates strongly disapproved of the violence but tried to understand the social factors that produced it. Louis Benes pointed out that the Civil Rights laws had not brought justice, voting rights were not secure in the South, and white power was often used unjustly and violently. It was hypocritical for whites to condemn the Black Power movement when conditions of inequality still existed.[71] Benes also asked if a law could be valid if it deprived people of their right to vote or be educated.[72]

The *Church Herald* printed several articles in the spring of 1968 that offered a sympathetic analysis of the riots.[73] Benes urged Christians to read the Bible more carefully. "God forgive us if we can think and talk about God's deliverance of Israel from bondage and not recognize or speak for the oppressed today. God forgive us if we read the thousand scriptural texts that call for justice and concern for the poor, and think that this has nothing to say to us about what justice and compassion mean today." Benes suggested specific actions such as making donations, developing personal relationships, and working in justice organizations. He concluded by noting that the Reformed Church had a particular responsibility to work for change, since so many of the cities where riots occurred (Harlem, Newark, Paterson, Detroit, Chicago, Watts) had once contained Reformed churches, although many of them had fled to the suburbs with their white congregants.[74]

---

70   John W. Beardslee III, Donald DeYoung, letters to the editor, *CH*, Nov. 13, 1964, 16.
71   Editorials, "So Many Have Learned to Hate Before We Have Learned to Love," *CH*, Sept. 17, 1965, 6-7; "Black Power," Sept. 9, 1966, 6-7.
72   Editorial, "That All Men Are Created Equal," Feb. 11, 1966, 6. Howard Hageman posed similar questions in "A Footnote on Law and Order," *CH*, Oct. 8, 1965, 9.
73   Lewis Smedes, "The Other Half of the Half-Truths," *CH*, April 26, 1968, 17; Joseph Muyskens, "Separate But Unequal Societies," May 10, 1968, 10.
74   Editorial, "You Must Do Something!" *CH*, May 24, 1968, 6-7. The RCA did take some positive actions to combat racism. The denomination conducted a fund drive during the summer of 1968 that raised almost $100,000. The money was used by churches in Chicago, Newark, New York, and Oakland, CA, to fund summer programs for children, support a community recreation center, and create college scholarships. News article, no title, *CH*, April 11, 1969, 13.

Martin Luther King Jr. provided a powerful presence and voice during these years, and Central College invited him to speak on campus in the spring of 1967. A.W. Gysen, from Bellflower, California, questioned the action, not because King was a Negro, he said, but because King was such a controversial figure and many of his actions were inconsistent with Christian leadership. Gysen warned Central to make sure its speakers agreed with the principles of those who supported the college.[75]

Unfortunately, racism was alive and well in Iowa in 1967, as it was in many southern and northern states. When King came to speak at Central, he flew into the airport in Ottumwa rather than Des Moines, as expected. He therefore missed seeing that the road from Des Moines to Pella was lined with burning crosses.[76]

Louis Benes had always spoken highly of Martin Luther King Jr. The day after King was assassinated, Louis Benes wrote a powerful essay in his memory. It said in part:

> I could cry. I could cry for his family. I could cry not only from sorrow that so worthy a leader, filled with the spirit of the prophets and the spirit of Jesus Christ, has been prematurely snatched from this life, but I could cry from shame and from anger, that anything like this could happen in my country. And I could cry not only because of the demonic and damnable nature of this tragedy, but because of all the piled up wrongs of my race that made it necessary for Martin Luther King and thousands of others to plan and plead and maneuver and march, just to obtain for their own people those freedoms and privileges which my people have always had in this "land of the free." I could cry, for shame, that so many of us good Christians see and know about this injustice all about us, and yet say so little and do so little to rectify it; that our white communities are so smug, and our white churches so contented, that we are people of good will who do nothing; that we make it necessary for the wronged black people to fend for themselves. Today I stand with my black brother, and I cry."[77]

Some readers thought it was the best piece Benes had ever written. On the other hand, Ronald Brown protested that King could not be

[75] A.W. Gysen, letter to the editor, *CH*, March 10, 1967, 14.
[76] Informal conversation with Arend Lubbers.
[77] Editorial, "I Could Cry," *CH*, April 19, 1968, 6.

considered a Christian because he did not sufficiently affirm the deity of Christ. R. Kuypers of Chicago called the editorial a "sob story" which wrongly imputed collective guilt to white people.[78]

Reformed Church members continued to wrestle with racist attitudes. Robert DeHaan, the advice columnist at the *Church Herald*, received a letter that claimed that white people justifiably feared Negroes because of their alleged violence. The writer suggested that Negroes could earn social acceptance if they engaged in appropriate behavior. In response, DeHaan noted that white society created and maintained the ghetto when white churches moved out of the city, white Christians removed their children from public schools, and white citizens showed no concern about justice for the poor. De Haan then chided the questioner, "Your proposed remedy is the kind that enrages black people. Such promises [of social acceptance] have frequently been made but never carried out. And why should white people presume to decide what is appropriate behavior?"[79]

The problem of racism could not be ignored. Reformed Church members disagreed about timing and legislation, but there were significant theological issues as well. Were all people created in the image of God? If so, how could unequal treatment be justified? Was racism a relatively minor individual sin or a systemic social evil? Would redemption and transformation occur as a result of individual conversion, or did society itself need to be radically changed? Was the role of the church to transform individuals or the society? Such strongly rooted disagreements would not easily be resolved.

Social Issues

Like the society around it, the Reformed Church was conflicted in its response to a host of other difficult social issues. Reformed Church members did not agree on *whether* the denomination should talk about politics or economics at all, and, when the church did choose to discuss an issue, members did not agree on *how* they should go about that conversation. Reaching a consensus on any social issue was even less likely. Debates occurred at all three of these levels: whether to converse, how to converse, and the outcome of the conversations.

During these years the Reformed Church was blessed or cursed (depending on one's perspective) with a very active Christian Action

---

[78] Letters to the editor, *CH*, May 10, 1968, 14, 20; R. Kuypers, letter to the editor, May 17, 1965, 24.

[79] "Sir I Have A Problem," *CH*, April 18, 1969, 8.

Commission (CAC), composed of laypeople and ministers who wanted the Reformed Church to have something meaningful to say about social issues. The commission regularly brought to the General Synod lengthy reports that contained dozens of recommendations. The reports raised difficult questions that produced vigorous debate. Moderates generally appreciated the commission's work and agreed with most recommendations, while purists resented the commission's influence and disagreed with its conclusions. Purists did not think the church needed a Christian Action Commission, because it was not the appropriate role of the church to express a position about China or Vietnam or poverty or gambling. Moderates insisted that the church should indeed express such positions as part of its role in transforming society, and that the commission helped the church do this.

In 1966 the Christian Action Commission's report discussed race, law and order, capital punishment, Communist China, Vietnam, poverty, and gambling. The synod approved the commission's recommendation in support of China's request to join the United Nations.[80] When the *Church Herald* reported the action, critics complained that General Synod meetings were so dominated by social issues that there was not enough time for the gospel. Robert Schuller wrote a letter protesting the "nonconstructive, strife-generating" political activity. Schuller noted that while little good could come of these actions, they created divisiveness when the Reformed Church needed unity.[81]

In 1967 the Christian Action Commission caused controversy even before the synod met. After discussing the war in Vietnam at its spring meeting, commission members wrote directly to President Johnson, encouraging him to go to Hanoi for peace talks. When the report of this action was published, a flurry of letters to the editor protested that the commission had no right to speak for the denomination and lacked the credentials to advise the president of the United States. One writer requested that the names and addresses of commission members be published so that corrective information could be shared with them directly. Another writer asked how the commission had been formed and who had given it the authority to speak independently.[82]

Winfield Burggraaff defended the work of the Christian Action Commission by noting that its role was not to arrive at predetermined

---

[80] *Acts and Proceedings*, 1966, 215-36.
[81] Robert Schuller for the Consistory of the Garden Grove Community Church, letter to the editor, *CH*, Aug. 26, 1966, 20-21.
[82] "Reformed Church Urges President: Go to Hanoi or Send Envoy," *CH*, March 17, 1967, 2. Carl Shafer, Russell Johnson, Lester White, letters to the editor, *CH*, April 7, 1967, 16, 22-23.

conclusions or to please those who held a particular perspective but to help the Reformed Church think through difficult social issues. Burggraaff noted that Reformed Church members had a right to disagree with the conclusions of the commission but not to discredit its integrity or to question its Christian commitment.[83]

Central College had sparked a similar debate and generated some anger within the Reformed Church when it invited Martin Luther King Jr. to speak on campus. In Central College's report to the synod in 1967, Central's president, Arend (Don) Lubbers, observed that in a time of social upheaval, students were eager to address social questions, and the role of the Christian college was to help students think through these issues. Some faculty and students had been working in a largely African-American section of Des Moines, and the college invited King to help them reflect on the issues raised by this experience. Lubbers encouraged the Reformed Church to focus on larger issues rather than become bogged down in petty disagreements.

> How minor the differences in our denomination (these same differences are reflected on our campus), among all Christians, and among all men, appear when stacked against the social imperative we face together as Christians in casting out prejudice and uniting the world in mutual understanding and mutual respect!...Time is too short for us to dissipate our energies on anything less crucial. We would appear ludicrous, and we would indeed be less Christian if we did otherwise.[84]

The Reformed Church did not take this advice to unite around the cause of social justice.

The most divisive social issue at the end of the 1960s was the war in Vietnam. In 1968 the *Church Herald* published a symposium that illustrated the range of opinion on this issue within the denomination. John H. Muller, formerly a chaplain in the Korean War, wrote, "Communist aggression must be answered by force, as this is the only language they understand. As citizens of a free land, we cannot let this godless ideology be forced on any people....Christians have a responsibility to be their brother's keeper. We cannot allow this godless tyranny to spread." On the other hand, Vernon Dethmers, a pastor in New Jersey, noted that the war was complex but that escalation of a very

---

[83] Winfield Burggraaff, "On the Right of Dissent," *CH*, June 2, 1967, 12-13.
[84] *Acts and Proceedings*, 1967, 63-64.

bad policy was not a good solution. Faithful Christians needed to seek ways to combat communism that did not involve war.[85]

In 1968 the Christian Action Commission brought to the General Synod several recommendations that received mixed responses. The commission encouraged the church to call for a nonmilitary solution in Vietnam. The synod referred the proposal back to the commission for rewriting. The commission recommended that the denomination distribute literature about Vietnam for churches to study. Synod delegates said no. The commission discussed conscientious objectors and asked the synod to affirm that the "first loyalty of a Christian is to the Lordship of Jesus Christ both in private and public living, and that dissent from public policy when based upon conviction is legitimate and necessary." The synod was willing to offer some support to conscientious objectors but not to affirm such a strong statement. Finally, the commission called for an end to the draft exemption for clergy and seminarians, because it unfairly privileged the pastoral role. Synod delegates said no. Perhaps this was because half of the delegates were pastors.[86]

There would be no easy resolution in the Reformed Church or the United States to the Vietnam War or to disagreements about it. Conservatives tended to emphasize the need to defeat communism and preserve democracy. They said that Christians ought to be loyal and patriotic. Moderates tended to emphasize the darker side of war—the violence done to civilians and the waste of young men's lives. They said that Christians ought to express their patriotism by asking hard questions and refusing to settle for easy answers. This unresolved conflict would affect the denomination—as it did the nation—for many years to come.

Angry Young Adults

During the late 1960s the baby boomers[87] exploded in frustration and rage over the challenges confronting American society. Many young adults were disenchanted with the direction of national politics and the

---

[85]   Herman Kregel, Norman Thomas, John H. Muller, Vernon Dethmers, "Vietnam: Conflict of Moral Responsibilities," *CH*, March 29, 1968, 12-13, 22.

[86]   *Acts and Proceedings*, 1968, 202-20.

[87]   The baby boomers are the children born between 1946 and 1962. The early boomers, born between 1946 and 1952, were between seventeen and twenty-three in 1969. They were the most active in the protests of the late 1960s and early 1970s. The boomers born toward the end of this period had a very different experience. The Vietnam War was over before they turned eighteen, and they did not face the uncertainty of being drafted.

virulent persistence of the Vietnam War. Some of them also rejected the values of affluence and success that had permeated the post-war period. They said that their parents' lifestyle was stifling, narrow-minded, and conformist. The boomers (or so the prevailing wisdom says) sought peace, love, and harmony but had little desire to become the conventional man in the gray flannel suit or the stereotypical housewife transporting four kids in a station wagon.

The boomers challenged the traditional authoritarian models of family life and education. Parents wondered why their young adult children rebelled against family religious values by dating peers of other faiths or by refusing to attend church services that seemed irrelevant to them. College students rebelled against *"in loco parentis,"* the standard policy in residential higher education that treated students more like children than adults.[88] The colleges affiliated with the Reformed Church in America—Hope (Holland, Michigan), Central (Pella, Iowa), and Northwestern (Orange City, Iowa)—experienced some student rebellion, although the incidents were not as dramatic as those that occurred at Columbia University or the University of Wisconsin.[89]

These challenges to tradition and authority were particularly threatening to adults, whose identities had been shaped by doing their patriotic duty in World War II and then working hard to "get ahead." Many parents felt as though they were losing not only their children, but their orderly, well-behaved society. Many adults thought that young people displayed astonishingly bad manners and a stubborn distrust of authorities and institutions. The youthful protestors challenged the rules of public discourse. They yelled at police officers, blocked university buildings, and refused to move when told.

These tensions and anxieties that were present in American culture affected church life as well. Many members felt a profound sense of loss. The values of the past were disappearing. Family, authority, and traditional views of religion were being supplanted by bad manners, bad behavior, and disrespect of authority. As these cultural bad manners

---

[88] Students resented dress codes, required chapel services, mandated hours for lights out, and rules governing dating that were more restrictive for women than for men. Students also protested unethical institutional policies, such as scientific research on napalm.

[89] In 1969 the acting president of Central College affirmed students for rebelling against meaninglessness and mindless tradition and demanding relevance. *Acts and Proceedings*, 1969, 45. When Kenneth Weller became president of Central in 1970, the students marched on Tulip Tower in the center of Pella as part of a protest against Vietnam. Oral history interview with Kenneth and Shirley Weller, Oct. 12, 2002, Pella, Iowa.

began to spill over into Reformed churches there was a growing sense of irritation, even anger, among members of the family.

The Restructure of Boards into the General Program Council

A few blocks away from the student protests at Columbia University, dramatic changes were occurring in the Reformed Church's offices at 475 Riverside Drive. These changes were quieter than the protests, but they had a profound impact on the life of the denomination. At the end of the 1960s, the structure of the Reformed Church received a massive overhaul. The change did not generate much open conflict, and yet it had a lasting effect on the denomination. The process began, as discussed in the previous chapter, with the formation of the General Synod Executive Committee. The Boards of Foreign Missions, Domestic Missions, Education, Pensions, and the Stewardship Council remained separate and independent. The GSEC, which included a number of powerful businessmen, found this arrangement with the boards to be untenable because no one was clearly in charge. Denominational executives answered to their boards and executive committees when they met, but during the rest of the year there was little supervision or accountability. The GSEC had been formed in part to coordinate and prioritize the work of the denomination, but it had no authority over the boards or their executives. There was no uniform chain of command, and no organizational chart showing who had authority over whom.

In 1966 the GSEC hired a consulting firm from Philadelphia, Edward N. Hay and Associates, to develop and implement a new structure. After two years of extensive discussion, the boards of mission and education were combined to form the General Program Council (GPC).[90] There were five major events in the transition process. First, the GSEC took over budget decisions from the Stewardship Council in 1966. Second, the members of the General Program Council met for the first time in 1968.[91] Third, in 1970 Arie Brouwer, secretary for program, became executive secretary, and both program and administrative units

---

[90]   This process sounds simple and straightforward, but it required years of conversation and negotiation. The papers of Robert Harrison (General Synod Archives), a staff member in the late 1960s, illustrate some of the finesse required. Staff members from each board were given aptitude tests to determine if and where they might fit into the new structure. Those who "passed" were given positions in the hierarchy of the new staff answering to the General Program Council. Others found positions elsewhere or retired.

[91]   The new GPC members included nineteen laymen, twelve laywomen, and twenty-nine pastors. Thirty-four of the sixty had previously belonged to a board or to the Stewardship Council. "The New R.C.A. Program Council," *CH*, Sept. 6, 1968, 17.

answered to him.[92] Fourth, the GPC took over the budget development process, including the responsibility to prioritize program allocations. Finally, the GPC developed regional "centers" in the early 1970s, which further diffused program autonomy and centralized oversight responsibility in Arie Brouwer's position as executive secretary.[93]

The General Program Council and the new staff structure completely reshaped the way the Reformed Church did its business. The real power in the New York office shifted from the general secretary of the denomination to the executive secretary of the GPC, Arie Brouwer. Brouwer gathered a team of smart, creative people as his inner circle, and under their leadership the Reformed Church began to function according to a more corporate model. Together these staff members planned several events and strategies that proved crucial in the life of the denomination in the 1970s.

Opinions varied greatly about the effectiveness of the new structure. Those suspicious of bureaucracy saw it as a dangerous move toward centralization and hierarchy that removed even more authority and influence from the grass roots. Others thought the new structure was long overdue; they insisted that the new model was outreach oriented, while the previous structure had merely maintained an inefficient status quo. Staff members experienced a high degree of turmoil, because no one was guaranteed a job in the new structure. Some church members asked why so much energy was being expended on a complicated restructuring, when the denomination was in the middle of merger talks that might make all structures outdated. The General Synod president, Harold Schut, replied that if merger was approved, the Reformed Church would have a better structure to combine with the Presbyterian Church. If the merger did not pass, then the RCA would be several years further along in the process of administrative upgrading.[94]

The new structure felt more like a corporation than did the old board structure. Some people lamented the loss of a "family" model of being church, and, indeed, some important values of community and

---

[92]   As secretary for program, Brouwer had supervised the staff for missions and education. General secretary Marion de Velder had supervised the administrative units, such as finance and human resources.

[93]   Laurie Mol, "A Case Study in Organizational Change: The Reformed Church in America, 1962-1972," graduate program, School of Social Welfare, State University of New York at Stony Brook, Jan. 11, 1973. Mol was a staff member at the time of restructure. For an extensive discussion of the development of the GPC, see Hoff, *Structures for Mission*, 148-99. The centers were located in Albany, NY; Hackensack, NJ; Grandville, MI; South Holland, IL; Orange City, IA; and Anaheim, CA.

[94]   Harold Schut, "Report to the Church on Reorganization," *CH*, April 12, 1968, 20-22.

connectedness and intimacy were lost in the transition. Certainly the new structure had its limitations. However, the presence of staff people who were loyal to the denomination as a whole, rather than primarily to their boards, probably helped the church survive the crisis it faced in 1969.[95]

Conclusion

What kind of church would the Reformed Church in America be? In 1969, there was no single clear answer. The moderates wanted the church to be ecumenical, involved in social issues (with a preference for progressive positions on those issues), and engaged with the world. The purists wanted it to avoid ecumenical entanglements, avoid dealing with social issues (or take only conservative positions), and maintain its purity by remaining apart from the world. The moderate and purist poles moved further apart. The conservatives were caught in the middle of a tug-of-war, stretched to the breaking point by competing factions. On some issues, there was no compromise position. The RCA would either merge with the PCUS or not; it would remain in the World and National Councils or not. No matter what the church decided, particularly regarding the merger, many people would be unhappy and some had threatened to leave. Tension, anger, and suspicion pervaded the denomination. Conversation within the Reformed Church family was increasingly mean spirited. The stage was set for a very painful conflict. Would the denomination continue as one church or divide into two?

---

[95]   For an overview of the role of bureaucracy in the RCA, see Donald A. Luidens, "National Engagement with Localism: The Last Gasp of the Corporate Denomination?" in *Church, Identity, and Change: Theology and Denominational Structures in Unsettled Times*, David A. Roozen and James R. Nieman, eds. (Grand Rapids: Eerdmans, 2005), 410-35.

CHAPTER 5

1969-1970: Breaking Up Is Hard To Do

In January 1969, the Reformed Church was about to make one of the most significant decisions of its history. In June 1968, the General Synod had voted by a large majority to approve the proposed merger with the Southern Presbyterians. Between January and March, each classis had to vote as well. Supporters of merger were encouraged by the favorable synod vote and hoped that the classes would confirm that decision. Both sides continued to debate the issue in the pages of the *Church Herald* and in other venues. Would the Reformed Church choose to remain separate and preserve its history and identity? Or would it choose to merge and be part of a larger body with potentially more influence and a better chance for long-term survival? If the Reformed Church chose to merge, would the purists leave? If it chose not to merge, would the moderates leave?

Several writers in the *Church Herald* made last-minute arguments. Howard Hageman promoted merger as an opportunity for mission, arguing that, on its own, the Reformed Church was inadequate to the task. "If we neglect this opportunity to join hands in the common task of witnessing to the Lord Jesus Christ and his Kingdom, what will become

of us and what account of ourselves shall we give to Him?" This was an
uncharacteristically anxious statement for Hageman, but it reflects the
depth of feeling and fear among eastern members that without merger
to give it a broader identity, the Reformed Church would lose what
little influence it still possessed.[1]

On the other side of the issue, Tom Stark, a pastor in East Lansing,
Michigan, feared a loss of identity and purity. He argued that if the
Reformed Church merged with the Southern Presbyterians, the next
step would be a merger with the Northern Presbyterians, which Stark
did not consider a confessional church.[2] Donner Atwood, a pastor in
New Jersey, responded that fear should not be the deciding factor.
The right question, Atwood said, was whether merger would help
the Reformed Church witness to Christ. The details about the future
should be left to God.[3]

The vote was announced in the *Church Herald* in April 1969.
Twenty-three classes voted for merger, and twenty-two against. This
was seven votes short of the thirty (two-thirds of the classes) needed
to approve the merger. Purists voted against merger in part because of
their loyalty to a relatively narrow vision of the Reformed Church as
a small, orthodox, separatist body. They questioned the orthodoxy of
the Southern Presbyterian Church, and they feared that the Reformed
Church would be swallowed up by the Presbyterians and eventually
by Rome. The moderates were also loyal to the Reformed Church, but
they wanted to see it survive and thrive, and they thought this could
be better accomplished in a merger. The conservatives in the middle
may not have been as skeptical about Presbyterian orthodoxy, but in
the end they voted against merger because the Reformed Church was a
family to them. They liked the sense of intimacy and connection they
experienced within the church, and they feared this would be lost if it
merged with the much larger denomination. For these reasons, then,
the conservatives voted with the purists against merger. Ironically, the
family ties they so appreciated were about to be tested.

In the same issue of the *Church Herald* that reported the results of
the merger vote, the Interchurch Committee announced that it would
recommend to the General Synod that the Reformed Church become
a full member of Consultation on Church Union (COCU).[4] Many

[1]   "To Unite or not To Unite," *CH*, Jan. 24, 1969, 10, 21-22.
[2]   "The Confessional Issues in Church Union," *CH*, Feb. 14, 1969, 12-13, 22-23.
[3]   Letter to the editor, *CH*, Feb. 21, 1969, 17, 23.
[4]   "Interchurch Committee Recommends R.C.A. Join COCU," April 4, 1969, 28-29.
       The Interchurch Committee's name was changed to the Commission on Christian
       Unity in 1976.

midwesterners were furious at what seemed to them to be yet another attempt to impose ecumenism. Gordon Girod, a pastor at the Seventh Reformed Church in Grand Rapids, wrote that the COCU proposal confirmed his fear that merger with the PCUS was merely the beginning of a long process of church union. He suggested that COCU was one of the major reasons for the defeat of the PCUS merger.

> Gentlemen, has it never occurred to you how much more the Reformed Church might accomplish if we had a leadership that led in the direction that our people want to go? You make many excuses for the lack of growth and impact in the Reformed Church: language, old methods and the like. A much more pressing reason is to be found in denominational leaders who are forever seeking to take our people where they refuse to go.[5]

A slim majority of classes had voted *for* merger, and yet Girod saw that as a mandate *against* ecumenical relationships.

Meanwhile, a number of eastern clergy charged that Midwestern parochialism limited their efforts to minister in a very diverse context. Lee Kester, a pastor in Oradell, New Jersey, announced the vote to his congregation on the back of a bulletin and observed that the Reformed Church in America was about to become the Reformed Sect in America. He suggested that divorce between the East and Midwest might be the best option, because this wound would not be easily healed.[6] Eastern ministers met informally several times to think and talk about their options for the future, particularly the possibility of the eastern churches aligning with the United Church of Christ or the Northern Presbyterian church.

Merger talks had consumed a great deal of time and energy for seven years. Tensions were high throughout the denomination and people were angry. The *Church Herald* attempted to redirect some of the anger into creative possibilities for the future. The editor invited readers to submit ideas for the future of the denomination. These various proposals illustrated the range of opinion in the Reformed Church.

Arie Brouwer, then the General Program Council's secretary for program, described two opposing views within the Reformed Church— one that said the church should save souls and the other that said the church should save society. It was difficult for the denomination to find middle ground or a compromise between them, in part because the

---

5   Letter to the editor, *CH*, May 2, 1969, 24.
6   A copy of this bulletin is in the PCUS merger papers in the General Synod Archives.

church was not a teeter-totter that could find a balance at the center. To overcome this apparent impasse, Brouwer encouraged the church to move toward a broader vision of mission that would help bring about the kingdom of God through both individual salvation and social transformation. He encouraged the church not to settle for a bland common statement but to seek out new ways to express the faith.[7]

Wesley Harmsen, a layperson from Brandon, Wisconsin, had little interest in new ways to express the faith but thought the Reformed Church should return to the old confessions. "If every member of our church would refresh his mind on the basic doctrines explained in the Heidelberg Catechism and the Canons of Dort and would hold these as the true understanding of Scripture, I would have no fear for our church....If we dare to witness to the doctrines we believe in, God will make us a blessing in the land."[8]

Moderate members believed that strict adherence to the Standards was part of the problem, not the solution. Carl Schroeder, Reformed Church minister for evangelism, observed that thinking pastors and laypeople were frustrated with what they saw as a complacent, ingrown quality in the denomination. "If there were more support for flexibility in our Reformed Church today, it would take much of the steam out of so-called liberal excesses."[9]

Some pastors were convinced that the two poles in the denomination had so little in common that division was the only solution. Ronald Brown, then serving in South Holland, Illinois, encouraged the Reformed Church to move away from mainstream ecumenical Protestantism, which he labeled faithless, modernistic, and not committed to scripture. Instead, Reformed churches should emphasize evangelism, Christian schools, the authority of scripture, and separation from the world. Brown saw little potential for compromise:

> I confess that I am no good for those who yearn for an ecumenical future. I, together with the chart which I have proposed, constitute a continuing drag upon the hopes of those who take the opposite view. And conversely, those who long for a deeper ecumenical involvement are a constant hindrance to the implementation of my chart for the future. Of course, I pray that the positions I have outlined above may, by the grace of God, triumph in the church.[10]

[7]   Guest editorial, "Beyond the Isms," *CH*, Jan. 31, 1969, 8-9. For a discussion of the growing emphasis on the kingdom of God in the RCA in the 1960s and beyond, see Heideman, *The Practice of Piety*, 211-63.

[8]   Letter to the editor, *CH*, Jan. 31, 1969, 17.

[9]   Letter to the editor, *CH*, March 14, 1969, 16.

[10]   "A Chart for the Future: One Pastor's Answer," *CH*, May 16, 1969, 10-11, 20-21.

Louis Benes suggested that a merger with the Christian Reformed Church was the next logical step, since it would restore the original unity of the two denominations. Randall Bosch, a pastor in New Jersey, noted sarcastically that such a merger would provide the ultimate enclave, a windmill in which Dutch people could find shelter from the world.[11] This merger may have seemed logical, but the RCA and CRC had grown further apart since their original separation, and reunion would have been neither simple nor obvious.

Norman Thomas, a pastor in Albany, New York, reminded the denomination that eastern clergy had preferred to merge with the Northern Presbyterians but compromised on the PCUS because it seemed more likely to be approved by the Midwest. That effort having failed, he wrote, many easterners thought that COCU offered the best step forward, because membership signaled that the Reformed Church was willing to cooperate with the wider Christian world. He hoped that, since the Midwest voted down the merger which the eastern churches wanted, midwestern delegates to the synod would in turn be gracious and vote in favor of COCU. Thomas knew critics labeled COCU "divisive," but he observed, "The cause of divisiveness lies not in an honest exploration with Christian brothers of the possibility of a united church, but in the tendency of many to view such an exploration with prejudiced distrust and unseemly fear."[12]

Robert Schuller, a pastor in California, made the most sweeping and unusual proposal. He encouraged the Reformed Church to re-form as an entirely new denomination called Christ's Church for America. It would be rooted in both the Reformed tradition and Norman Vincent Peale's positive thinking. This new denomination would not be burdened by bureaucracy, church politics, or negative thinking. It would appeal to the unchurched, encourage imaginative ministries, and downplay political debates in favor of direct involvement in society. It would welcome all who accepted Jesus as Lord and Savior. He suggested starting a walk-in-drive-in church in fifty, a hundred, and then two hundred of the most significant American cities. He believed God would provide the money as long as the idea was not defeated by impossibility thinking or the failure to pray big, believe big, think big, and plan big. Schuller proposed that when Norman Vincent Peale was elected president of General Synod in 1969, he should begin his

[11] Editorial, "Church Union—And Reunion," *CH*, May 30, 1969, 6-7; letter to the editor, June 27, 1969, 24-25.
[12] "The Future of the Reformed Church," *CH*, June 6, 1969, 13.

acceptance speech with "I have a dream" and then outline this vision of a new church, which would be inclusive yet very different from COCU.[13]

Clearly no consensus arose out of these suggestions. Harold Schut, past president of General Synod and chair of the General Synod Executive Committee, tried a more bureaucratic approach. He invited four ministers from each regional synod to meet in Chicago in April 1969 and asked them to discuss what each side needed from the other in order to stay together. The western ministers (from the synods of Michigan, Chicago, and the West) offered a purist agenda which showed no interest in compromise. They requested: (1) complete withdrawal from COCU; (2) complete separation from the National Council of Churches; (3) control of theological education; (4) control of the program and work of the denominational office in New York; and (5) full agreement of all clergy with the doctrines of the Reformed Church as the purists understood them.[14]

The eastern pastors (New York, Albany, and New Jersey synods) wanted the Reformed Church to place less emphasis on doctrinal uniformity and subscription and more emphasis on relationships, new ideas and approaches, and reaching out to the world. There was little if any common ground between the two groups and little possibility for compromise.

Harold Schut believed the denomination was at a critical crossroads. It appeared to him that the eastern clergy were willing to compromise, but the midwesterners had "a hardness which you could not move or get over or get around on the side of." Those who attended the Chicago meeting left thinking about a denominational separation, and someone had said explicitly that the Reformed Church could show the world how to disagree and divide in Christian friendship.[15]

The 1969 Meeting of the General Synod

Six weeks later the General Synod met on the campus of Rutgers University in New Brunswick, New Jersey. On the second evening, a Saturday night, a drama group from the Wyckoff Reformed Church performed T. S. Eliot's play, *Murder in the Cathedral*. They intended it as entertainment for the delegates, but the play may have been a bit more relevant than they anticipated. Although delegates did not resort to physical violence, they would see a great deal of political intrigue and

---

[13] "We Can Be Strong," *CH*, June 6, 1969, 15.
[14] Document located in the papers of Donner Atwood, General Synod Archives.
[15] Oral history interview with Harold Schut, January 18, 2000, Solon, Iowa.

maneuvering and hear many hurtful and angry words during the week the synod met.

Controversy began before the delegates arrived. On Thursday, June 5, the night before the synod began, James Forman and some colleagues from the Black Economic Development Conference[16] took possession of the Reformed Church offices at 475 Riverside Drive in New York. They simply moved in and announced that they would stay until they were allowed to speak at the synod. Established synod agenda items were tabled, and Forman was given the opportunity to address the synod on Friday night. He spoke at length, describing centuries of abuse of black people by white people and criticizing the complicity of many churches in such abuse. He presented a number of demands, based on the assumption that white churches controlled enormous financial resources and should share them. On Saturday morning, the synod appointed an ad hoc committee to draft a response to Forman.

The synod president, Ray Van Heukelom, gave a very different kind of speech on Saturday morning. He reported that the Reformed Church had been in limbo most of the year waiting for the decision on the PCUS merger. He regretted that he had not accomplished his goals for the year because he had spent his energies first in listening, and then "in an effort to interpret one section of the church to the other and to assure each section that it was loved by the whole church." He encouraged the synod to be positive and to celebrate the diversity of RCA churches. "Let us have done with the dishonest fiction that we are all alike in the Reformed Church. We aren't. Our history is different. Our problems are different. But let us alike give ourselves to Christ in obedience to his Word Written. What impressed us far more than our differences is the deep earnest devotion to mission we found everywhere."[17] Delegates, however, had little interest in celebrating anything, certainly not their diversity.

[16]   The Black Economic Development Conference was held in Detroit early in 1969. James Forman, director of international affairs for the Student Non-Violent Coordinating Committee, proposed a manifesto to the group that threatened sit-ins and seizures until religious bodies gave $500 million in reparations to various black projects including publishing, cable television, and a university. More than six hundred delegates were present, and the manifesto was approved 187-63. On May 4, Forman and six others appeared at Riverside Church in New York City and read their demands during the opening hymn. The senior minister led the choir and two-thirds of the worshipers out of the church, and Riverside later pledged financial support for disadvantaged people. Forman visited other denominations as well. "Religion in the News," *CH*, May 23, 1969, 2; "The Black Manifesto: Comments and Responses," May 30, 1969, 20-21; "Religion in the News," June 6, 1969, 2-3 (brief articles from the Religious News Service).

[17]   *Acts and Proceedings*, 1969, 317-18.

The synod spent much of Saturday discussing social issues. The report of the Christian Action Commission began by describing its own lengthy, honest, and respectful discussions of various issues. It did not anticipate full agreement from the synod, but it requested "reasoned consideration" and serious discussion of its proposals. The commission hoped that delegates would avoid labeling one another "Communist" and "fascist."[18]

The most controversial part of the Christian Action agenda occurred when five young men[19] tried to present their draft cards to the synod. In previous years, the synod had affirmed the principle of conscientious objection and questioned the morality of the draft. In light of these actions, it seemed logical to many people that the synod should support the men, and that giving the cards to the church was a better alternative than burning them. Others insisted that such action was illegal. The question of draft cards was referred to an ad hoc committee,[20] which offered a compromise recommendation that the young men be assured both ecclesiastical and legal counsel. An amendment from the floor of synod eliminated the legal counsel. This temporary committee also recommended the formation of a more permanent committee that would receive the draft cards and advise the draft resistors. The synod rejected this pastoral gesture by a vote of 109 in support of the recommendation and 123 opposed. The ad hoc committee included a statement that to carry or not carry a draft card was an individual's responsibility, but the synod approved an amendment from the floor that added the words, "but the church has a responsibility to share in whatever way it can in the agony which these individual decisions involve." Finally, there was a motion from the floor

---

[18] Ibid., 240-50. The commission was composed of eighteen people from all sections of the church and represented a range of theological perspectives. The commission made a recommendation that cautioned against a repressive law-and-order reaction against violence. It also recommended that denominational meetings use only hotels which offered equal employment and advancement to non-Caucasians. The synod approved these but denied a recommendation to request Congress to improve conditions for farm workers, particularly migrant grape pickers in California.

[19] Joseph Favale, John de Velder, Lewis Kain, Michael Moran, and Glenn Pontier. They had given their draft cards over to the Society of Inquiry at New Brunswick Theological Seminary, and the society asked the General Synod to take responsibility for them. The synod minutes are not consistent in naming the five. At times the list includes George Fitchett rather than Lewis Kain. Ibid., 249.

[20] This committee included Lester Kuyper, Vernon Kooy, Raymond Pontier, Herman Kregel, Joseph Favale, Glenn Pontier, and Arad Riggs. Ibid., 250.

that the synod accept the draft cards, but the synod said no.[21] The close vote, and the numerous amendments and motions from the floor, show that synod delegates were almost evenly split on the issue.

In the midst of the Christian Action Commission's report, another unusual event occurred. About thirty-five women with signs and banners marched through the synod protesting the Reformed Church's failure to ordain women. New Brunswick resident Edith Beardslee (wife of John Beardslee III, a professor at New Brunswick Seminary) spearheaded the organization of the march, in part out of frustration with the fact that women were encouraged to study at the seminaries but were not allowed to be ordained. The women also presented more than twelve hundred signatures on petitions asking for the approval of women's ordination.[22] The synod made no official response.

The vote on membership in COCU also occurred on Saturday afternoon. In addition to the recommendation from the Interchurch Relations Committee, two overtures requested full participation in COCU and two opposed it.[23] The Standing Committee on Overtures recommended full participation. But someone made a motion to postpone action indefinitely, and after a heated debate the synod voted 130 to 103 to postpone the vote. Some delegates protested the procedures immediately, and the president ruled that the vote would be taken again, without debate, on Monday.[24]

On Saturday night the synod met in plenary session after the production of *Murder in the Cathedral* to continue the discussion of ecumenical relationships. The committee[25] appointed in 1968 to study

---

[21] Ibid., 252. After the synod, twenty-five ministers and lay people formed an informal and unofficial ad hoc committee to receive the draft cards and support the men. Raymond Pontier, letter to the editor, *CH*, Aug. 22, 1969, 23. Pontier also wrote an article about the role of conscience in shaping the men's decisions, "Conscience and the Church," April 17, 1970, 11, 22-23. Glenn Pontier later served ten months in prison because he left the country while his draft status was under review. His father, Ray, pastor at the Allwood Reformed in Clifton, NJ, outspokenly supported his son, to the point that his relationship with the church soured and he resigned under pressure. In 1971 the synod voted to provide verbal support for Glenn Pontier but refused to designate the Ad Hoc Committee to Receive Draft Cards and Counsel Persons as an official RCA agency. *Acts and Proceedings*, 1971, 228-30. The Particular Synod of New Jersey had supported Pontier, urged the end of the war, and set up a legal defense fund.

[22] *Acts and Proceedings*, 1969, 250. Oral history interview with Carol Hageman, who also participated in the march.

[23] The Particular Synods of Albany and New Jersey requested full participation while the synods of Michigan and Chicago opposed it.

[24] Ibid., 137-39, 149-50, 153, 293-94.

[25] William Babinsky (chair), Louis Benes Jr., Raymond Brondyke, Frederic Dolfin, Albert Van Dyke.

membership in the National Council of Churches gave a very positive assessment of the council's educational work. In response to the criticism that the NCC made irresponsible and un-Christian political pronouncements, the committee reported that the council made controversial statements only after extensive study. These statements were not binding on member denominations. The committee concluded that the Reformed Church should stay in the National Council, because it would be extremely difficult to function in the twentieth century without cooperating with other churches. The committee did make two suggestions: first, that particular synods nominate NCC delegates (thereby assuring regional representation); second, that the assessment supporting the NCC be made an "asking," so that no church would be forced to support it.

Many delegates remained skeptical about the value of the National Council. The purists opposed to ecumenical entanglements may have seen the postponement of COCU deliberations earlier in the day as a victory for their side and a sign that the tide was moving against the NCC. But a motion to postpone the decision to remain in the council and a motion to recess both failed. The general secretary, Marion de Velder, asked for the floor and gave a lengthy speech in which he outlined his midwestern roots and the history of both his own and the denomination's involvement in ecumenism. He told the synod that if it chose to withdraw from the National Council, "I'll not have any interest in serving this church any longer." De Velder was a compelling presence and a passionate speaker, and his appeal probably influenced the outcome of the balloting. The synod voted to stay in the National Council and, somewhat surprisingly, rejected the proposal to make financial support for the councils an asking (voluntary) rather than an assessment (required).[26]

The debate over the National Council of Churches exacerbated the synod's tension. Midwestern delegates saw the vote to stay in the NCC as a generous compromise. Eastern delegates saw the very need to debate NCC membership as a sign of how insulated and provincial the church had become. The mood was not unlike that of a marriage gone bad. The two sides had little in common, holding completely opposite views on some of the most essential questions confronting the church. Members' perceptions of each other were equally distorted. Each side assumed the worst of the other, which was as deadly in a denomination

[26]   Ibid., 295-302.

as in a marriage. They did not trust each other or enjoy each other's company, and they could not talk to each other without difficulty.

On Monday, after the second vote on COCU had again resulted in postponement,[27] tensions were at their peak. Conservatives and purists refused to vote in favor of an ecumenical relationship that was very important to moderates. The two parts of the Reformed Church simply were not moving in the same direction. At that point, amid the anger and frustration, Harold Schut made the following motion:

> Fathers and Brethren: Whereas: 1. Discussion in the Reformed Church in America at many levels and at General Synod is revealing that division among us appears to be non-negotiable. 2. A separation of our denomination in anger is certainly not to the glory of God; 3. The continued existence of a particular denomination, especially one which is as fractured and fragmented as ours, is not necessarily to the glory of God; 4. The orderly dissolution of a denomination such as ours MAY BE to the glory of God; Therefore: Be is [*sic*] resolved that the General Synod of 1969 at this session direct the president of General Synod to appoint a joint committee of 24 with 12 representatives of the divergent views within the RCA to be assigned the task of drafting a plan for the orderly dissolution of the RCA to be reported to the General Synod of 1971.[28]

Thirty years after making this proposal, Schut reflected on the episode. He said that at the time he'd thought that, since the two sections of the church could not agree on the denomination's future, it would be better to separate with peace and dignity than to continue fighting. He said it was one of the hardest things he had done in his life.

The delegates were stunned. Fred Mold, a pastor in New Jersey, described it this way: "I can remember him [Schut] getting up and making his proposal with tears in his eyes, you know? It was a very emotional moment, and you know I remember him beginning about how he loved the church and saying, 'but it's obvious that we are moving in two different directions.'"

Carl Schroeder had served as a missionary in Taiwan and had recently been appointed minister of evangelism for the denomination. In an interview thirty-five years after this synod, he was almost in tears when he described the unfolding events. It was such a mess, he said.

---

[27]   The vote was very close, 133-126 in favor of postponement.
[28]   Ibid., 200-01.

There was so much sadness. Delegates wondered whether it would be worth the effort to put the church together again.[29]

John Nordstrom recalled that throughout the week there were a number of late-night gatherings of like-minded people to sort out strategy. "It was not a pleasant time. People were suspicious of one another. We were stubborn, frustrated, and not kind to our brothers, whether they were from the East or the West. There seemed little hope for reconciliation."[30]

Schut's proposal sparked a lengthy debate. Some delegates begged synod members not to divide the church. Others said the divisions were already so great that there was no other choice. In retrospect, the motion to dissolve was a brilliant strategy, because it called the whole church to account. Rather than resolving their differences by having one disaffected side or the other leave the denomination, the resolution suggested that the Reformed Church would cease to exist. One side would not force the other side to leave; instead, the whole church would decide that it could no longer be a church together. This made the delegates (and the entire denomination in the wake of the synod's decision) think about the Reformed Church's future in a far more complex and serious way. The proposal was sent to the Committee of Reference for further consideration.[31]

That night, Norman Vincent Peale, the recently elected president of General Synod,[32] moderated the synod's plenary session. Carl Schroeder recalled that Peale completely altered the mood. He told jokes, many of them about his lack of knowledge of Robert's Rules of Order. He disarmed the synod with his wit and candor, and he tried to conclude the meeting in such a way that the delegates would not go home angry.[33]

---

[29] Interview with Harold Schut. Oral history interview with Fred Mold, May 14, 2001, Manasquan, NJ. Informal conversation with Carl Schroeder.

[30] Personal correspondence with John Nordstrom. At the time of the synod, he had served an eastern church for several years but had recently moved to Second Reformed, Zeeland, Michigan. He still met with the easterners.

[31] Ibid., 200-01.

[32] Peale was elected vice-president in 1968 but was somewhat reluctant to assume the office of president. He had been embarrassed in print in late 1968 when he wrote that merger with the PCUS would keep the RCA out of COCU, and several leading Presbyterians said this was inaccurate. Peale had many other commitments and speaking engagements and he was already past seventy years old. Marion de Velder, Donner Atwood, and others convinced him to take the job. Peale was not the most active president, but he had a healing presence about him that was good for the denomination in a time of crisis.

[33] Conversation with Carl Schroeder.

Tuesday afternoon the ad hoc committee assigned to respond to the Black Manifesto brought a lengthy report to the floor. It began by acknowledging centuries of white complicity in slavery and racism. The report noted that the greatest progress in human history occurred in the time of greatest upheaval, and that the church was now in just such a time of upheaval "when we are being shaken to the very foundations of our life and our Christian faith." The report expressed appreciation for the ways that Forman had helped the Reformed Church better understand both the plight of black people and its own racist actions, in particular its ignorance and lack of attention to human relationships. Finally, the report offered twelve recommendations for change, including the development of a Black Council, a fund of $100,000 for that council to disperse as it saw fit, and measures to promote greater minority participation in decision-making structures.

Given the tension over race during the previous fifteen years and the tension generated at this synod, it is amazing that this document passed without a dissenting vote.[34] Perhaps this was a small sign that delegates could recognize the value of cooperation on a significant issue that transcended theological differences. *Christianity Today* reported that it was probably the most significant racial action of any church during the year.[35] Carol Hageman observed later in the summer at a meeting of the General Program Council Executive Committee that the wisdom and value of the action had not been fully recognized at the time because of all the controversy.[36]

The Committee of Reference responded to Schut's proposal Tuesday morning. It recommended appointing a "Committee of Eighteen" to study the issues and report to the synod in 1970. If this committee found no hope for reconciliation, a new committee would be appointed to work out the dissolution. The synod approved these steps.[37]

At the closing session, Norman Vincent Peale told the story of a judge who proposed tearing apart the wedding picture of a couple seeking a divorce. Peale said: "Can you imagine taking a pair of scissors and cutting down through the Reformed Church in America? Sure, we have differences; that's as it should be. So let's let the better elements of our natures take over—and not cut the picture apart."[38] Some people

---

34 Ibid., 98-105.
35 James Huffman, "After Bitter Debates, the Positive Thinker," *Christianity Today*, July 4, 1969, 36.
36 Minutes of GPC Executive Committee, July 17, 1969.
37 *Acts and Proceedings*, 1969, 200-04.
38 Huffman, "After Bitter Debates," 35.

agreed strongly with Peale. Others would have been happy to wield the metaphorical scissors and divide the denomination as quickly as possible. Either way, the synod was emotionally exhausting for those who attended. Leonard Kalkwarf said he was so tired when he returned home that he could have slept for days afterward.[39]

The synod may have ended on a slightly more positive note than it began, but some people thought the church would not survive. Harold Schut said he believed at the time that, "if the thing is going to come apart anyway, let's do it orderly like."[40] There were still many strong feelings. Easterners felt alienated, as if their church had been wholly taken over by a conservative power bloc. Many midwestern people could not figure out what all the anger was about and didn't understand how some parts of the church had become so radical. Both sides shared a deep sense of loss.

The Aftermath of the Synod of 1969

Following the synod, President Van Heukelom reported to *Church Herald* readers that delegates had set a moderate and safe course rather than an imaginative and bold one, because at the time it seemed to be the only way the two factions of the denomination could live and work together. The divided church had a long road toward unity.

> The actions of Synod indicate that the delegates were unwilling either to limit the range of activity of any servant of Christ or to compel anyone to go in a direction repugnant to him. We may be reaching that degree of maturity that permits diversity within unity. Unfortunately, we have not matured sufficiently to so appreciate those who differ as to give God thanks for them and their gifts. By the grace of God this too may come. It cannot come too soon.[41]

The shock of the motion to dissolve the denomination may have induced a brief era of good feeling, but the underlying differences continued to fester. Many people expressed their discontent with the denomination. Some midwestern purists maintained that Eastern ministers were all liberals in dying churches, and good riddance to them if they wanted to leave. Gordon Girod articulated this view in an article for the conservative Christian Reformed journal, *Torch and Trumpet*.

---

39   Oral history interview with Leonard Kalkwarf.
40   Oral history interview with Harold Schut.
41   Guest editorial, "The 1969 Synod," *CH*, July 25, 1969, 6.

Many in the Midwest would be happy to see the Eastern Liberals, along with their Midwestern counterparts, leave the denomination, but we want it to be done in that way. We want them to leave, not to disrupt or dissolve the denomination.... We find no fault with the doctrinal basis of the RCA. If, then, the Eastern Liberals cannot and will not live with the doctrinal standards of the RCA, let them withdraw from the RCA....We see no reason to enter into a conspiracy with them that would end in the dissolution of the RCA. This would imply that the RCA has no further reason to exist as a denomination. In the Midwest we can agree to no such thing. True, we want to remold the RCA to bring it into greater conformity with its doctrinal standards, but this does not mean that we are prepared to scuttle the ecclesiastical ship. To the contrary, we would be happy to take over the rudder and controls of the ecclesiastical ship, if those who are not satisfied with the Reformed Faith would simply depart and take their dissatisfaction with them.[42]

The Midland, Michigan, Reformed Church consistory was also willing to allow eastern churches to leave. It wrote, "Such a provision at this time would allow individual congregations to act according to their convictions and consciences on an issue crucial to their life, making the way clear for the continuing R.C.A. [*sic*] to act responsibly and unitedly without a resident party of dissent."[43]

Several purists expressed a willingness to reconcile the two factions of the church but insisted that it be on their terms. Tom Stark called the Reformed Church to theological unity, which he defined as obedience to the tenets of the denomination's Standards and the Constitution. In a letter to the editor, Stark noted that a minister from Schoharie Classis had said during the synod debate that he did not believe in the Virgin Birth. Stark also complained that a church in the Classis of Mid-Hudson had installed women as members of consistory. If the Reformed Church were to survive, he wrote, it could not tolerate defiance of its central tenets.[44]

Louis Branning, a pastor in Wyoming, Michigan, wanted the denomination to set limits on disagreement. He wrote,

many who are supposed to build believers up in the faith do not urge them to believe in an infallible Bible as Jesus Christ did....

---

42   "What about CRC-RCA Merger?" Oct. 1969, 4.
43   Paul Hostetter and Thomas Werkema for the consistory of the Reformed Church of Midland, Michigan, letter to the editor, *CH*, Sept. 5, 1969, 21.
44   Letter to the editor, *CH*, Dec. 5, 1969, 16.

Therefore, I contend that there is no unity in the Reformed Church in America because there is no unity in the biblical faith among its theological leaders....There is no unity in the Reformed Church in America because many classes have failed in their judging and passing upon ministerial candidates who are required to believe the biblical doctrines contained in our confessions.[45]

The consistory of the Alsip, Illinois, Reformed Church also stated its terms for reconciliation.

We insist, however, that all reconciliation be on evangelical terms of adherence to the Word of God and the Standards of the Reformed Faith. This simply means that we want this level of commitment, in sincerity and honesty on the part of the theological schools of the denomination, the boards and agencies of the church, and the ministers of the denomination....Further, it is our firm belief that real unity within the denomination will not become a reality until all relations are severed with the National and World Councils of Churches and the Consultation on Church Union.

They wrote that they did not wish to dissolve the denomination, but they would permit the malcontents to leave.[46]

A few members protested the response the synod had made to James Forman. They were angry that Forman had been given the podium to advocate revolution and demand reparations. One letter to the *Church Herald* called his demands "insane," and the writer added that she hoped Forman would receive nothing further.[47] For African-American Reformed Church members, though, Forman's action enabled the gathering of the Black Caucus, an informal network comprised of thirty-one delegates from throughout the church. They met in August 1969 and organized the Black Council.[48]

Two Native American Reformed Church members asked if they should adopt Forman's strategy in order to bring about a similar change in the way they were treated. The denomination had reduced funding for their churches and, with minimal consultation, closed the Children's Home in Winnebago, Nebraska. Although the Reformed Church claimed to encourage self-determination among minority

---

[45]   Letter to the editor, *CH*, Oct. 10, 1969, 17.
[46]   Arthur Scheid and Frank Shock, letter to the editor, *CH*, Sept. 26, 1969, 22.
[47]   Mrs. Nicholas Van Wingerden, July 26, 1969, 16.
[48]   "Black Caucus Organizes Black Council," *CH*, Sept. 5, 1969, 24.

groups in the denomination, many members of these groups thought it frequently demonstrated paternalism instead.[49]

Given the controversy from so many quarters, it was no wonder that many easterners believed there was little possibility for reconciliation. Most of the voices cited above represented the purist minority rather than the more mainstream conservative position within the Reformed Church, but the comments were certainly disheartening. They defined reconciliation as victory for the purists with the possibility of departure for the moderates.

Donald Bruggink, professor of church history at Western Seminary, offered a thoughtful analysis of the different historical and cultural roots of the two sections of the Reformed Church. The eastern churches were more ecumenical and diverse and the midwestern churches were more separatist and Dutch because of history and social context. That did not mean either expression of the faith was defective:

> It is not a matter of the East's being liberal and the West's being reactionary. It is a matter of fact that both sections of the church cling so tenaciously to their form of the Christian life because it is that particular form of Christian experience in which they have life in Christ....Neither part of the church is without fault, but neither part of the church is without Christ, and to keep this church of such varying experience together is to give some evidence of the success of Christ's reconciling love in our lives.[50]

The dissension in the Reformed Church was strong enough to elicit wider media interest in the Midwest. A Grand Rapids, Michigan, station televised a discussion between Charles Wissink, professor of Christian education at New Brunswick Seminary, and William Brownson, professor of preaching at Western Seminary, moderated by Reformed Church staff member Peter Paulsen. Wissink and Brownson reported that neither side felt heard, understood, or trusted by the other. Eastern members did not think the *Church Herald* represented their perspective accurately or provided an open forum for discussion by the whole church. Midwestern members thought that the East dismissed them as provincial and isolated, while they saw themselves as

---

[49] Gordon Beaver and Edward Cline, "Is a Show of 'Red Power' Next? Or...An Open Letter to the Reformed Church in America," *CH*, Dec. 26, 1969, 12.

[50] "Differences within Our Church," *CH*, Jan. 16, 1970, 12-13. A more extensive analysis can be found in Bruggink, "Sociological Separation and Unity," *Reformed Review*, Winter 1970 (23:2), 106-21. This issue was devoted to the topic of reconciliation in the RCA.

loyal to a historic faith. Brownson wanted discussion to occur without threat of schism, but Wissink said Eastern members were committed to the denomination but not to peace at any price, so they could not unconditionally promise to stay. Brownson replied, "I think it almost needs to be demonstrated that the church has become apostate, has completely abandoned the historic Christian faith, before we can justify breaking off from it." He believed the Reformed Church's problems would not be solved by dissolving.[51]

At the end of this rather tumultuous year, most Reformed Church members fell into one of three groups. On the theological and social right were the purists, who insisted that their church had to affirm a literal view of scripture and a sixteenth-century interpretation of the Standards. They opposed ecumenism and generally held conservative views on social and moral issues. They thought the answer was that everyone should believe as they did, and those not willing to do so should leave the denomination. On the other end of the spectrum was a group of mostly eastern, moderate members, who believed that the Reformed Church should be much more flexible and open to change. They did not believe there was only one way to think, and they resented efforts to impose a narrow identity upon the church. They believed that the future for the denomination depended upon relationships. If people got to know each other, they would become more tolerant of different perspectives.

Between these two poles was a large group of conservatives who did not necessarily expect everyone to believe or act as they did. They did not want to eliminate all dissent, but they were concerned lest dissent undermine the integrity and continuity of the Reformed Church.[52] This large middle group would play a significant role in deciding whether or not the church would stay together.

During the year following this divisive synod meeting, one process and two events helped Reformed Church members discuss some of their conflicts and envision a possible way forward.

[51]   Peter Paulsen, William Brownson, Charles Wissink, "For Understanding through Dialogue," CH, Oct. 24, 1969, 12-14, 24-25.
[52]   In their analysis of the various groups in the RCA, Don Luidens and Roger Nemeth labeled this middle group the "Loyalists" and described their significant contributions to the RCA at several points in its recent history. Donald A. Luidens and Roger J. Nemeth, "'Public' and 'Private' Protestantism Reconsidered: Introducing the 'Loyalists,'" Journal for the Scientific Study of Religion 26, no. 4 (December 1987): 450-64.

The Committee of Eighteen

In the fall of 1969 the General Synod Executive Committee appointed the Committee of Eighteen to decide whether reconciliation was possible or if the Reformed Church in America needed to move toward dissolution. Each particular synod had been asked to nominate one minister and one male and one female layperson to serve on the committee.[53] The first few meetings were difficult, in part because the denomination's differences and tensions were reflected in the committee. There were power struggles and disagreements over process. Donner Atwood complained that some of the laypeople did not understand why they were meeting or what the issues were. Some of the more conservative members identified the problem simply as the reluctance of the eastern ministers to agree to all points of the Standards. The chair of the committee, Elko Stapert, thought (both at the beginning and at the end of the process) that the denomination simply needed to uphold uniformly orthodox beliefs. Donner Atwood was much more interested in the committee's process and whether it could help people listen to and understand each other.[54]

As the meetings unfolded, the committee identified five points of tension, all rooted in historical differences: *theology*—particularly the interpretation of scripture and the relationship between scripture and the Standards; *polity*—the distribution of power and authority; the roles of women, laypeople, and youth; and the location of headquarters; *ecumenism*—the relationships with other churches and with the National and World Councils of Churches; *mission*—the communication patterns in the *Church Herald* and the priority of evangelism or social action; and finally *attitudes*—suspicion of people and programs, distrust of leadership, and lack of courtesy.[55]

In an effort to provide a common worship experience, the committee formulated a litany for all churches to use on Pentecost

[53]   Albany: the Rev. Robert Hoeksema, John Hintermeier, Mrs. Rudolph Snyder. Chicago: the Rev. Frederic Dolfin, Ralph De Kock, Chester Evers. Michigan: the Rev. Raymond Rewerts, Elko Stapert, Richard Machiele. New Jersey: the Rev. Donner Atwood, Merhl Shoemaker, Mrs. Fred Van Doren. New York: the Rev. Franklin Hinkamp, Robert Williams, Ruth Dickson. West: the Rev. William Miller, Willard June, Henrietta Van Wyhe. (The synods of Michigan and Chicago appointed three males.) "A Plan for Understanding," *CH*, Aug. 8, 1969, 19.

[54]   For correspondence among Stapert, Atwood, and other members of the committee, see the papers in the General Synod Archives. Donner Atwood deposited a number of letters and other documents about the Committee of Eighteen in the Archives. His frustration with the interpersonal dynamics of the committee is very evident in these papers.

[55]   *Acts and Proceedings*, 1970, 188-92.

Sunday (May 17, 1970). The committee hoped that the litany would emphasize denominational unity, but it employed very traditional, conservative language to affirm belief in scripture, the Standards, and the atonement. It confessed that doubt and disobedience had contributed to the current tensions. It called the church to bring "men" to conversion.[56] Some members found the tone heavy handed, even if they agreed with its sentiments.

In addition to this liturgical effort, the committee presented specific recommendations to the 1970 General Synod, which it hoped would create "an atmosphere of understanding in which reconciliation may be accomplished." The first recommendation suggested that the entire Reformed Church adopt the Goals for Mission of the General Program Council (the first of which was evangelism), because a shared effort to implement the goals would encourage reconciliation. As in the 1950s, a common mission appeared to offer a way to transcend theological disagreements.

The committee also recommended that the denomination develop a new statement of faith, cooperate with many different groups to achieve mission goals, and offer instruction for laypeople in leadership and evangelism. It made several suggestions designed to foster more trusting relationships, such as pulpit exchanges and interactions among youth groups and church members. It asked that people of differing views, especially delegates to the General Synod, be given opportunities to converse without needing to debate an issue. Finally, it suggested that regionalization was the best way for the denomination to do much of its work, which meant that each area could make its own decisions about ecumenical relationships, evangelism, and mission. The Synod of 1970 adopted all these recommendations.

The Committee of Eighteen was not a resounding success. The personalities on the committee were so strong and resistance so high that people remained somewhat suspicious of each other throughout the process. There were no heartwarming stories of group bonding. But the gritty process of committee members trying to get to know each other, develop trust, and build relationships may have been a realistic reflection of the larger situation. The denomination as a whole was not going to gather around the campfire, link arms, and sing "Kum-bay-ah." The work of reconciliation would be painful and time consuming. In the end, the denomination stayed together not because the different groups felt deep love and connection with each other, but because they

---

56   "A Day of Commitment," *CH*, May 15, 1970, 6.

wanted to keep the family together. The Committee of Eighteen served as a model for a process that would be long and difficult. Despite the personality conflicts and theological differences among committee members, they believed reconciliation was possible, both for them as a committee and for the denomination as a whole.[57]

The Congress on Evangelism

One significant event that contributed to reconciliation was more accidental than intentional. In September of 1969 about a hundred Reformed Church members attended an interdenominational Congress on Evangelism in Minneapolis, Minnesota. The organizers of the congress defined evangelism as concern for both souls and society, and the program offered a diverse set of speakers and practical workshops.[58] This was the first time a significant number of Reformed Church members had come together since the General Synod, and the recent upheaval was still fresh on their minds. Carl Schroeder, the recently appointed secretary for evangelism, attended the meeting and was surprised at the level of hurt and anger still present. He decided to gather the Reformed people together, tell his own story, invite them to express their anger and sadness, and then pray together. Many participants believed the congress in general, and this evening in particular, provided significant healing, in part because their stereotypes were challenged. Midwestern clergy found that eastern clergy did believe in evangelism, and eastern clergy found that midwestern clergy were not completely opposed to social action.[59]

Herman Luben was an eastern pastor and enthusiastic supporter of merger with the Presbyterians. When that effort failed, he was so frustrated and angry that he hoped the Reformed Church would dissolve and that the eastern churches would join the United Church of Christ or the Northern Presbyterians. He wrote, "Sometimes the feeling of being boxed in, of not being free to go with Christ into his new tomorrow, is so oppressive that almost any alternative looks good." Luben experienced a change of heart at the RCA gathering at the congress. He reflected, "We left that room with a new realization that wherever we were from, geographically or theologically, we were all broken and hurting." In this face-to-face setting, participants had

---

[57]   *Acts and Proceedings*, 1970, 188-92.
[58]   Louis Benes, editorial, "Much is Given—Much Is Required," *CH*, Sept. 26, 1969, 6-7. Organizers were connected with the Lausanne Movement, which organized a number of similar events throughout the world.
[59]   Conversation with Carl Schroeder.

spoken honestly and gotten to know the person behind the position. The experience convinced Luben that the Reformed Church could not be easily divided. But he was equally convinced that the path to reconciliation could not be based on doctrinal uniformity. "When we want to investigate one another's orthodoxy, we cease being brothers; we then become detectives and the hunted." Those who talked so openly in Minneapolis, he thought, became brothers.[60]

Carl Schroeder later wrote about the aftermath of the Synod of 1969 that it had been frightening to discover the deep gulf between Reformed Church members. Some people had ignored or belittled their opponents; others had tried to legislate them out of power. He encouraged people to be honest, but he realized that honesty required trust, which was in short supply. "If we believe that to expose our real selves will result in more hurt than healing, the cause is already lost."[61] In part because of Schroeder's leadership and honesty, trust began to be rebuilt at the Congress of Evangelism. The positive movement continued at the third event, the denominationally sponsored Festival of Evangelism.

The Festival of Evangelism

Denominational staff members had discussed the possibility of a church-wide festival in 1968, and after the Synod of 1969, they believed it was even more important to offer the church a venue for constructive dialogue. The Congress on Evangelism demonstrated that a mass gathering could be meaningful, if it provided a balance between speakers and small groups.[62] Consequently, Reformed Church staff members decided to develop an event that would give the church a chance to celebrate.

Donald Van Hoeven, a chaplain at Western Michigan University, served as chair of the planning committee for this gathering, called a Festival of Evangelism. The festival was held April 1-4, 1970, at Cobo Hall in Detroit, with fifteen hundred people registered for the full program and five hundred people for part of it. Detroit was selected as the site because it was a prominent urban area with a long-standing Reformed Church presence, and because it was located midway between the East and the Midwest. A banner on the front of the podium captured the wistful, yet hopeful theme of the gathering: "Do a new

---

60   Guest editorial, "Pilgrimage from Chicago to Minneapolis to..." *CH*, Oct. 31, 1969, 6-7.
61   "Some Thoughts on Reconciliation," *CH*, Nov. 14, 1969, 11.
62   Isaac Rottenberg, "A Festival of Evangelism: What, Why, When, Where?" *CH*, Feb. 6, 1970, 7, 20-21.

thing among us, Lord." The festival was oriented to young people and emphasized the arts and contemporary music. Along with a number of contemporary bands and vocal groups, the Hope College Chapel Choir provided traditional music.

A diverse group of speakers addressed the audience, mirroring the diversity of theological and experiential perspectives in the Reformed Church. John Anderson was the executive secretary of the Board of National Missions of the Presbyterian Church in the U.S. Leighton Ford served with the Billy Graham Evangelistic Association. Wyatt T. Walker was pastor of the Canaan Baptist Church of New York City and worked with the Southern Christian Leadership Conference. Tom Skinner was an evangelist. Howard Hageman was a Reformed Church pastor in Newark.

One of the most effective strategies of the festival was the use of assigned small groups that met throughout the four days. The composition of the small groups was intentionally diverse. As group members talked, they discovered that the people from other regions were neither heretics nor reactionaries. Deep relationships were built in these groups, in part because there were no votes or theological debates. The small-group format encouraged talking about faith and feelings, a practice which was atypical for many staid Dutch Reformed folk. At the final Communion service, each group received its own bread and cup, and members of the small groups served each other. Once again, this was a new experience for many of the participants, and this collective act of Communion seemed to aid the healing process. Benes reported that "God was near, the Holy Spirit was present, and many shed tears freely and openly."[63]

The festival was not without moments of drama and conflict. William Mason, an African American minister of education at the New Lots Reformed Church in Brooklyn, responded to the address by Wyatt T. Walker with a list of examples of racism within the Reformed Church. Mason claimed that the denomination did not actively welcome black people as church members, ministers, or college students. Black congregations that needed financial support were treated paternalistically, as mission churches rather than as equals. Black people had little voice in decision-making bodies. Mason noted that the first speaker had referred to the church as Christ's lily white bride, an image which he found offensive and unacceptable. Mason concluded his critique with this pointed request: "I ask not only for the

---

[63]   Editorial, "The Festival of Evangelism," *CH*, April 24, 1970, 6-7, 21.

privilege of loving you. I ask you to accept your full obligation of loving me, and leading my people to full liberation."[64]

One memorable event occurred after Tom Skinner described the poverty, despair, and violence he had experienced growing up in Harlem.[65] A number of young adult participants marched to the front of the auditorium carrying a large cross as a symbol of the many injustices meted out to racial minorities. They identified various social evils by saying, "I crucify race prejudice, I crucify a society church, I crucify indifference." The students then marched through the streets of Detroit carrying the cross, and a majority of the delegates followed. The action was a vivid example of the theme of putting one's faith into action. Faith became something to do, not just something to debate. Reformed Church members could engage in common action even if they lacked identical beliefs.

The festival succeeded in part because it attracted people of varied ages and perspectives. The planners designed a creative and effective process that was sensitive to group dynamics. Harold Schut thought the Reformed Church was ready to celebrate something after so many years of controversy. Louis Benes wrote, "There was a pervading enthusiasm, the thrill of seeing old friends and making new ones, a serious concern with how the Christian life really ought to be expressed, and a desire to come to grips with tensions, problems, and realities, in one's own life and in church and society." There were no votes, no decisions, and no debates. For four days, relationships were more important than theological precision. The festival emphasized personal religion, emotion, relationships, bonding, community, small groups, and the influence of the youth movement. All these factors proved extremely influential in the next decade of the life of the Reformed Church in America.[66]

The 1970 Meeting of the General Synod

The Synod of 1970 began at Hope College with considerably less drama than had the previous synod in New Brunswick. The Committee of Eighteen, the Congress on Evangelism, and the Festival of Evangelism had brought some unity and peace to the Reformed Church, and most people were willing to try to keep the denomination together. However,

---

[64]   William Mason, "For the Liberation of the Black Man," *CH*, May 1, 1970, 14.

[65]   Tom Skinner, "Evangelism: The Response of the Church," *CH*, April 24, 1970, 12-16.

[66]   Interview with Harold Schut; editorial, "The Festival of Evangelism," *CH*, April 24, 1970, 6-7, 21. For a more detailed description of the festival, see Hoff, *Structures for Mission*, 163-67.

the synod still faced a number of controversial issues related to social action and ecumenism.

The Vietnam War evoked heated discussion on several occasions. Delegates approved a Christian Action Commission recommendation calling for an end to the war. It was less sympathetic to a request from the Ad Hoc Committee of Reformed Church Clergy and Laity to Receive Draft Cards and Counsel Young Persons. The committee was holding draft cards from a half dozen Reformed Church students, and it asked the synod to receive the cards. The proposal was soundly defeated.[67] After the vote, a small contingent of delegates and observers marched out of Dimnent Chapel and pitched tents in the middle of the campus's Pine Grove. There the group held an impromptu "synod in exile" for three days, deliberating the issues which appeared before the synod.[68]

The Vietnam War also played a role in the perennial debate about membership in the councils of churches. Six overtures in 1970 asked the Reformed Church to withdraw from the councils. Two of these disapproved of the NCC's criticism of the Vietnam War. Zeeland Classis said the NCC statements did not reflect its members' opinions. Cascades Classis complained that many of the National Council's pronouncements, particularly those dealing with the Vietnam War, called for revolution rather than conversion, demonstrated "a soft attitude toward atheistic communism," and leaned toward a "liberal world-church along side of a socialistic world government." The World Council received even harsher criticism. West Sioux Classis insisted that the Reformed Church could not join hands with "delegates from Communist bloc countries who are seeking to destroy the church of Christ through the World Council of Churches."[69] Purist members thought the councils were little more than vehicles for Communist infiltration.

The Overtures Committee noted that the synod had probably spent more time discussing the councils than any other topic in the past decade but had always decided to continue the denomination's membership. The committee recommended that since these overtures did not present any new facts, the synod should declare a moratorium on debate about the NCC and WCC and save its time and energy for other issues. The committee also recommended that support for the

---

[67] *Acts and Proceedings*, 1970, 214-18, 220-21. The Ad Hoc Committee was formed after the synod meeting in 1969. The vote on the proposal to receive the draft cards was 50 in favor of receiving them, 190 against, and 15 abstentions.

[68] Conversation with Donald Luidens.

[69] *Acts and Proceedings*, 1970, 91-95.

councils should be voluntary rather than part of a congregation's assessment, so that members would not be forced to pay for something they opposed. The synod approved both proposals. In these votes on the councils, some conservatives voted with the moderates. They may not have agreed with everything the councils said or did, but they saw some value in ecumenical relationships and they were not willing to accede to the purist desire to separate the Reformed Church from all entanglements.[70]

The final controversial issue discussed by the 1970 General Synod was a plan for regional ecumenism. As they had said frequently during the discussion of the PCUS merger, the eastern churches wanted to be part of a larger body. When the Particular Synod of New Jersey met in May 1969 (about a month after the defeat of the merger), its delegates voted to ask the United Presbyterian Church/USA (Northern Presbyterians) to receive the particular synod as a Union Synod. The relationship would not be a full-scale merger, but it would allow cooperative work in church planting, Christian education, and youth camps. Administration would be united at the regional level, but classes would remain distinct from presbyteries and congregations would not merge.[71]

The proposal evoked considerable resistance. Several people protested that the particular synod had no right to form a union synod. There was a great deal of debate on the floor of the General Synod in 1970, but, in the end, the particular synod was allowed to proceed with conversations about the plan.[72] During the next year, some members of the New Jersey synod complained that they were being coerced into a relationship they did not want. Even the Particular Synod of Michigan weighed in on the debate. It submitted an overture asking the General Synod to prohibit union synods in order to "discourage division in our denomination." The synod took no action on this and adopted the Particular Synod of New Jersey's Plan of Union. Before it could be implemented, however, the Presbyterian Church restructured and enlarged its regional synods. The regional Presbyterian synod encompassing New Jersey was no longer comparable in size to the Reformed particular synod, and the union could not occur.[73]

[70] Ibid., 107-08.
[71] "Jersey Presbyterian and Reformed Churches Form United Synod," CH, May 29, 1970, 22.
[72] Acts and Proceedings, 1970, 90, 100-01, 116-24.
[73] Louis Benes, "The 165th General Synod: Actions and Reports," CH, July 2, 1971, 4-14; Acts and Proceedings, 1971, 94-96, 107, 110, 112.

This move toward regional decision making was a significant shift in the life of the Reformed Church. Allowing the regions more freedom helped move the denomination beyond its impasse, but it also sparked other problems. For example, Arnold van Lummel, a pastor in New Jersey, voted for voluntary support of the National Council of Churches in 1970 because he wanted to be conciliatory to those who opposed it. After further reflection, he changed his mind and wrote: "I favor reconciliation. A togetherness based on an accelerating voluntarism, however, can lead to fragmentation by installment. Voluntarism threatens to open a Pandora's Box of troubles more menacing to the peace and harmony of the denomination than the condition it seeks to correct."[74] He could see no valid reason not to belong to the council and believed that those opposed to it should not be able to determine denominational policy. People claimed their consciences would not permit them to support it, but he hoped that love for the Reformed Church would supersede conscience about the NCC.

The debate about the New Jersey Union Synod also demonstrated that those who wanted freedom for themselves were not always willing to extend it to others. Several classes in the Midwest had insisted on the right to leave the denomination with their property if the PCUS merger was approved, but they did not want to give the Particular Synod of New Jersey the freedom to enter into a regional cooperative agreement that seemed beneficial for its churches. Some purists and conservatives resented any disruption or division which might be imposed on them, yet they were willing to disrupt the plans and preferences of other parts of the denomination in the name of peace and unity.

Pandora's Box had indeed been opened, and voluntarism and regionalism became a significant part of Reformed Church identity. Still,

[74] Arnold van Lummel, guest editorial, "National Council of Churches and Assessments," *CH*, Aug. 28, 1970, 6-7. In 1971 the synod dealt with multiple overtures both supporting and opposing assessments for the councils. Clearly, the synod was ambivalent, as it voted 125-116 to restore the assessment for the World Council, but 127-117 against the assessment for the National Council. In 1972, classes complained about the WCC, insisting that churches forced to give to an agency they opposed would refuse to support other benevolences as well. The overtures claimed that the relationship with the councils created dissension within the denomination, and churches that disagreed should not be compelled to support them. For these purists, independence and freedom of choice were more important than the denomination's decision. Still, the WCC assessment was retained. In 1972 the synod voted to restore the assessment for the NCC. In the mid-1970s, perhaps weary of the battle, the RCA stopped assessing for the councils and used interest income and special gifts to pay for membership. *Acts and Proceedings*, 1971, 100; Benes, "The 165th General Synod," 4-14; *Acts and Proceedings*, 1972, 84-86.

in 1970 the Reformed Church chose to continue as one denomination. A number of factors contributed to that decision.

The first factor was the denomination's willingness to face the depth of the conflict. In this regard, the Reformed Church was indebted to pastors such as Harold Schut, Donner Atwood, Marion de Velder, and many others who did not ignore tension or pretend it did not exist or try to make it disappear. Several years after the Synod of 1969, Harold Schut received a note from a Nebraskan who had been a delegate. The man recalled that in the heated discussion that followed Schut's motion to dissolve the denomination, he had denounced Harold as arrogant and a fool. Now the man apologized and wrote, "I really think you were a prophet." John Nordstrom also spoke highly of Schut's leadership. "In retrospect, if ever there was a moment when the Holy Spirit addressed the RCA—not just the Synod of 1969, but the whole church—it was in Harold's motion. And now as I look back it is clear that from that moment the church was going to address the issues that faced it in a different way."[75] These leaders were deeply committed to the Reformed Church as a family, but they recognized that conflict was an unavoidable aspect of family life and believed it needed to be addressed honestly and openly.

The second factor that kept the family together was the loyalty of its members and clergy. Eastern ministers were angry and disillusioned in 1969. Their hopes for a more ecumenical future had been dashed, and they thought the denomination was moving in a direction inconsistent with its history and identity. Still, their loyalty proved stronger than their anger, and they chose to remain. Carl Schroeder was disappointed by the failure of the RCA-PCUS merger and saw little future for the Reformed Church as a separate denomination. He thought seriously about whether he wanted to stay in the RCA, and he finally decided that "who I was, where I came from, who nurtured me, who paid for my education, who paid my salary...it was the people I was so upset with, and I could not just pick up and leave."[76] In the end, his loyalty to the whole Reformed Church transcended his anger with some of its members and decisions.

Third, when Reformed Church members talked honestly together they found many points of agreement and shared experience. Although they did not agree on the details, East and Midwest shared a history, a

---

[75]   Interview with Harold Schut. Personal correspondence with John Nordstrom.

[76]   Interview with Carl Schroeder. During twelve years as a missionary in Taiwan, he had experienced a high level of ecumenical cooperation.

theological perspective, and a commitment to scripture. They felt like family.

Fourth, when they began to talk about evangelism and outreach and making a difference in the world, Reformed Church members found that they had a common purpose and that they needed each other. At festivals and in similar settings, they realized that when they engaged in faithful activities, their ideological difficulties became less urgent and divisive.

Finally, the Reformed Church made judicious use of avoidance as a way to manage conflict. As noted above, some people confronted head-on the significant differences that divided them. But many other issues were neither addressed nor resolved and perhaps could not have been. No amount of conversation or shared Communion services would create complete agreement about the morality of the Vietnam War or the validity of women's ordination. The church had to learn to live with significant disagreements. Some members developed a grudging tolerance of different perspectives. But unresolved issues such as ecumenism, biblical interpretation, and the role of women have continued to cause conflict.

At the time of his retirement in 1977, Marion de Velder looked back at this difficult time in the church's history. He recalled that one of his most meaningful experiences as general secretary occurred in the spring of 1970 when he traveled around the Reformed Church and met in seventy-six small groups with more than thirty-four hundred church leaders. Each group spent two or three hours discussing current denominational issues and the relationships of the group's members to other Reformed Church people. De Velder concluded, "I don't hear anybody saying today [1977] that the Reformed Church cannot live together as one family. I believe we have very important differences, and that these will persist as long as we are a group of diverse peoples who have come from many cultural backgrounds and geographical areas. We have learned to live together in that context.[77]

What kind of church would the Reformed Church in America be? It would be one church, not two, but it would have to give up the cozy notion that family meant everyone thought and looked the same. It would have to learn to live with conflict and diversity rather than expect uniformity.

---

[77] John Stapert and Marion de Velder, "Sixteen Years of Creative Struggle," *CH*, June 10, 1977, 6-8.

CHAPTER 6

1970-1983: One Church or Many?

At the 1970 General Synod, the two wings of the Reformed Church in America chose to stay together despite the painful institutional crisis of the previous year. Reformed Church members had decided that their connections were stronger than their conflicts and that they should continue as one church. Once the immediate crisis was resolved, the next task was to find ways to enable people with serious disagreements to work together productively. One popular strategy permitted different sections of the church to make their own choices and to continue their own regional patterns, rather than force every decision to a vote. Herman Luben, a pastor in Utica, New York, believed that a significant shift had occurred and that in the future the denomination would be more open and flexible. He wrote:

> The synod of 1970 ushered us into a new way of life. No longer will we insist on uniformity in the denomination....We're embracing a diversity we formerly frowned on. One hopes that we are not just being tolerant of one another, but affirming that our common discipleship to Jesus Christ may be leading us into different modes

and strategies of service. Hopefully, we'll affirm one another and celebrate each other's discipleship as authentically directed by the Holy Spirit.[1]

The strategy was successful in the short-term, but over the next decade it led to significant fragmentation and loss of identity. In 1970 some Reformed Church members felt such strong loyalty to the denomination that they were willing to fight to preserve its purity, identity, and integrity. By 1983, an increasing number of members would react to denominational statements or conflicts with a resounding, "Who cares?"

There were three trends in American religious life during the 1970s that also affected the Reformed Church. The first was a move from social activism toward inner spirituality. During the late 1960s, young adults had protested against the Vietnam War, racial injustice, poverty, and authority in general. In the 1970s, especially after the war ended, Americans seemed to grow weary of protesting. Many turned inward in a quest for personal growth and emotional nurture. This shift also occurred in religious life, and the 1960s' interest in social issues faded for a time in favor of individual spirituality.[2]

The second trend in American religious life was the loss of members in mainline denominations during the 1970s. The Reformed Church dropped from 233,000 confirmed members at its peak in 1967 to 214,000 in 1982. Other denominations showed similar losses. Some members may have left the mainline and joined more independent churches, but most of the membership decline occurred because people did not join. Many congregations continued to do things the same way they had always done them, but the culture had shifted.[3] Some young adults (baby boomers) found these congregations boring and irrelevant.

---

[1]   Guest editorial, "How to Be Different and Enjoy It," *CH*, July 17, 1970, 6-7.

[2]   Bruce Schulman, *The Seventies: The Great Shift in American Culture, Society and Politics* (Cambridge: Da Capo, 2002). In 1973, the Religion Newswriters Association identified the move from social activism toward more personal religion as the second most important religious story of the year. Religion News Service article, no title, *CH*, Jan. 11, 1974, 4. The top story was dissension in the Lutheran Church-Missouri Synod.

[3]   For studies of mainline decline and baby boomer spirituality see Dean Hoge, Benton Johnson, and Donald Luidens, *Vanishing Boundaries: The Religion of Mainline Protestant Baby Boomers* (Louisville: Westminster/John Knox, 1994); Jackson Carroll and Wade Clark Roof, *Beyond Establishment: Protestant Identity in an Post-Protestant Age* (Louisville: Westminster/John Knox, 1993); Wade Clark Roof, *American Mainline Religion: Its Changing Shape and Future* (Louisville: Westminster/John Knox, 1987); Wade Clark Roof, *A Generation of Seekers: The Spiritual Journeys of the Baby Boom Generation* (San Francisco: HarperSanFrancisco, 1993).

Young adults in the Reformed Church offered similar critiques of their congregations. In 1969 the *Church Herald* conducted a survey of Reformed Church college students attending the three denominational colleges (Hope, Central, and Northwestern), along with Western Michigan University, Michigan State, and the University of Michigan. The results were not encouraging for the church's future. Students reported that their churches did not take them seriously or ask for their opinions but instead ignored them. Churches resisted change and new ideas, the students said. Churches did not answer the questions students were asking or prepare them to live in the world. Instead, the churches portrayed the world as a dangerous place that should be avoided. Finally, the students saw little love or compassion in their congregations, especially for people who thought or acted differently from the norm.[4]

John Gould, a member of the Plainview Community Church in New York and president of the Reformed Church's Youth Council, offered a blistering analysis of traditional religious practice:

> The church is a glittering example of super-structure. We are led by the hand in worshiping God, repeating meaningless prayers, reading ancient responsive readings, singing strange old hymns, and generally following a strict method and format....the church has become a giant institution concerned primarily with physical problems and methods of operation.[5]

The generation gap was widened further when young people who tried to integrate their faith with contemporary culture were criticized. Paul Doring, from Daytona Beach, Florida, wrote that he was astonished to see a Christian rock group pictured in the *Church Herald*. He wondered "whether the kind of young people who would prefer rock and roll to the traditional hymns of the Christian church are likely to be won as converts to Christ on any sort of permanent basis."[6]

The third trend was that, in addition to losing members in the 1970s, many churches feared that they were losing influence in society. Religious values may have once shaped morality and values, but it seemed that fewer people listened to religion or took its advice. This was poignantly expressed by the editor of the *Church Herald* when he asked:

---

[4]   Karen McFall, "The Church's Forgotten People," *CH*, Oct. 17. 1969, 12-13, 20-22.
[5]   John Gould, et. al., "Youth Speaks Out," *CH*, Oct. 2, 1970, 8.
[6]   Letter to the editor, *CH*, May 16, 1969, 17.

Is there not a vital correlation between the virility of our faith and our obedience to the truth on the one hand, and the moral and social and economic condition of our society on the other? Were we not meant to be a salt and a leaven in it? What has happened? Where has all the power gone? Time was when the church was a force to be reckoned with; when it had an impact on society, in education, communications, morals, and politics. And that was when she was poorer, had smaller numbers, and was less sophisticated. Now that same church is largely ignored, or merely tolerated. Where has all the power gone?

This was a profound and essential question, but Benes provided a rather simplistic answer. The church had lost influence, he said, because individuals no longer lived strong Christian lives. They did not spend time with God. They watched too much television. They did not demonstrate quality Christian living.[7] Benes and others repeatedly called the church to go back to its old way, to restore the evening service and the midweek prayer meeting and emphasize conservative doctrine and piety. These practices might restore the church's influence in the world. Ironically, at the very time that young people complained about too many constraints, Benes assumed that the church had lost its young members because it had been too lenient, too reluctant to take a stand, and too relaxed about its traditions.

Moderates in the Reformed Church and others parts of the Christian tradition also bemoaned the loss of power and influence but offered a very different diagnosis and prescription. They said the church had lost power because it had been fixated on minor moral issues like movies and dancing and failed to address the important questions of justice and human welfare. Moderates suggested that the church could regain its influence if it became more involved in social issues, especially those that young people cared about. If the church offered profound and helpful insights about the war in Vietnam, the plight of migrant grape pickers in California, and the race riots in the cities, perhaps young people would rediscover the relevance of the church.

All of these larger trends would make an impact on the Reformed Church during the next decade and beyond, but in 1970 it was occupied primarily with internal issues. After conflict had nearly torn the church apart in 1969, it turned inward, spending a considerable amount of time and energy in the following years finding ways to deal with its internal diversity. It made a number of institutional adjustments that

---

7   Editorial, "Quality Christian Living," *CH*, Sept. 19, 1969, 9.

enabled its members to live a bit more graciously with their differences. In 1975, however, the president of the General Synod observed that the Reformed Church had lost about seventeen thousand members in the last decade. He challenged the denomination to focus much more of its attention outward by emphasizing evangelism and church growth. In the late 1970s, the Reformed Church also spent more time and energy on social and political issues. However, overshadowing all of its actions throughout the 1970s was a persistent conflict over the ordination of women. That issue will be discussed separately in chapter seven.

Looking Inward: Rebuilding Relationships

One significant issue after the difficult Synod of 1969 was whether the very different groups in the denomination could reduce the conflict between them and learn to work together productively. To facilitate greater congeniality and provide a broader perspective, a number of changes were implemented at the Synod of 1971. Delegates began to be seated alphabetically rather than by personal preference, so they were less able to engage in regional caucusing. Two students from each college and seminary attended as corresponding delegates—with a voice but not a vote.[8] Each delegate, visitor, and staff member participated in an "exchange group" of twenty people who listened to one another without debating issues. These conversations eased the argumentative mood that synod meetings had developed.

Denominational meetings also became more harmonious because they avoided divisive issues such as the Vietnam War.[9] The synod president in 1974, Donald DeYoung, recalled in his report to the synod that, during the 1960s, relationships in both church and nation had been issue-centered and confrontational. The issues of merger, race, and Vietnam had caused conflict and polarization, but in the early 1970s,

> the Lord saw fit to send us a number of festivals, mini-festivals, Lay Witness Missions, and many other gatherings which helped us address the inner needs and strengths of the Body of Christ. The church became appreciated as a source of power and

[8]   There are two photos on the same page of the report on this synod in the *Church Herald*. One shows eight students with long hair, wearing blue jeans, sandals, and print shirts. The other shows a group of men aged fifty to seventy-five wearing dress shirts and ties. Louis Benes, "The 165th General Synod: Actions and Reports," July 2, 1971, 9.

[9]   Louis Benes, "The 166th General Synod: Actions and Reports," *CH*, July 14, 1972, 4-14. Howard Hageman, "A Word on Synod," *CH*, July 14, 1972, 15.

renewal, instead of a sociological obstacle to change. While not compromising our differences on issues, we discovered it is hard to feel alienated from a Christian brother or sister with whom you share, sing, pray and even cry.[10]

These changes contributed to a more congenial atmosphere at General Synod meetings. Louis Benes thought that the Synod of 1973 may have been the finest he ever attended. He noticed a new spiritual climate and a desire to demonstrate mutual respect.[11] George Magee, a missionary in Japan, attended synods in 1968 and 1973 and observed that in the latter meeting people debated the issues just as avidly but seemed open to other positions and affirmed their unity in Christ. Jerome DeJong, a pastor in Grand Rapids, mentioned the "genuine brotherhood" he experienced at the closing Communion service in 1973. Charlotte Harvey, an elder from Utica, New York, while not a "brother," also considered the service a highlight of the week.[12]

Looking Inward: Rethinking Missions

For more than a century, the Reformed Church had identified itself as a denomination that was committed to world mission. Church members attended mission conferences and listened to missionaries wearing native dress tell stories and show slides about their work in Africa or Arabia or Asia. As television news expanded to include routine coverage of other parts of the world, however, foreign mission work lost its exotic, dramatic quality. With increasing frequency, church members could read about world events in the newspaper or watch live news coverage on television from the places the Reformed Church had missionaries. During the 1950s the *Church Herald* devoted the bulk of its February and November issues—and many other pages throughout the year—to articles about domestic and foreign missions. During the 1970s it published a few scattered articles each year on mission-related

---

[10] *Acts and Proceedings*, 1974, 273-74. DeYoung was an Anglo pastor serving an African American church in Harlem. He would not have advocated that the church avoid difficult issues in order to keep people happy. His point raises an important question, however. Should the church emphasize its role as a source of spiritual and personal renewal and avoid social issues and the conflicts they generate? It may be pragmatic to do so, but is that the church's calling? Reformed Church members did not (and do not) agree on the answer to this question.

[11] "The 167th General Synod: Actions and Reports," *CH*, July 13, 1973, 4-14. The most controversial issue was voting to give the professorial certificate to Joyce Stedge. See chapter seven.

[12] "Observations and Impressions," *CH*, July 13, 1973, 18-20.

matters. Mission work had changed dramatically also. For example, in 1920 fifty Reformed Church missionaries served in India, but by 1970 there were only four.[13]

The denomination's identity as a mission-minded church was challenged in the late 1960s on two fronts. Funding for denominational missionary work lagged as congregations redirected resources to local missions. At the same time, difficult questions were being raised in the broader Christian community about the value of missionary work. Some critics said that it was an arrogant and racist attempt to impose western values and religion on other countries. While avid supporters of missions continued to insist that the "heathen" must be converted by missionaries whose main role was evangelism, a growing number of missionaries and other church leaders argued that mission work must be culturally sensitive and concerned with meeting human needs along with saving souls.[14]

To provide a forum for conversation about these issues and to build on the success of the Festival of Evangelism in 1970, denominational staff members planned a mission festival for October 1971. Organizers hoped to discuss some of the difficult questions, inspire more giving to the denominational program, and offer opportunities to build community among the different sections of the Reformed Church.

The 1971 Mission Festival created more controversy than many had expected, but it still proved to be a positive experience for the denomination. Nineteen hundred people attended the entire event, including a large number of young adults attracted by a coffee house and bands. Participants attended workshops and engaged in dialogue groups with people from other regions, ages, and theological perspectives.

The most memorable and controversial element of the festival was the speech by the Reverend John Gatu, general secretary of the Presbyterian Church in East Africa, entitled "Missionary, Go Home." He stated bluntly that many missionaries had damaged the culture, self-esteem, and sense of responsibility of people in the Third World. Missionaries had said implicitly or explicitly that Third World people were uncivilized, pagan, and incapable of church leadership. This had been so destructive, Gatu said, that the only way to strengthen the indigenous churches in the Third World was to withdraw Western

---

[13] John and Bernadine Siebers De Valois, letter to the editor, *CH*, Dec. 17, 1971, 24-25, 30.

[14] Arie Brouwer, "Why Mission Festival '71?" *CH*, May 7, 1971, 11.

missionaries completely so that local Christians would take the responsibility for evangelism, administration, and education.[15]

Jose Miguez-Bonino, a professor in Buenos Aires, Argentina, gave a similarly challenging speech. In Latin America, he said, people lived in economic oppression caused in part by low prices for American consumer goods and high returns for American stockholders. If missionaries simply preached redemption for souls while tacitly supporting the economic status quo, it would be better for them to leave. If they could support the cause of liberation, as defined by the people themselves, he said, then the missionaries would be welcomed enthusiastically.[16]

Some festival participants were appalled that these speakers were so critical and ungrateful for all that Western churches had done for Third World countries and equally upset that they had been invited to speak at the festival. Why criticize missions rather than celebrate and encourage them? Did denominational leaders agree with the speakers they had invited? Arie Brouwer responded that Gatu had expressed a thought-provoking opinion that did not represent the view of all missionaries or the view of the General Program Council. When the Reformed Church sent fewer missionaries, it was due to reduced income, not a new mission philosophy. Church members could send more missionaries by increasing their giving.[17]

Peter Boogaart, a student at New Brunswick Seminary, acknowledged the shock church members felt but also agreed with the speakers. He wrote, "The R.C.A. absorbed a staggering blow in Milwaukee. We were told that the rest of the world didn't want our money, didn't want our programs, and didn't even want our missionaries. To a denomination which takes pride in its mission work, this came as a dumbfounding declaration." The rejection seemed harsh, Boogaart continued, but "the world has little respect for Christians who deplore social injustice from the safety of comfortable homes, who send missionaries to do the work they themselves should do, and who don't really accept other Christians as brothers."[18]

The mission festival ended on a high note despite the controversy. The final Communion service took place in the small dialogue groups that had met for several days. People described the service as a "lovefest"

---

[15]   *CH*, Nov. 5, 1971, 4-5, 20-21.
[16]   "The Present Crisis in Mission," *CH*, Nov. 12, 1971, 12-14, 20-22.
[17]   Louis Benes, "The Milwaukee Festival and Mission In The R.C.A.: An Interview with the Rev. Arie Brouwer," *CH*, Nov. 12, 1971, 4-7.
[18]   Multiple authors, "What Did Mission Festival '71 Mean to You?" *CH*, Nov. 5, 1971, 8.

in which genuine expressions of confession and appreciation occurred.[19] John Piet, a professor at Western Seminary and former missionary to India, offered a more critical analysis:

> That service illustrated what muddled and hurt people generally do, namely, turn in upon themselves....For two days, the delegates were told to direct their attention to those structures of life which dehumanize millions and to become involved as a church in the political, social, and economic dynamism of human existence. The one body of Christ gathered around the table of our Lord, however, said nothing about the "cosmic powers of this dark age," but concentrated on personal sin, reconciliation, and love. Granted, these are essential, but is this what the Festival was about?[20]

The festival raised questions about the Reformed Church's identity with regard to world mission. It did not provide sufficient time to process these questions or consider what it might mean if one of the most important tasks of a denomination was no longer necessary. Louis Benes wished that more concrete proposals had resulted from the conference. "It may be, as someone said, that the Reformed church seems often not as much interested in really coming to grips with our problems, and in actual commitments, as in just feeling good about being together and learning to know one another better."[21] While it was true that the Reformed Church had frequently avoided dealing with difficult questions, given that two years earlier the denomination had nearly divided, "feeling good about being together" was quite a significant accomplishment.

Worship at the festivals emphasized personal faith and feeling and fostered small group connections, and the people who attended these gatherings seemed starved for this emotional and relational experience of the faith. The Reformed Church had a history of emphasizing doctrine, and its worship style could feel rather formal and stiff. The small groups offered a change from the constant debate about doctrine and social issues. Participants were invited to converse rather than debate and to experience rather than analyze. They saw evidence of deep faith in people who came from a different region of the country. The

[19] Ibid., 6-9.
[20] Ibid., 7-8. For a similar critique, see Harlan Ratmeyer, letter to the editor, *CH*, Oct. 29, 1971, 17, 22-23.
[21] Editorial, "The Milwaukee Mission Festival: A Postscript," *CH*, Nov. 19, 1971, 8-9. For a more detailed description, see Hoff, *Structures for Mission*, 167-71.

lengthy discussion of merger had created a high level of defensiveness, but once merger had been voted down, the purists did not need to try so hard to preserve a Reformed Church identity, and the moderates did not need to insist that merger was the only way the church could survive.

Looking Inward: Institutional Adjustments

After deciding neither to merge nor divide, the Reformed Church needed to make a number of decisions about its future and the structures that would support it. Three issues demanded attention. Moderates expressed concern about a negative tone that had become common in the denomination. Purists complained that staff members in the New York headquarters did not reflect the views of grassroots members. Both sides worried about the long-term financial viability of the denomination and particularly its two seminaries. Behind these questions were larger, unstated questions about how denominations would be funded, who would make decisions, and, ultimately, whether denominations were necessary.

One of the first adjustments appeared minor but had powerful symbolic effects. All Reformed Church clergy recited a "Declaration" when they were ordained or installed to a new ministry. Its language emphasized the fear of being wrong and the need to preserve Reformed identity and keep dangerous ideas out of the church.

> We believe the Gospel of the grace of God in Jesus Christ as revealed in the Holy Scripture of the Old and New Testaments, and as truly set forth in the Standards of the Reformed Church in America, and we reject all errors which are contrary thereto. We promise that we will exert ourselves to keep the church free from such errors. We promise that should we ever have any doubts as to this Gospel, or as to the Standards of our faith, we will neither propose nor teach the same, but will first communicate our views to the classis to which we belong, and will subject ourselves to its counsel and decision, under penalty, in case of refusal, to be *ipso facto* suspended from our office. We do further promise to be ready always to comply with a request from the consistory or the classis for an explanation of our views respecting any particular article of our Standards, under a penalty of censure or suspension from the ministry.

Arnold van Lummel, a pastor in Asbury Park, New Jersey, called for a change in this formulation. He acknowledged the importance of defending the gospel, but he believed the Declaration wrongly emphasized theological purity and penalties over the joy of welcoming a new minister. He concluded, "We don't need a rewrite. We need a new Declaration, less apologetic, more evangelical in tone, alive to the thrill and joy of serving our Servant Lord."[22] Moderates objected to the Declaration because it conflated the Standards and the Bible. The Standards were a sixteenth-century attempt to articulate the Christian faith, but they did not necessarily "truly set forth the gospel" or possess the same degree of inspiration and infallibility as the Bible.[23] Purists, on the other hand, insisted that twentieth-century ministers were indeed bound to sixteenth-century interpretations.

There was enough support for revision that one was approved by the General Synod in 1971, but it did not receive enough votes in the classes. A second version removed the testing and evaluative components and instead emphasized outreach and service. Clergy were asked to affirm the Standards as historic and faithful witnesses to the Word of God. The Declaration still attempted to protect orthodox belief, but this concern was expressed more communally and less punitively.[24] This new Declaration was approved by the classes in 1973.

The second structural issue dealt with the location of the denominational headquarters. When the General Program Council was planned in the late 1960s, the consultants advising the process recommended that the Reformed Church relocate its headquarters and seminary education to somewhere within the triangle bounded by Chicago, Cleveland, and Cincinnati. Theoretically, this idea provided a much needed middle ground for a divided church, but there was no natural location for such a headquarters within this triangle. The church's headquarters had long been located in New York City and attempts to move the offices had always failed. Eastern members thought it was important to maintain an urban headquarters with ecumenical connections lest the offices move to the Midwest and become entirely enmeshed in a more conservative, parochial mindset. The location of the office said something about identity; it did not simply provide an address.

Several overtures in 1971 asked the denomination to consider moving its headquarters to a more central site, such as Kalamazoo,

---

[22] Arnold van Lummel, guest editorial, "Wanted: A New 'Declaration' For Ministers!" *CH*, March 5, 1971, 7.

[23] William Hanousek, "For Honesty's Sake, Let Us Change Our Forms of Declaration," *CH*, Feb. 11, 1972, 14, 21.

[24] Arthur Jentz, "The Proposed Creedal Declaration for Ministers," *CH*, March 2, 1973, 12-13. Compare Tom Stark, "Why We Need Our Creedal Declaration for Ministers," *CH*, Feb. 2, 1973, 12-13, 22-23.

Michigan. They argued that the Reformed Church could save money if it owned a building instead of paying rent at 475 Riverside Drive. The Classis of East Sioux claimed that a move would put staff members in "closer touch with the denomination itself and the leadership could provide programs which would receive the support of the entire church."[25] The reasons to remain in New York were similar to those offered in previous years: The Interchurch Center at 475 Riverside served as headquarters for a number of denominational and ecumenical organizations, and the rent was surprisingly reasonable. Tasks such as banking, communication, and caring for missionaries were all easier in New York City. Eastern churches strongly opposed a move, since the Midwest had four "affectional centers" (three colleges and Western Seminary) while the East had only one seminary in addition to the national headquarters. In the end, synod delegates decided it was more efficient and cost-effective for the office to remain in New York.

The decision was likely made easier because the General Program Council was already discussing a process of "regionalization," which would transfer many staff members out of New York and into "centers" in the most populated areas of the church. Regional staff members hoped to offer training programs that would help all members discover their gifts and engage in ministry.[26] The plan was quite effective, and congregations made many requests for help and appreciated the training. Staff members hoped that if they were closer to the people, churches would give more generously to the denomination. Congregations were happy to use the services of the denomination, but they remained reluctant to pay for them.[27]

Despite the efforts of denominational staff to engage with members and provide services, however, the denomination itself was becoming less relevant to the average church member. Congregations that had once given generously to the denominational benevolent program now gave more to local and regional mission projects or simply kept the money for themselves. In the Holland Classis, for example, between 1971 and 1972, congregational giving to General Synod benevolences increased $503, giving to other benevolences

[25] *Acts and Proceedings*, 1971, 97.

[26] Christian Walvoord, "Regionalization—Scenario for the Years Ahead?" *CH*, April 9, 1971, 14. Lois Joice, "Togetherness in Zion: The Fall Meeting of the General Program Council," *CH*, Dec. 17, 1971, 20, 29-30. Arie Brouwer presented a report at this meeting entitled, "A New Commitment—Available for Mission."

[27] Tom Bast, "The New Centers Concept in the RCA: An Interview with Some of Our Reformed Church Staff," *CH*, Sept. 6, 1974, 12-15.

increased $37,845, and giving for congregational purposes increased $74,134.[28] If even the most historically generous congregations were less interested in funding it, what was the future of the denominational mission program?

Some money previously given to the denomination was redirected to the regions. Particular synod programs had grown quickly over the last two decades, and when they needed money, they either levied assessments or made it clear that their "askings" were expected rather than voluntary. Many congregations met those appeals by giving money out of their General Synod benevolence budgets.[29] Local churches wanted to make their own decisions about the mission work they supported, and they often preferred local projects to national ones. An unintended consequence of regionalization was that, as congregations began to identify more with the region than with the denomination, they shifted their benevolent giving accordingly.

The shortage of funds was also a factor in a lengthy debate about a significant institutional issue: the number and location of the theological seminaries. By the 1960s, it was clear that the Reformed Church did not have enough students or money to support two seminaries. Both regions of the church valued their seminaries, but neither constituency funded them adequately. In an attempt to unify administration, the two seminaries adopted a single Board of Theological Education (BTE) in 1967, with one board and one president [1969-1973] for both seminaries. During the next few years the BTE developed an innovative Bi-Level Multi-Site (BLMS) program as a way to use the facilities and faculties of both seminaries and to reduce some East-West, liberal-conservative tension. Students spent the first two years at New Brunswick studying the foundational disciplines of the Christian faith, then moved to Western for two years to learn about the practice of ministry. In theory, this was an excellent program. Students experienced both regions of the church and learned from both faculties. In practice, students found it expensive and inconvenient (particularly during an economic recession) to move their families in the middle

---

28   Paul Colenbrander, letter to the editor, *CH*, July 13, 1973, 22.

29   This pattern raised enough concern that a national consultation was held in 1973 to discuss the growing tensions between national and regional funding, but it concluded only that RCA members had the potential to donate more than twice what they did. The denomination did not have the power to limit the assessments levied by particular synods and was reluctant to raise its own assessments to support the national program. Christian Walvoord, guest editorial, "Facing Issues Together," *CH*, May 19, 1972, 6-7. Lois Joice, "Consultation on Funding Ponders New Approach to Dollar Needs," *CH*, April 6, 1973, 16.

of the program and to add a fourth year of study. In addition, some Midwestern members thought the program gave too much advantage to New Brunswick. An overture from South Grand Rapids said, "We are concerned that the first two years will bring the students under the influence of some in the [eastern] area who will impede and discourage seminarians from coming back to serve harmoniously and enthusiastically in the western synods of our church."[30]

The seminaries adopted a transition period during which each offered its own M.Div degree along with overseeing half of the BLMS program. This meant the faculty of each seminary had to provide all of the courses for two different tracks. A number of students simply chose not to enter the BLMS program. In 1970 the seminaries announced that they would continue to offer both programs, but soon thereafter it became clear that the BLMS program was not economically viable. Despite all the advantages the program provided, the seminaries chose not to require all students to enroll in it. Freedom of choice prevailed at the expense of a thoughtful, innovative, unifying program of seminary education.[31] By 1973 the program was being phased out, and the last student graduated in 1977.

The uncertainty about the future of seminary education provoked a number of questions about seminary curriculum and theological identity. Louis Benes reported that some Reformed Church members wondered whether a single seminary would be "distinctly evangelical." If it was not, Benes said, "We are likely to find that many churches will not want to support it, that many young men will go elsewhere for their seminary training, and that many churches will look elsewhere for ministers to man their pulpits." He then added, "It seems to us that we will need to rethink our seminary curriculum, so that it will concentrate on preparing men for ministry in our churches." Future pastors in the Reformed Church did not need more scholarly work, he thought; rather they needed practical training under successful ministers who

---

[30]   *Acts and Proceedings*, 1970, 86-90, 105.

[31]   Louis Benes, "The 166th General Synod: Actions and Reports," *CH*, July 14, 1972, 12. For further discussion of theological education during this period see Norman J. Kansfield, "The President's Role in Theological Education: 1963-1971," in *Herman J. Ridder: Contextual Preacher and President*, ed. George Brown, Jr., HSRCA, no. 59 (Grand Rapids: Eerdmans, 2008), 21-52; Dennis Voskuil, "When East Meets West: Theological Education and the Unity of the Reformed Church in America," in *Tools for Understanding: Essays in Honor of Donald J. Bruggink*, ed. James Hart Brumm, HSRCA, no. 60 (Grand Rapids: Eerdmans, 2008, 201-28; Howard Hageman, *Two Centuries Plus: The Story of New Brunswick Seminary*, HSRCA, no. 13 (Grand Rapids: Eerdmans, 1984).

could teach personal evangelism, group ministry, and communication skills.[32]

The editorial sparked a number of letters. John Moerman claimed that the BLMS program was "far more mechanical, technical, and ecclesiastically diplomatic than soundly evangelical, highly evangelistic, and thoroughly practical." It was too expensive and the churches had not been consulted before it was implemented. Elko Stapert, a lay person from Kalamazoo, agreed that seminarians did not need more academic training. "We need strong evangelical, Bible-oriented pastors who will take care of their congregations and who are not experimenters with all the new and unproven gimmicks reputed to be revitalizers." In the same issue of the *Church Herald*, however, professor Donald Bruggink described the many ways that his colleagues at Western Seminary engaged in pastoral work and used those skills to train their students.[33] Two students finishing their first two BLMS years at New Brunswick described the emphasis there as "evangelical."[34]

Some critics suggested that seminary education itself had minimal value. Sam Hofman, a missionary in Chiapas, reported that Christians there identified people with gifts for ministry and gradually gave them more responsibility. He thought the Reformed Church should use a similar pattern.[35] The Classis of Orange, in an overture to the 1972 General Synod, asked that Hebrew and Greek be elective rather than required courses, because too much time was required to learn languages and pastors needed training in people skills more

[32] Editorial, "Crucial Issues in Our Reformed Church," *CH*, Jan. 21, 1972, 6-7. Benes also reported that some RCA members thought the denomination was too small to support even one seminary and should instead provide a professor at other seminaries to teach Reformed theology and polity. He suggested that Fuller, Trinity Evangelical, Gordon-Conwell, and Reformed Theological Seminary (Jackson, MS) would provide a suitably evangelical home for RCA students. Princeton and Columbia (Atlanta) would be more liberal, and Union (NY) and Harvard distinctly liberal. RCA members would have had significant disagreements over the meaning of the phrase "distinctly evangelical" and whether it should apply to an RCA institution.

[33] Letters to the editor, Feb 25/March 3, 1972, 24-25, 29.

[34] Allan Janssen and John Engelhard, letter to the editor, May 26, 1972, 17. The BLMS program produced a number of the RCA's brightest and most capable pastors.

[35] J. Samuel Hofman, "The Ladder System: How to Select and Train a Minister," *CH*, May 19, 1972, 4-5, 21. The RCA had always emphasized the need for an educated ministry, even during the colonial period when there was a severe clergy shortage. Hofman's ideas were not implemented in the 1970s, but two decades later the RCA decided to permit "commissioned pastors" without formal seminary training as long as they had demonstrated their gifts in a local congregation. That decision has already had a major impact on the denomination, but there is significant disagreement as to whether it is positive or negative.

than "book learning."[36] The synod referred the overture to the Board of Theological Education for study.

While the BLMS program was being phased out, GSEC leaders again asked if the Reformed Church could afford two seminaries. They concluded that it could not. But if one was sufficient, which one? Each had its advantages and loyal supporters. Western had more students and greater financial stability and was adjacent to Hope College. New Brunswick had recently completed a new building and was located in the middle of Rutgers University and near the New York metropolitan area. After holding a consultation in 1973 to discuss the issue, the GSEC decided that neither seminary could be eliminated without creating ill will and losing both financial support and students, who would opt to attend non-RCA seminaries. Both seminaries had something to offer to the broader church, and each region believed that it needed its own seminary. The seminaries had searched unsuccessfully for a shared president, but each began its own presidential search in 1973. Joint administration of the seminaries had proved too difficult.[37] Regional loyalties and identities took precedence over the desire for unity and efficiency.

One final institutional adjustment that resulted from the Synod of 1969 was another attempt to articulate a contemporary statement of Reformed faith. Moderates asked for this because they thought the sixteenth-century Standards did not address current issues adequately. The Commission on Theology agreed that it would be helpful to have a clear statement of theological identity and made several attempts to write a brief statement of faith. None managed to be succinct, orthodox, and interesting. Eugene Heideman, dean of the faculty of Western Seminary, was given the task and in 1974 produced "Our Song of Hope." The statement was about four pages long and written in poetic form. It articulated a moderate Reformed theology, with emphasis on the kingdom of God and the need for Christians to help transform the world. Despite its attempt to be accessible, "Our Song" was too theologically

---

36   *Acts and Proceedings*, 1972, 92-93.
37   Herman Ridder served as president of both institutions from 1969 to 1971, and Lester Kuyper served as interim president of both from 1971 to 1973. Both moved regularly between Holland and New Brunswick. The BTE offered the joint presidency to Arie Brouwer in 1972. He was willing to accept if he could continue his role as executive secretary of the GPC. He hoped this would unify the program of the RCA and the education of future ministers, but the proposal was criticized sharply because it gave a great deal of power to one person. He then declined the invitation. See "Arie Brouwer Offered the Seminary Presidency," *CH*, March 17, 1972, 19; Kansfield, "President's Role"; Voskuil, "When East Meets West."

sophisticated and subtle for some Reformed Church members, who simply wanted the historic tenets of Reformed Calvinism spelled out clearly. For example, one critic complained that the document treated many precious truths superficially or ambiguously. He thought that the new statement would cause confusion and division.[38] In response to purist criticism, the GSEC decided not to recommend "Our Song" as a doctrinal standard but encouraged its use in witness, teaching, and worship as a statement of the Reformed faith. The synod approved this ambiguous status in 1978.

Looking Inward: Denominational Communications

In the midst of these institutional changes, another major shift occurred. Louis Benes retired at the end of 1974, after twenty-nine years as editor of the *Church Herald*, and John Stapert was named to that role. Stapert grew up in Kalamazoo, Michigan, the son of Elko, the elder who had served as chair of the Committee of Eighteen in 1969-1970. Stapert attended Hope College, Fuller Seminary, and the University of Illinois, where he earned a Ph.D in psychology. He taught briefly at Northwestern College, then served as executive coordinator for the Particular Synod of the West. He was thirty-three when he became editor. Like Benes, Stapert had no prior professional experience as a journalist. Unlike Benes, Stapert lacked parish experience and received his theological training at a non-RCA seminary. While Benes expressed purist positions, Stapert was more of a moderate. He quickly encountered purist resistance.

Some Reformed Church members insisted on preserving not only the substance of the faith as it had been articulated in the Standards, but also the style or presentation of it. Under Stapert's leadership, the *Church Herald* tried to be more relevant and appealing to readers, but it received a great deal of criticism whenever it adopted new formats. If the magazine featured a contemporary nativity or Easter painting on the cover, critics said it was ugly or irreverent or unspiritual. In the spring of 1977, a cover featured a female student studying on a college lawn. A critic protested that the picture "doesn't convey a Christian flavor or direct my thoughts to God. She's pretty and her wind-blown hair makes for a sexy message. I'm aware the magazine is trying to indicate National College Day, but why print such a sexy symbol to celebrate it?"[39] Other readers were absolutely puzzled by this response.

---

[38] Wayne Hartman, letter to the editor, *CH*, July 26, 1974, 21. "Our Song of Hope" can be accessed at http://www.rca.org/Page.aspx?pid=313.

[39] Mrs. Gene Elliott, letter to the editor, *CH*, May 13, 1977, 22.

Some readers again saw sexuality run amok on the cover of the June 10, 1977, issue. The cover, celebrating summer, featured a photograph of a girl about ten years old who was waterskiing, dressed in a modest two-piece swim suit. A barrage of letters followed that labeled the photo lewd, obscene, and in poor taste. One writer said that the "half naked girls" implied a theological stance of liberal humanism. Another said the photo brought shame and embarrassment to the Reformed Church, and the magazine could not be left on the coffee table. Still another irate reader asked when the magazine would come out with a centerfold.

Subsequent issues of the magazine published a number of letters from readers who were shocked by this high level of shock. One writer observed that "beauty is in the eye of the beholder and so, it seems, is lewdness." Another wondered if the girl should be wearing a Victorian bloomer suit. Herman Ridder reported, tongue in cheek, that he had searched his back issues for the cover in question and found a little girl water skiing.

> Thus, what I suspect is that you have a policy of sending out the same issue but with two different covers! Should that be the case, I must register a firm protest. After all, we pay the same subscription rate and are entitled to the same treatment throughout. Please be advised that unless you adopt a uniform policy on the covers for all subscribers some of us will be forced to cancel our subscriptions. Nobody likes to be gypped![40]

During the early 1980s, the hotly debated moral topics were movie reviews rather than magazine covers. The magazine reviewed *On Golden Pond* in 1982 and *Tootsie* in 1983 and received numerous angry letters.[41] The writers could not understand why a Christian magazine would write positive reviews of movies which contained swearing and sexual themes. The critics often refused to attend the movies, yet they felt free to comment, as was the case with the writer who complained that Tootsie was wearing a very seductive outfit.[42]

---

[40]   Letters to the editor, *CH,* July 8, 1977, 22; Aug. 5, 1977, 22-23.
[41]   *On Golden Pond* featured Katherine Hepburn, Henry Fonda, and Jane Fonda and told a powerful story about aging and family, but Henry Fonda's character was a crusty man who swore a lot. *Tootsie* featured Dustin Hoffman playing an actor who could not get any roles until he dressed as a rather frumpy sixtyish woman and landed a key role in a soap opera. The movie raised interesting questions about gender and relationships.
[42]   Letters to the editor, March 4, 1983, 21.

The number of purist critics was relatively small, but this sort of debate made a significant impact in the church. Moderates shook their heads over what appeared to be rigid, even ridiculous moralizing. They wondered if this mentality was the dominant view among more conservative Reformed Church members. Moderates had little interest in being identified with this approach to Christianity. They did not think that naughty words were the form of sin and brokenness with which the Reformed Church should be most concerned. At the same time, purists wondered why so many members of their denomination did not appear to care about basic morality and piety.

Another extremely conservative and often caustic perspective on the Reformed Church came from the League of Christian Laymen. This loosely structured association, comprised of a small number of midwestern laymen and centered in Holland, Michigan, published a newsletter entitled *Facts!*, which regularly attacked Western Seminary, the *Church Herald*, the ordination of women, and the World and National Councils of Churches. Writers in *Facts!* were convinced that a liberal cabal ran the Reformed Church and that it was the league's duty to denounce the faith and integrity of individuals and institutions that advocated moderate positions. The newsletter at times wrongly accused respected ministers and professors of heterodox Christian faith.[43]

Significantly, even conservative classes and people found themselves at odds with the stridency of the league. In 1977, the classes of Cascades, Holland, and Zeeland submitted overtures that criticized the League of Christian Laymen and supported the institutions under attack. In an editorial, John Stapert provided several examples of the newsletter's misuse of facts and noted an inconsistency between the personal warmth and Christian commitment of some of the league's members and the harsh language they used against other Christians.[44] Once again, the Reformed Church as a whole refused to allow a narrow view of the faith and harsh criticism of others to reshape its core identity. But the persistence and hostility of the league's rhetoric made many moderate easterners wonder if this was what most midwesterners thought about the faith. Was this the new identity of the Reformed Church? The answer was no, but, clearly, this purist perspective had its followers.

Other Reformed Church members were not remotely interested in these purist agendas. Some were developing creative forms of ministry. Herbert DuMont worked at the Robert Taylor Homes in Chicago doing

---

[43] Some issues of the newletter can be found in the Joint Archives of Holland.
[44] "Facts?" *CH*, Feb. 18, 1977, 8-9.

community action and justice work. Trinity Reformed in Holland drew twenty-five hundred people to a coffee house it provided for three nights during the city's annual Tulip Time Festival. Harold DeRoo and the Good Samaritan Church in Gahanna, Ohio, developed an innovative ministry without a traditional building.[45] A number of congregations conducted small-scale mission festivals that improved their sense of community and connectedness. The third denominational festival, celebrating the family, was held in Estes Park, Colorado, in July 1972. This time, three thousand people attended, and most thought it was a very positive experience. The festival included family-centered entertainment, workshops, and covenant groups. It was less content driven than previous festivals because so many children were present, but it served as another bonding experience for the denomination.[46]

Looking Inward: Valuing All God's People

Reformed Church members discussed their different beliefs about theology, morality, and politics at great length during these years. They negotiated extensively about which views held more power and influence and who decided the future of the denomination. There were other kinds of differences however—skin color, ethnicity, language, country of origin—that were less often discussed. The church found it a considerable challenge to welcome and include these members who had long been consigned to the periphery of the denomination. During the 1970s, members of the ethnic communities organized and found a voice in the church. The Black Council was formed in 1969 after James Forman's speech at the General Synod. The American Indian (1972), Hispanic (1974), and Asian-Pacific American Councils (1980) soon followed. Forming the councils proved to be far easier than fully including their voices and giving them places of influence within the denominational structure. The General Program Council recognized in its 1974 report to the synod that it needed to listen to minority voices, develop authentic relationships, and avoid paternalism. This sentiment appeared admirably sensitive, but the councils noted that it was the listeners, rather than the speakers, who possessed the power to decide

---

45   James Hefley, "The Ghetto Is His Parish," *CH*, June 4, 1971, 4-6, 21-22; William Brownson, "The Fish Comes to Tulip Time," *CH*, July 17, 1971, 13, 23; Sue Ann Langdon, "A Church without a Church," *CH*, Nov. 30, 1973, 6-7, 27-28.
46   Louis Benes, "Our Family Festival," *CH*, Aug. 25, 1972, 4-9. A fourth festival was held at Slippery Rock State College (Pennsylvania) in August 1976. Although 1,150 people attended, the event merited only one page of coverage in the *CH*. "1,150 attend Jubilee/76 at Slippery Rock," Sept. 17, 1976, 24-25.

what to hear and how to act on what they heard.[47] Listening alone did not necessarily produce substantive change.

Each council had a very different agenda and leadership style. In 1976 John Stapert observed that when they reported to the synod, the councils appeared to differ more from each other than from the white majority. The Black Council emphasized the distinctive racial identity of its members, the need for black pastors, and the importance of self-reliance in black congregations. They spoke of themselves as "historic victims of exclusion" and often jarred the sensibilities of their mostly white audience. The representative from the American Indian Council greeted the synod with open arms and the words, "You are my friends," and the synod responded with spontaneous, warm applause. The Hispanic Council emphasized evangelism, church growth, and conversion—an agenda that echoed the denomination's priorities at that time. Stapert commented approvingly, "There may not be a more enthusiastically evangelistic group in the denomination."[48]

During the Synod of 1978, there was considerable controversy over racism and the role of the Black Council. Perhaps because there was relatively little to debate (indeed, the synod finished its work ahead of schedule[49]), this topic received a great deal of attention and created lasting controversy. Lacking other hard news, Stapert's General Synod report in the *Church Herald* gave significant space to the "occasional flurries of debate relating to racism."

The controversy began when Sarah Smith, chair of the Black Council, led worship on Tuesday morning. Smith warned the synod of "the threatening cloud in the sky that will bring destruction if we do not destroy racism." When the Christian Action Commission presented its report on South Africa, Smith protested that the report did not critique multinational corporations sufficiently, nor did it demonstrate full solidarity with the poor and oppressed. In response to this stinging criticism, the synod passed a motion from the floor asking for a study of the Reformed Church's investments in South Africa. Smith later presented the Black Council's report, which "spoke strongly against racial injustice and placed blame with the church for the sin of racism." The synod received the report and approved the

---

[47] *Acts and Proceedings*, 1974, 68. The councils were referred to collectively as "minority" councils. I will use this language because it is historically accurate, while recognizing the preference now for the term "racial-ethnic" councils.

[48] "The 170th General Synod: Actions and Reports," *CH*, July 23, 1976, 13.

[49] On Thursday afternoon, the synod was doing the work scheduled for Friday. Some delegates wondered if it was worth taking a week off from work to attend.

recommendations, but Stapert reported that delegates were irritated by the discussion. The other councils presented very different reports. The Hispanic Council described programs that had enriched spiritual life, and the American Indian Council described its self-study. Both were applauded spontaneously, perhaps in relief from the tension generated by the Black Council. The "better behaved" and less critical minority councils unmistakably received more approval from the predominantly white assembly.

Stapert's own irritation with the Black Council was evident throughout the section suggestively subheaded, "Black Assertiveness, Rights." Was he simply reporting the news and reflecting the synod's mood? Or did this account trivialize the debate and imply that the Black Council had overstepped institutional and cultural proprieties?[50]

In the midst of these judgments, however, Stapert identified an issue that the Reformed Church has still not fully resolved. How do the councils fit into the broader administrative structure of the denomination? Some people insisted that the councils and their staffs be accountable to a denominational executive, but the councils resisted this structural supervision out of fear that they would lose their independence and have their agendas determined by the white majority. Significantly, despite their theological and programmatic differences, all the councils agreed about the need to preserve their autonomy rather than be absorbed into a denominational staff structure.

The councils were rightly concerned about autonomy, since a number of Reformed Church leaders were eager to tell them how to behave. Synod president Harvey Hoekstra reported that when he worshiped with the Black Council, his heart had been warmed because they preached love for Christ and each other. This was what white people needed to hear, Hoekstra believed. He continued:

> I regretted that so frequently at a General Synod we have been exposed to that more militant, strident concern of our black brothers and sisters about injustice and suffering. We need to hear what our black brothers and sisters are telling us, and we must do something about it. This cannot be affirmed too strongly. At the same time, I must say that we also need to hear of their hopes and

---

50   "The 172nd General Synod and 350th Anniversary Celebration," *CH*, July 28, 1978, 4-12. The section on race is on pp. 7-8. In subsequent issues, several letters to the editor took Stapert to task for divisive reporting: Aug. 25, 15; Oct. 6, 18-19. Sarah Smith wrote a letter objecting that the portrayal of the Black Council was "disruptive, uncooperative, and belligerent," Sept. 8, 1978, 18.

dreams to share their love for Christ with those who may never come to know him without their witness.[51]

Another synod president, Harry Buis, also addressed the issue of racism in a *Church Herald* article in 1980. He had experienced a sense of joy and evangelical renewal while worshiping with the Black Caucus, he said, but he had also heard disquieting laments about discrimination and racism within the Reformed Church, American society, and South Africa. Buis concluded that black and white Reformed Church members needed to communicate more extensively, because they had much to learn from each other. But it must be a dialogue of equals, he wrote, which requires that "whites must get over their paternalistic attitudes and blacks must not be quick to label racist every idea with which they disagree."[52]

The Reformed Church had a great deal of work to do before it would be fully able to welcome people of various ethnic groups. One function of minority councils was to raise awareness of discrimination and injustice, but the examples above demonstrate how difficult it was for members of the white majority to hear a critical message. Many members of the white majority did not wish to be reminded about their complicity in racism, and they much preferred to experience pleasant worship and upbeat talk. They would rather discuss evangelism than advocacy and justice. Advocacy seemed to them to be selfish concern about the rights of a particular group, and white people often had difficulty acknowledging the degree of racism and white privilege that still existed in American society and churches.

Looking Inward: One Church with Many Choices

By the end of the 1970s it became clear that the strategy of allowing the midwestern and eastern regions to make their own choices had led to a great deal of fragmentation within the denomination. Warren Van Tongeren, who had recently joined the Fair Haven Reformed Church in Jenison, Michigan, wrote an essay about being a newcomer to the Reformed Church. He had hoped to find a clear Reformed emphasis, he said, but found instead that congregationalism and fundamentalism "have muted or distorted our Reformed character and witness. I think that we are Reformed, but at best we are somewhat unsure of what that means, and we certainly are not very enthusiastic about it." The

---

[51]   *Acts and Proceedings*, 1979, 28.
[52]   "The president considers...The Black Caucus," Jan. 9, 1981, 19.

congregation's hymnbook offered fundamentalist theology and hymns about infant dedication rather than baptism. The pews contained no copies of the Reformed confessions, despite the denomination's supposed commitment to them. Van Tongeren concluded, "I looked for a progressive, reforming church in the RCA, and now I read responsive readings in 17th century English and sing 'Heaven came down and glory filled my soul.'" He thought the Reformed Church needed to produce its own hymnbook.[53]

His essay and the responses it generated illustrate the degree of liturgical variety within the Reformed Church. A woman from Caledonia, Michigan, responded, "The spirit-filled services in fundamentalist churches far surpass those in any Reformed church. When you leave, you know you have felt the Spirit of the Lord (especially in their music). Nothing is less uplifting than liturgy, creeds, and written prayers."[54] Another writer thought the Reformed Church should use the sixteenth-century worship practices of singing the Psalms to the tunes in the *Genevan Psalter*. He wrote, "While fundamentalist influences tend to promote the idea that worship is for us—a show, an entertainment—the Psalms continually bring us back to the true focus of worship: God." Another writer complained that applause in response to musical performances demonstrated a growing spirit of irreverence in the church. The Reformed fathers had established a semiliturgical church with orders of worship that avoided innovations, gimmicks, and gadgets. "We should get back to the services the liturgy provides. Worship in the beauty of holiness is not in clapping, rapping, shuffling, and hand-shaking; rather it is in the blessed quietness in which one can feel the presence and hear the still small voice of God."[55]

The Reformed Church *had* a liturgy and a hymnbook, but many congregations and clergy chose not to use them. Some of the congregations that insisted most vehemently on maintaining the purity of the Reformed tradition (as they interpreted it) also preferred evangelical or even fundamentalist worship resources over those produced by the RCA. Many moderate congregations and pastors, on the other hand, insisted that liturgical worship and Reformed

---

53   Warren Van Tongeren, "I'd like to say...We Need a Reformed Hymnbook," *CH*, June 12, 1981, 13. The RCA had *The Hymnbook*, produced in the 1950s in cooperation with several other denominations, but despite its quality it was not widely used in the Midwest.

54   Marilyn De Vries, letter to the editor, *CH*, July 10, 1981, 21.

55   John DeKorne, letter to the editor, *CH*, July 24, 1981, 20. Nelson Slot, letter to the editor, Aug. 7, 1981, 13.

hymnody were central to Reformed identity. The moderates wanted to "conserve" the liturgy, while some conservatives and purists adopted worship practices and innovations that were more evangelical and fundamentalist than Reformed.[56]

As differences in theology and worship increased, some members began to question the role of traditions based on geography. For more than a century the denomination had been divided by ethos and origin into a more progressive East and a more conservative Midwest. The Reformed Church had developed a number of traditions to preserve a balance of power between the two. General Synod meeting locations alternated between East and West, vice-presidents of the General Synod were elected alternately from East and West, and advisory committee moderators and vice-moderators were carefully balanced. In 1982 John Stapert suggested that the East-West distinctions were no longer helpful, because issues discussed at synods were no longer decided along regional lines. The regions were not monolithic, he pointed out; there were urban churches in the Midwest and rural and suburban churches in the East. New churches in North Carolina, Texas, and Kansas did not fit into either category. Stapert concluded that these practices may once have enabled Reformed Church members with different views to remain in the same denomination, but he thought they had outlived their usefulness. "We don't need the East-West tradition any more, and I think we should make a point of abandoning it....The artificial constraint of geography can be put behind us."[57]

Stapert suggested that the denomination end the practice of East-West alternation in the selection of the vice-president, but in 1982 the synod followed tradition and elected an easterner as vice-president (Leonard Kalkwarf) during the East's year. Stapert reiterated his suggestion in 1983, this time with a more shaming approach. He noted that the geographical tradition made the church vulnerable to covert practices and private arrangements that did not honor the Holy Spirit. Some ministers—all of whom are slated to attend General Synod in rotation—had juggled their years, hoping to be elected vice-president when it was their region's "turn." In previous generations the practice

---

[56]   An analysis of the theology of many of the hymns sung by RCA congregations would show some of these theological contradictions. For example, "I Have Decided to Follow Jesus" does not reflect the Reformed belief that God first extends grace to sinful people and enables their response. Calvin would argue that no one is capable of deciding to follow Jesus without God's grace first transforming them. Numerous other examples could be cited.

[57]   Editorial, "Let's Start a New Tradition," *CH*, April 2, 1982, 4-5.

may have eased tensions between two segments of the church, but now, Stapert believed, the selection process needed to be more open. He also thought that the Far West deserved to be a third entity in the mix.[58]

If the East-West traditions were simply about geography, and all other factors had been equal, then Stapert may have been right. But East and West in the Reformed Church did not simply refer to one side of the Alleghenies or the other. Instead, East and West had become shorthand for moderate and conservative theological positions. The words represented a mind-set, not simply a location. In the late 1940s, after Henry Bast complained about geographical inequities, the denomination instituted practices that would balance power more evenly between East and West, even though the East had more members at that time. By the early eighties, with membership in the Midwest larger than in the East, it seemed that the Midwest wanted to return to the practice of "majority rules."[59] Geography may not have mattered any more, but moderate/conservative differences certainly did. The Reformed Church had been able to maintain courtesy and balance when the issue was framed in geographical terms. It was more difficult for the denomination to acknowledge that there was a tenuous balance between moderates and conservatives that needed to be honored.

However, the addition of the Far West as a third distinctive region significantly changed the dynamics. The Reformed Church moved from two focal points to three. If it were simply a matter of geography, this would not have had much impact. But because churches in the Far West were generally conservative, and often more evangelical than Reformed,[60] the identity of the Reformed Church began to shift. Whereas the East-West dichotomy had been roughly even in terms of power and influence, adding a third entity that was more like the Midwest than the

---

[58] Editorial, "It's Still Time for a Change," *CH*, June 3, 1983, 4. In 1982 Leonard Kalkwarf (Pennsylvania) was elected over Harold Leestma (California) by two votes. In 1983, William Brownson (Michigan) won over Herman Ridder (California). In 1984 Californian Kenneth Leestma won. Only delegates to synod can be nominated for election as vice-president.

[59] In 1980 the Classis of South Grand Rapids and the Particular Synod of Michigan sent overtures asking that representation to GSEC, commissions, and agencies be determined more equitably, based on the RCA population. The Particular Synod of Michigan had 25 percent of RCA membership, the West 26 percent, Chicago 12 percent, Albany 10 percent, New Jersey 15 percent, and New York 12 percent. The three western synods contributed 79 percent of denominational benevolent funds. It did not seem fair to them that Albany and the Far West had the same number of representatives. The overtures were referred to the GSEC, which recommended denial, and the synod agreed. *Acts and Proceedings*, 1980, 279-82.

[60] The Far West churches will be discussed more extensively below.

East clearly shifted the balance of power and theological perspective. The conservatives had two "blocs" as it were, while the moderates had one. This would have a significant impact on the church in the next two decades.

By the mid-1970s a new trend had also become evident: congregations became increasingly detached from the denomination. The Reformed Church had an excellent missionary program, but congregations could choose not to support it. The seminaries developed the Bi-Level Multi-Site program, but students could choose not to enroll in it. The denomination could realistically support only one seminary, but, because of the realities of two constituencies, two seminaries remained. The main theme in denominational life appeared to be, "You can't tell me what to do." Some people argued that this was as it should be. Denominations were voluntary organizations that could not compel congregations to act or believe in certain ways. Other people insisted that congregations were not entities unto themselves but part of a larger body from which they received benefits and to which they owed certain responsibilities. This question of how much loyalty, financial support, and obedience congregations owed the denomination would be debated for the next thirty years.

The above discussion may have given the impression that this was a relatively congenial period within the Reformed Church, and in some respects it was. But during the decade of the 1970s and beyond, the denomination engaged in persistent and painful debate about whether women could be ordained as elders and deacons.[61] The themes of diversity, fragmentation, and "you can't make me" were much in evidence. As it had done in 1950 after another significant period of conflict, the Reformed Church looked to church extension as an opportunity to transcend conflict with a common sense of mission.

Reaching Out: The World beyond the Reformed Church

By the mid-1970s the Reformed Church had moved beyond the crisis of 1969 and resolved several internal issues. As in the early 1950s, church growth appeared able to unite people with very different beliefs. But church growth also took on a new sense of urgency. At the General Synod meeting in 1975, Ray Rewerts said in his "President's Report" that the denomination faced a real crisis. It was not only small, but it had a "negative growth rate." He wondered why a church with such a

---

[61]   See chapter seven for a detailed discussion of the process.

rich theological heritage was so ineffective at outreach and evangelism, and he urged the synod to make evangelism and church growth a priority. The synod agreed, and this decision gave the denomination a clear task and focus for the next several years.[62]

During this decade there was a migration of people from the Rustbelt in the Northeast and Midwest to the Sunbelt of the South and West. This meant a loss of population where most Reformed Church congregations were located, and growth where there were very few Reformed churches. The churches in the Particular Synod of the West actually added members in some years, while other regions declined. In the statistical year between 1975 and 1976, the Reformed Church grew by about 1,500 members for one very simple reason: the Particular Synod of the West reported an increase of almost 3,000, and most of that came from the Garden Grove Community Church, which said it had grown from 3,992 to 6,229.[63] The growth seemed to be in the Sunbelt, and the denomination increasingly looked to that region as a place to start churches.

To raise money for these efforts, the Reformed Church Growth Fund was launched in 1977. It set a goal of five million dollars and promised that the money would be used to reach people who needed Christ. About half the money funded new sites and facilities, and the rest was used to strengthen existing churches and start a new mission in Venezuela.[64] The drive raised about six million dollars, in part because it

---

[62] *Acts and Proceedings*, 1975, 241-51. Rewerts offered a very thoughtful analysis. He insisted that kingdom growth meant helping people find the wholeness that only God could provide. The Reformed perspective made clear that it was God who invited and drew people into the kingdom. Rewerts also noted that the RCA had failed to take the world seriously enough. The church did not listen well to the questions people were asking or to the depth of their pain. Rewerts said, "We think in terms of our theology and our churchianity rather than of their spiritual loneliness and frustration. We communicate effectively in the language of the theologian but we fail to communicate effectively in the language of human hurt" (245). For a slightly different perspective on church growth, see Luidens, "Between Myth and Hard Data." Luidens argued that the RCA (along with other mainline denominations) saw the decline in numbers as an internal problem that could be solved by a new structure or increased commitment or more money or a clearer identity. In reality, he said, mainline decline was a matter of demographics and other issues beyond a denomination's control.

[63] John Stapert, editorial, "Looking into the Church Growth Numbers," *CH*, Oct. 15, 1976, 10-11. These statistics could be slippery. Two years earlier, in 1974, Garden Grove reported a drop in membership from 5,377 to 3,500. Some people wondered if the church adjusted its numbers based on the amount of assessments it was willing to pay.

[64] Lois Joice, "A Time To Plant," *CH*, Feb. 18, 1977, 18-19.

was effective in inspiring individuals to give. It fostered a sense of pride, confidence, unity, and commitment.[65]

Some of the money was earmarked for a new strategy of multiple church starts in Dallas, Texas. Peter Paulsen was hired as the executive pastor, and he selected locations for three churches in the suburbs of Plano, Carrolton, and North Dallas. After three pastors were hired, Paulsen returned to the denominational staff. The churches grew steadily, in part because they tried to appeal to northerners moving to Dallas by offering a distinct alternative to the Southern Baptists and Methodists who dominated Texas church life.

Reformed Church members in general were encouraged when church starts succeeded in new communities, because it meant that people who were not Dutch or previous members of the denomination actually found Reformed churches attractive. Some spirited debate did occur over the type of members deemed desirable in new churches. Peter Paulsen was quoted in the *Washington Post* and the *New York Times* saying that the new churches in Dallas were looking for "the Reformed Church type—a well paid, well-educated family." Critics wondered whether the Reformed Church had a similar passion to start churches in poor or ethnic neighborhoods.[66]

In 1978 the boundaries of the particular synods were redrawn in order to clarify geographical areas of responsibility for new church starts. Maine, for example, was placed within the Synod of Albany. The Synod of the West supervised church growth in the entire western half of the United States. Richard Welscott, director of new church development, considered this a defining moment in church growth

---

[65] Russell Redeker, "Church Growth Fund Discoveries," *CH*, Dec. 15, 1978, 14-15. Fund-raisers believed that the drive's success demonstrated the need for a good stewardship program. Most churches had given up the every-family stewardship visits they conducted fifteen years earlier, but had not replaced them with another means of inviting generous giving to the denomination. LeRoy Koopman, "The Reformed Church Growth Fund: How It All Came Out," *CH*, March 20, 1981, 3-7.

[66] Daniel Plasman, John Paarlberg, letters to the editor, *CH*, Feb. 23, 1979, 19. One of the church growth gurus at the time was Peter Wagner, who had developed the Homogeneous Unit Principle as a guide to church growth. He said that churches grew by attracting similar people, and that new churches needed to be explicit about the kind of people they were trying to attract. Families who lived in larger homes in suburbia were particularly appealing customers for new church starts. Wagner's idea worked, in that these kinds of churches did grow and thrive, but critics asked whether homogeneity was really the best idea for a church. This was one of many times when pragmatism (what worked) clashed with the ideal biblical and theological vision of what the church should be.

because each regional synod had clear responsibility for starting churches in a designated part of the country.[67]

The most creative and well-known church growth effort in the Reformed Church was Robert Schuller's development of the Garden Grove Community Church and its walk-in, drive-in sanctuary. Schuller's "possibility thinking" was controversial, but no one could argue with his success. A reporter observed that worship services at the church did not emphasize guilt or self-abasement but created an atmosphere of confident Christianity that knew that with God all things were possible. "Theologians might argue the pros and cons of this approach. What no one can dispute, however is that *something is happening there*. The church is gloriously alive, reaching the normally unreachable and restructuring lives. Whatever they are doing at Garden Grove, it is working."[68]

Louis Benes also gave a glowing report of the church after attending its Institute for Successful Church Leadership. Benes concluded that the secret to the church was the enthusiasm members demonstrated about the church and Jesus Christ. They had encountered God in a meaningful way and wanted to share what they had discovered.[69] This report illustrates a significant shift in Benes's thinking over the preceding three decades. He had become far more open to creative ideas and far less rigid and purist in his attitudes about church life. The denomination had also become more pragmatic since the 1940s. Insisting on precisely orthodox theological beliefs no longer seemed as essential as fostering practices that led to more members and great commitment and enthusiasm. A few questions were raised about the money Schuller spent on buildings. One letter writer lamented, "Oh, that all this money could be used to make this world a better place to live in rather than a monument to a Lord who never knew luxury, never cared about buildings, but was dedicated to recognizing the humanity of all people."[70] In general, though, Schuller was much admired and imitated.

By 1976, the Garden Grove congregation had outgrown its worship space and announced plans for a new "Crystal Cathedral." Stapert attended the dedication of the Crystal Cathedral in the fall of

67   "New Particular Synod Boundaries," *CH*, July 28, 1978, 13. Conversation with Richard Welscott. Prior to this, two regional synods might start churches in one area, such as Florida, while other parts of the country were neglected. Logistically, it was far more challenging to start a church at a distance from the regional synod office or the sponsoring church.

68   Lois Joice, "The Glass Cathedral that Grew in an Orange Grove," *CH*, April 16, 1971, 4-5.

69   "New Hope for the Church," *CH*, April 16, 1971, 6-8, 22.

70   Mrs. Stephen Bienkowski, letter to the editor, *CH*, May 7, 1971, 14.

1980. The building had 10,000 windows, 91,500 square feet of space, 2,890 seats, and an 18 million-dollar price tag. It was dedicated debt free, and the offerings taken at the dedication were slated to be used to build a hospital in Chiapas, Mexico. Stapert was impressed with the ministry. "It helps people to see themselves and to see others in ways that are a little bit more like the way God sees them and a little bit less like the way humans see them." Stapert also noted a potential problem: "Whether the cathedral will be a help to the gospel or not depends a great deal on whether the cathedral glorifies Schuller or God."[71]

There was a dark side to church growth that sometimes clouded the general euphoria: a lack of supervision over the new congregations being organized. For decades Reformed Church congregations had raised money for new buildings by selling promissory notes through ads in the *Church Herald*. This was the case with the RCA congregation in San Dimas, California, which began in 1965 with a big vision and a very young pastor. The church published advertisements that showed plans to develop a drive-in church, a retirement community, and a television program. The ads offered notes for sale at an interest rate about two percent higher than other churches. In 1974 a member of the fund-raising staff wrote to the note-holders advising them that the church was in deep financial trouble. It is unclear how the church spent the five million dollars it received, but it probably paid salaries and ongoing expenses rather than paying off the mortgage. The Classis of California, in which San Dimas was located, had approved a maximum of $800,000 in note sales, but apparently it paid no attention to the amount that the church actually sold.[72]

Noteholders filed suit. The pastor had left that year, and the classis appeared to know nothing about the church's finances. It was unclear who was responsible to pay on the defaulted notes. This financial fiasco raised serious questions about Reformed Church polity and the classical oversight of new church starts. Should investors who received such a high rate of return accept the risks, as they would in the stock market? Should the *Church Herald,* which advertised the note sales from 1966-1973, be responsible for bad notes? Some letter writers thought the denomination should reimburse investors, perhaps using

---

[71] Editorial, "Robert Schuller Is from La Mancha," *CH*, Oct. 17, 1980, 8-9. "Garden Grove Dedicates Crystal Cathedral," Oct, 17, 1980, 22-23.

[72] John Stapert, editorial, "Unmentionables," *CH*, May 27, 1977, 8-9. According to the *Historical Directory of the Reformed Church in America* (Eerdmans, 2001), the pastor, David Ray, had been ordained Congregational in 1964 and was attending Fuller Seminary when he began working as a student pastor at San Dimas.

money from the Reformed Church Growth Fund.[73] No one appeared to be legally liable, and everyone refused to take moral responsibility.

At the Synod of 1977 the Overtures Committee recommended that the synod form a committee to study the matter, but Harry De Bruyn, former General Synod president and a lawyer, persuaded delegates to reconsider this recommendation. Forming a committee implied that the denomination had responsibility for the San Dimas debacle, an admission which could cost the Reformed Church a lot of money.[74]

In 1982 a civil court awarded the San Dimas noteholders $3.4 million—$2.9 million against the church and $501,000 against the Association for Inspirational Living, an off-shoot of the church's ministry.[75] Neither institution had any money or assets. In a letter to the *Church Herald* in March 1983, West Coast pastor Murray Moerman suggested that the synod give or loan money to the San Dimas church from the current fund drive or ask ten dollars per member from Reformed churches to cover the court-ordered payments. "It is inconsistent to insist on theological, liturgical and functional conformity and then not be a family when trouble comes. If it doesn't mean this, then we should lighten the fatherly hand which insists on conformity in other areas also."[76] The Reformed Church chose not to pay the congregation's debts, and, in the face of insurmountable expenses, the San Dimas church disbanded in 1984.

There were multiple system failures in this congregation. The pastor was young and inexperienced and had minimal connection with the Reformed Church. His piety and enthusiasm had persuaded a couple of prominent lay leaders that he would be a good person to start a church, even though he had not finished seminary. He was given a great deal of freedom, perhaps with the hope that he would be able

---

[73] Letters to the editor, *CH*, May 27, 1977, 20; June 24, 1977, 23; June 10, 1977, 23. The papers of Louis Benes in the Joint Archives, Holland, Michigan, contains a folder of angry letters written to him by noteholders. The General Synod Archives also contains documents about the church.

[74] *Acts and Proceedings*, 1977, 117, 119-20. Louis Benes, president of the General Synod, recommended the formation of an aid committee to provide financial assistance to those whose retirement savings had been particularly affected. The synod approved. *Acts and Proceedings*, 1977, 30-31, 35-36.

[75] Reformed Church News, "Court Awards Noteholders $3.4 Million," *CH*, Dec. 17, 1982, 20. The article erroneously gave the figures of $2.9 million and $501, but the error was corrected in the Jan. 7, 1983, issue, p. 26.

[76] The two pastors in place when the church disbanded, Melvin DeVries and Richard Decker, received a call from the Classis of California to start the New Hope Reformed Church in San Dimas. "New Hope Reformed Holds Services in San Dimas," *CH*, April 6, 1984, 23-24. Murray Moerman, letter to the editor, March 18, 1983, 22.

to develop a ministry like the Crystal Cathedral. There were very few checks and balances and little if any supervision by the classis or the regional synod. In the end, the excitement which seemed to drive the new church movement lost some luster—and future ventures received more supervision.

Reaching Out: Raising Money for Mission

The Reformed Church in America had stressed the importance of world mission for more than a century, but both enthusiasm and funding for missions had declined by the late 1970s. In his 1979 presidential report, Harvey Hoekstra (a former missionary to Africa) lamented the decrease in support for missionaries since 1968, when the Board of World Mission became part of the General Program Council. He feared that the structure of the GPC (five functionally organized committees[77]) did not foster the relationships between congregations and particular missionaries or areas that produced effective fund-raising. Hoekstra proposed that the GPC be reorganized so that world mission would be defined clearly and visibly and administered by people with specific expertise. He also argued that the denomination lacked a clearly stated priority and that its work had become fragmented. He suggested that if the Reformed Church put all of its energy into evangelism abroad and church growth at home, then the money would follow.[78]

An example of this fragmentation was evident at the Synod of 1980. The Evangelism and Church Growth Advisory Committee called on the General Program Council to develop a ten-year plan for starting new churches, to give a high priority to urban *and* rural ministry, *and* to attend to the needs of small churches. The Hispanic Council asked that GPC develop a plan to start new churches in the thirty areas of the country with the largest Hispanic populations. Although the synod approved these tasks, the Reformed Church simply did not have the financial resources or personnel to accomplish all of them.[79]

In response to Hoekstra's speech the GPC developed a new structure with three divisions—World Mission, Christian Discipleship,

---

[77] The committees were Evangelism and Church Growth, Christian Community, Human Welfare, Personal Growth and Relationships, and Social Issues. Lois Joice, "Togetherness in Zion: The Fall Meeting of the General Program Council," *CH*, Dec. 17, 1971, 20, 29-30.

[78] *Acts and Proceedings*, 1979, 31, 38.

[79] *Acts and Proceedings*, 1980, 199-209. Synod advisory committees; the president; and all agencies, councils, and commissions could propose that the synod perform a certain task. Delegates often found these ideas inspiring and approved them, without necessarily thinking about what was possible or what should have priority.

and Church Planning and Development—and hired seven new executives.[80] The GPC also proposed a relatively modest assessment to fund the Discipleship and Planning divisions.[81] In response, both the Classis and the Particular Synod of Chicago protested that congregations did not want or use denominational programs and should not be forced to pay for them.[82] The GPC discarded the assessment idea[83] and instead asked each congregation to contribute 2 percent of its congregational purposes budget for Christian Discipleship and 1 percent for Church Planning and Development. Everett Zabriskie, executive coordinator of the General Program Council, presented the request as a matter of identity:

> The glue that holds the RCA family together is the work of the divisions of World Mission, Christian Discipleship, and Church Planning and Development. Without our common work we are merely a heap of congregations with a common past, a disjointed present, and no future. Support shares and the responsibilities and opportunities that go with them will keep us together in the work of the gospel today and in the days to come.[84]

Congregations were not convinced and did not provide enough funding for the new structure. In the fall of 1981, the GPC predicted a $900,000 deficit for the year. Churches had increased their giving over 1980, but not enough to meet a budget that was 13 percent higher than the previous year.[85] In the spring of 1982 the GPC made major budget cuts and eliminated several staff positions.[86]

---

[80]   Everett Zabriskie, executive coordinator; John Buteyn, World Mission; Bert Van Soest, Christian Discipleship; Russell Redeker, Church Planning and Development; Robert White, Social Witness; and Warren Henseler and Dick Vander Voet, Missions.

[81]   Jack Boerigter (Yes) and Ronald Geschwendt (No), "A Proposal for Assessments," *CH*, March 21, 1980, 10-12. The amount of the assessment would be based on spending for congregational purposes. All churches would pay at least $52, but no church would pay more than $5,200.

[82]   Arie Brouwer, "A Proposed Assessment for Denominational Services," *CH*, Feb. 8, 1980, 15. *Acts and Proceedings*, 1980, 224-26. The overtures included several additional reasons. Assessments were a form of taxation contrary to the historic method of voluntary giving. Congregations should be able to choose their programs (and some churches preferred the curriculum from the Christian Reformed Church). More money did not mean more quality programming. Assessments were unbiblical because giving in the Bible was always voluntary.

[83]   "GPC Approves Restructure, Budget," *CH*, Apr. 18, 1980, 22.

[84]   "GPC Designs Support Share Financing System," *CH*, Sept. 4, 1981, 17; Everett Zabriske, "Support Shares for the Family," *CH*, Sept. 18, 1981, 18.

[85]   "GPC Approves $7 Million Drive," *CH*, Dec. 11, 1981, 21. The actual deficit for 1981 was more than $800,000. "GPC Deficit Exceeds $800,000," *CH*, Feb. 19, 1982, 23.

[86]   Arie Brouwer, "Reducing Staff and Continuing Mission," *CH*, April 16, 1982, 19, 29; "General Program Council Rejects Division Merger," *CH*, April 30, 1982, 23-24; John Stapert, editorial, "No Rubber Stamp," April 30, 1982, 5.

John Stapert suggested several reasons for the large deficit. The new structure was expensive to implement, and the request for support came too late to include in congregational budgets. Additionally, churches waited until the last minute to send contributions, which made the deficit look worse than it was. The Reformed Church had been affected by a bad economy with high unemployment, inflation, and interest rates. Finally, he noted that "dollars have gained a whopping kind of control over denominational program—a sad state for any Christian body to be in." Some cutting of expenses is appropriate, but "if we make a habit of scaling down our witness—at any level of the church—so that it fits our financial resources, we've lost our visionary faith."[87]

A few letters to the editor suggested that the deficit was not about money so much as a lack of confidence in denominational leadership. Paul Nulton, a pastor in Calgary, Alberta, claimed that churches did not give to the Reformed Church

> because we have lost the confidence that the Lord Jesus Christ is preeminent in the programs and among the leadership of our denomination....Could it be that in the RCA today we are drifting into congregationalism because a whole lot of people genuinely feel that it does us no good to raise our spiritual and biblical concerns to the leadership—that they will find another reason to justify decline and failures anyway?[88]

Don den Hartog of Orland Park, Illinois, argued that the financial crisis was actually a good thing because it had forced the denomination to eliminate a number of unnecessary positions. He also believed that Reformed Church congregations would give far more to the denomination if it stopped giving money to the World and National Councils of Churches. [89]

Ironically, after all the hand-wringing, job-eliminating, and debating, the General Program Council ended 1982 with a $55,000 surplus. Contributions from churches increased about 13 percent, and an additional $253,000 came from the sale of property.[90]

In addition to this extensive and expensive bureaucratic re-structure in 1981, the Reformed Church's development staff announced a new campaign later that year for a Church Building Fund, with a

[87]   "Lessons from the Deficit," *CH*, April 16, 1982, 4-5.
[88]   May 28, 1982, 19.
[89]   June 25, 1982, 21.
[90]   "Treasurer Reports 1982 GPC Surplus," *CH*, March 4, 1983, 24.

goal of seven million dollars. Many of the churches begun in the late 1970s were meeting in schools or theaters and lacked resources for their own buildings. Some churches had outgrown their facilities and needed to expand. Older churches needed money for repairs. Property and construction costs were extremely high in the early 1980s. The denomination did not have enough money available for churches to borrow, and churches could not qualify or pay for commercial loans. The assets of the Church Extension Fund came from the sale of promissory notes, and the Reformed Church could not attract enough investments when money market certificates offered nearly twice the interest rate the denomination could afford.

As part of the campaign, particular synods were given fund-raising goals and were told they could use the money they raised to make the first loans in their own regions. Each congregation also had a goal based on membership and income. Unlike the Reformed Church Growth Fund a few years earlier, this drive did not reach its goal. By September 1983 only $3.8 million had been pledged. The Synod of the West exceeded its goal and raised $2.4 million, but this included a million-dollar pledge from Robert Schuller on behalf of the Crystal Cathedral that had been earmarked for a church his son would start in San Juan Capistrano.[91] Michigan churches pledged only $375,000 of a $2 million goal.[92]

One reason given for the lack of support was that some churches preferred to support missionaries rather than construction. Russell Redeker, the director of the fund drive, responded that establishing new congregations was a form of missionary work, because mission was accomplished through people in congregations. "Mission is not only the sending of people to other places or providing money for the relief of hunger, injustice, and oppression. Mission takes place at home, too, and our mission here requires facilities." Some churches preferred to give to church growth efforts sponsored by their own regions. Redeker noted that denominational loan money had historically been given by the eastern churches and used by the western churches. Now there were several new projects in the synods of New York and New Jersey, so it was appropriate for the funding to flow in the opposite direction. "The Reformed Church needs every part of the denomination if it's going to grow, and assisting the church in the East is a step in the right

---

91   "GPC Approves $7 million budget," *CH*, May 6, 1983, 20. The GPC granted an exception in Schuller's case to the usual loan limit of $300,000.

92   "CBF Drive Lowers Projections," *CH*, Sept. 16, 1983, 22.

direction."[93] None of these arguments moved the Reformed Church to match its generosity to the Church Growth Fund of the late 1970s.

Both world mission and church growth had historically been sources of unity within the Reformed Church as people from all regions shared a common goal. By the early 1980s, however, regionalism, a growing independence ("you can't tell me what to do"), and anger over women's ordination combined to produce a rather fragmented denomination that struggled to pay its bills.

Reaching Out: Making a Difference in the World

Religion and spirituality may have become more individual and personal during the 1970s, but churches could not avoid pressing social issues. Two new issues, abortion and homosexuality, had received almost no attention in the past but became deeply divisive in both politics and religion at this time. The war in Vietnam continued to cause controversy, as did the Watergate scandal. Toward the end of the 1970s, the Religious Right mobilized under the leadership of Jerry Falwell and others, and some Reformed Church members found that stance on social and political issues more appealing than that of their denomination. As the Reformed Church wrestled with these issues at General Synod and in other venues, sharp differences of opinion became increasingly evident.

Political Issues

The Vietnam War gave the Reformed Church multiple topics for discussion during the first half of the 1970s: draft cards, amnesty, Vietnamese-American children, and refugees. The synod denied a recommendation to abolish the draft but voted to support both those who refused military service and those who accepted it, acknowledging that both were exercising Christian conscience. This may have been the path of least resistance, but it also recognized that there was no single answer to the question of military service for Christians.[94]

The news about Vietnam became especially troubling and divisive during the summer of 1971, when the *New York Times* began publishing the *Pentagon Papers*, a set of secret government documents analyzing the United States' involvement in Vietnam. The papers described two decades of deception, particularly by then president Lyndon Johnson. In the face of these stark revelations of government manipulation,

Louis Benes sympathized with the government and condemned the media for the underhanded nature of the leaks. He criticized both national leaders and the American people for failing to rely on God in their decisions. He wondered whether the agony over Vietnam and the loss of confidence in the government "is a judgment of God upon our country for our national failure and refusal to recognize him as we should in our public life." Benes suggested that if government officials had sought God's wisdom, they might have found a better way to deal with Vietnam. If people prayed more diligently, perhaps the guidance of God would be evident in national affairs.[95] The *Pentagon Papers* showed the depth of human sin and brokenness in political structures, but Benes advocated personal prayer as a response.

Benes responded similarly to revelations about Watergate. This scandal began with a break-in at the offices of the Democratic National Committee in the Watergate complex in Washington, D.C. Further investigation revealed numerous illegal activities on the part of Nixon's staff. In May 1973 Nixon claimed that he had been misled but that he would accept full responsibility. Benes found it very difficult to believe that a Republican president could have engineered these events. He wrote,

> We can hope that as all the facts come out, they will show that the President was not himself involved, and that he was indeed misled by his aides. We want to believe, as we trust the nation wants to believe, that our president was not personally involved in this ignominious web of evil. We want to hold, with many of his friends, that his moral and ethical principles would not have allowed him to share in such shame.

Benes was disappointed that Nixon had surrounded himself with so many immoral people, but he called for patience, prayer, and the suspension of judgment until more facts emerged.[96]

Benes wrote another editorial at the end of August 1973 after more corruption was revealed. He was shocked by the revelations, but he saw Watergate as a symptom of the permissiveness and lawlessness that had affected all of society. Better laws were necessary, but, in the end, society would only be improved with better men who had been reborn. "America's only hope lies in a return to the God of the Bible and to the ways he has laid out for mankind in it. It lies in the life that

95   Editorial, "The Pentagon Papers," *CH*, July 16, 1971, 6-7.
96   Editorial, "The Watergate Scandal," *CH*, May, 25, 1973, 6-7.

comes alone from the Son of God, and in the new obedience that flows from that life."[97]

Jerome De Jong, a pastor in South Holland, Illinois, wrote a guest editorial in May 1974 asking readers to respect the office of the presidency and give people in authority the benefit of the doubt.[98] Other Reformed Church members were far less willing to excuse Nixon and the Republican Party. Harry Ver Strate, a retired pastor from Metuchen, New Jersey, suggested that respect and honor could be restored only after a thorough cleansing of the White House. The tapes did not show a president who deserved respect. Ver Strate also noted that he had paid three times the income tax Nixon did in 1970.[99]

In August 1974, after Nixon had resigned in disgrace, Benes wrote about Nixon's profanity and the obscenities that had to be deleted from the transcript. "It had been a sickening and disillusioning experience to read in these documents language without dignity, without a single reference to an ethical standard or a God of righteousness and truth.... The name of God was not sacred to our former President. Was anything sacred? Was morality or integrity? The transcripts reveal an amoral man participating in amoral discussions." Benes felt sorry for Nixon and hoped that he would ask forgiveness from God. Benes then broadened his analysis and noted that Nixon's crimes were likely widespread. Neither his critics nor anyone else was free from the sinfulness of the human race. "And whether we like it or not God's tape recorder is going all the time, recording not only our words and actions, but our thoughts and intentions as well." All will need forgiveness.[100]

There is wisdom in this ability to see sin as a widespread problem, rather than to focus solely on the guilt of a very public sinner. But Benes reflected a rather selective and individualistic view of sin. Nixon and his henchmen did not trust God, they used bad language, and they made bad choices. These are individual moral failings, and Benes called Nixon and other politicians and the whole nation to personal repentance. One of the insights of the Reformed tradition, however, is that sin is much larger than individual actions; sin is pervasive and systemic and transcends personal moral failings. Correspondingly, the remedy for sin is not simply individual conversion and personal piety, but the transformation of social structures. Benes chastised Nixon for his bad language and immorality, but he did not see any need for

---

[97]   Editorial, "More Thoughts on Watergate," *CH*, Aug. 24, 1973, 6-7.
[98]   "Respect and Honor," *CH*, May 3, 1974, 8.
[99]   Letter to the editor, *CH*, May 31, 1974, 24.
[100]   Editorial, "The Need for a New Sensitivity," *CH*, Aug. 23, 1974, 10-11.

systemic change in the political system (except for more prayer). He did not ask how the government had reached this level of criminal behavior or what could be done to prevent it in the future. Benes believed that if everybody turned to God, such corruption would not exist. Even if this unlikely event did occur, history has shown that personal piety is not sufficient to deal with systemic corruption on this level. The arrogance and the violation of both the office of the president and human decency demanded structural transformation, not just prayer.[101]

Abortion and Homosexuality

When Nixon resigned in 1974 and the Vietnam War ended in 1975, the political unrest in America seemed to ease for a bit. Two new social issues emerged that would fuel the culture wars for decades. The first issue was abortion, and the key event occurred in 1973 when the Supreme Court legalized abortion in the Roe v. Wade decision.[102] By this time the issue had already come before the General Synod several times. In 1968 the Christian Action Commission recommended, and the synod agreed, that abortion should be legal in cases of grave birth defects, when pregnancy impaired the mother's health, or if the pregnancy resulted from rape or incest.[103] In 1971 the Christian Action Commission drafted guidelines for the church to use in thinking about abortion. The commission noted that there was a broad spectrum of Christian opinions about abortion, no definitive instruction from scripture, and no scientifically proven time when life began. Given this ambiguity, the commission concluded that in the context of Christian freedom, every woman had a right to decide for herself whether to have a legal abortion, and this right should not be constrained by financial circumstances or the imposed moral positions of others. The decision should never be forced, but should be made prayerfully and in the context of a Christian community.[104] The synod approved these guidelines.

Much debate ensued during the next year. In a statement whose language exhibits bizarre irony, the Particular Synod of Michigan asked

---

[101]   After Nixon resigned, Gerald Ford, a native of Grand Rapids, Michigan, became the nation's only unelected president. Ford pardoned Nixon so that the nation could get on with healing and rebuilding trust, but many questions remained unanswered.

[102]   Before this decision, states could decide whether or not to permit abortions. The court ruling meant that states could no longer prohibit all abortions.

[103]   *Acts and Proceedings*, 1968, 217-18.

[104]   Louis Benes, "The 165th General Synod: Actions and Reports," *CH*, July 2, 1971, 4-14.

the Synod of 1972 to revise the guidelines because: "We believe the Bible teaches the sanctity of human life. Men are given the precious gift of life from God and are created in the image of God."[105] The synod did not alter the guidelines but referred them to the Christian Action and Theological Commissions for further study.

In the fall of 1972, citizens in Michigan voted on an amendment to the state constitution which would permit abortions up to twenty weeks. Before the vote, the Christian Action Commission published a statement in the *Church Herald* supporting the amendment and citing the 1971 guidelines that allowed freedom of choice. In the same issue, the Particular Synod of Michigan published its belief that abortion was wrong except in the case of rape or incest or to save the life of the mother. It encouraged a "no" vote on the amendment.[106] Several angry letter writers protested that the Christian Action Commission had no right to make a statement in this way and should be disbanded. General Synod president Harry DeBruyn, GSEC chair William Babinsky, and general secretary Marion de Velder reviewed the synod actions and concluded that, although the Christian Action Commission often served as the conscience of the church, this particular action was inappropriate. The three officers encouraged Reformed Church members in Michigan to study the issues and vote their conscience as guided by scripture and the teachings of the church.[107]

This incident offers an example of regional autonomy in the face of denominational pronouncements. The General Synod of the denomination approved guidelines advocating choice, on the basis of which a denominational agency (the CAC) issued a formal statement. However, when church members from Michigan did not agree, they were certainly not bound to it. The Christian Action Commission only had authority if church members agreed with it.

The second hot-button social issue of the 1970s was homosexuality. In the late 1960s, movements in support of gay rights had begun to gather steam but received a great deal of resistance from both churches and broader American society. Lars Granberg, president of Northwestern College and a psychologist, offered the explanation commonly accepted by professional therapists at the time: that being

---

[105] *Acts and Proceedings*, 1972, 102.
[106] "RCA Commission Urges Yes Vote in Michigan Abortion Referendum," "Michigan Synod Recommends No Vote on Proposal B Legalizing Abortion," *CH*, Nov. 3, 1972, 15.
[107] For critical letters see *CH*, Nov. 3, 1972, 17, 22-23; Nov. 10, 1972, 10; and Nov. 24, 1972, 30-31. One letter in the Nov. 24 issue defended the commission. "Statement Re: Christian Action Commission Action," Nov. 17, 1972, 19.

gay was not a choice but resulted from a dysfunctional family. He described the ideal family as consisting of "a strong, tender father, one who enjoys being a man, who loves his sons, and who also loves his wife and daughters and values them for their femininity; and a warm, loving mother who enjoys being a woman, loves her children and values manliness in her husband and sons." Gay and lesbian children were likely to come out of families that lacked these characteristics. Granberg went on to explain that if homosexuality was not a choice, it could not be easily given up. Extensive and expensive therapy would be required to undo the family damage. There were no quick and easy cures. Given these realities, he concluded that homosexual people deserved to be treated with kindness and honesty, and the Reformed Church should "take a responsible approach" to the disorder.[108]

In 1974 the Christian Action Commission recommended that churches study the issue of homosexuality and "provide the compassionate acceptance of such persons within the life and mission of the church." Synod delegates were ambivalent. On the one hand, an amendment to delete "such" and insert "these confused" was defeated. On the other hand, the entire section was deleted after the synod debated whether "acceptance" meant that homosexual people could be ordained as ministers and elders. In the end, the synod adopted a motion from the floor which encouraged churches to affirm the biblical teaching against homosexuality. It did not recommend "compassionate acceptance."[109]

In 1977 the issue became very public in American society when Anita Bryant led a fight to repeal an ordinance in Dade County, Florida, that outlawed discrimination of gay and lesbian people. John Stapert thought that repeal was the right decision and wrote, "Regarding homosexuality, we have to be understanding and helpful. But giving 'rights' to homosexuality is like hospitals giving 'rights' to diseases."[110] Other responses were more compassionate. Harriet de Velder, a long-time missionary, insisted that homosexuals were human beings who

---

[108]   Lars Granberg, "Biblical Perspectives on Homosexuality," *CH*, Jan. 19, 1968, 14-15. Forty years later, research has shown numerous problems with this explanation. Both "dysfunctional" and "healthy" families produced both heterosexual and homosexual children. A number of questions have also been raised about the social construction of masculinity and femininity assumed in this description. It is important to recognize that despite its limitations, this analysis did not see homosexuality as a choice.

[109]   *Acts and Proceedings*, 1974, 221-22; Louis Benes, "The 168th General Synod: Actions and Reports," *CH*, July 12, 1974, 9.

[110]   "Losing and Winning," *CH*, June 24, 1977, 12-13.

should be insured their rights. Phyllis Naylor (a regular *Church Herald* columnist on family life) described a pastor who said that a lesbian woman was a child of God even if she was confused, disturbed, or warped, and must be accepted as a child with a handicap. A reader responded that the article was in poor taste and that writing about homosexuality would encourage it. Another said that homosexuality should not be equated with a birth defect, because there was nothing sinful about lameness or blindness.[111]

Donald Lindskoog, a psychology professor at Northwestern College, wrote a guest editorial advocating a somewhat more accepting view. Homosexual behavior was not life at its best, he said, but sexual preference was shaped early and mysteriously and may not be changeable. Somewhat paradoxically, he then said that heterosexual interest could be developed, and that homosexual people could choose to engage in heterosexual relationships. He concluded by insisting on the need to treat people decently. Gay and lesbian people had the right to be honest about themselves without fear of consequences, and diverse viewpoints must be respected.[112] The article sparked several critical letters. Bev Arp of Inwood, Iowa, insisted that homosexuality threatened children and should be "put in the closet where it belongs." Arp went on to say that she believed homosexuality should be made "such an intolerable burden that the homosexual would feel the pressure to seek help."[113]

In 1978 and 1979 the Theological Commission prepared a two-part paper on homosexuality that concluded, "Heterosexuality is not only normal; it is normative. Homosexual acts are contrary to the will of God for human sexuality." After saying this, the 1978 report went on to make two significant observations that have often been overlooked. First, the paper said that some homosexual people do not decide to be gay or lesbian. Their orientation comes from genetic, hormonal, or psychological factors over which they have no control. They do not choose this any more than heterosexuals choose their orientation. Second, the paper insisted that the church was responsible to support full civil rights for homosexual persons, even if it did not approve of their orientation or behavior. Denial of human and civil rights to homosexuals, the paper concluded, was "inconsistent with the biblical

---

[111] Harriet de Velder, letter to the editor, *CH*, Aug. 5, 1977, 23. Phyllis Naylor, "An Accepting Heart," *CH*, Aug. 5, 1977, 14-15. Muriel Aalfs, letter to the editor, Sept, 2, 1977, 18. Mrs. Randal Lubbers, letter to the editor, Sept. 16, 1977, 18.

[112] "The Church and Homosexuality," *CH*, Jan. 13, 1978, 8-9.

[113] Letter to the editor, *CH*, March 10, 1978, 21. See other letters Feb. 24, 1978, 20.

witness and Reformed theology." These reports were approved for study.[114] The church then avoided the topic for several years.

Communism and Human Rights Issues

In the early 1980s, after the election of Ronald Reagan to the presidency and the growth of the Religious Right, the culture wars intensified in both religion and politics. Tensions increased between the United States and the Soviet Union because of the build-up of nuclear weapons. It was a conflicted era in America and in the Reformed Church as well.

Under the leadership of the general secretary, Arie Brouwer, and the minister for social witness, Robert White, the Reformed Church paid more attention than usual to world events and crises, particularly the plight of people in El Salvador, the Soviet Union, and South Africa. The synod approved several actions and papers that could be termed progressive or moderate, and these were met with a great deal of resistance. Some members were more concerned about swear words in the movie *On Golden Pond* than they were about mass murders in Central America. They saw the primary role of the church as fostering personal piety, not criticizing the government.

During Ronald Reagan's presidency there was a great deal of conflict and warfare in Central America. Nicaragua had been taken over by Communists, and the United States feared a "domino effect" with other countries in the region. As a result, the United States government was providing substantial aid to the governments in Guatemala and El Salvador to prevent a Communist takeover and keep the right-wing governments in power.[115]

---

[114]   *Acts and Proceedings*, 1978, 235-39. The full reports are in *Acts and Proceedings*, 1978, 229-40, and 1979, 128-35. They may also be found in Cook, *The Church Speaks*, 243-66. The Synod of 1977 had referred to the Commission on Theology a motion that the RCA affirm civil rights for homosexual people. The papers were written in response to this motion and the broader discussion of the issue in American society. The first paper dealt with biblical texts and theological issues, and the second discussed pastoral care for homosexual people. Although individual authors were not identified in committee reports, it was widely recognized that Lars Granberg played a significant role in writing this report and particularly in emphasizing the genetic nature of homosexuality. The commission returned to the issue in the 1990s, and these reports and a study guide can be found on the RCA website at www.rca.org/sslpage.aspx?pid=2264 and in James I. Cook, ed., *The Church Speaks, Vol 2: Papers of the Commission on Theology, Reformed Church in America, 1984-2000*, HSRCA, no. 40 (Grand Rapids: Eerdmans, 2002), 269-90.

[115]   These countries had long been governed by combinations of the military, large business interests, and conservative politicians. A few families of European descent were rich and powerful, while the vast majority was extremely poor. When

In the spring of 1981, Arie Brouwer participated in a multidenominational meeting that culminated in a three-hour march in Washington D.C. and an offering of letters of protest to the president about the U.S. government's policies in Central America. Despite this demonstration of widespread religious concern, President Reagan twice refused to meet with denominational leaders. Brouwer reported on these activities in the *Church Herald* and also encouraged pastors to study the issues and write letters to government officials.[116]

Mr. and Mrs. Bob Berens of Hamilton, Michigan, expressed disappointment that the money they had given to the denomination to be used for God's work was used instead to mail biased opinion packets and fund Brouwer's travel to a demonstration in Washington. They wrote:

> We elected President Reagan to office, and I [*sic*] believe God placed him in this position for such a time as this, so we as Christians should support him. The Communists are masquerading in El Salvador as they have done in all the other countries before they took them over, and if we don't take action now our own dear North America will be next. In early Christian times, [*sic*] God commanded the Israelites to destroy their enemies, and now I believe we should help the El Salvadorans against Godless communism.[117]

Mrs. Cliff Dykstra of Friesland, Wisconsin, asked why Brouwer opposed the president's policy. She had received information from "various evangelistic and conservative publications" that the United States was desperately trying to stop the spread of communism in Central America. She trusted the secretary of state, Alexander Haig, to know

---

indigenous people tried to organize for better pay or housing or the opportunity to own land, the movements were labeled Communist and violently destroyed. In El Salvador, most of the peasants lived in desperate poverty, while the military government used any means necessary to preserve its power. Death squads tortured and killed agrarian reformers, politicians, and priests who sided with the poor. Archbishop Oscar Romero was assassinated March 24, 1980, and four American women church workers were murdered in December 1980. Still, the United States government authorized $25 million to support this repressive government, arguing that this action was necessary to prevent a Soviet takeover. The Society of Inquiry and the Faculty, New Brunswick Theological Seminary, letter to the editor, *CH*, May 15, 1981, 22.

[116] Arie Brouwer, "Siding with the Suffering," *CH*, April 17, 1981, 18, 30. "Brouwer Campaigns to Halt Aid to El Salvador," April 17, 1981, 24-25, "Brouwer Marches in Washington, D.C.," May 15, 1981, 21.

[117] Letter to the editor, *CH*, May 15, 1981, 22.

what was in the best interest of the country. Nicaragua had already experienced a "Communist invasion" by the Sandinista Liberation front, and the United States was arming El Salvador to prevent a similar action there.[118]

A few members expressed support for Brouwer. Vietnam Veteran Keith Taylor of McBain, Michigan, noted that during the Vietnam War, people looked to the church for moral leadership but found none. He appreciated Brouwer's courageous stand, which "points us to Scripture rather than to the easy half-truths of patriotism."[119]

The Hispanic Council supported Brouwer as well and recommended that the Synod of 1981 communicate to President Reagan its opposition to continuing military aid for El Salvador. In the debate which followed, some delegates argued that the synod did not have enough information and should trust the government's expertise. Another delegate argued that the church should not take political action because President Reagan had drawn the line on communism in El Salvador and Christians as good citizens should support his position. Delegates then debated whether a denomination had the right to speak to government leaders or if that overstepped the proper boundaries of church behavior. Finally, Samuel Solivan, a missionary to Venezuela, pointed out that the Salvadorans had specifically asked for a halt to military aid. Solivan's firsthand experience carried considerable weight with the delegates, and the recommendation passed by a 3-1 margin. The Reformed Church had chosen to side with the suffering rather than the preferences of the Republican Party.[120]

The fear of communism pervaded American society in the early 1980s, as both the United States and the Soviet Union continued to build their supplies of nuclear weapons.[121] In the midst of this tension, Arie Brouwer spent three weeks in Russia in 1981. He later asked why Americans were so afraid of Russia when America had so much more

---

[118] Letter to the editor, *CH*, May 29, 1981, 21.

[119] Ibid.

[120] John Stapert and Laurie Baron, "Canadian Setting Enhances 175th General Synod," *CH*, July 24, 1981, 6-7. Not all missionaries would have agreed, but it is significant that here a missionary demonstrated a clear understanding of the connections between social and evangelistic emphases. These denominational statements are often dismissed as irrelevant, since it is unlikely that Ronald Reagan cared what the RCA thought about the issue. The recommendation did say something significant about the RCA and its identity as a church which chose to support those who were suffering, even though it was politically unpopular.

[121] For a profound and insightful analysis of the arms race, see the paper by the Theological Commission, "Christian Faith and the Nuclear Arms Race, *Acts and Proceedings*, 1980, 117-29.

freedom, wealth, and power and the Soviets were actually afraid of America. Brouwer wrote,

> This climate of fear has stimulated the search for an enemy within as well as without. Apparently, we need a scapegoat. If our appetite for arms is to be satisfied, someone will have to starve. It appears that the poor have been chosen....I am afraid that these two great engines of fear—fear of the enemy without and fear of the enemy within—may be out of control, that their momentum may be too great to stop.[122]

In 1982 the classes of Raritan, Pella, and Albany and the Particular Synods of Michigan and Albany submitted overtures asking the Reformed Church to endorse a proposal that the United States and the Soviet Union freeze the testing, production, and deployment of nuclear weapons at current levels."[123] Earle Ellis, a professor at New Brunswick Seminary, proposed an amendment calling for a freeze at balanced levels of forces, because he believed that the Soviets had a far larger arsenal. Emotional debate followed. Those who supported the amendment argued that the Soviets wanted to take over the world, and one speaker referred to the Russians as the anti-Christ. Elder delegate Ray Shoff compared the arms limitation proposal to his experience at Pearl Harbor in December 1941. "I looked on men I ate with and slept with and saw only bits and pieces. We had nothing to fight with. Now we're talking about laying down all our resistance so that another nation can come in and take over. I'm appalled. I'm overcome." But James Stackpole, a pastor in Brooklyn, argued against the amendment because it would perpetuate fear, which had already failed the world. "It's time for the Christian church to try faith." In the end, the amendment (to freeze at balanced levels of arms) was defeated 168-74 and the original recommendation (to freeze at current levels) was approved. Once again the denomination affirmed a moderate stance despite the fearful rhetoric.[124] Some delegates remained unconvinced. On the last day of

---

[122] "Re-entry from Russia," *CH*, Sept. 18, 1981, 15. The role Brouwer played in talks with Russian Orthodox Church leaders about nuclear containment is demonstrated in several essays in Arie R. Brouwer, *Ecumenical Testimony*, HSRCA, no. 21 (Grand Rapids: Eerdmans, 1991). This memoir contains accounts of Brouwer's firm leadership on a number of social issues, including his testimony regarding apartheid in South Africa. It also bears witness to his substantive concern for Reformed worship and theology.

[123] *Acts and Proceedings*, 1982, 91-94.

[124] John Stapert and Margaret De Ritter, "Social Concerns Dominate General Synod," *CH*, July 23, 1982, 8-9.

synod in 1982 some delegates complained that the synod spent too much time on social issues such as El Salvador and the nuclear freeze and not enough on prayer and evangelism. Minister delegate Jerry Sittser suggested that the synod "could be prophetic by spending two or three hours on our knees this afternoon."[125] The request illustrates the persistent uncertainty within the Reformed Church as to the best way to make a difference in society.

Abortion Revisited

In response to the public efforts of the Moral Majority,[126] the Reformed Church revisited the topic of abortion during the early 1980s. In 1981 the Classis of Zeeland argued that previous synodical pronouncements on abortion had been ambiguous. The classis called on the synod to affirm the Human Life Amendment being debated in the U.S. Congress, which stipulated that life began at conception.[127] The delegates that year were more willing to live with ambiguity than the Classis of Zeeland. Many of them opposed abortion but refused to support the Human Life Amendment because it removed a woman's freedom of choice. Delegate Joan Tolliver argued that the Human Life Amendment would not stop abortion, but it would harm poor women who would be forced into illegal and dangerous alternatives. Those with the financial resources would still be able to find safe abortions outside the country. The *Church Herald* reported: "Although the synod had previously been cautioned against applause, a spontaneous burst of clapping began for Ms. Tolliver's speech. The applause was quickly silenced by the chair but it spoke revealingly about many delegates' persuasions."[128] The synod denied the Zeeland overture, but this moderately pro-choice mood proved to be the exception rather than the rule.[129]

---

[125]   Ibid., 18.

[126]   An organization formed in 1979 by the Rev. Jerry Falwell to give conservative Christians more influence in politics.

[127]   In 1979 Rep. Romano Mazzoli proposed an amendment that said the right to life began at fertilization. In 1981 Senator Orrin Hatch introduced an amendment which said the right to abortion was not guaranteed by the Constitution. These and similar proposed amendments that attempt to restrict abortion are usually referred to collectively as the Human Life Amendment.

[128]   Stapert and Baron, "175th General Synod," 4-16.

[129]   In the months after the Synod of 1981 met, debate resumed in the *Church Herald*. Ray Pontier, coordinator of the New Jersey Religious Coalition for Abortion Rights, wrote an article in which he described several scenarios in which a woman should have the right to choose whether to continue a pregnancy. He opposed the Human Life Amendment because it gave the fetus absolute priority and placed the woman

In 1982, the General Synod spent more time discussing abortion than any other issue. This time it took a more conservative position, approving an overture from the Classis of Cascades that asked governments to discontinue the use of public funds for abortion. Some delegates argued that this action would discriminate against the poor and drive abortion underground, but there was no applause for this view, as there had been in the previous year.[130]

In 1983 the conversation about abortion seemed particularly urgent and anxious. The Classis of Cascades sent an overture asking that the Reformed Church communicate its disapproval of the massive number of abortions to the governments of the U.S. and Canada. A motion to refer it to the Theological Commission for study was denied, and the synod approved the overture by a 2-1 margin. The synod also adopted an overture from Cascades opposing abortion in all but the most exceptional circumstances. Murray Moerman, a pastor in British Columbia, argued that as many as 97 percent of abortions were done for reasons of convenience. He said that his wife counseled pregnant women and reported that "wanting to look good in a bikini, wanting a new car, or finding pregnancy inconvenient this year," were reasons some women had offered for abortions. Stapert reported only a few opposing voices, and none from women as had been the case in previous years.[131] On this issue, the moderate voice gave way during the early 1980s to a purist one, reflecting the shifting currents of the national debate.

Membership in the World and National Councils

Finally, in the early 1980s the Reformed Church spent significant time revisiting an old issue: its membership in the World and National

---

in the role of a non-person without a voice. Fifteen letters followed; only three agreed with Pontier. Critics argued that women had a choice whether to be sexually active and whether to use birth control, but no choice once they were pregnant. Others insisted that the fetus was a person. One writer argued that there was no middle ground for a true Christian, and no place for a pro-choice organization in the RCA. Another accused the RCA of cowardice for refusing to take a stand. Raymond Pontier, "Abortion: Thinking of the Woman," *CH*, July 10, 1981, 6-7; Letters to the editor, *CH*, Aug. 7, 1981, 13; Aug. 21, 1981, 20-21.

130 John Stapert and Margaret De Ritter, "Social Concerns Dominate General Synod," *CH*, July 23, 1982, 6-8.

131 "The Synod and Its Festival," *CH*, July 15, 1983, 4-6. Statements about abortion were not based on theological principles but rather arose on an *ad hoc* basis, which depended on the nature of overtures received and the presence of delegates who were passionately opposed to abortion. In 1983 the Theological Commission presented a paper that did deal with some of the moral and spiritual issues, but the majority of delegates thought that the language was too complex and needed revision.

Councils of Churches. As in the 1950s and 1960s, critics of the councils were partially driven by the fear of communism. In August 1982 the *Reader's Digest* published an article about the WCC entitled, "Karl Marx or Jesus Christ?" It argued that the WCC supported violent actions and Marxist governments and refused to criticize the Soviet Union for any human rights violations. Arie Brouwer responded that many Christians in Communist countries—including those who were members of the World Council—lacked the freedom that Americans had to speak without punishment.[132]

In January 1983 the *Reader's Digest* followed its earlier critique with a piece entitled, "Do You Know Where Your Church Offerings Go?" The author accused the National Council of Churches of promoting Marxist causes and revolutionary behavior through its relief agency, Church World Service. John Stapert and Margaret De Ridder pointed out the long-term record of Church World Service as an efficient group with low overhead that actually provided substantive care. They also wondered whether Christians should trust the *Reader's Digest* or the NCC and Reformed Church leaders.[133]

James Cook posed a similar question about trust in 1983. He reminded readers that both Marion de Velder and Arie Brouwer, past and present general secretaries, had worked closely with the councils. Should Reformed Church members trust their leaders, missionaries, and staff who had actually worked with the NCC, or should the Reformed Church members trust outside critics with their own agendas? [134] It was ironic that some of the most conservative Reformed Church members, who would quickly decry the "media" as secular and untrustworthy, chose to believe the media rather than their denominational leaders.

Council membership was hotly debated at the General Synod in 1983. Eight classes submitted overtures asking for withdrawal from the World Council, and six from the National Council.[135] Those opposed argued that membership in the councils hampered church growth, destroyed unity within the denomination, and was generally irrelevant to most members. In the end, the overtures to leave the councils were defeated by margins of 2-1. The synod did vote to explore affiliation

---

[132] John Stapert, editorial, *"Reader's Digest* or World Council?" *CH*, Sept. 3, 1982, 4-5; Arie Brouwer, "Distorted Images," Sept. 17, 1982, 19.

[133] Margaret De Ridder and John Stapert, editorial, "Truth in Journalism: *Reader's Digest* vs. NCC," *CH*, Feb. 4, 1983, 4-5.

[134] "The RCA and the Councils of Churches," *CH*, April 1, 1983, 19. It was clear from the letters and overtures that a number of members distrusted denominational leaders precisely because they had been so involved with the councils.

[135] Letters to the editor, *CH*, June 3, 1983, 18; *Acts and Proceedings*, 1983, 135-44.

with the National Association of Evangelicals, despite the fact that that association did not allow its members to belong to the National or World Councils.[136]

The Reformed Church's commitment to ecumenism received considerable criticism. Kenneth Kroll of Anacortes, Washington, argued that Arie Brouwer's defense of the World Council illustrated the confused thinking of many church liberals.

> He makes an eloquent appeal for unity of all men but creates disunity within the body of Christ. President Reagan is a born-again Christian, yet Rev. Brouwer does not even display the spiritual maturity to treat the president as a brother in Christ. Instead he marches with other WCC members to support the Soviet-supplied leftist terrorists in El Salvador and flaunts President Reagan's policies openly in public....I believe we are blessed in America with a Christian president by the will and grace of God and that our church's obligation is to support him in prayer, offer constructive criticism where differences occur, and live in the faith that God will prevail through his presidency.[137]

For a few years in the early 1980s, the Reformed Church made statements and took actions on social and political issues that were unusually progressive. Arie Brouwer and Robert White offered significant leadership in this direction. They were articulate, persuasive, and profoundly shaped by Reformed theology. Their leadership was deeply appreciated in some quarters of the church but strongly resisted in others. In 1983, after fifteen years on the denominational staff, Arie Brouwer announced that he was leaving the Reformed Church to become deputy general secretary for the World Council of Churches.[138]

---

[136] John Stapert, "The Synod and Its Festival," *CH*, July 15, 1983, 6-7, 10. Stapert later observed that these two apparently contradictory actions (staying in the NCC but reaching out to the NAE) reminded him of a bridge. The RCA had often served as a kind of intermediary agency, particularly on the mission fields, between liberal and conservative groups that would talk to the RCA but not to each other. The decision to remain in the councils suggested that the RCA saw itself as an ecumenical body rather than a narrow and isolated one. Stapert hoped that the NAE would change its membership policy, which excluded those who belonged to the NCC and WCC, but the NAE was unwilling to do so. "The RCA as a Bridge," *CH*, July 15, 1983, 19.

[137] Letter to the editor, *CH*, Aug. 12, 1983, 22.

[138] Arie Brouwer, "Why Work for the WCC?" *CH*, April 15, 1983, 18-19. "Arie Brouwer Accepts WCC Nomination," April 15, 1983, 24. About a year later Brouwer was the leading candidate for the position of general secretary of the World Council. He withdrew his name when an anti-Soviet statement by President Reagan forced the Russian Orthodox representatives to withdraw their support from an American

The next general secretary would guide the church onto a very different course.

Conclusions

What kind of denomination would the Reformed Church become? In the early 1980s, there were many different answers to that question and many ways to be Reformed. Various members and congregations wanted the denomination to emphasize social justice or evangelism or church growth or Reformed theology or strict personal morality or a conversion experience. Some members were passionately committed to the denomination and concerned about its identity, but there were others who would respond to the question of identity with "Who cares?" The denomination seemed increasingly intrusive or irrelevant to them. In their view, a denomination should not tell members what to think or do. It should not require members to pay for programs they did not support. It should not take stands on difficult social issues. Instead, each region, congregation, and individual should decide what it meant to be Reformed. For church members who thought this way, the denomination carried little authority to encourage common action or belief.

Denominational identity was fragmented. There had been attempts to articulate a Reformed position on issues such as apartheid and nuclear weapons. However, people did not necessarily listen; in fact, they frequently listened more carefully to non-Reformed voices.

A loss of members, along with the accompanying fear that the denomination was losing its influence and appeal, created a great deal of anxiety. Some people suspected that the identity and efforts of the past had not been sufficiently evangelical/conservative. Other members insisted that the Reformed Church needed to recover its Reformed identity, not adopt Baptist hymnbooks and theology.

The family was held together in large part during these years by strong and gifted denominational staff leadership. Most of them were very bright, articulate, loyal, open to new ideas, and yet deeply Reformed (moderate) in their theological positions.

Given the political and social polarization in America during the 1980s, it is not surprising that the church experienced conflict over these

candidate. In the fall of 1984, he was named general secretary of the National Council of Churches. "WCC Elects Uruguayan New General Secretary," *CH*, Aug. 10, 1984, 20. "NCC Nominates Brouwer New General Secretary," *CH*, Oct. 19, 1984, 20. Robert White became president of New Brunswick Theological Seminary in 1985.

issues as well. The cultural and political tension was compounded by the fact that many conservatives and purists were still very angry about the ordination of women. Some pulled away from the denomination, while others encouraged the Reformed Church to take more conservative positions. The persistent shortage of funding in the early 1980s made it difficult for members to unite around exciting new programs as they did with the Church Growth Fund in the late 1970s.

The Reformed Church had worked through the conflicts of 1969 enough to survive as a denomination, but the heated debate over women's ordination showed the persistence of deep differences that had not yet been resolved.

CHAPTER 7

1970–1994: Do Women Belong? The Debate over Ordination

Photographs of General Synod delegates from the early years of the twentieth century are rather remarkable, because in them the delegates all look alike. They are all dressed in black suits, white shirts, and black hats. Most are over forty. And, of course, they are all men.

During the 1950s and 1960s, every July the *Church Herald* published a General Synod issue that reported on the meeting and included a number of photographs of delegates and visitors. The dress code gradually became more varied, but most of the delegates were still over forty. And, of course, they were still all men. Women did appear occasionally in the photographs. They joined their husbands for meals, held a prayer meeting in the ladies' lounge, and watched from in the back of the meeting room in the visitors' row. But they did not participate in any official business.

In the General Synod issue which followed the tumultuous Synod of 1969, the *Church Herald* included a photograph of women walking through the meeting room carrying signs that protested the Reformed Church's failure to ordain women. They also carried petitions with more than a thousand signatures from women protesting their lack of voice, role, and status in the denomination.[1] Given the amount of conflict and controversy at this synod, their action did not have much immediate impact, but it was clear that women were no longer willing to remain segregated in the ladies' lounge and the visitors' row. During the next ten years, the issue of the ordination of women would cause significant conflict within the Reformed Church in America.

By 1969, efforts to gain the ordination of women to the offices of minister, elder, and deacon had occurred sporadically for fifty years,[2] but the denomination continued to resist making the necessary changes to the *Book of Church Order*. Those who opposed women's ordination usually cited four reasons. The most frequently cited rationale was the Bible. Read literally, it provided multiple texts that prohibited women in leadership. "Women should be silent in the churches....For it is shameful for a woman to speak in church" (1 Cor. 14:34-35). "I permit no woman to teach or to have authority over a man; she is to keep silent" (1 Tim 2:12). "Wives, be subject to your husbands as you are to the Lord" (Eph. 5:22). These instructions seemed straightforward.

Proponents of women's ordination argued that there were many other biblical texts that affirmed women in leadership roles. Some of these references were subtle and easily missed without the assistance of biblical scholarship. Acts 2 reported that the Holy Spirit fell on both women and men at Pentecost. Paul insisted that in Christ there was no male or female (Galatians 3). He referred to Phoebe (a *diakonos*), Priscilla, Mary, Junia, Tryphaena, and Tryphosa as his coworkers in Romans 16.

---

[1]   Since 1945, women's official roles in the RCA had gradually been reduced. For decades women ran the Woman's Board of Foreign Missions and the Women's Board of Domestic Missions, which supervised both male and female missionaries. When these boards were absorbed into the denominational boards in 1946 and 1951, women were given about one-third of the seats on those boards. But when the boards were integrated into the General Program Council, women comprised about 20 percent of the members. Women were excluded from the General Synod Executive Committee because of the requirement that members be ministers or elders. For an overview of women's roles in the RCA see House and Coakley, *Patterns and Portraits*. For a discussion of the Woman's Board of Foreign Missions, see Kansfield, *Letters to Hazel*. For an overview of women in office see Edwin G. Mulder, "Full Participation—A Long Time in Coming!" *Reformed Review*, Spring 1989, 42/3, 224-46. It is available on the RCA website at http://images.rca.org/docs/archives/longtimecoming.pdf. See also a paper by the Commission on Theology, "The Role and Authority of Women in Ministry," *Acts and Proceedings*, 1991, 435-49. It is available on the RCA website at http://images.rca.org/docs/women/authoritywomen.pdf.

[2]   See the discussion of these efforts above, pp. 79-83. Attempts to change the *BCO* in 1964 and 1967 had also failed.

Jesus challenged a number of restrictive rules about women and valued them as intelligent, spiritual beings. It is true that Jesus did not ordain women, but he did not ordain any men either. Those who supported women's ordination thought their beliefs were equally rooted in the Bible.

Second, some ministers and laypeople rejected women's ordination on the grounds that it was unconstitutional in the Reformed Church. The *Book of Church Order* (*BCO*) was ambiguous on this issue. It said that elders and deacons must be chosen from among the *male* members of the congregation, but when it described candidates for minister of Word and sacrament it said *persons* could be ordained. Supporters pointed out that persons meant men and women. Opponents insisted that *persons* in this context had always meant males. These semantic issues sparked endless debate during the 1970s and beyond.

The third common argument was that women's ordination was not good for the church. This response was used by the review committee almost every time overtures asked to delete the word male from the requirements for elder and deacon. In 1918 a review committee said such an amendment would "work injury through friction and division out of all proportion to any possible good that might accrue." In 1921 the review committee said "the time was not yet proper," and in 1932 it said that "strong objections may arise." In 1936 the review committee professed high regard for the qualifications and consecration of women but feared that men would let the women do all the work. In 1951 a committee said that the need [for women elders and deacons] was "not apparent" and "the church was not yet ready."[3] Similar arguments recurred during the 1970s as the debate intensified, and they occasionally reappear three decades later.[4]

Finally, the least explicit but perhaps the most influential argument against the ordination of women insisted that women were not fit to be ministers or church leaders because it was not in their "nature" to exercise leadership. In this view, women were called to raise children, maintain their homes, and support their husbands. They could not hold authority over the souls of men.[5] Lucille VanWyk of Lynnville, Iowa, criticized women who dared to step out of their traditional role.

---

[3]   For a list of these actions see Mulder, "Full Participation."

[4]   In 2010, after a woman minister was elected vice-president of the General Synod, a blogger on the RCA web site opined that churches led by women did not thrive.

[5]   These arguments appeared repeatedly in letters to the editor, *Church Herald* articles, and debates. For a more extended summary and analysis of the arguments, see Lynn Japinga, *Feminism and Christianity: An Essential Guide* (Nashville: Abingdon, 1999), 127-44.

"What has come over the once attractive confusion-free helpmate of man to make her so dissatisfied with her God-instituted tasks even though God has given her such a beautiful origin and position?" She wondered how women could hire baby-sitters and thereby forfeit the right to shape their children. She was appalled that so many women worked in order to provide for their wants, rather than their needs, and wore manlike clothes, even to church. She concluded that God's Word said men should rule over women.[6]

Another woman suggested that her happiness in her role as a wife and mother should be the norm for all women.

> My husband is our family's leader, protector, and provider. He also manages the money and does the necessary worrying. I feel "liberated" being able to go out to coffee with friends, taking time to read God's Word during the day, and being able to go to Mothers' Club at school....If a mother must be off to work by 8 a.m., how can she have devotions with her children? And when she gets home she is tired. But so is the husband. Is it his job to wash and make supper?...A woman's presence lights a home. Husbands in the busy world, full of problems, look forward to coming home to a delicious meal and happy kids. I feel fulfilled watching my children find their way in life....Let us recognize that a man has superior strength and ability, then honor his right to be the leader that God meant him to be.[7]

The combination of the Bible, the *Book of Church Order*, biology, and tradition presented formidable obstacles to the ordination of women. Still, some women felt called to ministry and leadership, and a number of men felt equally called to support them.

After a half century of attempts to change the *BCO* through the "proper" channel of overtures and classis votes, and a half century of resistance, some congregations and classes took matters into their own hands. In 1970, the Rockaway Reformed Church of Whitehouse Station and the Middlebush Reformed Church ordained women as elders and deacons. The Classis of Raritan approved their actions and submitted an overture asking the synod to show cause why the churches should not have done this. The Overtures Committee noted in its response that the synod had indeed said in 1958 that there was no biblical reason to deny ordination to women. Still, the Overtures Committee did not think

---

6   Letter to the editor, *CH*, March 17, 1972, 23.
7   Mrs. Howard Vande Bunte, letter to the editor, *CH*, April 14, 1972, 18-19.

that the classis had acted correctly: "This violation is a disruption of the orderly process within the church and contributes to consternation in the church. It is the opinion of the committee that this violation should not serve as precedent in future procedures by the Classis of Raritan in this matter." The committee did not choose to discipline the classis or attempt to revoke the ordinations. It simply recommended no action and the synod agreed.[8] Its desire to avoid "consternation" ironically caused the Reformed Church a great deal of consternation in the next decade.

The Bible was used by both sides of the debate, the *Book of Church Order* was ambiguous, and the synod did not approve of civil disobedience but did not punish it either. These ambiguities led to several other inconsistencies in Reformed Church polity. Women could exercise authority by voting for elders and deacons but could not hold the offices themselves. A woman could serve as a voting member of the General Program Council and report its actions to her classis, but she could not vote at a classis meeting. Women served on the Committee of Eighteen, but they were not allowed to vote on its recommendations. Women missionaries could be ordained as elders in churches overseas, but not in their home churches in the United States. The Reformed Church claimed to recognize the calling of the Holy Spirit but insisted that women could not be called. The church affirmed scripture as its authority and approved a report that said scripture did not exclude women from office, and yet it refused to permit women to hold office.[9] Despite the leaps in logic, most Reformed Church members seemed able to live with the status quo.

The Particular Synod of New York asked for a change in the *Book of Church Order* that would allow each classis to decide whether or not to ordain women as ministers, and each consistory to decide whether to ordain woman as elders and deacons. The Overtures Committee affirmed the overture on the grounds that allowing the different regions and judicatories to decide would give a greater sense of freedom and unity within the denomination. The General Synod agreed. In the winter of 1971, classes voted on these amendments: "With the approval

---

8   *Acts and Proceedings*, 1970, 99, 111. This decision appeared to establish the *BCO* as a higher authority than the Bible. The synod had already affirmed that the Bible did not prohibit the ordination of women. The *BCO* did. The Overtures Committee chose to be guided by the *BCO* rather than the synod's interpretation of the Bible in 1958.

9   Marie Walvoord, "On the Ordination of Women," *CH*, Aug. 14, 1970, 8. She was an observer at the General Synod from the National Department of Women's Work and made these points in a speech to the synod.

of its classis, a church may select its consistory from such men and/or women who are qualified" and "The classis may ordain and install to the office of minister of the Word such men and/or women who are qualified." A majority of the classes approved these changes, 28-16 and 26-18 respectively, but not the required two-thirds majority.[10]

In 1972 the classes voted again, and this time two-thirds of them voted to remove the word "male" from the *BCO* and permit the ordination of women as elders and deacons. By the time the synod met to take the declarative action, several congregations had already ordained women, some churches had sent women as delegates to classes, and three female elder delegates came to the synod.[11] Those opposed to women's ordination considered this a blatant disregard of church order. A motion from the floor asked that the synod declare its disapproval of the illegal action of consistories and rededicate itself to exercising Christian charity toward those who disagreed. The motion was not adopted. Twenty-three delegates asked that their names be published in the minutes recording their opposition to the declarative action.[12] Meanwhile, other delegates celebrated the change. The synod president, Chris Walvoord, noted in his report that the ordination of women would be good for the church and concluded, "Only one problem remains for this assembly: what do we substitute for that melodious phrase, 'Fathers and brethren?'"[13]

The change in the *Book of Church Order* caused a major shift in denominational practice and considerable disagreement about how the new language should be implemented. Marion de Velder, then general secretary, interpreted the change to mean that women were now eligible for the offices of elder and deacon even if a congregation had bylaws that limited the offices to males. Such bylaws needed to be changed and could not supersede the denomination's position. Congregations could determine their own methods for nominations, but they could not disallow nominations based on gender.[14] By the time of the

---

[10]   *Acts and Proceedings*, 1970, 101, 112. Thirty classes had to approve a change to the *BCO*.

[11]   Mrs. Harold Rose from Palisades Classis, Joyce Regier from Paramus, and Jean Wells from Mid-Hudson. *Acts and Proceedings*, 1972, 4-5.

[12]   *Acts and Proceedings*, 1972, 297.

[13]   Ibid., 276.

[14]   Marion de Velder, "Women Serving as Elders and Deacons: An Explanatory Statement to Pastors and Consistories," *CH*, March 16, 1973, 17. Anecdotal evidence suggests that almost three decades later, some congregations continue to disregard this advice. There are still congregations which have by-laws or practices that prevent women from being elected to office.

synod in 1973, 275 women were serving as elders and deacons in 141 congregations.[15]

Hotline, the newsletter of the General Program Council, celebrated the decision by publishing the names and congregations of newly ordained women. What some celebrated, others lamented. Russell Horton, a pastor in Lansing, Illinois, asked if *Hotline* was trying to rub salt into an open wound. Why advertise an unbiblical procedure? Why discriminate against new male consistory members?[16]

This change theoretically resolved the question of women elders and deacons, but the Reformed Church continued to debate the ordination of women as ministers of Word and sacrament. The first direct challenge to denominational policy occurred in 1973, when the Review Committee on Theological Education recommended that Joyce Stedge be granted a dispensation from the professorial certificate.[17] Those in favor of women's ordination noted that the *Book of Church Order* said "persons" could be ordained as ministers. Joyce Stedge was a person. Those opposed made the argument from tradition that "persons" had always been interpreted as men.

The synod's president that year was Harry DeBruyn, a lawyer. He ruled that it was constitutional to grant a dispensation because the term "persons" included women. DeBruyn and General Secretary de Velder stated that the professorial certificate allowed Stedge to preach, but it did not permit her or other women to be ordained as ministers of the Word.[18] The synod voted to grant her a dispensation. This declaration and action might have been sufficient to end the debate about how to interpret the word "persons." Instead, the synod sent the amendment to the classes for a vote, along with a letter informing the classes of its decision that "persons" included women, and its belief that the *BCO* simply needed to be clarified. Opponents of women's ordination were not convinced.

Joyce Stedge was subsequently ordained by the Classis of Rockland-Westchester in October 1973 and installed as pastor of the

---

15 Louis Benes, "The 167th General Synod: Actions and Reports," *CH*, July 13, 1973, 11.

16 Letter to the editor, *CH*, July 13, 1973, 22.

17 The professorial certificate was granted by the faculty of Western Seminary and New Brunswick Seminary to their graduates deemed fit for ordination. Students who attended a non-RCA seminary had to apply to the General Synod for a dispensation from the professorial certificate in order to be ordained. Stedge graduated from Union Theological Seminary in New York and therefore needed the dispensation.

18 Louis Benes, "The 167th General Synod: Actions and Reports," *CH*, July 13, 1973, 9-10. DeBruyn's decision was appealed, but the synod supported it by a vote of 152-83, well beyond the simple majority required to sustain his ruling.

Rochester Reformed Church in Accord, New York, by the Classis of Mid-Hudson. The article reporting these actions noted that she had six children, perhaps to assure anxious readers that she had not entirely abandoned her feminine role.[19]

The vote in the classes on the amendment in early 1974 was 23 in favor, 18 against, and 3 abstentions. This was less favorable than in 1973 when it had been 27-14-3, only three votes away from the 30 required. There was evidently some backlash against the Stedge ordination as reflected in this letter to the editor: "The liberals have played their game of defiance again and have proved once more their incessant desire to sabotage the doing of things 'decently and in order' according to constitutional government."[20]

When it became clear that the amendment had failed in the classes once again, the General Synod Executive Committee authorized the synod's president, Donald DeYoung, to hold a consultation in April 1974. Participants included the General Synod officers, four representatives appointed by each particular synod, six from GSEC, six delegates to the 1974 synod selected by the president, four denominational staff members, the editor of the *Church Herald*, and one person from the Commissions on Theology, Christian Action, Church Government, and Judicial Business. No women were listed as participants. The discussion demonstrated that people interpreted the actions of the synod quite differently. Some believed that granting the dispensation opened the office to all women or at least to this particular woman. Some thought all offices should have been open to women when the word "male" was deleted in 1972. Others argued that when the synod sent the amendment (to substitute members for persons) to the classes again, it indicated that the BCO still needed to be changed. The consultation wanted to identify an action that would unify the church, so it recommended to GSEC that because of the confusion surrounding the previous vote and the synod's decision on Stedge's professorial, another amendment (to change "persons" to "men and women") should be sent to the classes.[21] The Synod of 1974 voted in favor of this, but once again the vote in the classes fell just short: 28-15-1 (tie). People on both sides were growing increasingly frustrated and angry, and there seemed to be no good solution to the impasse. John Stapert observed that if five people had voted yes instead of no, the amendment

[19] "Ordination," *CH*, Oct. 26, 1973, 20.
[20] Arthur Scheid, letter to the editor, *CH*, Nov. 16, 1973, 31-32.
[21] Louis Benes, "A Report on the President's Consultation," *CH*, May 17, 1974, 22-23.

would have passed. He insisted that the worst possible outcome would be to "move away from orderly constitutional processes," because to abrogate good and proper order would be divisive. The denomination needed a peaceful, orderly resolution.[22]

In 1975, Ray Rewerts, then synod president, also encouraged the synod to keep the peace. He noted in his report that Reformed Church polity had become twisted. Women were allowed to be elders and deacons but not ministers, and this challenged the traditional parity of the offices. Some classes had taken female seminary students under care but voted against the change in the *Book of Church Order*. He acknowledged that some advocates of women's ordination wanted to force the issue, but Rewerts insisted that this would be disastrous and divisive. He pleaded for constitutional loyalty, continued study, and patience.[23]

The Synod of 1975 received two very different overtures that might have resolved the impasse. The Particular Synod of Michigan asked the synod to set aside the Joyce Stedge ordination, while the Particular Synod of New Jersey asked the synod simply to declare that "persons" meant men and women, as Harry DeBruyn had done two years earlier with the synod's approval.[24] Before the synod took action on these overtures, the Review Committee on Theological Education recommended an amendment to the *BCO* that substituted "men and women" for "persons." The synod adopted this recommendation with little debate. The Committee on Overtures reported that afternoon. It recommended no action on the overture regarding Stedge's ordination. In an apparent victory for advocates of women's ordination, the synod voted 158-97 to take no action. Enthusiastic applause was quickly stifled by President Rewerts, who said that the church needed understanding and patience rather than expressions of victory. Theoretically, this could have ended the stalemate. The definition of "persons" had been

---

22 Editorial, "Women's Ordination Voting," *CH*, May 2, 1975, 8-9.

23 *Acts and Proceedings*, 1975, 249. Rewerts also noted a great deal of selective loyalty to the *BCO* among RCA churches. Some who insisted it be obeyed regarding women's ordination were far less committed to its instructions about supervision of churches, use of the Liturgy, and care for ministers and congregations.

24 The Overtures Committee needed to consider and give advice on about twenty-two overtures, so the chair, Fred Dolfin (pastor in Kalamazoo), divided the forty members into subcommittees. The one assigned to the Michigan overture had six delegates from the Midwest and one from the East, while the subcommittee that discussed the New Jersey overture had five delegates from the Midwest and one from the East. A number of committee members opposed what seemed to be a stacked deck in opposition to women's ordination. By a vote of 20-17 the committee decided that the whole committee would discuss these two overtures.

tested, an ordination of a woman had occurred, and the synod upheld it. But it was not enough.

The synod then considered the overture from the Particular Synod of New Jersey to declare definitively that "persons" meant men and women. Such a declaration would not have required a *BCO* change or a vote in the classes. The Overtures Committee recommended approval. Delegates debated the measure and then went to dinner and the evening program without having taken a vote. On Friday morning, apparently after some back-room consultation, Rewerts ruled the overture out of order because the synod had voted earlier to send the *BCO* amendment to the classes on the recommendation of the Review Committee on Theological Education. His ruling was challenged but supported by a majority of delegates, 178 to 71.[25]

The vote on the amendment in early 1976 was again extremely close: 29 yes, 15 no, and a tie; one vote short of the thirty required. The tie occurred in the Classis of Cascades, where delegates voted 14-14. John Stapert predicted another year of contention, especially since women were graduating from seminary. He wrote, "Again this year endurance and patience with each other is what we must pray for."[26]

The Synod of 1976 received proposals from several different groups. The president, Bert Van Soest, recommended that the synod send a pastoral letter urging the classes to vote for the change in the *Book of Church Order*. The Christian Action Commission recommended that the synod support the right of choice for women who felt called to be ministers. The Theological Commission had prepared a paper on maleness and femaleness that concluded that men and women were equally fit for church office. The synod adopted both the commission's recommendation and the paper.[27]

Opponents of women's ordination had their own ideas. The Classis of Illiana asked for a two-thirds vote at the General Synod before a proposed amendment could be sent to the classes a second time, because "the classes are weary of facing the same decision year after year: e.g. ordination women [*sic*] for the fifth time; and, classis or synod spends too much time with such issues."[28] The Overtures Committee

[25] John Stapert and Karen Vogel, "The 169th General Synod: Actions and Reports," *CH*, July 11, 1975, 6-17. Prior to the closing Communion service, a motion was made from the floor to prohibit all classes from ordaining women during the coming year in order to prevent divisive actions while the vote was still being taken. A storm of debate followed. The motion was finally withdrawn on a technicality, because no women were eligible for ordination.

[26] Editorial, "It Couldn't Have Been Closer," *CH*, April 30, 1976, 8.

[27] *Acts and Proceedings*, 1976, 28-29, 34, 190-91, 235-45.

[28] Ibid., 103.

recommended no action on the Illiana motion, because one synod should not be able to restrict future synods. The committee also added that suspending constitutional practice because of weariness was "not in accord with the best traditions of legislative theory and practice. These traditions demand that no pains be spared in an unceasing search for truth and justice." The synod agreed with the committee and took no action. A delegate asked to postpone consideration of the ordination of women until 1980 on the grounds of collective exhaustion, but the motion was ruled out of order.

The Particular Synod of New Jersey tried a unique but rather convoluted approach. It asked the synod to change the *Book of Church Order* so that it explicitly read "men" rather than the ambiguous "persons." This overture offered a way out of the impasse since, presumably, the majority who supported women's ordination would reject this limited interpretation when the classes voted, and the more inclusive meaning would be clarified. The synod took no action, however, because the president had proposed and the synod approved another vote in the classes.[29]

Rodger Dalman, a pastor in South Holland, Illinois, expressed his frustration in a letter to the editor in the summer of 1976. When the *Book of Church Order* was amended to allow ordination of women as elders and deacons, he wrote, opponents were assured that this would not necessarily lead to women ministers, but now they were told that the RCA was in an illogical and inconsistent situation. He went on,

> Those who oppose the ordination of women do not desire to be divisive or chauvinistic, they simply want to be obedient to Scripture. They also want to be listened to as well as admonished to listen. Constitutions exist for the protection of those who adhere to the historical point of view. I am content to let the Holy Spirit lead us as a church in the matter, but I find it difficult to believe he leads through coercive methods.[30]

The vote in the classes in the fall of 1976 again failed by one vote (29-15-1 with a tie in California).[31] Stapert reported that there were

---

[29] John Stapert, "The 170th General Synod: Actions and Reports," *CH*, July 23, 1976, 6-17. *Acts and Proceedings*, 1976, 115-16.

[30] Aug. 20, 1976, 22.

[31] Van Soest had recommended that the vote be taken earlier than usual, at the fall classis meetings in 1976 rather than the spring meetings in 1977. He hoped that the vote would be merely a formality and that classes would receive the pastoral advice of the synod and vote to make the clarification that "persons" meant men and women.

high levels of aggravation at the classis meetings he attended, which may have led to a backlash. He summarized the state of the debate: over half the church favored women's ordination, the votes in classes had been close, women were completing their training in seminary, and the Reformed Church was inconsistent in ordaining women elders but not ministers. He then offered this pessimistic conclusion: "It is apparent that proposals to ordain women ministers, no matter how frequently set forth, are bound to lose." He thought it would have been better not to have voted for the fifth time, because "all the church has accomplished this time is a heightening of the frustration and irritation on both sides." He thought the church needed relief from the constant debate, so he proposed a three-year moratorium during which the Reformed Church would study not only the issue of women but also broader questions about ministry and ordination. He also wondered if the women currently in seminary might be commissioned as missionaries until the church sorted out the issues.[32]

The editorial sparked a number of critical letters. The Classis of Mid-Hudson defended its installation of Joyce Stedge as both consistent with the *BCO* (she was a person) and biblical (based on the paper approved in 1958). Donald Healy, a minister in Hopewell Junction, New York, pointed out that the denomination had already studied the issue and produced papers, but the church ignored them. He considered it procrastination and sexism to make women wait a few more years. A female seminarian suggested that a moratorium on ordination ought to apply to both genders. Tom Stark pointed out that the word "persons," in Reformed Church history and tradition, had always meant men, or else it would not have been voted on so many times.[33] Arnold van Lummel replied that many supporters of women's ordination considered the amendment unnecessary because "persons" meant men and women, but they had tried to keep the peace by following proper procedure. He protested, "Now to be told that our acquiescence was tantamount to conceding 'amendment' as the *only* way is grossly unfair and historically inaccurate."[34]

The Synod of 1977 did not listen to Stapert's advice but voted to send the amendment to the classes once again. The vote was 26-19, which meant it received less support than in the fall of 1976.[35] Tensions

---

[32]   Editorial, "Whither Now the Ordination of Women?" *CH*, March 4, 1977, 8-9.
[33]   See letters by Donald Hicks, Donald Healy, and Everett Zabriskie III, *CH*, April 15, 1977, 23, and by Anne Moshier and Tom Stark, May 13, 1977, 22.
[34]   Letter to the editor, *CH*, June 10, 1977, 23.
[35]   "Proposal to Ordain Women Fails to Pass for Sixth Time," *CH*, May 18, 1978, 24. The classes of Chicago, Ontario, Pleasant Prairie, and West Central voted no in 1978 after voting yes in 1977. Illinois switched from no to yes.

over the issue began to affect fund-raising and church unity. Russell Horton, a pastor in Lansing, Illinois, reported that his consistory had voted to challenge the congregation to raise $30,000 for the Church Growth Fund Drive because, "Finally our leaders had come along with something worth supporting." But when the Synod of 1977 proposed a sixth vote on the *BCO* change and tried to elect a woman vice-president, the consistory rescinded its action. "Has the Holy Spirit not spoken five times in a row or will he only have spoken when we have twisted his arm to get our way?" Horton said he resented the fact that those wanted to be true to God's Word had this issue forced on them every year, and he wondered what would happen to those who could not participate in the ordination of a woman when the liberals finally got their way. He wondered if it might be time to reconsider the recommendation from 1969 that the two sections of the RCA go their separate ways.[36] Horton and other purists worried that the purity of the church would be compromised by the ordination of women and that the purists would be forced to do something they did not want to do.

The Reformed Church in America celebrated its 350th anniversary in 1978 with a fairly high level of good will. There were no overtures or recommendations regarding women's ordination and thus no votes scheduled for the winter of 1979. Nevertheless, John Stapert observed that delegates felt pressured by pro-women's ordination forces. "A display booth featured women's ministries and distributed lapel buttons favoring women's ordination. (Few delegates wore them.)" Supporters of women's ordination held a worship service off-site, he reported, but few delegates attended. Pieces of the litany from that service (thanking God for progress toward women's ordination) were incorporated into the synod's closing worship service. Stapert noted that several delegates took offense at this.[37]

Less than a month later, two classes chose to move ahead with the ordination of women despite the lack of official approval. On June 25, 1978, the Classis of Brooklyn ordained Valerie DeMarinis. On July 23, the Classis of Bergen ordained Louise Ann Hill-Alto. Both women said that ordination was not an act of defiance but an attempt to follow the call of God.[38]

36   Letter to the editor, *CH*, Aug. 19, 1977, 19. Elsie Lamb, an elder from Hope Church in Holland, MI, received one-quarter of the votes in the election for vice-president.
37   "The 172nd General Synod and 350th Anniversary Celebration," *CH*, July 28, 1978, 9-10.
38   "Ordain Two Women as RCA Ministers," *CH*, July 14, 1978, 26. DeMarinis graduated from Princeton Seminary and was enrolled in a doctoral program at Harvard University. She received a dispensation from the professorial certificate in 1977, and

In an editorial in August, 1978, Stapert reported that in addition to these two candidates, the Classis of Raritan had approved the ordination of Constance Longhurst, and the Classis of Albany that of Joyce Borgman de Velder. He also noted that a formal complaint had been filed with the Particular Synod of New Jersey against the ordination of Hill-Alto. Stapert explained the difference between the legislative and judicial processes and pointed out that the Reformed Church members who had approved the ordinations were not anarchists but had acted in a manner approved by the *Book of Church Order*.[39]

News of the ordinations sparked many letters. One critic objected that the spirit of the ordination requirements had been violated. "Everyone knows that ordinarily the word 'persons' means men and women. However, for many years our denomination has given a special interpretation to this word as meaning 'only men.'...The only intelligence required to understand the interpretation our denomination has given to the word 'persons' is the ability to read."[40] Some critics insisted that the perpetrators of the ordinations be disciplined.

Warren Henseler, a pastor in Hasbrouck Heights, New Jersey, asked that discussion remain civil with the assumption that all parties were honest and sincere Christians. Supporters of ordination did not wish to destroy the *Book of Church Order*, he said, but believed that custom and tradition needed to be changed and not the *BCO* itself. He pleaded for calmness, civility, and charity in the midst of differing opinions.[41]

J. Groetsema, a retired minister from South Holland, Illinois, suggested that the Reformed Church could take a cue from the practice of the Roman Catholic Church when a new pope was elected. When balloting commenced, a three-fourths majority was required, but if no one was elected after a certain time, the requirement shifted to a two-thirds majority and then a simple majority, lest the cardinals spend the rest of their lives in the Sistine Chapel. The *BCO* wisely required a two-thirds majority to enact change, he reasoned, but lacked a provision to deal with repeated votes where a minority controlled the majority. He

---

the minutes show no evidence of debate over this (*Acts and Proceedings*, 1977, 162, 166, 168). She received a call from the faculty at Harvard to study working mothers. Hill-Alto graduated from New Brunswick Seminary in 1977 and was working at the Glen Rock Community Church in New Jersey. She reported that the Classis of Bergen had approached her about being ordained. Personal correspondence with Louise Hill.

39 Editorial, "Women's Ordination: Now It's a Judicial Process," *CH*, Aug. 25, 1978, 7.
40 Clarence Vande Zande, letter to the editor, *CH*, Sept. 22, 1978, 18.
41 Letter to the editor, *CH*, Oct. 20, 1978, 19.

suggested that the order be changed to permit amendments with only a simple majority after five years of voting.[42]

Meanwhile, the judicial actions continued. Along with the formal protest lodged against the Particular Synod of New Jersey, the Synod of 1979 received several other formal complaints[43] about these ordinations. The process had become judicial. The synod would vote yes or no on the validity of the complaints. Had the two classes erred in ordaining women as ministers? The decision would be made by a majority vote among synod delegates and did not need to be sent to the classes.

The Judicial Business Committee heard arguments and discussed the complaints during two meetings in May 1979. The committee ruled that the major issue before the synod was the meaning of "persons" in the *Book of Church Order*. It found no compelling reason to interpret the word other than "men and women." The committee also noted that the synod had declared in 1958 that there was no biblical reason to prohibit the ordination of women. History and tradition may have kept the offices closed to women, but these were not sufficient reasons to continue excluding them. The Judicial Business Committee concluded that the classes had acted appropriately when they ordained women and had not defied or violated the *Book of Church Order*. The BCO did not need to be changed because it had never prohibited the ordination of women as ministers. The repeated votes in the classes were clarifying, not substantive changes. The committee recommended that the ordinations be upheld and the complaints be dismissed.[44]

The synod delegates discussed this recommendation at great length. William Thompson, a conservative pastor from Denver, was a particularly influential voice in the debate. He did not believe in women's ordination, Thompson said, but his reading of the account of the Council of Jerusalem in the book of Acts led him to urge the synod to uphold the ordinations. Women's ordination was a matter of conscience, not salvation or the purity of the gospel. He thought that people could disagree about the issue.[45]

---

42 Letter to the editor, *CH*, Nov. 3, 1978, 14.

43 Martin Weitz filed a complaint against the Particular Synod of New York for upholding the Classis of Brooklyn's decision to ordain Valerie DeMarinis. Henry Griswold filed a complaint against the Particular Synod of New Jersey for upholding the Classis of Bergen's decision to ordain Louise Ann Hill-Alto. The Classis of Albany filed two complaints against the Particular Synod of Albany for refusing to allow the classis to ordain Joyce de Velder. Mulder, "Full Participation." *Acts and Proceedings*, 1979, 65-70.

44 John Stapert, editorial, "Big Issues Face 1979 General Synod," *CH*, June 1, 1979, 8.

45 John Stapert and Laurie Baron, "The 173rd General Synod," *CH*, July 27, 1979, 4-6.

Finally, in a historic and controversial decision, the synod voted 150 to 115 to uphold the ordinations of women as ministers. Delegates agreed with the Judicial Business Committee that neither the Bible nor the *Book of Church Order* prohibited women from serving in this capacity. The decision did not end the conflict, however.

The vote sparked a barrage of letters to the editor of the *Church Herald*. A few were positive. In a more extended opinion piece, Christian Walvoord encouraged women to take themselves seriously as leaders.

> I hope that the women of the Reformed church will live up to their new estate. I'm not thinking just about women's ordination but about the whole decade in which women have come into their own in the councils, proceedings, and the decision-making process as they never did before. They must not slip back into the old cookbook and rummage-sale mode.

Walvoord exhorted women to get out of the kitchen. They didn't all need to become preachers, but he said, "Please run for office, stand for it, compete for it. Have confidence in yourselves....I expect you to say to your husbands, 'You get in the kitchen too! I've been there long enough.'...The men ought to know the joys and pains of peeling potatoes....Why should only the women be saddled with it?" He observed that in his experience having women on consistory improved the atmosphere and the decision-making process. He advised, "Don't be coy in your dealings with men. Never use your charms to win a point or cover a weak argument. Don't fall into 'us girls' talk. Shun sexist jokes. In other words, come straight at us and be honest." He referred to the Apostle Peter's words about being a chosen race and a royal priesthood and concluded, "Peter wasn't talking only to men."[46]

But most writers were troubled by the decision. David Bast, a pastor in Hamilton, Michigan, argued that it represented a new way of reading the *Book of Church Order*. Instead of interpreting the language as the authors meant, the synod had forced the text to say what it wanted. Bast asked, "Does this action of General Synod establish a new hermeneutical principle for our church? If we no longer interpret

---

[46] "I'd like to say...Stop Selling Cookbooks!" *CH*, Aug. 10, 1979, 13. A year later, Walvoord reported that he had worked in the kitchen of the Third Reformed Church in Holland, Michigan, during a Tulip Time meal and appreciated the hard work, efficiency, and sense of community he found there. "I'd like to say...Potato Peeling Could Be Worse," Aug. 8, 1980, 13. Walvoord served on the denominational staff, as president of the General Synod, and as pastor of primarily eastern churches. He retired in Holland, Michigan.

the *BCO* on the basis of the meaning of its language in historical and cultural context, is the same true of scripture?...Do we now assert that the meaning of scripture can change in the same way that the meaning of the *BCO* can change?"[47] Bast raised a significant point of disagreement. Moderates believed that the *BCO* was a human document, subject to change when it became unworkable or needed clarification. Conservatives, purists in particular, were more reluctant to change it.

Some critics of women's ordination appealed to the authority of scripture. Timothy Santinga, a pastor in Florida, argued that the Bible taught the principle of women's subjection. Women might pray in public, but they "simply do not have the right to get up and address the assembly, nor have they ever had that right. To take to themselves that right violated the principle of subjection and mocked God's divine order." Women cannot hold positions of authority over men.[48] Robert Jackson, a pastor in Hawthorne, New Jersey, pointed out the many ways that the principle of subjection had been misused, particularly as a justification for slavery and the Jim Crow laws. God is doing new things, he said. "Simply because the Holy Spirit leads us in ways that are new, different, and unique, does not warrant anxious return to some 'principle of subjection.'"[49]

Some Reformed Church women had harsh words for other women who felt called to ministry. Betsy Rosema from Grand Rapids insisted that women should not serve as a pastor or an elder because the offices would give them authority over men.

> It amazes me that any woman who is a proclaimed follower of Christ should even aspire to lording herself over men, but then it is understandable as simply another example of human nature exerting its selfishness. Certainly these women are not even in tune with God's spirit let alone allowing him to fill them for use to his honor and glory.

Mary Arnessen from New Jersey insisted that the ordination of women would weaken the church just as the women's movement had challenged the traditional family structure.[50]

Some critics took issue with the judicial process. One letter pronounced the vote one of the "most devious pieces of business ever

---

47   Letter to the editor, *CH*, July 27, 1979, 22.
48   Letter to the editor, *CH*, Aug. 10, 1979, 21. Santinga attended the very conservative/ purist Dallas Theological Seminary and served as pastor of a Baptist church before he entered the RCA.
49   Letter to the editor, *CH*, Sept. 7, 1979, 22.
50   Betsy Rosema, Mary Arnessen, letters to the editor, *CH*, Sept. 7, 1979, 22.

perpetrated in the history of the Reformed Church. Many of us who do not oppose the ordination of women to the ministry are saddened that it was found necessary to resort to acts of chicanery to obtain this goal. Every fair and right-minded person must be offended by what has taken place." The author pronounced the decision an abuse of minority rights.[51]

Elton Eenigenburg, a professor at Western Theological Seminary, defended the judicial process. He read the synod's action as a declaration that "more important than the literal reading of pronouns is a broader reading—one that takes into account a significant change in the church's attitude toward women as ministers of the Word....It is not unusual for judicial bodies to bring current practice into line with historical reality without changing the wording of the law." The Supreme Court has done this with the U.S. Constitution, he pointed out. The intent of the judicial process was to determine whether the laws of the church were violated. The synod concluded that they were not.[52]

Opponents of women's ordination did not find this reassuring. In 1980 the General Synod Executive Committee heard from fourteen individuals, eleven churches, and eleven classes who disapproved of the 1979 action. The Classis of South Grand Rapids declared that it would not enroll women as candidates nor ordain, license, or admit them to classis membership as long as the *Book of Church Order* had not been amended. The Classis of Zeeland took a similar action. The First Reformed Church in Oostburg, Wisconsin, declared that it would not be bound by the synod's action.[53] Six classes overtured the synod to change its 1979 decision, but the overtures were ruled out of order on the grounds that a synod cannot rescind a previous synod's disciplinary action. Opponents of women's ordination were particularly worried that the Reformed Church would adopt the practices of the United Presbyterian Church, which *required* churches to include women on the sessions (consistories).[54]

By the time the synod met in 1980, more than a dozen women had been ordained. In an effort to deal with the sharp polarization within the church, two members of the Advisory Committee on Church Order, Robert Wildman and Tom Stark, drafted "A Proposal to Maintain Peace

---

51   Howard Davis, letter to the editor, *CH*, Aug. 10, 1979, 21.
52   "I'd like to say...The Judicial Process is Legitimate," *CH*, Sept. 21, 1979, 13. Eenigenburg had opposed the ordination of women in the past but had changed his mind.
53   "Classis and Consistories Oppose Synod Action," *CH*, Feb. 22, 1980, 23.
54   *Acts and Proceedings*, 1980, 274.

in Diversity in the RCA Concerning Women as Church Officers." The proposal included yet another vote by the classes to change "persons" to "men and women." It also offered two amendments which became known as the "conscience clause." Those who opposed women's ordination could not be penalized or forced to participate in any decision or action which went against their consciences, but they could not obstruct by unconstitutional means the movement of women into church offices.[55]

A key phrase in this compromise resolution was that no one would be penalized for his or her minority position on the ordination of women. In reality, the greater problem was that women were frequently "obstructed." What if a woman believed herself to be called to the ministry but attended a church where consistory members would not vote to recommend her to the classis? Did she have to find another church? Anecdotal evidence suggests that this occurred several times.[56] Some churches retained by-laws that said only men could hold office. In other churches, less formal constraints inhibited women's involvement, such as nominating committees that refused to put women on the slate.

Purists rejected the compromise because they thought it signaled that the church had sacrificed its integrity and commitment to scripture for social acceptance. Russell Horton wrote, "Since the Bible does not permit the exercise of authority of women over men in the church and therefore the ordination of women to the offices of the church," he could not approve a proposal which contradicted the Bible. He intimated that the Reformed Church no longer acknowledged the Bible as the only rule of faith and practice.[57]

Despite these objections, the classes approved both the conscience clause and an amendment to the *Book of Church Order*. But the victory was a narrow one, for the change in language barely passed by a vote of 30-15. A major victory had been won by the advocates of women's ordination, but the skirmishes continued.

The next challenge for women was how they would be received by churches and parishioners both during and after seminary. As president of the synod, James Cook, a professor at Western Seminary, addressed

---

55 John Stapert and Laurie Baron, "The 174th General Synod," *CH*, July 25, 1980, 4-6. *Acts and Proceedings*, 1980, 274-76.

56 One woman considered going to seminary, but she attended a church in South Grand Rapids Classis that would not take her under care and recommend her to the classis. She became a gifted teacher and administrator. How much has the denomination lost by denying her and other women the opportunity to attend seminary to become pastors?

57 Letter to the editor, *CH*, Sept. 5, 1980, 22.

the reluctance of churches to accept women as ministers and argued that the real issue was not reverence for the Bible (since both sides took it seriously), but experience. Congregations that had encountered women as students, preachers, and pastors were much more accepting of their ministry. "Experiencing women in ministry is just another example of the truth that we all live our way into our thinking as much as we think our way into our living." Cook cited Peter's growing acceptance of Gentiles in Acts 10-11 as a biblical example of the process.[58]

Acceptance was slow to arrive. Women did receive calls, although a larger proportion of women than men served in specialized ministries, often because they could not find positions as pastors. One sign of the degree of acceptance of Reformed Church women could be found in the number of women delegates to the synod. Out of roughly 290 voting members in 1985, 39 were women; in 1986, 29; and in 1987, 17. Perhaps women elders were asked to attend but found it too difficult to give up a week of their lives to participate. It was more likely, however, that they were not being elected to the office, especially in the Midwest and Far West.

The Particular Synod of New York overtured the General Synod in 1987 to change the *Book of Church Order* to require every classis to send at least one woman delegate to synod. The Advisory Committee on Church Vocations thought this would interfere with classical rights and recommended against the overture. It reasoned that the change would "place undue pressure upon individual classes and churches to insure the ordination of women as elders and their selection as delegates, thereby being insensitive to local realities of working women, women not desirous of serving in such capacities, and the normal rotation of churches providing elder delegates." The advisory committee did not believe there was a clear need for increased representation of women or that this was the appropriate way to raise consciousness about the role of women in the church.[59]

During the debate, Marchiene Rienstra, a pastor at Hope Church in Holland, Michigan, said that she had expected the General Synod to look more like a congregation on Sunday morning. She was stunned by the preponderance of men in the room and said, "While it's true we can't legislate hearts, sometimes people learn by seeing something different." Ruth Wilson, president of the long-standing program body for women, Reformed Church Women, thought that the overture did

---

[58]   James Cook, "From Willingness to Welcome," *CH*, Oct. 1, 1982, 19.
[59]   *Acts and Proceedings*, 1987, 211.

not go far enough to address the discrimination that still occurred in the church. "I find it disappointing that at this synod we have 17 women out of 291 delegates. When those numbers more accurately reflect our membership, then we will truly be 'a people who belong.'" The overture was denied, but the synod instructed the general secretary to remind the classes of the importance of appointing women delegates.[60]

Later that year the synod's president, Robert Wise, suggested specific changes that would yield a better representation of women. Women delegates could be elected from Reformed Church Women. A woman from each congregation could attend classis meetings and be eligible to serve as a delegate to the General Synod. Each regional synod might send five women to a General Synod. Wise recognized the limits of coercion, but he also knew that proposals without "teeth" did not bring any change. He concluded, "Representative inclusion of women in the judicatories of the church is a basic, fundamental right. Let's do something now when delegates are selected. Women belong. We need them at General Synod in greater numbers."[61]

Harry Buis, a pastor in Hudsonville, Michigan, protested that a quota system undermined the conscience clause, which was intended to protect the rights of both sides. "Now there are those who favor taking away the vote or diluting the vote of some men and women in our churches in order to let others have their way. To require classes to send a certain number of representatives depending on their sex or to add other delegates from Reformed Church Women would interfere with the principle of representative government." He thought the only fair method was to encourage classes that believed in women's ordination to send more women to the synod. But violating the rights of those opposed to women's ordination "could only lead to a lessened support of our denominational program and, more seriously, to a division in the church which we all ought to do everything to avoid."[62]

The proposal was criticized on other grounds as well. Calvin Heyenga, an elder from Stout, Iowa, agreed that women needed to be involved in the church, but they did not belong in leadership roles. "True, a female pastor or consistory person is not inconsistent with the *Book of Church Order*, but it is inconsistent with God's order of things." Russell Horton thought the proposal was coercive. Since the *Book of*

[60]   Christina Van Eyl, "Synod Discusses Quota for Women," *CH*, July 17, 1987, 14.

[61]   Robert Wise, "Who Speaks for The 53 Percent Minority," *CH*, Oct. 16, 1987, 14-15. Wise said that women from the RCW would not necessarily be ordained and therefore should not offend those opposed to women's ordination.

[62]   Letter to the editor, *CH*, Nov. 20, 1987, 22.

Church Order was circumvented in 1979, he said, subtle pressure had been imposed on those who thought that women's ordination went against the Bible.[63]

In 1988, the Commission for Women[64] recommended that each particular synod send two women corresponding delegates to the synod (with voice but not vote). Much to the surprise and delight of the commission, the General Synod instead approved an amendment to the *BCO* that each particular synod send two women as voting delegates. While this change seemed generous, it had little chance of being approved by the classes and indeed was not.[65] The General Synod of 1989 returned to the initial proposal of two corresponding delegates, and this was approved by the classes in 1990.[66]

Occasionally a male minister in a position of power and influence recognized the slow pace of change. Louis Lotz, a pastor in Iowa and a regular columnist for the *Church Herald*, wrote about a girl in his church who said she wanted to be a minister. Lotz was not sure what to tell her, he wrote, because he did not think the Reformed Church had been very supportive of women clergy, but he hoped the church would become more accepting. He concluded his column,

> I know, I know, you can't force social change. You can't snap your fingers and expect generations of tradition to disappear. We're making progress, slow but sure. There are more women ministers today than there were five years ago, and five years from now there will be more than there are today. These things take time. Rome wasn't built in a day. Maybe we haven't yet achieved the goal of equality, but we're getting close. I agree. All those things are true. And they sound good. To a man.[67]

Two significant events occurred at the Synod of 1991 that signaled changes in the status of women. Beth Marcus, a long-time denominational executive in domestic missions, communications, and Reformed Church Women, was elected vice-president. This meant she would likely be elected president in 1992. Slightly less momentously, but still indicative of the changes afoot, Renee House, librarian at New

63   Calvin Heyenga, Russell Horton, letters to the editor, *CH*, Nov. 20, 1987, 22.
64   The Commission for Women was formed in 1978 to minister to the needs of women in Christian ministry. *Acts and Proceedings*, 1978, 52.
65   Jeffrey Japinga, "Women, Deacons, Professors: Maybe Next Year," *CH*, July 22, 1988, 12-13.
66   *Acts and Proceedings*, 1990, 41, 278.
67   "Before You Follow Your Dream," *CH*, Oct. 1990, 50.

Brunswick Seminary and an ordained minister, was the first woman to preach at a General Synod. Even conservatives had to admit that she was a gifted preacher.

Women were also more visible on the floor of the synod, thanks to the two female corresponding delegates sent by each particular synod. This practice caused some skepticism. Jeanette Baas, an elder from the Hope Reformed Church in Grand Rapids, applauded the election of Beth Marcus as vice president. She was less excited about the fact that women had "appeared" as corresponding delegates. Since they could not vote, she feared that appearances in this case were misleading. It looked as if the representation of women had improved when in fact it had not. She urged women to decline the invitation to attend the synod as corresponding delegates.[68] The Synod of the Far West also opposed the presence of the corresponding delegates, not because it was misleading, but because that synod did not want to pay the women's expenses when they had no vote.[69]

In the early 1990s, Don Luidens and Roger Nemeth surveyed Reformed Church members and their beliefs about the role of women and sorted the answers by regional synod. In the eastern synods, nine out of ten parishioners believed that women should be allowed to be elders and deacons. In the other synods, about two-thirds affirmed women as elders and deacons. More than eight out of ten easterners supported ordained women ministers, but barely half of the midwestern and far western members concurred.[70] Given these differences, it was not surprising that the debate continued to simmer.

In a March 1993 letter to the editor in the *Church Herald*, Patrick Shetler, a pastor in Grant, Michigan, argued that women should not be ordained because the Belgic Confession did not permit it. Elder Scott Christiansen of Omaha, Nebraska, responded: "I know several God-called ministers of the gospel who happen to be female. The fact that God does bless the ministry of women should say something powerful to us as we debate this issue." Experience does not supersede scripture, Christiansen continued, but where scripture is difficult to understand or where multiple interpretations are possible, "we must also acknowledge that God didn't stop working when the canon was completed. God is

---

68   Jeannette Baas, Flak and Flattery (letters to the editor), *CH*, Sept. 1991, 4.
69   *Acts and Proceedings*, 1992, 385-86. It was customary for the travel expenses of corresponding delegates to be paid for by the commission or agency that they represented.
70   "In Search of the RCA, Part 3: How We Stand on Social Issues," *CH*, Nov. 1992, 8-10.

not silent; he speaks in and through the lives of female ministers every day. Praise God that our Reformed faith can keep reforming."[71]

Shetler revisited the issue a year later:

> A debate is going on for the very soul of the denomination. It is a debate between those who believe the RCA is reformed according the Word of God and hold to Scripture-alone authority, and those who are re-forming who have a quest for continued inspiration from the Holy Spirit from sources like personal experience....The issue of authority is at the very essence of the Christian faith. Unless there can be agreement as to where authority lies there can be no unity in the RCA....Our constitution clearly declares that the Scriptures alone are authority.

Shetler thought that too many Reformed Church members did not believe this.[72]

Albert Vander Meer, stated clerk of the Regional Synod of Mid-America, asked several congregations in that synod how they used women in leadership. He received a range of responses. Some churches called ordained women as pastors. Other congregations conducted special programs for women encouraging friendship, prayer, and discipleship. A few had elected women as deaconesses. Many more found nonordained roles for women in the life of their community. The Faith Reformed Church in Lanark, Illinois, said that women comprised half the Sunday school teachers. In addition, "all the women of the congregation are divided into three service groups for help during special events." "Although we don't have any women as consistory members, we do solicit their advice and counsel."[73]

The lengthy, tedious, and frustrating process described here suggests that perhaps this way of dealing with conflict in the church had not been the best course of action. During the decade of the 1970s, both conservatives and moderates were angry with the pace of change. Conservatives thought the ordination of women was being forced on them, while moderates thought the Reformed Church was entirely too cautious. The denomination displayed a deep devotion to proper order and polity. There were several times when it would have been possible for the synod simply to make a declaration as to the meaning of "persons"; however, the synod insisted repeatedly that the *Book of Church Order* must be amended, even though it already specified that

---

[71]   Flak and Flattery, *CH*, March 1993, 4; May 1993, 5.

[72]   Flak and Flattery, *CH*, Feb. 1994, 6.

[73]   Albert Vander Meer, Regional Spotlight: Synod of Mid-America, "Women's Roles Continue to Emerge," *CH*, Nov. 1994, 47.

"persons" meant men and women. There was a constant concern for keeping the peace so as not to cause "consternation" or offense. Despite all this caution, there was no peace. Both sides were offended. In the end, when some classes simply went ahead and ordained women, the issue was finally resolved. The denomination did not fall apart or divide. Certainly, the conservatives and purists were angry, but they were, after all, in the minority. They continued to resist the ordination of women and insisted on their right to do as they chose. They insisted that the denomination could not tell them to take a course of action that the Bible prohibited.

The conflict is not fully resolved, however. There are still debates about the conscience clause and the actions it permits congregations and consistories to take (or fail to take.) There are still congregations that do not allow women to serve as elders and deacons and refuse to permit a woman to preach in their pulpits. There are still people who believe that women cannot possibly be called to church leadership or exercise it effectively.

On the other hand, the Reformed Church has been gifted with a number of extraordinarily talented women who have been excellent elders, deacons, preachers, pastors, and teachers. Congregations and individuals that are willing to experience women as leaders almost always become enthusiastic supporters of them. Hope Church in Holland, Michigan, has had male and female pastoral teams sharing leadership for almost three decades. Churches with female pastors do not wither and die. Still, the more subtle forms of resistance, particularly the idea that women are not meant to be leaders, continues to encourage opposition.[74]

On this matter, as on so many others, the Reformed Church was willing to give people a great deal of freedom. It was very sensitive to the concerns of the conservative minority, in part because the threat of schism was never far from the surface. Some conservatives insisted repeatedly that the denomination could not make them accept women's ordination, and they have continued to resist, citing the need to protect their consciences. Many parts of the denomination have accepted the leadership of women, but the Reformed Church still has not reached the point where it is clear that women belong fully, on an equal basis with men.

---

[74] At the Synod of 2012, delegates approved a recommendation to eliminate the conscience clause. The classes will vote on this *BCO* change in early 2013. Some opponents of the recommendation argued at the synod and on various blogs that they were "complementarians," who believed that women's "complementary" giftedness with men does not include holding leadership positions in the church. Several threatened to leave the denomination if the conscience clause is eliminated.

CHAPTER 8

1983–1994: Fragments or Family?

An unofficial theme of the Reformed Church in America in the 1970s was, "You can't make us do that; we'll do it our own way." The denomination allowed the ordination of women, but many churches justified their resistance with the Conscience Clause. The general secretary opposed repressive and violent political regimes in Central America, but some church members preferred to follow more conservative religious and political authorities. The Reformed Church remained a member of the World Council and National Council of Churches, but congregations could decide whether to provide financial support for them. Congregations decided what it meant to be Reformed and chose their worship practices accordingly. This strategy of encouraging freedom and diversity worked for a time, but by the early 1980s the editor of the *Church Herald* and other leaders observed that the denomination was now so diverse and fragmented that it was not clear what held it together. The denomination had let people go their own way in order to keep the peace, but peace came at a price. The Reformed Church lacked a coherent sense of identity. The deep sense of denominational loyalty evident in the 1960s began to wane as congregations increasingly saw themselves as self-sufficient. Some considered the denomination to be irrelevant or even an impediment to growth. The Reformed Church would expend a great deal of energy in the 1980s attempting to bring all these fragments together into a family.

That process began in 1983 with a major shift in denominational leadership and emphasis. Arie Brouwer joined the staff of the World Council of Churches, and Edwin Mulder was chosen as the new general secretary. Arie Brouwer was passionate about social issues, ecumenism, and church structures and possessed an authoritative leadership style. Ed Mulder was more of a pastor than a bureaucrat and a prophet, although he developed a deep commitment to racial reconciliation in South Africa.[1] Mulder saw the denomination not as a structure that needed to be made creative and productive, but as a family that needed to be nurtured, strengthened, and unified. He was a people person, not an organization man.[2]

Mulder came to the position of general secretary with thirty years of varied pastoral experience. He grew up in small towns in Minnesota and Iowa, where community members and extended family had a positive impact on a boy whose father died when he was young. Mulder attended Central College[3] and Western Seminary. He served a variety of congregations in both the East and Midwest: an older, urban church in Ridgefield, New Jersey; a new church in Holland, Michigan (Christ Memorial); Marble Collegiate in New York City; Second in Hackensack, New Jersey; and again at Christ Memorial. He also served as the Reformed Church's minister for evangelism in the mid 1960s and as president of the General Synod in 1979.

---

[1] Mulder visited South Africa during his term as General Synod president. While he was general secretary, he participated in several protests against apartheid. He visited again and fostered significant ecumenical relationships between the RCA and the Uniting Reformed Church of South Africa (the black and colored churches). He was instrumental in the process of making the Belhar Confession a fourth standard for the RCA. For more information on the RCA's relationship with churches in South Africa, see the DVD, *The RCA and South Africa*, which is available through the RCA Archives. Cf. Brouwer, *Ecumenical Testimony*, 56-77.

[2] There were several leadership transitions in the early 1980s. Howard Hageman retired from New Brunswick Seminary in 1985 and was succeeded by Robert White, formerly the RCA secretary for social witness. John Hesselink resigned the presidency of Western Seminary to teach theology there, and he was replaced by Marvin Hoff, a former national staff member. Several other professors of theology retired, as did three particular synod executives: Bert Bossenbroek (NY), James Schut (MI), and Albert Ten Clay (West).

[3] Some of Mulder's fellow students at Central included John Hesselink, Leonard Kalkwarf, Eugene Heideman, and Alvin Poppen. All exercised significant leadership in the RCA during the 1970s and 80s.

As general secretary, Mulder promised both a pastoral style and a team approach to the position. In an interview with John Stapert, Mulder identified a theme that would shape his work: "We need a renewed appreciation for each other and an increasing awareness of our need to be united in a common witness. We belong to a family. We need to be committed to each other and to the tasks which the Lord of the church is calling us to do in today's world." Mulder brought no particular agenda to the office, he said, but intended to listen and learn in order to shape an agenda shared by the whole church. He hoped the denomination would learn to celebrate its life together.[4]

Mulder began the new position at a time when the Reformed Church was not sharply divided into two distinct factions but fragmented into multiple opinions and practices. In 1983 John Stapert noted that Reformed Church congregations used forty-three different hymnbooks. A decreasing number of congregations purchased subscriptions to the *Church Herald* for their all members. A growing number of students attended non-RCA seminaries. Stapert thought this freedom of choice weakened the bonds that connected Reformed Church congregations.[5]

Other Reformed Church members preferred to have more freedom of choice, not less. Murray Moerman, pastor of the New Life Community Church in Burnaby, British Columbia, argued that new Reformed churches needed some elbow room. Congregations should pay assessments, participate in classis, and support Reformed Church mission, but they should not be required to baptize infants, use prescribed liturgy and traditional hymns, or restrict the pulpit to seminary educated and ordained clergy. It was misleading to call a church a community church if only Reformed practices were permitted.[6] Robert Wise, the pastor of a relatively new RCA church with "Community" in its name, responded that being a community church within the Reformed Church meant moving away from the old pattern

---

[4] John Stapert, "Expecting to Listen: An interview with Dr. Edwin Mulder," *CH*, Oct. 7, 1983, 10-11. Brouwer had been very active in ecumenical work, but Mulder chose to delegate most of that work to a staff member in order to have more time to provide a pastoral presence to the church. After Mulder had been in office eighteen months, Stapert praised his servant leadership. Mulder had been meeting with people throughout the church and helping them talk to each other when they disagreed. He praised people, encouraged positive actions, and tried to defuse potential explosions. Editorial, "Quiet Leadership," *CH*, Feb. 1, 1985, 5.

[5] Editorial, "Self-Actualization Run Wild," *CH*, April 1, 1983, 5.

[6] "I'd like to say...Let Community Churches be Community Churches," *CH*, May 20, 1983, 20.

of Dutch ethnicity and being open to all people and to the community itself. It did not mean surrendering Reformed identity.[7]

Many of the diverse practices occurred in the Synod of the West, particularly the Classis of California. That classis was considered a model for successful church growth because it had started several new congregations during and after the rapid influx of people to the state in the 1960s and 1970s. Chester Droog, field secretary in the Synod of the West, observed that most newcomers to California had never heard of the Reformed Church in America, so the new congregations had to be innovative and daring. They adopted the possibility thinking, drive-in worship, and church growth ideas developed by Robert Schuller. They called themselves "community" churches in order to differentiate themselves from the very conservative (often southern-based) denominations that were also starting congregations. For advice and ideas about ministry, they turned not to RCA institutions thousands of miles away, but to Fuller and Talbot Seminaries, Biola and Westmont Colleges, Campus Crusade for Christ, and World Vision.

Droog noted that the new congregations often acted very independently, "each doing what it deemed best to accomplish its mission." For example, some congregations practiced both infant and adult baptism (immersion).[8] Unlike the purists of the 1940s, they were not concerned about preserving Reformed beliefs and practices. They were pragmatic, willing to use whatever methods attracted new members into their churches. Some leaders believed their congregations had grown *because* they had not been confined by a specifically Reformed identity.

In 1969, the synod president, Ray Van Heukelom, had asked Reformed Church members not only to tolerate but also to value diverse expressions of the Christian faith. Reformed churches did begin to welcome more diversity, but by 1983 John Stapert and others wondered if the denomination had become *too* open. Should a Reformed church

---

[7]   Letter to the editor, *CH*, July 15, 1983, 27.
[8]   Chester Droog, "The RCA: Growing in the Southwest," *CH*, June 7, 1985, 16-17. The RCA encouraged adult baptism (by immersion if desired) for those who had not been baptized previously. It discouraged the practice of infant dedication and labeled adult rebaptism a doctrinal error. See Cook, *The Church Speaks*, 56-74, 101-11. Twenty-five years later the RCA is still debating appropriate baptismal practices. Some congregations have allowed members to choose baptism or dedication for their children, and whether to be rebaptized as adults. They say they do this to give flexibility to members from Baptist traditions. It raises the question, however, of the meaning of Reformed identity and whether there are any limits to tolerance of practices which are not particularly Reformed.

practice infant dedication? Use a Baptist hymnbook? If the Reformed Church was ecumenical, should members be so critical of the National Council? If the denomination ordained women, should churches be permitted to refuse to do so? Some members insisted that there should be a great deal of freedom, and no member or congregation should be forced to do anything. Some members insisted that these differences of opinion did not matter, and that a denomination could encompass very different beliefs and practices. But if members and congregations could act as they chose, what did it mean to be part of a denomination? What held the disparate parts together? What was the denomination's identity?

Identity Crisis?

In 1984, as president of the General Synod, Leonard Kalkwarf visited Reformed churches in many different areas of the country and saw at first hand their growing diversity in worship style and beliefs. In his report to the synod, he raised a question that the denomination would address for the next three decades.

> The issue seems to be, "What is the glue that holds us together?" Early in our history, the answer to this question might have been our Dutch heritage. As one visits different congregations, one is struck by the variety of worship forms, vestments, liturgies, architectural styles, and even theological emphases. Surely these are not what we have in common, and perhaps they ought not to be. Perhaps it is to be found within that beloved old document which affirms that *our only comfort in life and in death is that we are a people who belong.* Yet, somehow it seems as if that is not the case. I do not have the answer. However, since the issue continues to surface, and since there are those who believe that until we are able to determine who we are as a denomination we will not be able to move forward together, I recommend: To instruct the General Synod Executive Committee to give high priority during the next three years to the study of the issue of denominational identity.[9]

Kalkwarf's speech sparked a flurry of study and activity. The General Program Council selected the phrase, "A People Who Belong," as a theme to shape the work of the denomination. Edwin Mulder

---

[9]   *Acts and Proceedings*, 1984, 28-29.

explained that many groups within the church—singles, youth, women, specialized ministers, ethnic congregations, laity—felt as though they did not belong. The theme would serve as a "covenantal hug" to remind everyone that they were part of a family.[10] Still, the Reformed Church found it easier to *declare* that everyone belonged to the family than to fully welcome everyone into the fold.[11]

The more formal institutional response to Kalkwarf's question began when the General Synod Executive Committee appointed the Identity Task Force to develop a three-year focus on identity. The task force adopted this directional statement: "To be a church which will encourage in all members a sense of identification and belonging, which will aid the RCA in celebration, witness, and ministry." It declared as its purpose, "To engage RCA members in a process of experience and reflection, leading to a sense of identity and belonging." The task force proposed a number of gatherings and studies to help discern this identity.[12]

The first major denominational identity event was held at the General Synod in 1986 at the Crystal Cathedral in Garden Grove, California. The synod held a worship service during the presynod festival, and this service was transmitted live via satellite to groups of Reformed Church members who had gathered at various locations in all the regional synods. The goal of the event was not to reflect on denominational identity per se, but to bring members into a shared experience. This expanded family reunion included music and speakers and an acknowledgment of Edwin Mulder's wedding anniversary. To

---

[10]   Edwin Mulder, "People Who Belong," *CH*, Oct. 5, 1984, 6-7.

[11]   In 1984 the Council for Pacific and Asian American Ministries reminded the denomination that "Crossing Cultural Barriers: Reaching and Receiving in Christ" had been adopted as the denomination's priority for the decade of the 1980s but had not yet been implemented, *Acts and Proceedings*, 1984, 81. Other members pointed out that the denomination was willing to minister to people of different skin colors when they lived in other parts of the world, but not when they lived in U.S. cities. The RCA spent a great deal of money on world mission and church extension in suburbs, but very little on urban churches. Eugene Roberts, "I'd like to say... Support Urban Missions," *CH*, Jan. 3, 1986, 19. Roberts wondered why an urban church received only $5,000 a year for a salary supplement, while the denomination spent $60,000 a year to support a missionary in Mexico. He also noted that urban mission work was overseen by the Division of Church Planning and Development, and these efforts were evaluated by the same criteria for success as new church starts, which usually made them look unsuccessful, despite the good work they did.

[12]   *Acts and Proceedings*, 1985, 43-44. Members of the task force included Gregg Anderson, William Brownson, Robert Hess, Nella Kennedy, Louis Lotz, James Neevel (chair), Peter Paulsen, Sonja Stewart, and staff members Jhonny Alicea-Baez, Wayne Antworth, Eugene Heideman, and Edwin Mulder.

create a tangible sign of denominational unity, each congregation had been invited to a make a quilt square. Almost five hundred congregations did so, and these were combined into an enormous quilt that was raised dramatically to the peaks of the Crystal Cathedral. It was a striking image of family and connectedness.[13]

The Identity Task Force realized that despite this apparently congenial family reunion, Reformed Church members held diverse and complex identities. To quantify the degree of difference among them, the task force asked Donald Luidens and Roger Nemeth, sociologists at Hope College, to conduct an extensive survey of Reformed Church members. The data showed significant differences between eastern and western regions of the denomination. Western members attended church more often and contributed more, despite having smaller incomes than Reformed Church members in the East. They were more likely than eastern members to believe the Bible was the actual Word of God and should be read literally. Yet the two regions shared an unquestioned commitment to their religious faith: 91 percent of all Reformed Church members said religion was extremely or quite important.[14]

Luidens and Nemeth concluded from this data that Reformed Church members had no cause to be suspicious of one another. "For any one section of the denomination to point to another section and suggest that its beliefs or practices are wrong, or that Christ is not being worshiped there, or that Christianity is not being taken seriously by its members, is dismissive at best and destructive at worst." Instead, the Reformed Church should celebrate the fact that its members were committed to their Christian faith, regardless of region.[15]

---

[13] Kim N. Baker, editorial, "It's Fun to Belong," *CH*, July 25, 1986, 5. There was considerable tension behind the scenes of this event generated by a conflict over a member of the African National Congress who had been invited to address the synod. This event will be discussed below.

[14] More than half the members in Michigan, Mid-America, and the Heartland attended church five or more times a month. More than half the members in the Albany and New York synods, and 40 percent in Mid-Atlantics, attended fewer than four times. Almost half the midwestern members, but less than one-fourth of easterners, believed the Bible was the actual Word of God and should be read literally. Most others said that the Bible was the inspired Word of God, but not everything should be read literally. Ninety-five percent of midwestern and 82-84 percent of eastern members said that religion was important.

[15] Suspicion of the quality of faith in the eastern Reformed churches began almost immediately after the immigrants arrived in the United States and reappeared frequently, particularly in conflicted periods like the 1940s and late 1960s. Not all midwestern RCA members shared this sentiment. Cf. Voskuil, "When East Meets West," 201-28.

A more sobering result of the survey was that clergy and laity did not value the Reformed confessions as much as was often assumed. The Apostles' Creed was ranked as very or quite important by more than 80 percent of all clergy and laity, including East and West. The Heidelberg Catechism was considered very or quite important by 75 percent of clergy and 50 percent of laity. The Nicene Creed was important to about half the respondents, but the Belgic Confession, Canons of Dort, and the *Book of Church Order* were important to less than a quarter of respondents.

The survey also found that that only half the laypeople considered membership in the Reformed Church to be extremely or quite important. Luidens and Nemeth observed,

> The relative weakness of this support should be of major concern to the denomination. The task of renewal ahead is a formidable one, and the level of resolve is not uniformly strong....if one out of two current members of the denomination has little personal commitment to the denomination, it will be virtually impossible to generate the necessary enthusiasm to make the renewal efforts succeed....Without a strong drive to make the denomination work the RCA will have some difficult years ahead. Our differences will become divisive, and our small size will increase the intensity of that division."[16]

Neither Reformed theology nor denominational commitment was able to provide sufficient glue to hold the denomination together.

The Identity Task Force continued gathering data by organizing twenty-two regional consultations, which met October 31, 1987 (Reformation Day). These groups were asked to determine the Reformed Church's task for the next century.[17] In January 1988 one representative from each regional meeting, plus representatives of commissions and agencies, gathered for a national consultation whose purpose was to "provide the data needed for the formulation of a statement on the vision for the future of the RCA and an evaluation of the three-year identity focus to be presented to the General Synod in 1988 by the Identity Task Force."[18] This rather convoluted purpose statement produced a rather

---

16   "The RCA Today: Painting a Portrait," *CH*, Feb. 6, 1987, 5-7; "The RCA Today: Beliefs and Behaviors," Feb. 20, 1987, 12-14; "The RCA Today: Seeking Unity amid Diversity," March 20, 1987, 11-14.

17   Reformed Church News, "Identity Task Force Schedules Consultations," *CH*, Oct. 2, 1987, 23.

18   *Acts and Proceedings*, 1987, 141-42.

convoluted meeting. The desire to discern denominational identity had been reduced to a vague celebration of diverse perspectives and a need to create a feeling of connection for Reformed Church members with the denomination and each other.

Participants in the January consultation developed a list of nearly forty items that would facilitate these connections, such as promoting cultural diversity, developing better lay training, and enhancing communication within the denomination. One group said, "We call the Reformed Church in America to be a community which accepts and trains all whom God calls into leadership from our diverse culture and various life stages." Other groups mentioned inclusivity, ethnic diversity, and sending the *Church Herald* to every household. Stapert observed, "Most participants finished the consultation without knowing how their weekend activities would contribute to the RCA's articulation of an identity. In many, however, there was the sense that the identity would be forged as the church brought its heritage, resources, and energy to bear on specific contemporary issues."[19]

The summary of the consultation that appeared in the *Church Herald* was entitled "RCA Pursues Identity." "Pursues" was a telling choice of verb, suggesting that the RCA was chasing something that continued to elude it. The process generated some interesting proposals, but no clear sense of identity. The consultation participants wanted the Reformed Church to be more inclusive, and rightly so. But seeking inclusivity was not the same as discerning identity. Genuine inclusion would probably be attained only after RCA members reflected on why its identity had made it so difficult to be inclusive in the past.

The task force processed the data from the consultation and proposed twelve identity affirmations. These rather generic statements described the Reformed Church in America as rooted in God and scripture, guided by the *Book of Church Order* and the early creeds and Reformation confessions, valuing worship and mission, and being a family but not an exclusive clan. The task force also noted five areas of tension: (1) Some members felt alienated from their fellow members. (2) Confessions were theoretically important, but people did not know them well. (3) Some members emphasized mission and evangelism while others emphasized peace, justice, and ecology. (4) The *BCO* provided guidance for discipline, but the denomination found it difficult to set boundaries which might exclude some practices or ideas. (5) A common

---

[19]　Reformed Church News, "RCA Pursues Identity," *CH*, Feb. 19, 1988, 25.

Reformed tradition had produced a great variety of expressions of faith, but not all were clearly Reformed.[20]

Given the significant time and money that was invested into this study of identity, the results were disappointingly minimal. The statements of the task force were accurate, but they were not particularly insightful or engaging. They could have described the Reformed Church before the lengthy study of identity was initiated. Some critics thought that the denomination asked a superficial question and got a superficial answer. Early in the process John Stapert wrote, "With the demise of this ethnic [Dutch] identity and with our current theological diversity, it's no wonder that we're experiencing an identity crisis. I think this is the opportunity for this denomination to set forth a singular purpose around which all its members will rally."[21] Stapert's use of the phrase "identity crisis" intimated that the Reformed Church was a self-indulgent adolescent trying to find him or herself. But the denomination needed to sort out its identity because the diversity which had long pervaded the denomination had led to fragmentation. During the 1700s, the Reformed Church had embraced both revivalism *and* a more cerebral faith. In the 1800s, it had included midwestern separatists *and* the ecumenical easterners. In the 1900s it welcomed evangelists *and* social activists. Perhaps it was impossible to discern or pursue a single identity because no single identity existed. From the outset the Reformed Church had embraced diversity and diversity had caused conflict. But no one was willing to say this.

Since the Reformed Church seemed to lack a clear, common identity, the next logical emphasis quickly became what *does* tie the RCA together rather than what *should* tie it together. Banners at General Synod meetings proclaimed the denominational theme: A People Who Belong. But what did they belong *to*? The first question of the Heidelberg Catechism said that we belong not to ourselves but to our faithful Savior Jesus Christ, but the task force increasingly emphasized belonging to the *denomination*. The task force hoped that individuals who felt they belonged would be more committed to the Reformed Church. This made the identity of the denomination dependent on

---

[20] *Acts and Proceedings*, 1988, 164-72. The task force sent many of the consultation's proposals on to denominational committees or agencies. For example, the task force encouraged the archives to continue gathering the denomination's collective memory, and it urged the *Church Herald* to publish a historical column, which it did for a year.

[21] Editorial, "Reformed Glue," *CH*, Jan. 15, 1988, 4-5. For a critique of the identity emphasis, see Paul R. Fries, "Confessing Is Identity: Reflections on a Denominational Identity Crisis," *Perspectives*, June 1988, 407.

how its members felt about each other and the institution. A more Reformed view of the church might have emphasized that the RCA was part of the body of Christ and defined by what Christ does, not what people feel.[22]

Despite the ambiguity inherent in the study of identity, one of the strengths of the Identity Task Force report was its broadly inclusive portrayal of the Reformed Church. It recognized and valued multiple viewpoints and emphases. The report might have had a more lasting impact, however, if it had connected diversity more clearly with Reformed theology. For example, the breadth of belief and practice in the church reflected the Reformed conviction that human beings do not know the mind of God and should not blithely equate their programs with God's will. Many different strategies and gifts could be used to help bring about the kingdom of God. Christians did not need to agree about every issue. This approach might have generated a clearer and more compelling sense of identity.

The task force said that it had tried to help the denomination experience identity rather than define it. This meant that the process was relatively open-ended and avoided finding answers too quickly. But simply experiencing identity did not provide substance to the process. Specifically, the task force did not incorporate much theological or historical reflection about the reasons for diverse opinions in the Reformed Church. It did emphasize that the denomination was part of a larger Christian tradition, although it might have said more explicitly that the diverse and often conflicting perspectives within the Christian faith were similarly reflected in the RCA.

In the end, the focus on identity did not produce major insights or changes. It was a feel-good process, which was not a bad thing for a denomination inclined to self-doubt and conflict. It did not find a profound new metaphor or theological concept to give shape to the church. Instead, it concluded that the Reformed Church's identity was its diversity,[23] and that should be celebrated.

---

[22] The revivalist and evangelical strands in American religion tended to emphasize that congregations were collections of individuals who chose to worship in a particular church. In this view, the congregation was primarily a voluntary organization rooted in freedom of choice. A more Reformed view emphasized that the church was rooted in God's action and God's grace and that being part of a denomination reminded believers that the Christian tradition was larger than their personal faith or their congregation's life.

[23] In 2011, "diversity" in RCA bureaucratic speech usually refers to primarily to multicultural and multiracial perspectives. In the late 1980s, the Identity Task Force used the word much more broadly to refer to a variety of theological perspectives

Ways to Deal with Diversity

The Reformed Church in America did celebrate its diversity, but it became ever clearer that these multiple perspectives made it difficult to be a unified denomination. Consequently, the church sought ways to allow different models and strategies but to avoid complete fragmentation.

Different but Equal

The first strategy was to recognize that different approaches were equally valuable. This was particularly useful in responding to social issues about which there was no clear biblical mandate. In his presidential report to the General Synod in 1985, William Brownson tried to find common ground between the purists on the right and the moderates on the left. The two groups were concerned about different social problems and took very different approaches to outreach and social witness, but they shared a desire to be good neighbors, like the Samaritan in Luke 10. Brownson wrote,

> There are many wounded and endangered ones along the roadside. Some of us are inclined to notice the ones on the left. We care about oppressed people in South Africa, about the hungry in Ethiopia, about the victims of war. Some of us are moved by wounds on the right. We're concerned about the plight of unborn children, about lives soiled by pornography, blighted by drugs and alcohol, about families wasted through unfaithfulness, abuse, and divorce. That diversity of concern is okay. The suffering is grievous, and the ditch is deep on both sides of the road. No one can stop by all those wounded travelers. How sad it is when we act like all the real neighbors are working our side of the street! I thank God we've got neighbor-hearted ones on the right and the left and others in the middle. Don't despise the other man's issue, the other woman's concern. We've got to love each other, and you can't love me if you sneer at my cause, if you dismiss as trivial what is breaking my heart.[24]

This strategy of allowing diverse practices was also used for issues which had more impact on local congregations than on the

---

within the RCA. The task force recognized and valued the growth of ethnic groups within the RCA, but its use of the term referred more to ideas and practices than to race and ethnicity.

[24]   *Acts and Proceedings*, 1985, 30.

denomination as a whole. For example, in 1988 the synod approved a proposal to allow children to participate in the Lord's Supper. Because of the close vote (139-132) and the high level of resistance, the policy was made optional so that congregations would not be required to include children.

Those opposed to allowing children at the Table argued that scripture required a greater intellectual grasp of the theology of the Lord's Supper than was possible for small children. They insisted that young people were less likely to make profession of faith if they were not enticed by Communion. One delegate called the Supper "a feast of the totally committed" and claimed that children were incapable of that. Those who wanted to include children at the Table insisted that children did indeed have meaningful faith and that if total commitment and a complete intellectual understanding of the sacrament were required, most adults would be excluded as well.[25]

The synod debated the issue again in 1989, after several overtures asked that the decision be rescinded or made more restrictive. Jay Van Sweden, an elder from Grand Rapids, said, "I am unalterably opposed to allowing children at the Lord's Supper without a [prior] confession of faith. I don't want the Lord's Table profaned. The Lord's Table is not a picnic table."[26] Other critics suggested that if children professed their faith at an earlier age, they could be welcomed at the Table. The synod chose not to make any changes.

Allowing these choices appears to offer a simple way to keep peace in the denomination, but these were not minor differences in practice. The two options arose out of very different beliefs about the nature of the church and the sacraments. Those opposed to children at the Table cited the Apostle Paul's warning not to profane the sacrament. They wanted to protect the Table from being defiled by immature believers. The Lord's Supper was a privilege given only to those who had demonstrated their faith and earned a place at the Table. The church needed to protect the purity of the Supper.

In sharp contrast, those who wanted children to be welcomed at the Table saw the sacrament more as participation in a community than as individual privilege. They cited biblical imagery of feasts and banquets that welcomed everyone. God invited God's people to a meal, not because of their correct beliefs or good behavior but because God

---

[25] John Stapert, "Permission Granted: Table Opened to Children," *CH*, July 22, 1988, 4-5.

[26] John Stapert, "Synod Keeps the Table Open," *CH*, July 1989, 8-9.

was gracious. Children should be included and welcomed as well. The Table did not need to be so carefully protected.

For issues such as this one, when there was no compromise position that would satisfy each side, it seemed wise to let each congregation decide on its own, rather than force half the people to adopt or continue a practice they did not believe in.

Limited Choices

A second strategy for handling the denomination's diversity was to allow choices but attempt to manage and limit them. This strategy shaped the formation of the Theological Education Agency (TEA) in 1984. There was growing concern in the early 1980s about the number of students who chose not to attend New Brunswick or Western Seminary. Only one of twenty-four students from the Far West attended a Reformed Church seminary. Thirty-three RCA students attended Fuller Seminary in Pasadena, California. Some students chose non-RCA seminaries for geographical convenience, so as not to move their families. Some chose seminaries that they thought would be more liberal or conservative than the Reformed Church institutions. Many of these seminaries were located in areas that lacked Reformed churches, where students might complete internships and develop a sense of denominational identity and connection.

Assessing the fitness of these students for ministry also caused considerable work for the RCA seminary faculties. In order to be ordained, students at New Brunswick and Western had to receive the recommendation of their professors in the form of a professorial certificate (later called the Certificate of Fitness).[27] Students who did not attend the two RCA seminaries needed to apply for a dispensation from the professorial certificate and demonstrate their fitness to the faculty. They wrote papers on Reformed Church history and Standards, took a polity test, and submitted sample sermons, orders of worship, and lesson plans and then discussed these with Western or New Brunswick faculty. This made a large workload for the faculty, who processed fifty-four dispensations between 1979 and 1983. As the number of Reformed Church ministers grew and their opportunities for pastoral positions decreased, some ministers asked whether these "outsiders" should be

---

[27]   Both the professorial certificate and the Certificate of Fitness were a kind of quality control of seminarians. Some students performed well enough academically to receive a Master of Divinity degree, but lacked the gifts for ordained ministry. Seminary faculty could grant such students the degree without endorsing them as potential RCA pastors.

ordained in the Reformed Church if they refused to attend an RCA seminary. Was there room for them in the RCA? Did they belong?

In addition to these concerns about theological education, James Cook observed in his president's address to the General Synod in 1983 that Reformed churches in the Far West often felt isolated from the rest of the denomination, in part because their pastors had not attended RCA seminaries and lacked connections to and knowledge of the denomination. He proposed the formation of an ad hoc committee to study the possibility of RCA theological education in the Far West.[28] During the next year the committee drafted a plan for a Theological Education Agency (TEA), which would be housed at Fuller Seminary but would supervise students at all non-RCA seminaries. These students would earn certificates of fitness for ministry from TEA, just as Western and New Brunswick students did from their faculties. The director of TEA would teach Reformed Church polity and Standards to students at Fuller Seminary but would not be a full-time professor. The agency would not own property or have its own faculty, but it would provide an affectional center for the Reformed Church in southern California. It would help all its students develop a stronger sense of Reformed Church identity, theology, and polity.

John Stapert, a graduate of Fuller, observed that TEA would "change our view of seminarians who go to schools other than New Brunswick or Western. In the past, they have been viewed as wanderers (or, perhaps, rebels) who needed to obtain permission to be allowed back into the Reformed Church." Under TEA, students would receive the church's blessing from the beginning, and an antagonistic relationship would become cooperative.[29] Not everyone agreed with his optimistic assessment, however, and vigorous debate ensued at the synod. Critics said TEA was expensive, gave too much authority to California churches, and encouraged students to attend non-RCA seminaries. An amendment suggested that Cook's proposal be studied for a year, but the synod rejected this amendment and approved the proposal.[30]

---

[28] Two recent overtures had raised related issues. In 1981 the Classis of Cascades asked the synod to study why RCA students chose to attend non-RCA seminaries. The Classis of California asked that ministerial students under its care who completed a Reformed heritage course at Fuller Seminary automatically receive a dispensation from the professorial certificate and not be required to do additional work at an RCA seminary. *Acts and Proceedings*, 1981, 227-28; James Cook, "The Unfinished Gospel," *CH*, June 17, 1983, 112-17.

[29] Editorial, "A Time for TEA?" *CH*, May 4, 1984, 4-5.

[30] John Stapert, "Synod Says 'Yes' to TEA," *CH*, July 13, 1984, 6-7.

The Theological Education Agency did attempt to provide the seminarians under its supervision with more knowledge of the Reformed Church in America. However, by the late 1980s, there were seventy students in the TEA program scattered among twenty seminaries around the country, and the director found it difficult to supervise them all. To complicate matters, students could still attend any seminary regardless of its theology or location. The Board of Theological Education attempted to implement guidelines mandating that seminaries should be of compatible Reformed theology and located near Reformed Church congregations, but even these modest guidelines created a great deal of debate. The criteria for compatible theology were not made clear, so both moderates and purists feared that their preferred seminaries would be ruled out. The lack of a definitive list of approved seminaries left people wondering if the church was moving toward a policy where only Western, New Brunswick, and Fuller would be approved.

Several overtures in 1989 opposed any guidelines that would rule out certain seminaries. They argued that the *Book of Church Order* specified only that students must attend an accredited seminary and that only the classis had the right to supervise seminary selection. The role of the synod through TEA was to manage the diverse choices, not limit the options. In the end, the denomination chose not to establish any theological criteria.[31]

The discussion of theological education raised several important questions about Reformed Church identity and its sense of family. Should students who refused to attend an RCA seminary be ordained and employed in the Reformed Church? Should students be permitted to attend a seminary that taught theology or polity that was inconsistent with the Reformed tradition? If a student considered the RCA seminaries too liberal or too conservative, did he or she belong in the denomination? In the end, the church allowed almost complete freedom of choice, in part because it could not agree on narrower guidelines.

---

[31] *Acts and Proceedings*, 1989, 237, 259-65; 1990, 260-61. The Board of Theological Education seemed rather secretive about this policy. Its report to the synod in 1987 mentioned the criteria but did not specify what they were. It did say that TEA was not intended to encourage attendance at other seminaries, and students needed to be well trained in the Reformed tradition, *Acts and Proceedings*, 1987, 183-84. In 1988 the BTE reported that the Commission on Church Order had affirmed its authority to put a selection policy in place, and that the policy had been sent to people in classes responsible for candidates. It did not publish the policy.

James Cook hoped that TEA would reaffirm the core identity of the Reformed Church and connect seminarians and congregations with the denomination and one another. However, the result has been very different. Since TEA began, some Reformed Church ministers educated at non-RCA seminaries (and some from RCA seminaries as well) have encouraged their congregations to be more independent and congregational and less Reformed. They have encouraged infant dedication rather than infant baptism, resisted paying assessments, refused to ordain women, and threatened to leave the denomination. TEA was proposed as a way to manage diversity with the hope that greater unity would result, but in some ways it simply solidified and institutionalized the fragmentation.

The Family That Pays Together Stays Together?

A third strategy that helped promote a stronger denominational identity was fund-raising. The Reformed Church faced several budget problems that had not been resolved by either restructuring or eliminating staff.[32] The divisions of Christian Discipleship and Church Planning and Development consistently failed to bring in sufficient contributions to support their programs.[33] In order to assure the long-term viability of these programs, the General Program Council asked the 1987 General Synod to levy an assessment of $2.43 to pay for staff costs.[34] Opponents insisted that assessments would breed distrust and hostility within the denomination. Supporters believed that education, church extension, and social witness were essential denominational activities that members ought to pay for. In the end, the synod approved the assessment.

[32] Reformed Church News, "GPC Wrestles with Finances," *CH*, May 6, 1988, 24. In 1987 the GPC had a $473,000 deficit.

[33] John Stapert wondered if this pattern resulted from a "crusader" mentality, which meant that RCA members might be more eager to convert people than to educate them. They gave money to evangelize Africans in Africa but not to educate African Americans in Brewton, Alabama, at the Southern Normal School. Editorial, "Tourists, Crusaders, Servants," *CH*, Jan. 2, 1987, 4-5. Whether or not Stapert was correct in his analysis, it was a rare attempt to discern the cause of the consistent pattern of generous giving to foreign missions and less generous giving to other RCA projects.

[34] Reformed Church News, "GPC Endorses Funding Through Assessments," *CH*, May 1, 1987, 25; *Acts and Proceedings*, 1987, 245-65. When the GPC discussed this, Ed Mulder pointed out that $2.43 equaled the price of a burger, fries, and soda. He said, "The church has asked us to do a job but then hasn't provided the funding. We may not agree with all the things that are being done in some areas, but let's not undercut all the good things that are also happening. We must stand together."

In the same year, the Board of Theological Education proposed a new assessment of $1.80 per member to fund the president, dean, and business manager at each seminary, plus the director of TEA.[35] The synod approved this as well.[36]

Congregations were more resistant, and complaints began immediately. Elder Ernest Wood predicted that assessments would lead to the death of small congregations. They were already required to pay a pastor a minimum salary, annuity, and medical insurance, and they could not manage any more. A minister analyzed the statistics for Ernest Wood's church and concluded that if each family gave five percent of its income, their donations would indicate that the average family income was about $6,700 per year, well below the national poverty line. The minister wondered if Wood's fellow parishioners all lived below the poverty line or exercised poor stewardship.[37]

A number of classes submitted overtures in 1988 asking that the assessments be repealed. Palisades Classis was "spiritually uncomfortable" with funding programs through a tax and predicted a backlash of decreased local giving. Illiana Classis believed "there are better ways to raise the necessary funds and that those ways would create more spiritual enthusiasm rather than the human tendency to rebel when we are ordered to do something." South Grand Rapids feared that "the agencies and institutions involved will be less responsive to the needs and perspectives of the local church." Zeeland Classis claimed that "assessments may cause giving not to be the result of a cheerful heart. They also may cause division among RCA members because some members in good Christian conscience may not support the underlying rationale of the use of an assessment."[38] Despite a heated discussion in the Financial Support Advisory Committee, the overtures were easily defeated by the synod.[39] The "you can't make me" theme was much in evidence in the overtures, but, in the end, delegates concluded that if the Reformed Church was going to be a family and survive as an institution, then everybody needed to pay a fair share. Assessments

---

[35] John Stapert, "The Assessment Synod," *CH*, July 17, 1987, 5-7.

[36] Delegates to General Synod during the period from 1987 to 1992 were remarkably willing to fund denominational projects. Serving as a delegate was often reported to be a very positive experience for both clergy and elders. The elders in particular encountered the denomination in a very different way and came away with a much broader understanding of the work of the RCA.

[37] Ernest Wood, "I'd Like to Say...Assessments Hurt Small Churches," *CH*, Sept. 4, 1987, 19; James Foster, letter to the editor, Oct. 16, 1987, 20.

[38] *Acts and Proceedings*, 1988, 345-51.

[39] Jeffrey Japinga, "Paying the Price: Synod Confirms Assessments," *CH*, July 22, 1988, 8-11.

asked everyone to support the denomination at a basic level so that the essential work could be completed. Most congregations found the resources to pay the increased assessments, despite all the complaints.

Assessments helped meet the ongoing expenses of the denomination, but for big projects the Reformed Church turned to fund drives. In 1986, denominational staff members identified several major projects that needed to be financed. In the past, boards and agencies had conducted separate and often competing fund drives, but this time the denomination tried a unified approach. It combined the major projects (student housing at New Brunswick Seminary and renovations at Camp Warwick, New York) and invited congregations and other groups to submit proposals as well. Putting People in Mission (PPIM) was born. This fund drive occurred concurrently with the study of RCA identity, and thus in many ways Putting People in Mission functioned as a goal—or the glue which held the denomination together for a time.[40]

The fund drive also illustrated the wide variety of ministries that flourished around the Reformed Church. The range of proposals offered congregations a way to learn about other parts of the denomination. A church in California wanted to reach out to gang members. An Anglo congregation in suburban Philadelphia wanted to build an addition so that it could hold concurrent worship services with the Korean congregation that shared its space. Churches in the West could learn about the work of New Brunswick Seminary and Camp Warwick.[41] Energized by this display of vital ministries, the synod approved the PPIM goal of $25 million in 1988.[42]

John Stapert and others expected a great deal from PPIM. Stapert wrote,

> Facing the growing realities of regional programming and the constantly advancing individualism of North American Christianity, this denomination has decided it will fight for

---

[40]   Edwin Mulder, "A Unified Endeavor," *CH*, April 3, 1987, 26-27.
[41]   More than one hundred proposals were submitted totaling $32 million. Focus meetings were held across the denomination that encouraged participants to vote for the proposals they thought should be included in the fund drive. A few proposals were eliminated (a national legislative office in Washington, and a short-term every household distribution of the *Church Herald*), and some large requests were reduced (Warwick Camp and Conference Center, and a magazine for Reformed Church Women).
[42]   Reformed Church News, "GSEC to Recommend $25 Million Fund Drive Goal," *CH*, June 24, 1988, 23.

cohesion by seeking every member's participation in this church-wide drive. The more members who become involved, regardless of the amounts of money pledged and contributed, the more RCA cohesion we'll have.[43]

Not only would the drive raise money, there were hopes that it would unify the denomination and give it a sense of identity.

Resistance to the fund drive appeared almost immediately. The Particular Synod of the Far West allowed its staff members to spend 10 percent of their time consulting, but they could not solicit contributions.[44] The Particular Synod of Michigan also limited the involvement of its staff members. This insistence that regional interests took priority over the needs of the denomination did not set a very positive example.

A number of congregations also refused to participate. Some cited their own building programs or their disagreements with the denomination. One pastor did not like the suggested method of visiting every member. Some pastors were reluctant to allow their most generous givers to be approached for major gifts. Other pastors simply refused for reasons that were not clear.

One month before the pledge period began, a news article in the *Church Herald* praised PPIM as an exciting way to share resources and get people involved in mission, but the article also reported these hesitations and concluded on a sober note. "If those favoring the priority of local efforts and those expressing dissatisfaction with the direction of the RCA combine to cut into a huge denominational program like PPIM, the loss may be greater than lack of money. Rather, it will point to another broken thread in the tapestry called the RCA."[45] Critics said the article was negative, poorly timed, and gave too much attention to naysayers in the denomination. Others said it simply named the lack of unity that existed in the church. James Brumm, a pastor in New Jersey, noted that families fight, and the reporting of disagreement should not be equated with disloyalty to the denomination.[46]

During the pledge period of PPIM in the spring of 1989, 487 congregations gave or pledged about $13 million, including about $2.5

[43]   Editorial, "The RCA's Big Decisions," *CH*, Sept. 2, 1988, 4.

[44]   Reformed Church News, "PSW Honors Droog, Installs DeMaster," *CH*, Nov. 4, 1988, 22-23.

[45]   Reformed Church News, "Putting People in Mission: Raising Money, Raising Loyalties," *CH*, April, 1989, 30-31.

[46]   Flak and Flattery, *CH*, July 1989, 6. Some members thought that the role of the magazine was to promote denominational projects, not report bad news.

million in major gifts. When the leaders of the fund drive reported to the synod in June, they remained optimistic about the possibility of meeting the goal of $25 million. This did not happen. By 1991, about 800 churches had contributed a total of about $15 million, well short of the goal.[47]

Toward the end of the fund drive, Edwin Mulder asked Peter Norman, president of the consulting firm assisting with the drive, to give his impressions of the Reformed Church, and Norman readily agreed. First, Norman said, the Reformed Church is very self-critical. "I have been impressed with the thoroughness with which you undertake a task, but it never seems to be good enough. You make a decision, and then proceed to second-guess yourselves....Instead of saying 'That is really great!' you say 'that's not so bad.'" Second, Norman saw a great deal of congregational autonomy. "When we entered into a contract with the Reformed Church in America, we thought that we would be working with a connectional church and that the decisions of its assemblies would be carried out." But many pastors and congregations refused to participate. Finally, Norman observed that the disgruntled members received too much attention. A minority was able to immobilize the majority. Mulder agreed with this assessment. The Reformed Church was supposed to be a family, and yet too many family members thought they could do as they pleased, which led to fragmentation. Mulder appreciated constructive criticism, but he noted that some people were angry about everything and dragged down a good cause.[48]

In spite of the hesitation and resistance, Putting People in Mission raised a significant amount of money that was put to very creative use. It did unite the denomination to some degree around a common

---

[47] Leaders of the fund drive said that some churches were still receiving pledges, which could reach $5 million. In all, 236 congregations said they would participate later and this offered potentially another $7 million. Sixty-four congregations had given no response and their goals totaled $1.8 million. One hundred fifty-six congregations simply refused to participate. *Acts and Proceedings*, 1989, 52, 324-27. The Rev. Cornelis Van Kempen wrote later that his congregation had implemented the fund drive differently than had been encouraged. Rather than individual solicitations of all members, the congregation gathered to view the videos and discuss the projects. They reached 104 percent of their goal, but the story raises the question of why there was such resistance to the every-member visit program. "It's Not Too Late for PPIM," *CH*, Nov. 1989, 5. For later reports see *Acts and Proceedings*, 1990, 367-68; 1991, 336-37; 1992, 439-40.

[48] Edwin Mulder, "Through the Eyes of Another," *CH*, July 1989, 5. In his subsequent correspondence, Mulder frequently cited Norman's first point about the high degree of self-criticism within the RCA. Mulder Correspondence, General Synod Archives. Seven staff members from the consulting firm provided advice to the RCA, and administrative expenses totaled $2 million.

project. It built connections among people involved in different kinds of mission in all parts of the church. It brought the family together, but it also demonstrated that some people did not want to be part of the family. It also showed some potential for denominational unity and identity centered on outreach and mission.[49] Reformed Church members could come together around concrete and interesting mission projects. They could set aside some of their geographical differences and theological disagreements in order to fund and carry out ministry to people in all parts of the church and the nation.

Testing the Limits of Diversity

The Reformed Church was clearly willing to permit a wide range of congregational and personal beliefs and practices to coexist without enforcing uniformity. Most members could accept the fact that other members took different stances on women's ordination, children at the Lord's Table, and the choice of hymnbooks. There were other areas, however, where the purists in particular believed that the denomination was making an intolerable choice that they could not support. Significant conflict and debate ensued.

The African National Congress vs. the Crystal Cathedral

A major test of family ties occurred at the Synod of 1986, held at the Crystal Cathedral in Garden Grove, California. After years of discussing apartheid in South Africa, the Synod of 1985 voted to invite Oliver Tambo, president of the African National Congress (ANC), to address synod delegates in 1986.[50] When Tambo accepted the invitation in the spring of 1986, several people protested. Howard Hoffman, a layperson from Zeeland, Michigan, claimed that the ANC was a terrorist organization funded by the Soviets. Howard Davis, a pastor in Grand Rapids, wrote that it was "unbelievable, unconscionable, and unacceptable" for Tambo to address the General Synod because of the violent actions the ANC had initiated. Don den Hartog, a pastor in Chicago, wondered why the Reformed Church was paying for Tambo's body guards. John Hubers, a pastor in New York, and John Beardslee III, a professor at New Brunswick Seminary, asked the Reformed Church to listen to Tambo. Hubers noted that the American government had

[49]   *Acts and Proceedings*, 1991, 336-37; 1994, 34-35.
[50]   In 1986 apartheid was still the law of the land in South Africa. Nelson Mandela was still in prison. Critics said the African National Congress was a terrorist group. Supporters said it sought civil rights.

used violence in many situations. Beardslee reminded readers that the United States had accepted Soviet help in World War II and wondered why black South Africans should be denied similar aid.[51]

The issue became even more complicated when Robert Schuller, pastor of the Crystal Cathedral, barred Tambo from speaking there, lest Tambo's remarks damage the church's public relations or incite violence. Schuller's abrupt decision raised numerous logistical questions only a month before the synod. It also raised the issue of authority. Did the host church have the right to control the guests of the General Synod? The Reformed Church staff and General Synod officers considered moving the synod to a different location, but no appropriate site could be found on such short notice. Moving the synod out of southern California would have been very costly. Staff and officers finally decided to move the speech and that session to the Doubletree Hotel, where the delegates were staying. Meanwhile, Tambo was invited to speak to the United Nations International Labor Organization in Paris during the week of synod, so the ANC sent its secretary general, Alfred Nzo, in Tambo's place.[52]

When the synod began its work, Howard Davis called for a boycott of the Nzo session and received some applause. Eugene Sutton, an African American pastor from an inner city church in Muskegon, Michigan, received even more applause when he asked delegates to have the dignity and compassion to listen. Most delegates attended both Nzo's speech and a question and answer session following it. Nzo insisted that the African National Congress was not a terrorist organization. Delegates listened carefully. No one disrupted the presentation from Nzo or boycotted the daily worship services led by Robert Schuller.[53]

The synod's actions sparked several critical letters to the *Church Herald* insisting that the Reformed Church should not involve itself in political and social issues like the cause of the African National Congress, because delegates did not understand political issues and frequently took actions that supported communism. These writers believed that the Reformed Church was losing members because of its misguided

---

[51] John Stapert, editorial, "Explicit and Implicit Endorsements," *CH*, May 23, 1986, 5; Howard Hoffman, letter to the editor, May 23, 1986, 21; Howard Davis, letter to the editor, June 6, 1986, 19; Don den Hartog, John Hubers, John Beardslee III, letters to the editor, June 27, 1986, 16-17.

[52] John Stapert, editorial, "Synod's Sites," *CH*, June 27, 1986, 5. See the collection of letters regarding this issue in the General Synod Archives.

[53] John Stapert, editorial, "A Splendid, Even Temper," *CH*, July 25, 1986, 4-5; "ANC Rejects Terrorist Label," June 25, 1986, 6-7.

commitment to social issues. If it focused on the fundamentals of its relationship to the Lord and scripture, it could again be a "winning team." Don den Hartog suggested that if the synod had invited Billy Graham to speak instead of Nzo, the denomination might have been helped to reverse its declining numbers.[54]

This event demonstrated that the Reformed Church still had major disagreements about the role of the church in politics and economics. Robert Schuller advocated an apolitical stance for his congregation, and many members agreed that the church had no business meddling in South Africa. Others insisted that the Christian faith required them to take a stand against the degradations of apartheid.

Consultation on Church Union

A second divisive issue in the late 1980s rehashed an old ecumenical debate in the Reformed Church about the appropriate level of participation in the Consultation on Church Union (COCU). The consultation began in the 1960s with a grand plan to merge several mainline Protestant denominations. By the mid-1980s, COCU had adopted the more modest goal of cooperation. The Reformed Church had always held observer status in COCU but defeated every proposal for full membership.

The Commission on Christian Unity discussed COCU in 1987 but decided the Reformed Church was not ready for full membership. Meanwhile, the Particular Synods of New York and Mid-Atlantics did think the church was ready and submitted overtures to the Synod of 1987 asking that the Reformed Church become a full member of COCU.[55] At the synod, the advisory committee somewhat surprisingly voted 13-11 to recommend full membership. In the ensuing floor debate, supporters argued that ecumenical relationships were important and that full membership would give the RCA more input into the documents and the process that the consultation produced. They cited Jesus' prayer for unity in John 17.

Critics of full membership said that the Reformed Church already had influence as an observer and did not need to be further entangled in the process. One delegate feared the creation of a super church, and another argued that Jesus was not talking about bureaucratic unity in John 17 but about unity of spirit. These arguments were nearly identical

---

[54]   T. E. Werkema, Arnold Albers, Don den Hartog, letters to the editor, *CH*, Sept. 5, 1986, 19.

[55]   Full membership meant ten members rather than three observers, and the privilege of comment and vote.

to arguments for and against ecumenism used in 1949 and 1969. The recommendation to become a full member in COCU lost by two votes.[56]

The Commission on Christian Unity interpreted this close vote as a sign that the Reformed Church might indeed be ready for full membership, and the commission began to educate the church through mailings, classis presentations, and articles in the *Church Herald*. The opponents persisted as well. One letter writer pleaded, "With all due respect to the sincerity of those who are pushing COCU again, please, enough is enough. Exciting things are happening in the Reformed Church, and further controversy over COCU will merely further polarize our church and divert our energy."[57] Critics saw COCU as a highly bureaucratic and outdated idea that would not bring unsaved people to Christ.[58]

Despite these objections, the Commission on Christian Unity proposed full membership to the Synod of 1988. Two delegates predicted (or perhaps threatened) that the Putting People in Mission fund drive would fail if the denomination joined the consultation. Another delegate denounced that as blackmail. The synod voted against full participation for the second time.[59]

The denomination debated full membership in COCU again in 1990, but by that time critics had become angrier and hinted at schism. Howard Davis, a pastor in Grand Rapids, Michigan, said,

> We have been increasingly pushed away from fellowship and life in the Reformed Church. This issue may become the proverbial straw that breaks the camel's back. I only hope that when the denomination splits that it will [be] amiable and that we will be allowed to keep our buildings and our people....If you want the RCA to persevere as a separate denomination, vote against COCU; if you want church union, vote for it.[60]

---

[56] John Stapert, "RCA Edges toward COCU, Stays in WCC," *CH*, July 17, 1987, 10-11.

[57] Clinton Baker, letter to the editor, *CH*, May 6, 1988, 21.

[58] John Stapert, editorial, "What COCU Membership Means," *CH*, April 15, 1988, 4-5; Tom Stark, Morris Kronemeyer, letters to the editor, *CH*, May 20, 1988, 21. Critics of COCU disliked some of the practices that had been proposed for the Uniting Church, particularly the hierarchy of the bishops, the lack of ordained lay offices, and the need for previously ordained people to experience a new laying on of hands with the bishop present.

[59] The Classis of Columbia-Greene overtured for full membership in COCU, and the classes of Zeeland and Illinois and the Synod of Mid-America asked that the RCA not become a full member. *Acts and Proceedings*, 1988, 187-90, 202-03; Christina Van Eyl, "Still Watching: Synod Says No to COCU," *CH*, July 22, 1988, 6-7.

[60] Christina Van Eyl, "Information Please: COCU on Hold until 1992," *CH*, July 1990, 16.

The synod postponed its decision, and in 1992 the Commission on Christian Unity recommended that the Reformed Church postpone indefinitely the question of full membership because of the vigorous opposition and clear lack of consensus within the church. The purists had prevailed with the support of the conservatives. Moreover, since COCU no longer included observers as part of its deliberative process, this decision ended the Reformed Church's involvement.[61]

The Consultation on Church Union was a lively and intriguing idea when it was first proposed in the heyday of the mainline denominations in the early 1960s, but it did not capture people's imagination when it took institutional form. The concept was vague and abstract and required a great deal of debate about structures and offices. It did not offer much "pay-off" in the way of mission or relationships. Denominations were convinced that they could manage on their own. Purists in the Reformed Church thought that COCU endangered the church's identity and doctrinal integrity, and many conservatives agreed. Moderates were not opposed to COCU, but even they were not certain it was a cause worth fighting for.

The Limits of Salvation

The third issue that tested the limits of diversity during this period was theological. In the mid 1980s, Richard Rhem taught preaching at Western Seminary while continuing to serve as pastor of one of the largest churches in western Michigan, Christ Community Church in Spring Lake. Rhem published an article in *Perspectives,* a theological journal published jointly by the Reformed Church and the Christian Reformed Church, citing biblical and theological evidence for universal salvation. The article sparked a great deal of criticism, despite the fact that it was a position which could be supported by Reformed theology. Rhem chose not to enter the fray of debate and simply resigned his position at Western Seminary. He may have concluded that he would not receive much support from either Western Seminary's administration or the Board of Theological Education. Rhem was one of the most creative theologians and successful pastors in the Reformed Church, but the controversy sent a rather chilling message that some kinds of thinking were not welcomed. At the same time, if Rhem had chosen to defend himself and his position at the seminary, the furor

---

[61]   N.a., "COCU: The End is Here," *CH,* July/Aug., 1992, 13; *Acts and Proceedings,* 1992, 208. For a history of COCU, see *Acts and Proceedings,* 1992, 248-57.

might have died down without further incident. The purists may not have had sufficient influence to remove him from teaching.[62]

Homosexuality

During the 1970s, the Reformed Church discussed the controversial topic of homosexuality several times, and the Commission on Theology produced two papers which did not approve of the "homosexual lifestyle" but advocated civil rights for gay and lesbian people. In the mid-1980s, however, the rapid spread of the AIDS virus sparked considerable anxiety and discussion within the denomination. Kim Baker, managing editor of the *Church Herald*, encouraged Christians to respond compassionately to the AIDS crisis. He wrote, "AIDS is also not the result of God's righteous anger toward homosexual behavior. Even if one believes that homosexuality is sinful, God does not inflict illness as punishment." Several angry letters responded that AIDS was indeed God's judgment on the sin of homosexuality.[63] Lu Ann Ritsema, of New York City, was discouraged by the callous tone of these letters. While Christians debated whether homosexuality was sinful, she said, people were dying. They needed to know that God loved them, and they needed to be treated with dignity and compassion.[64]

In their report to the synod in 1987, the Christian Action Commission encouraged education about AIDS.[65] Arnold Albers, a layperson from California, responded, "Trying to cure AIDS while ignoring the cause is like trying to cure a high fever while ignoring the infection that caused it." He labeled AIDS a "deadly terrifying disease brought on by perversion" and advocated striking at its source—the homosexuals and drug users.[66] In 1988, the Christian Action report discussed the relationship between disease and sin, recommending that the synod "reject the perception that AIDS is the judgment of God on

---

[62] Richard A. Rhem, "The Habit of God's Heart," *Perspectives*, Sept. 1988, 8-11. A number of responses followed in subsequent issues: William Brownson, "Hope for All," Oct, 1988, 13-15; letters, Jan, 1989, 14-15, Feb. 1989, 14, March 1989, 12-13. Less than a decade later, purists again complained about Rhem, this time because a group of gay and lesbian Christians were given worship space in Christ Community's building. Much debate followed in the Classis of Muskegon, and eventually the church left the RCA, with its property, setting a new precedent for denominational polity.

[63] Kim Baker, editorial, "The AIDS Challenge," *CH*, Jan. 16, 1987, 4-5; Letters to the editor, *CH*, Feb. 20, 1987, 22; March 7, 1987, 19.

[64] Lu Ann Ritsema, letter to the editor, *CH*, April 3, 1987, 18.

[65] Christina Van Eyl, "General Synod Tackles Social Witness Agenda," *CH*, July 17, 1987, 12-13; *Acts and Proceedings*, 1987, 58-59.

[66] Letter to the editor, *CH*, Aug. 14, 1987, 20.

homosexuals, drug users or any other group of people." Critics wanted to delete the phrase because they believed that AIDS *was* the judgment of God. After lengthy debate, the synod approved an amendment which said, "To reject the perception that AIDS, among the variety of tragedies that can follow upon actions of fallen humans, is in any particularly discernable sense a judgment of God."[67] The commission also made a recommendation that called on those in at-risk categories to refrain from practices that may further spread the disease. It was amended to ask "everyone" to do this, and then was adopted.[68]

A year later, the Synod of 1989 made a more inclusive and gracious statement about gay and lesbian people. The Task Force on Racial Justice[69] submitted a long list of recommendations to the synod. When the Advisory Committee on Christian Action discussed the task force's report, it added an additional recommendation that members of the Reformed Church "create a climate within the church whereby all persons will be truly accepted and treated as God's children." When the entire synod discussed this recommendation, an amendment was proposed which specified the inclusion of women, people with disabilities, and people of various language groups, ages, and sexual orientations. A number of delegates spoke in opposition to the reference to sexual orientation, but an amendment to delete this phrase was not approved. The synod approved both the recommendation and the more inclusive and specific amendment. It had explicitly welcomed all of God's children.[70]

Two letters in the September issue of the *Church Herald* reflected sharp differences in opinion about this statement. One letter thanked the Reformed Church for helping create an accepting environment for people of homosexual and bisexual orientation. The other insisted

---

[67]   Christina Van Eyl, "Christian Action: Social Concerns Fuel Debate," *CH*, July 22, 1988, 14-16; *Acts and Proceedings*, 1988, 76.

[68]   *Acts and Proceedings*, 1988, 77. This raises an important question about the purpose of a General Synod recommendation. Did commission members and synod delegates believe that members of high-risk groups were eagerly waiting to hear what the RCA would tell them to do?

[69]   The Task Force on Racial Justice was formed in 1986 to propose specific actions which would make RCA leadership and structure more inclusive of its racial/ethnic members.

[70]   *Acts and Proceedings*, 1989, 72-82. The amended recommendation read: "To call upon the members of the RCA to create a climate within the church whereby all persons will be truly accepted and treated as God's children, particularly women; persons with physical and mental disabilities; persons of various ages, language groups, and sexual orientation; and persons of other categories commonly discriminated against."

that this action wrongly encouraged homosexuality by suggesting that it was an acceptable lifestyle. "The RCA must not compromise its values by attempting to appease every type of behavior in the world. Some things are wrong and it must be clearly stated they are wrong and the RCA does not approve."[71] For the next five years (and beyond) the Reformed Church debated the meaning and implications of this radically inclusive action that said that everybody was welcome in the family.

The question Leonard Kalkwarf posed in 1984, "What is the glue that holds us together?" appeared relatively straightforward, but it proved remarkably difficult to answer. The search for identity did not produce a clear and compelling biblical, theological, or ecclesial image or concept that could serve as glue for the Reformed Church. The denomination returned to its default mode, as it were, and emphasized that it was a family. Members were linked by kinship and connection and to some degree by ethnicity. The Identity Task Force also emphasized the diversity within the Reformed Church and claimed that RCA members could think differently about ecumenism, biblical interpretation, theology, and social issues, yet still be part of a family. That claim was challenged more sharply, however, as tensions increased. Opponents of COCU threatened to withhold money from PPIM and even mentioned the possibility of schism. Could the family hold together when people did not get along? What if some members cared more about demanding purity than preserving relationships? How much diversity could the Reformed Church handle?

1990-1994: The Mood Shifts

If the theme of the 1980s was "we are [trying desperately to be a] family," the theme of the 1990s might be "we are a family frayed and stretched." There was a sense of increasing desperation in the Reformed Church during the early 1990s, in part due to a growing sense of loss. There were 207,474 active communicants in the denomination in 1987, but 202,959 in 1989. Fifteen years of church growth initiatives had not reversed the decline. The denomination in general and congregations in particular felt pressure to grow in order to survive. Some purist voices re-emerged and suggested that the denomination would grow if it returned to biblical literalism and emphasized personal morality rather than social issues. Some leaders committed to church growth argued that the denomination should focus most of its energy on starting new

---

[71]   Todd VerBeek, Donald Cowell, Flak and Flattery, *CH*, Sept. 1989, 8.

churches rather than waste resources on irrelevant or controversial issues. Still other members were concerned about the loss of loyalty and connections within the denomination. As in previous decades, there were several different ideas about what kind of church the Reformed Church should be.

Those who suspected that Reformed Church members had become more diverse had their suspicions confirmed after another denominational survey. Hope College sociologists Donald Luidens and Roger Nemeth again surveyed RCA members in the early 1990s.[72] They found that 65 percent of easterners and 93 percent of those from the Midwest and Far West believed that humans were sinful by nature. Fifty-nine percent of easterners and 90 percent of others regarded the Bible as authoritative for their faith. Thirty-four percent of easterners and 59 percent of others believed their salvation was determined by God before birth. Easterners were less likely to support banning abortion and more likely to support homosexuals as school teachers.[73] In all of these measures, there was a significant difference between eastern members and those from the rest of the denomination.

When Luidens and Nemeth reported their data to the General Synod, they drew more explicit conclusions than in the articles.

> The regional differences which have long crosscut the RCA are now very plain; there are clearly different perceptions of what it means to be an active RCA member. While this paper does not call for the creation of uniformity or unanimity, it is imperative that the RCA reaffirm the differences and find ways to creatively encourage their healthy interaction. Left to the present pattern, it is very likely that one segment of the denomination will assert its hegemony over the other, thereby alienating a significant segment of the RCA and undermining the denomination's viability.[74]

---

[72] The data showed more women than men at all ages. Twice as many young women were confirmed as young men. Since 1976 the number of women in the denomination had grown from 116,000 to 137,000, but the number of men dropped from 100,000 to 65,000. The RCA had also become somewhat more Dutch, probably because more non-Dutch members had left.

[73] Donald Luidens and Roger Nemeth, "In Search of the RCA," *CH*, Sept. 1992, 8-11; "In Search of the RCA, Part 2: What We Believe," Oct. 1992, 8-10; "In Search of the RCA, Part 3: How We Stand on Social Issues," Nov. 1992, 8-10. In the three eastern synods, from 9-21 percent supported banning abortion and 26-36 percent supported homosexuals as teachers. In the western synods, 48-62 percent supported a ban on abortion and 10-21 percent supported homosexuals as teachers.

[74] *Acts and Proceedings*, 1992, 414-19.

Luidens and Nemeth concluded that despite the regional differences, Calvinism was alive and well in the Reformed Church. The majority of clergy and lay people affirmed God's involvement in history, the authority of the Bible, and the covenant between God and Christians through Christ. They were committed to worship and shared a common faith. "The test of the RCA for the near future will be its members' commitment to continue to pull together despite the differences highlighted in these studies, as the Reformed Church seeks to faithfully serve Jesus Christ."[75]

This approach to family differences was cautiously optimistic. Luidens and Nemeth believed that Reformed Church members did not all have to think and act alike in order to be part of the family. The denomination did not have to be monolithic in order to function well. The denomination had always encompassed diverse opinions, and it had survived. The danger was not diversity but trying to eliminate diversity in favor of a single point of view. The Reformed Church could be a family, these analysts thought, even if not all members were the same. Other members disagreed strongly. They did not approve of this kind of flexibility and tolerance, and they urged the Reformed Church to adopt a narrower identity that would exclude some people and perspectives.

Denominational unity and identity would be tested during the next few years by several topics: (1) a debate about homosexuality, (2) church growth initiatives, (3) the growth of Canadian churches, (4) a new denominational governing body, (5) a new policy for distributing the *Church Herald*, and (6) the issue of homosexuality revisited.

Homosexuality: Part I

The period from 1990 to 1994 began and ended with debates over homosexuality. In general, most Reformed Church members took one of three positions. Some members insisted that homosexual people had made a sinful choice to be gay or lesbian. Others differentiated between sexual orientation and sexual activity. They were willing to be gracious to those who were gay or lesbian in their orientation as long as they were not in a relationship. Still others saw a homosexual orientation as an in-born trait. This meant that it was perfectly natural for them to be in a relationship with someone of the same sex.

In March 1990 the *Church Herald* printed an essay about homosexuality in "Platform," a frequent op-ed column written by

---

[75] *Acts and Proceedings*, 1993, 376-82.

various authors. Author Todd VerBeek challenged several stereotypes about gay people. They do not choose their orientation, he said, and can rarely, if ever, change it. Children cannot be recruited to become gay. Homosexuality is not a mental disorder. Long-term monogamous relationships are possible. He briefly discussed some of the biblical passages cited against homosexuality but noted that when the Bible condemned homosexual behavior it did not refer to mutual, loving relationships. VerBeek did not believe God would exclude people from grace for feelings they did not choose to have. Many Christian homosexuals prayed to be different, but God did not change them. He concluded, "Society shouts that the love we feel is wrong. But prayerful meditation quietly assures me that mutual love in the context of a greater love for God can only be good. My faith is in the loving God who speaks to me in that still, small voice."[76]

The *Church Herald* printed two pages of negative letters in response to the article. These critics said VerBeek had twisted scripture. They insisted that gay people do choose their lifestyle, children can be recruited, and those who choose to continue in homosexuality are not welcome in the church. Abe Vander Weide, a layperson from Florida, wrote, "When we start saying homosexuals are born that way, we take away the sinfulness of their actions." Several writers took the magazine to task for publishing the essay, even though "Platform" articles included a disclaimer that they did not necessarily represent the views of the magazine or the denomination. Art VanderMeulen, a minister from Canada, wrote, "By allowing that article to be printed, you are contributing to the erosion of our denominational unity by challenging the General Synod through improper channels." The elders of the Calvary Reformed Church in South Holland, Illinois, said that there may be two sides to many issues, but not to this one. The consistory of the Unity Reformed Church in Kentwood, Michigan, said that the article "has surely done much harm by upsetting and confusing people and has certainly not been edifying to our church as a whole.... Many will see it as an expression of acceptable Reformed theology and that is certainly regrettable."

Two positive letters praised the essay and the magazine for re-examining an issue in the light of current medical and biblical scholarship.[77] Two months later, Nancy Meehan Yao argued that homosexuality was *not* a choice:

[76] "Living in Sin?" *CH*, March 1990, 7.

[77] Flak and Flattery, *CH*, May, 1990, 4-7. The writers who defended VerBeek were John Beardslee III and John de Maagd, both in their seventies and respected figures in RCA missions and education.

If, as most research shows, homosexuality occurs as a genetically induced characteristic, then to ask people to give up their "sexual perversions" would be the same as asking people with other genetic diseases to give them up in the name of Christ—as if it were a matter of will alone. It behooves us as children of God, as well as members of the church in the twentieth century, to accept these people as they are. God certainly does, and Christ certainly died for their sins too. Is homosexuality a sin? That is for God to decide, not we fallible humans.[78]

The debate continued at the General Synod in 1990. The Classis of Illiana and the Particular Synod of Mid-America asked the synod to amend the statement adopted in 1989 that specified acceptance regardless of sexual orientation. Both offered as a reason, "It is an exploitation of women, persons with physical and mental disabilities, persons of various ages and language groups to be linked by association with people of various sexual orientation—a group which is frequently distinguished by public advocacy of sinful behavior." The connection "sets back efforts to reduce discrimination against these other groups." The synod did not rescind the 1989 statement but voted "to call upon the members of the Reformed Church in America to create a climate within the church whereby all persons commonly discriminated against will be truly accepted and treated as human beings created in God's image."[79]

The Classis of Cascades overtured the synod to adopt the 1978 paper on homosexuality as the Reformed Church's official position. After lengthy discussion the advisory committee recommended instead, "To adopt as the position of the RCA that the practicing homosexual lifestyle is contrary to scripture, while at the same time encouraging love and sensitivity toward such persons as fellow human beings."A motion to refer the recommendation to the Commission on Theology for study was defeated. In the discussion on the floor of synod, Jonathan Gerstner, executive secretary of the Council of the Reformed Church in Canada, "called the issue of homosexuality a *status confessionis*, that is, a non-negotiable, non-debatable part of Christianity." He claimed that if the Reformed Church said clearly that homosexuality was sinful, a number of United Church of Canada congregations might join the denomination. A few voices protested what they saw as the misinterpretation of scripture or the exclusion of certain people,

---

[78]   Flak and Flattery, *CH*, July 1990, 6.
[79]   *Acts and Proceedings*, 1990, 459-60.

but most delegates agreed with Tom Stewart, a pastor in Oklahoma, who insisted that if the synod delayed a decision, "people will say we are wishy-washy on sin." The synod approved the recommendation disapproving of the "homosexual lifestyle" but encouraging love and sensitivity.[80]

It was a rather odd process. The synod first refused to refer the issue to the Theological Commission for further study. Instead, it made a definitive statement driven by the fear of being "wishy-washy on sin" and by the desire to draw new members to the Reformed churches in Canada. After adopting the statement, the synod allowed that perhaps the issue should be studied after all and recommended that the Commission on Theology conduct a new study on homosexuality.

The 1978 and 1979 papers on homosexuality included some perceptive biblical and theological reflection, but after a decade they were already dated. They used offensive and inappropriate language (perverts and inverts) to describe gay and lesbian people, and they did not reflect research and insights from the intervening decade. To their credit, however, the papers recognized that some gay and lesbian people were not able to change their orientation and they insisted on full civil rights for homosexual people.[81]

Over the next two decades, a growing number of Reformed Church members argued that being homosexual was not a choice but a biological given, and that people who did not choose their orientation should not be punished with required celibacy or the constant judgment that they are wrong, "disordered," psychologically unhealthy, or sinful. As more members began to articulate this belief, the conflict increased as well.[82]

---

[80]   Jeffrey Japinga, "Policy: Reject Lifestyle, But Not Gay Persons," *CH*, July 1990, 10-11; *Acts and Proceedings*, 1990, 460-62.

[81]   Some RCA members continued to resist further study and discussion. A *Church Herald* columnist raised some questions he thought the church should consider, but letter writers immediately responded that the RCA did not need to ask these questions because it was obvious that homosexuality was a "curse and a detestable sin." The RCA did not need a committee to study the question. Gay people simply needed to repent and change. Gregg Mast, "Questions of Homosexuality," *CH*, Sept. 1991, 49; Flak and Flattery, Nov. 1991, 4-5, Dec. 1991, 5.

[82]   A group called Room for All was founded in 2005 to provide support and advocacy for gay, lesbian, bisexual, and transgendered people. In 2009 Room for All held a conference at the Central Reformed in Grand Rapids, MI, and local chapters continue to hold monthly meetings in a number of cities with multiple RCA churches. One of the most controversial events in the recent history of the RCA has been the trial and suspension of the Rev. Dr. Norman Kansfield, former president and professor of theology at NBTS. This occurred at the synod meeting in 2005. He had conducted the marriage of his daughter to her female partner in a state that

Church Growth

The Reformed Church had devoted significant resources and attention to church extension since 1975. The Particular Synod of the West had been the most successful in starting new churches. Between 1974 and 1986 it started fifty-eight churches, and by 1987, fifty-one of them had meaningful ministries with full-time pastors. Eleven congregations spoke other languages, primarily Korean. Chester Droog, the field secretary, attributed the synod's success to population density, an inflow of people into southern California, a clear target group, and the right leadership. Droog said, "Church planters must be positive, optimistic, loving people. They must be people with a dream. They must have an incredible desire to succeed, must be risk takers, willing to work, and be motivators of people. I doubt whether you can teach these to people who do not demonstrate these qualities."[83] The synod had tried a variety of models, but Droog said, "We do best when we do our demographic home work, select the right leadership, purchase a site of three to five acres, and help the young congregation—through denominational loans—to construct its first phase building within five years. This has resulted in the most self-supporting, growing churches in the RCA." Church growth was actually quite predictable, he concluded. Failures usually resulted from choosing the wrong leadership or thinking there was an exception to one of the rules.[84]

The fact that the Synod of the West had been so successful at starting and retaining new churches meant that it became a role model

---

recognized gay marriage. For a discussion of the issues raised in the trial, see Donald J. Bruggink, "Extra-Canonical Tests for Church Membership and Ministry," in *A Goodly Heritage: Essays in Honor of the Reverend Dr. Elton J. Bruins At Eighty*, ed. Jacob Nyenhuis, HSRCA, no. 56 (Grand Rapids: Eerdmans, 2007).

[83] This model of a young, energetic, creative, hard-working, entrepreneurial pastor was becoming something of a norm or ideal. While there were certainly many other ways to be faithful pastors, this model tended to be the most acknowledged and rewarded. In 1990, the 98 by '98 proposal for new church development said that "the most important ingredient in any new church start is the founding pastor." In 1991, church start pastors began to be introduced at the synod as missionaries had been in the past. *Acts and Proceedings*, 1990, 317; 1991, 30-31.

[84] Chester Droog and John Stapert, interview, "Lessons from RCA Church Growth," *CH*, May 1, 1987, 16-17. Between 1973 and 1983, the Synod of the West organized one more church than all the other synods combined. Population growth contributed to its success, as nine of the ten fastest-growing counties in the U.S. were within the synod's borders. The Synod of the West included the classes of California, Cascades, Central California, Rocky Mountain, Southwest, Central Plains, Dakota East Sioux, Minnesota, Pella, Pleasant Prairie, Red River, and West Sioux. In 1990 this large synod divided into two: Heartland and Far West.

for the entire denomination. Some Reformed Church members argued that the denomination would be far healthier if all regions adopted the evangelical, pragmatic, and entrepreneurial emphases that had worked so well in the West. This argument often failed to consider the dramatically different patterns of population growth and decline in the East and Midwest where Reformed Church congregations were present.

The church growth movement also gained influence as members of the Far West were put into positions of leadership. Beginning in 1984, several General Synod presidents were elected from this region.[85] The formation of the Theological Education Agency gave pastors in southern California more authority to shape seminary training. In 1990, the particular synod split in two, and the Synod of the West became the Synod of the Heartland and the Synod of the Far West.

Church growth seemed to be a unifying force, but some of its assumptions and strategies raised serious theological questions. The Synod of 1990, for example, adopted a directional statement entitled "Building the Church for the 21st Century." It included these pledges: "We will add to the church a great company of believers in Jesus Christ"; and, "In obedience to our Lord's Great Commission and in reliance on the Spirit's power, we seek to enlarge and extend our community of faith, as all our members are nurtured, educated, and equipped for ministry and witness."[86] This statement illustrates a recurring theological tension between Reformed and evangelical perspectives. The Reformed doctrine of predestination had always insisted that God was responsible for church growth. God would save those whom God had chosen.[87] The phrase "we will add," on the other hand, suggests that human effort brings members to the church. Critics said it was presumptuous to tell God to start ninety-eight churches in a decade, because God worked mysteriously and freely, not necessarily according to human plan. Supporters of church growth insisted that they relied on God's Spirit, but they also wanted to obey the Great Commission in

---

[85]   Kenneth Leestma, Robert Wise, Harold Korver, Steve Brooks.

[86]   *Acts and Proceedings*, 1990, 350.

[87]   For the first two centuries after John Calvin, churches in the Reformed tradition were not particularly focused on missions. Their belief in predestination led many of them to believe that God would save those whom God had chosen. The belief in predestination could also lead to a sense of superiority among those who considered themselves God's chosen people. Despite these significant drawbacks, the strength of the Reformed belief in predestination was the reminder that salvation was God's work, and that Christians did not need to be so anxious about it. Under the influence of evangelicalism, the RCA's view of church growth has shifted further away from the Reformed side (which seemed too passive) and more toward the idea that church growth is solely the church's responsibility.

Matthew 28. They believed that God worked through human structures to start churches and save souls and that Christians were called to cooperate with God in that work.[88]

Despite these differences in theological emphasis, denominational leaders hoped that purist, conservative, and moderate members could find unity in this common mission of building new churches.[89] But the emphasis on church growth actually sparked considerable debate and highlighted some of the major differences among the regions in terms of social context, economic resources, and beliefs about the role of the church.[90]

In 1990, the General Synod considered an extensive proposal for church growth called "98 by '98: A Plan for New Church Development in the Reformed Church in America." The goal was to start 98 churches by 1998. The proposal began with a summary of RCA membership numbers. From 1950 to 1967, the denomination grew from 187,257 to 232,978 communicant members. In 1990 the RCA had 204,545 members. The three western synods had started 59 churches between 1965 and 1988 and gained 24,211 communicants, while the three eastern synods had lost 52,252 communicants and 27 churches. The report acknowledged that these statistics did not take population shifts into account, and yet it concluded that because the Reformed Church grew in regions where new churches were started, that meant new church development must be given top priority.[91] It was not said explicitly, but there appeared to be an underlying suspicion among some Reformed Church members that eastern churches did not grow because they lacked doctrinal purity and a deep commitment to evangelism.[92]

[88] The statement, "Building the Church for the 21st Century," reflected some of this tension. It said, "Aware that the future is in God's hands and in reliance on the Spirit's power," and yet clearly emphasized the responsibility of the church to add new members. *Acts and Proceedings*, 1990, 350.

[89] Richard Welscott, "Choices for the Future," *CH*, April 1990, 18-19. Welscott led church growth efforts in the Particular Synod of Michigan during the 1980s and later took on the leadership of church growth for the entire denomination.

[90] Compare, for example, the goals that each region set for growth in 1987. The Synod of Mid-America hoped to start twelve new churches by 1995. The Synod of Michigan planned thirty-two in the next decade. The Synod of the West planned to start thirty churches every decade. The Synod of the Mid-Atlantics had recently started four new churches. The Synod of Albany was nurturing its congregations and teaching people how to evangelize. The Synod of New York focused its resources on supporting its fifty-four city churches, including eighteen Asian congregations that had recently been started and the twelve to fifteen more the New York Synod hoped to start in the next decade. "Regional Church Growth Programs," *CH*, May 1, 1987, 18-19.

[91] *Acts and Proceedings*, 1990, 313-20.

[92] Henry Bast said this explicitly about eastern churches in 1946.

The emphasis on church growth sparked debate about the recipients of the denominational growth efforts. Who was the Reformed Church trying to reach? The 98 by '98 proposal noted that the denomination had traditionally appealed to people who valued doctrine and education. "The RCA has not done well in terms of maintaining self-sufficient, indigenous congregations in the lower socio-economic strata or the higher socio-economic strata. Historically speaking, this means that the RCA has drawn its members primarily from people who live in homes that have one and one-half to two and one-half bathrooms."[93] Delegates raised a number of questions about this assumption. Did it mean that the Reformed Church was not particularly interested in starting congregations in urban areas and less financially stable neighborhoods? If the denomination had focused specifically on middle-class people because they were a good "fit," was that evidence of clear "branding?" Or had the denomination failed to welcome and include people who did not share the same economic resources?[94] These questions were vigorously debated at the Synod of 1990 but not resolved.

The proposal to establish ninety-eight new congregations within the next decade passed unanimously. Reformed Church members at all points on the theological spectrum could support church growth.[95]

John Stapert noted that delegates at the 1990 synod were feisty and argumentative. They frequently challenged the chair and called for divisions of the house in voting.

> Still, these were not unpleasant delegates. They engaged in the warmest of conversations over coffee and lunch. Vigorous opponents on the floor became chatty compatriots during recesses. Some who disagreed about homosexuality joined each other in late-evening prayer. In other years, people of like mind would have joined only their friends at lunch and would not have built bridges during the evenings.

He concluded that diverse opinions had become the norm in the denomination. Tolerance and patience needed to be the norm as well.[96]

---

[93] *Acts and Proceedings*, 1990, 317.

[94] John Stapert, "A Plan to Grow," *CH*, July 1990, 8-9.

[95] During the next two decades, the RCA put more and more of its resources and energy into starting new congregations and revitalizing existing ones. This emphasis has indeed helped unify the denomination, but it has also raised questions about priorities. As church growth receives more resources, education, worship, social witness, and world mission seem to receive less. It has been a challenge to retain balance.

[96] Editorial, "A Landmark Synod," *CH*, Aug, 1990, 4. As noted above, however, it was at this synod that Howard Davis predicted a split in the RCA if COCU was approved. Van Eyl, "Information Please," *CH*, July 1990, 16.

Not everyone was as hopeful as Stapert. There were a number of examples in the early 1990s of growing anxiety about the fraying of the family. Some people suggested that more love and kindness would keep the family together. Others emphasized the need for Reformed Church members to obey the rules and believe the right way.

In an effort to pull the family together, the denomination returned to a strategy that had worked well following the Synod of 1969. In 1988, the synod's president, Robert Wise, proposed that the Reformed Church hold another festival, and a committee developed the Praise and Promise Festival to be held in southern California in July 1991. When Edwin Mulder invited Reformed Church members to attend the festival, he used the theme of family. Relationships were fragile, he wrote, and the denomination needed civility, forgiveness, understanding, and encouragement. "As never before we need to be committed to the church as family. In this day of individualism it is possible for individuals to think that they do not need family. They are wrong. No Christian exists in isolation from the rest of the family; neither should congregations exist apart from other members of the family." The RCA is a connectional church, Mulder wrote, and if it is to be vital, its members need to be committed to its life and witness.[97]

The Praise and Promise Festival was a positive event, with keynote speeches by Louis Lotz and Henri Nouwen. Only six hundred people attended, which was one-third to one-half of the number expected initially. It was neither as transformative nor as controversial as some of the earlier festivals. In part, attendance was low because California was not centrally located. Nearby Disneyland did not draw families as organizers had hoped, and the California heat was less appealing in July than it might have been in January.[98] A vacation with the Reformed Church did not attract members in 1991 as it did in the 1970s.

Oh, Canada

Another significant denominational conflict in the early 1990s arose out of the growing influence of the Reformed churches in Canada.[99]

---

[97] Edwin Mulder, "All in the Family," *CH*, June 1991, 18. Early in the planning process, Robert Wise went on sabbatical and then left his church, so the initiator of the idea was no longer part of the planning.

[98] John Stapert, "Six Hundred Gather for Praise and Promise," *CH*, Sept. 1991, 36-38.

[99] There were about thirty-five RCA churches in Canada in 1990. Nineteen were in the Classis of Ontario and one was in the Classis of Lake Erie (both part of the Regional Synod of Michigan). Fifteen were in the Classis of Cascades and part of the Regional Synod of the Far West. These churches had about seven thousand members. As part of the restructure, two new classes were formed from the old

In 1989 the Emerging Synod of Canada hired Jonathan Gerstner[100] as executive secretary and established two goals. It intended to form a new regional synod for the churches of Canada, and it wanted to increase the Canadian churches' numbers and influence within the denomination. One way to expand the numbers was to bring in already established churches. On September 24, 1989, four congregations and six pastors from the United Church of Canada (UCCan) transferred into the Reformed Church. They had been anxious about the direction of their former denomination and were particularly angry when the Canadian denomination had declared that membership and ordination were open to all Christians regardless of sexual orientation. Gerstner assured these congregations and pastors that the Reformed Church in Canada offered them a more congenial (and theologically conservative) home. This action raised a number of questions about ecumenical propriety, but the denomination as a whole could do nothing to prevent Gerstner from recruiting disaffected churches, because classes had the right to receive new congregations.[101] Gerstner's supporters believed that they were acting graciously in welcoming displaced congregations into the Reformed Church family.

In May 1991, ecumenical officers from the United Church of Canada criticized Gerstner and Gordon Ross (the newly hired director for church development in the Emerging Synod of Canada) for encouraging UCCan congregations to join the Reformed churches in Canada. Such ecclesiastical "sheep-stealing" was not considered good manners in ecumenical relationships. Gerstner dismissed the charge, claiming that commitment to the gospel was more important than honoring the ecumenical old boys' league of either the World Alliance of Reformed Churches or the Canadian Council of Churches. Gerstner thought the United Church of Canada had given up essential

---

Classis of Cascades: British Columbia and Canadian Prairies. Each had fewer than a dozen churches and a thousand members.

[100] Gerstner received a BA degree from Michigan State and an MA from the University of Chicago. He spent a year studying in Utrecht and a year at Stellenbosch, then earned a Ph.D at Chicago. He was ordained by the Classis of Chicago and held several short-term jobs. He left the RCA in 1995. Gerstner did not grow up in the RCA but probably made the connection while at Michigan State. He presented himself as a strong leader with the answers for Canada, but he did not know the whole of the RCA very well. After a few years in his position, some Canadians (and certainly many others in the denomination) found his leadership rather authoritarian. See letters and papers in the General Synod Archives.

[101] Case Koolhaas, with Jeffrey Japinga, "A Growing Family: Classis Cascades Welcomes New Members," *CH*, Nov. 1989, 33-34. Congregations that left the UCCanada could not take their buildings with them and needed money to build.

parts of the gospel; therefore, the Reformed Church should welcome those who could no longer live within it. John Stapert observed that Gerstner also had a larger agenda—to reform the Reformed Church in America. "Theologically, Gerstner sees the addition of conservative UCC [Canada] congregations as an opportunity to help the RCA clarify its thinking about the core issues of the Christian faith."[102] Gerstner had a great deal in common with the purists of the 1940s, although he was not raised in the Reformed Church. He did not approve of the church's broad and inclusive identity. He wanted it to be much more conservative and narrow.

A number of moderate Reformed Church members disapproved of Gerstner's actions and attitudes regarding the United Church of Canada. At the Synod of 1991, Arie Brouwer asked that the delegates be given Stapert's editorial about Canada and copies of all denominational correspondence with the United Church of Canada so they could be adequately informed. The president, John Hiemstra, ruled the request out of order but the delegates overruled him. The Advisory Committee on Christian Unity discussed the issue at length. The committee offered this recommendation: "To affirm the efforts of RCA denominational staff and the Commission on Christian Unity to resolve the complex ecumenical concerns with the United Church of Canada and the Reformed Church in Canada."After much debate and repeated attempts to amend and postpone, this and other recommendations were approved. The synod also approved a motion from the floor which said, "To welcome our new brothers and sisters in Canada and assure them of our love and support as they enter the Reformed Church in America family of faith."[103] Gerstner was not satisfied with these statements and asked the Reformed Church to admonish the United Church of Canada for supporting the homosexual lifestyle and call it back to purity and biblical Christianity. Several delegates said this action was inappropriate because delegates had not read the United Church's position papers on the issue. No admonition was sent.[104] Church growth that resulted from welcoming unhappy members of other churches was clearly a mixed blessing.

Six months after this synod meeting, the Emerging Synod of Canada used its page in the *Church Herald* to introduce one of the new pastors. A.G. Skelly, a former UCCan pastor who transferred to the

---

[102] "Migrating UCC Churches Swell RCA Ranks in Canada," *CH*, May 1991, 43-45.
[103] *Acts and Proceedings*, 1991, 191-93.
[104] "Canada and The Right to Know," *CH*, July/Aug, 1991, 10-11.

Reformed Church in Canada, had visited the General Synod meeting in 1991 and was discouraged by what he called a "family squabble" over the reception of UCCan pastors and congregations. He had not realized there was so much diversity in the Reformed Church. Skelly explained that he did not leave the UCCan but realized that the denomination had left him when it questioned the uniqueness of Jesus. He insisted that he came to the Reformed Church in Canada on his own initiative. "I was not approached or bribed or wooed. I am aware that there has been some concern at the ecumenical level about 'sheep stealing' on the part of the RCA, but I have not seen a single shred of evidence of such activity."[105] It is telling that Skelly spoke of entering the Reformed Church in Canada and not the RCA as a whole and then was surprised by the diversity he witnessed at the synod. Perhaps Gerstner had implied that everyone in the Reformed Church believed just as he and some of the Canadians did, rather than present a more nuanced portrait of a denomination that disagreed about significant issues.

Paul Nulton, a pastor in New Jersey who had previously served an RCA church in Alberta, wrote a "Platform" essay defending the Reformed churches in Canada. He believed that some United Church pastors showed a "lack of sensitivity for the Scriptures and little comprehension of Christ as Savior." If some of the conservative pastors made the costly and painful decision to leave the UCCan because of its stance on the Bible and homosexuality, Nulton said, Reformed churches should welcome them, not quibble about ecumenical niceties. The RCA should not try to defend the actions of the UCCan, he said, but confront them with their sinfulness and try to lead them to repentance. That would be true ecumenicity.[106]

The Regional Synod of Canada was formed in the fall of 1993. It was the largest geographically and the smallest numerically with seven thousand members. Gerstner wrote that one of the goals of the new synod was to

> help the whole RCA move into the future as an evangelical denomination with a vision for the future....All of us need to invest to insure that the General Synod keeps making decisions which are faithful to Scripture, please the Lord, and further his kingdom. The Regional Synod of Canada has grown because of the RCA's uncompromisingly biblical stand on sexual ethics. It

---

[105]   A.G. Skelly, "A New Beginning" (Regional Spotlight: Emerging Synod of Canada), *CH*, Jan. 1992, 44.

[106]   Paul Nulton, Platform, "Ecumenicity and Sin," *CH*, Oct. 1991, 6.

is in everyone's interest to be faithful to Christ and to seek his guidance.[107]

In 1994 Gerstner accepted a call to Knox Theological Seminary in Fort Lauderdale, Florida, to become a professor of church history and apologetics. Looking back over his five years in Canada, he reflected that welcoming the congregations from the United Church of Canada had been a highlight of his ministry. It demonstrated that Christians had a right and responsibility to leave a communion that denied basic Christianity. He considered the formation of the Regional Synod of Canada another high point. "I am convinced the synod will be a leader in the RCA in spiritual and theological issues, indeed, as the conscience of the denomination."[108] Gerstner was a purist who did not trust other denominations and perspectives, but the Reformed Church as a whole largely resisted his efforts to lead it in a more purist and evangelical direction.

General Program Council Restructure

The denomination continued to struggle with financial issues. Although the synod had approved an assessment to fund discipleship and church extension, the General Program Council still did not receive enough contributions. At the same time, the dual GSEC/GPC structure had become increasingly unwieldy and required a great deal of meeting time and preparation for both staff and committee members. The General Synod Executive Committee appointed a committee of lay and clergy leaders to explore a possible new structure for the denomination.[109]

The initial proposal envisioned a single structure, the General Synod Council (GSC), composed of about thirty people who would also be voting delegates at the General Synod. The General Synod would

[107] Jonathan Gerstner, "A New Creation," *CH*, Oct. 1993, 43. The formation of a new synod was important because a number of committees/commissions in the RCA were composed of representatives from each regional synod. The Reformed Churches in Canada wanted to be a distinctive entity and not be subsumed in and divided among synods composed primarily of American churches.

[108] Regional Spotlight: Synod of Canada, "Gerstner to Leave Regional Synod of Canada," *CH*, June, 1994, 55. It is interesting that Gerstner tried to introduce a certain kind of evangelicalism into the RCA, much as Henry Bast and Louis Benes had in the late 1940s.

[109] Members of the committee included Wilma David, Jeanette Doyle, Edwin Mulder, Eugene Pearson, Herman (Bud) Ridder, George Smith, Donald Troost, Marlin VanderWilt, Carl Ver Beek, and Kenneth Weller. Alvin Poppen and Ellen Mers staffed the committee. *Acts and Proceedings*, 1991, 57-79.

meet every other year, and all delegates would attend two consecutive synods. The Editorial Council for the *Church Herald* would be eliminated, and the editor would answer to a denominational vice-president for communication. The president of General Synod would travel less and would no longer make a report to the synod. Assessments would increase about three dollars per member in order to fund all of the denomination's work except world mission.[110] This new structure met with resistance from many quarters. Although it would have promoted efficiency, it also reduced representation in favor of a highly centralized and powerful body.

After a great deal of discussion throughout the church,[111] the proposal was changed to expand the General Synod Council from thirty-six to sixty, so that each classis could elect a representative. A third of the members would be women,[112] and half lay people, with proportional representation from the ethnic groups. Council members would not be voting delegates at synod. There would not be a new assessment. The *Church Herald* would maintain an independent editorial board. The synod would shrink from 277 to 189 delegates but remain an annual event for at least three years. The general secretary would give an annual report, but the president would continue to travel and also present a report, in order to continue a non-staff voice in a position of influence.[113] With these changes in place, the synod approved the new structure in 1992.[114]

The General Synod Council was supposed to save the denomination $170,000 a year, but this was not enough to solve the budget problems. In late 1991 the General Program Council said it might have to bring seven missionary couples home because it lacked the resources to pay them.[115] Congregational giving in 1991 had increased only 1.4 percent over 1990. In response to the shortfall, the GPC conducted an unprecedented direct mail solicitation at the end of 1991, sending

---

[110]   John Stapert, "Key Issues in RCA Restructure," *CH*, June 1991, 6-7.

[111]   Thirty-seven meetings drew fifteen hundred people during the fall of 1991.

[112]   Clarence Toren argued in a letter to the editor that only the most qualified people should serve on GSC, and gender should not be a criterion. If membership in GSC was strictly based on the proportions of denominational membership, a two-thirds quota of women would be more appropriate than one-third. But quotas were not a biblical method of choosing leaders. Clarence Toren, Flak and Flattery, *CH*, Sept. 1992, 4.

[113]   Jeffrey Japinga, "New Structure Takes Shape Slowly," *CH*, Feb. 1992, 36.

[114]   "A New Look: Restructure Ratified," *CH*, July/Aug., 1992, 11-12; *Acts and Proceedings*, 1992, 42-80.

[115]   Jeffrey Japinga, "Budget Crisis Threatens GPC Programs, Positions," *CH*, Dec. 1991, 37-38.

appeal letters to 5,600 people (ministers, missionaries, members of GSEC and GPC, and names submitted by members of GPC and GSEC). The appeal brought in $241,000, but it also generated considerable criticism that direct solicitation undermined congregational giving. Supporters insisted it was a necessary counter to the dozens of appeals church members received from other, nondenominational agencies. Reformed Church members needed to know what the denomination did, Mulder said, and have opportunities to support it.[116]

The Synod of 1992 approved a new $1.50 assessment for the Discipleship and Church Planning Divisions of the General Program Council, and $.75 for a staff position for youth and young adult ministry. But perhaps the most significant issue at the 1992 synod was a proposal made by its president, Louis Lotz, regarding the *Church Herald*.

Changes at the *Church Herald*

In 1991, John Stapert had resigned as editor of the *Church Herald*, and managing editor Jeffrey Japinga was named as his replacement.[117] The magazine had become a monthly in 1988 and had won several awards for design and content, but circulation continued to decline as churches cut costs by discontinuing the practice of purchasing a subscription for every member.

Louis Lotz, a pastor in Sioux City, Iowa, and a regular columnist in the magazine, had been elected president of the General Synod in 1991. When he gave his report in 1992, unlike some presidents who named a dozen problems and made a dozen recommendations, Lotz diagnosed one problem in the Reformed Church and offered one solution. The problem, he thought, was fragmentation within the denomination. Congregations and individuals were not linked to each other or to the larger church. The Reformed Church needed sidewalks that would connect Florida to Canada and East to West. Lotz offered as a solution what he called a marvelous but enormously unpopular idea. He proposed that the Reformed Church send the *Church Herald* to every household as a benefit of membership, just as organizations like AAA and AARP automatically sent magazines. The tab of $4.87 per member was admittedly significant when the denomination and local churches were struggling to make their budgets, but Lotz pointed out that, for

---

[116] Edwin Mulder, "A People Who Respond," *CH*, April 1992, 11.

[117] Japinga was trained as a journalist, worked for *Guideposts* magazine, and graduated from NBTS in 1987. He had no experience as a parish pastor other than a brief but successful period as the pastor's husband.

a couple, this was less than the price of a pizza.[118] To the amazement of skeptical observers, the advisory committee recommended approval, and there was relatively little debate on the floor. Vice-president Beth Marcus asked for a standing vote, and a large majority of delegates rose to vote yes. A radical proposal, especially in the face of the long-term and steady decline of subscriptions, was approved with little dissent because of the president's persuasive power.

Louis Lotz was a personable and engaging leader. He focused his entire report on one recommendation, thereby accentuating its importance and urgency. His leadership throughout the week of synod was easy-going and humorous. The synod caught his passion and good will and approved his idea. Indeed, the synod conducted itself as a united family.

The editor likely had some impact on the decision, as well. Lotz asked Jeff Japinga to lead worship during the week. Some delegates saw this as an inspired move; others saw it as manipulative. Most delegates agreed that worship was thoughtful and innovative and created a favorable impression for the magazine.[119] The Every Family Plan was a significant move toward greater denominational identity and loyalty.

The synod continued this generous positive spirit as it dealt with more than a dozen overtures from South Grand Rapids Classis asking for specific cost-cutting measures. The classis proposed eliminating the archivist position, the part-time ecumenical officer, and full-time positions for the racial-ethnic councils. The reasons repeated in most of the overtures were greater efficiency and cost-savings, but the delegates were not impressed with the attempt to micromanage. Most overtures were minimally debated, if at all, before being voted down, but not before they had created anxiety among the staff people whose positions were at stake.[120]

The Synod of 1992 was marked by good will and generosity, but it was much more difficult to convince those who had not been present that the new assessment was a "marvelous idea." Tom Stark called it "fiscal irresponsibility" to raise assessments while failing to replace retiring missionaries.[121] Several people argued that the idea had been rushed through and needed more study. Others insisted that people needed to be free to choose whether to receive the magazine themselves. Mulder's correspondence files contain dozens of angry letters

---

[118] *Acts and Proceedings*, 1992, 28-31.
[119] "The President's Report: Building a Sidewalk," *CH*, July/Aug., 1992, 8-9.
[120] *Acts and Proceedings*, 1992, 80-91.
[121] Tom Stark, *Flak and Flattery, CH*, Sept. 1992, 4.

complaining about the expense and the imposition. To each of these complaints he responded that members of the synod had voted for the assessment because they thought it was a good idea. He encouraged people to give the magazine a chance, to trust each other, and to see themselves as part of a family.

The *Church Herald* hired a journalist from outside the Reformed Church to write an article about the debate. He reported that people complained most frequently about the cost and whether this was the best use of a million dollars. Small churches said they could not afford it. Some people wondered whether the magazine would retain its editorial freedom or if it would become a mouthpiece for denominational bureaucrats or be dominated by purists or moderates. Others protested that the decision had been imposed on church members without giving them a choice. Some critics suspected that Lotz had pushed the idea through at the General Synod because delegates had only a few days to consider it. Mulder pointed out that it was a democratic decision made by a representative government. All 287 people from 44 classes had time to discuss and review the proposal, and the majority voted for it. No one was coerced. Louis Lotz framed the debate in terms of community and individuals. "Do we intend to remain a choir, or are we going to become more and more a collection of soloists?"[122] The debate about the magazine touched on questions about money, power, trust, and what it meant to be a denomination.[123]

At the Synod of 1993, eighteen classes sent overtures to abandon or change the assessment.[124] The reasons given were similar to those noted above, with a few additional arguments: the magazine did not always represent the moral and doctrinal positions of the congregations; people had no interest in the magazine and many copies were wasted when sent in bulk to churches that would not release their mailing lists; the Canadians wanted to receive their own magazine, the *Pioneer*, instead; the money should be used for mission; one brand of theological

---

[122] Ed Golder, "Cracks in the Sidewalk," *CH*, April 1993, 8-10. The author was the religion editor for the *Grand Rapids Press*.

[123] In 1992 the GPC received income of $445,000 more than it spent, due to a 5 percent increase in contributions and a 2 percent decrease in spending. Despite all the complaints about not having enough money, people were able to give. RCA News, "GSEC: The Financial News is Positive," *CH*, May 1993, 10.

[124] Albany, California, Columbia-Greene, Florida, Greater Palisades, Illiana, Lake Erie, Mid-Hudson, New York, Passaic Valley, Pleasant Prairie, Red River, and Schenectady asked that the assessment be discontinued. Cascades, Montgomery, New Brunswick, Ontario, and Rockland-Westchester asked that the assessment be changed or that the question be studied further.

thinking could gain control; people should not be forced to pay for something they did not choose.

Assessments had increased 246 percent in five years, which placed a heavy financial burden on congregations. Pleasant Prairie Classis wrote, "The constantly increasing assessments are contrary to the biblical concept of stewardship. Giving should be done gladly, regularly, sacrificially, and out-of-the-heart as God has given to us. Giving should not be legislated and demanded as RCA assessments are doing." Some of the angry responses seemed disproportional, as when the Classis of Columbia-Greene wrote that having the magazine forced on them had led to "major difficulties, angry feelings, and extreme reactions." To force people to receive it was at worst reprehensible, at best ill-advised, and not tactful. The classis concluded, "This situation is appalling and carried denominational authority to dangerous and potentially self-destructive extremes."[125]

Despite this criticism, the advisory committee assigned to consider these overtures gave thirteen reasons to continue the assessment for the magazine. Communication was important, and the magazine was of high quality. Moreover, in the face of the fragmentation about which Lotz warned, the *Church Herald* could build unity and identity. Congregations who could not pay could receive relief from assessments. The magazine was worth the cost.[126] Those who read it appreciated it, and they recognized that the magazine did provide the kind of information about the denomination that was helpful for members to know. The discussion on the floor of synod was relatively brief, because after about eight speakers, someone called for the question. The synod voted 170 to 81 to continue the assessment for the magazine.[127]

Nevertheless, debate persisted for another year. The General Synod Council hired the Gallup organization to study the content of the magazine and hold five town meetings across the country. The council concluded that the magazine was of high quality and that people were willing to work with the Every Family Plan, so they recommended that it continue. At the Synod of 1994, Marilyn Rottschafer, a delegate from the Christ Community Church in Spring Lake, Michigan, said she came from a large ecumenical church and wanted the right to choose. The church sent a letter to all the delegates that read, "To be forced to promote the denomination is to betray our vision and the sense of who we are." The letter also stated that the magazine had become

---

[125]   *Acts and Proceedings*, 1993, 189, 180-81.
[126]   Ibid., 168-69, 179-91.
[127]   "*Herald* Plan Stays," CH, July/Aug., 1993, 13.

an institutional promotional piece which should not be forced on congregations. Despite the criticism, the synod concluded once again that "the *Church Herald* has earned its place as a significant vehicle of communication in the denomination."[128]

Homosexuality Revisited

At the General Synod of 1994, the issue of homosexuality was reengaged. In 1992 the Commission on Theology had formed a Task Force on Homosexuality to conduct the new study that the synod had requested in 1990.[129] The task force held a forum at the synod in 1993 during which 150 people talked in small groups about how their perceptions of homosexuality had been formed. The task force decided not to present a formal paper to the synod in 1994, in part because the conversation at the 1993 synod and the committee's process led the members to conclude that the Reformed Church needed conversation about the issue rather than another position paper. The task force and the Commission on Theology recommended that congregations, classes, and synods "enter into a season of discovery and discernment guided by study, prayer, listening, and discussion." The key term in this list was the notion of "discernment," during which all options were theoretically open.

The advisory committee discussed the topic for three hours and finally voted 10-7 to recommend that the General Synod deny the proposal from the task force. An article in the *Church Herald* summarized the essence of the discussion: "The time for talking about this issue is past, the majority said; we know what we believe, and we cannot compromise those beliefs. We need simply to act on them." The

---

[128] Jeffrey Japinga, "Keep the Presses Rolling," *CH*, July/Aug., 1994, 12-13. The magazine went to every family for about fifteen years until 2007, when the assessment was redirected into church extension and the magazine again had to operate by subscription. Despite the fears expressed in the 1990s that the magazine would become a "house organ" or a public relations piece rather than continue as an independent entity, in 2007 a frequent complaint was that the magazine did not promote the denominational program adequately. In 2009, the synod voted to cease publication of the magazine. Some of the assessment money was given to fund the production of a "house organ," *RCA Today*.

[129] Todd VerBeek asked if there would be gay and lesbian people on the task force, noting that the denomination would not constitute a task force on women or ethnic minorities or people with disabilities without including them. But there were no gay or lesbian people on the task force. Flak and Flattery, *CH*, Sept. 1993, 5. Fourteen years later another committee was formed to design a process to discuss the issue, and it had no gay or lesbian people either.

minority believed there was always time for serious inquiry into the Word, and that the church must always be open to new insights.[130]

When the proposal came to the floor, discussion continued in the same vein. Steve Hoogerwerf, chair of the task force, pointed out that the discernment process offered an opportunity to listen and learn. It was not a process that would inevitably lead to the adoption of a secular gay rights agenda, but a way to begin to overcome years of misunderstanding. Opponents insisted that the church did not need such a process because it already knew the answer, and discernment was simply an underhanded way to change the church's position. Encounters with gay and lesbian people did not matter. Personal feelings and experience did not matter. Homosexuality was sinful, and although the church should minister lovingly to gay people, the church must be clear in its condemnation.

There was no consensus and little room for compromise between purists and moderates. The synod recessed for lunch and afterwards decided to follow its stated agenda rather than return to the debate. That night Hoogerwerf (professor of Christian ethics at Hope College), David Timmer (professor of philosophy and religion at Central College and chair of the Theology Commission), Jim Brownson (professor of New Testament at Western Seminary), and pastors Dave Van Lant (California), Dave Landegent (Illinois), and Ken Korver (California) met to try to find a compromise. The next morning, Hoogerwerf and Korver stood together at a microphone and presented a substitute recommendation that called Reformed Church members and churches to a place of repentance for failing to live up to its pastoral statements on homosexuality, and to a process of prayer, learning, and growth in ministry. The recommendation asked the Commission on Theology to develop a study guide and collect models for ministry to help local congregations. Discussion was brief, the recommendations were approved, and delegates sang the doxology.

John Hesselink, the newly elected vice-president, called the decision not only the high point of this General Synod but of any he had attended. Kevin Korver called it a miracle and said it established the Reformed Church as a leader of denominations. "For one shining day," Jeffrey Japinga wrote, "the church came together on an issue that has been deeply divisive."[131]

The 1994 miracle got the delegates through the week, but not through the issue itself. Unity was achieved temporarily by finding

---

[130] Jeffrey Japinga, "Maybe a Miracle Happened," *CH*, July/August, 1994, 7-8.
[131] Ibid.; *Acts and Proceedings*, 1994, 370-78.

a basic point that all could agree on. Certainly the church could and should agree on repentance and the value of learning and prayer. But the denomination had already decided in 1990 that homosexual practice was sinful, not as a result of a new study of the biblical texts or a process of discernment, but in reaction to the AIDS crisis and increasing cultural discussion about gay rights and inclusivity. A study guide[132] was published and discussion has been encouraged, but the Reformed Church has not formally changed the basic position it took in 1990.[133]

Since the 1994 action, some Reformed Church members have sharply criticized other denominations that have taken a more inclusive stance on this issue. This criticism has affected ecumenical relationships with the United Church of Canada and the United Church of Christ. The debate also sparked several serious questions that have not yet been answered: How does the Reformed Church read the Bible? Who can be welcomed into the Reformed Church? Why is there so much conflict about this issue? How much dissent can the denomination accept? On what basis are critical issues debated and denominational positions determined?

A Final Note on the RCA as Family

Edwin Mulder announced in 1993 that he would retire in 1994. In his last year as general secretary, he was still trying to encourage the Reformed Church to act like a family. He wrote several articles about denominational identity. He noted in February 1993 that some congregations refused to send their membership lists to the *Church Herald* because they did not want them used for fund-raising. Mulder wrote, "The local congregation and the denomination are not adversaries. We are family. We are partners." Mulder emphasized that the denomination was not trying to steal money from congregations but wanted to offer individuals the opportunity to give to denominational causes.

---

[132] *Homosexuality: Seeking the Guidance of the Church* (Grand Rapids: Reformed Church Press, 1996).

[133] In 1997 the synod approved the Formula of Agreement between three Reformed denominations (the RCA, the United Church of Christ, and the Presbyterian Church/USA) and the Evangelical Lutheran Church in America. A number of overtures in the next few years protested the relationship because the UCC allowed gay and lesbian people to be ordained. Similar overtures were sent in 2010 after the ELCA decided to allow the ordination of gay and lesbian ministers in committed relationships. For a more extended discussion see Norman J. Kansfield, "The Reformed Church in America: One Denomination's Response to Same-Sex Marriage," in *Defending Same-Sex Marriage*, ed. Traci West, Vol. 2 (Westport, CT: Praeger, 2007), 191-210.

The following month, Mulder described the declining relevance of denominations. In the past, he wrote, denominations had identified themselves by ethnicity or ethical conduct (no drinking, dancing, movies, etc.) or by what made them theologically distinct, but now Christians emphasized their religious experiences and talked about similarities rather than differences. Still, Mulder believed denominations had a role. "The denomination is us. It is 967 congregations comprised of 340,000 baptized members. It encompasses our history, liturgy, standards, polity, programs, and institutions." Just as human beings cannot live without a body, he continued, the church cannot be a spiritual being without a body. The church has taken concrete form in denominations, and it is through these concrete forms that God's mission is carried out in the world.[134]

The search committee for the next general secretary announced in May 1994 that it had nominated Wesley Granberg-Michaelson. Granberg-Michaelson was raised in an evangelical family with Swedish roots. His parents went to Wheaton College. He went to Hope College, where he met Karin Granberg, whom he would later marry. He worked in Washington D.C. for Senator Mark Hatfield and was affiliated there with the Church of the Savior. He graduated from Western Seminary in 1984, worked with the New Creation Institute in Montana, and joined the staff of the World Council of Churches in Geneva in 1988. He had not served as a pastor of a Reformed church.[135]

The choice of Granberg-Michaelson as general secretary says a great deal about the church's shifting identity. The fact that he was not RCA-born and bred and had little pastoral experience and little connection to the Reformed Church suggests that the search committee believed that traditional RCA connections and practices were not essential for the leader of the next phase of denominational life. One reader protested that selecting a candidate who worked for the World Council of Churches was a slap in the face to conservatives, especially "those in the Midwest and West who make up a majority of the membership and do most of the bill paying for the denomination. To have a WCC executive running the day-to-day business of the RCA is simply not in the best interests of our denomination."[136]

---

[134] "Jesus and Me, but What about You?" *CH*, Jan. 1993, 12; "The Reformed Connection," Feb. 1993, 11; "Constantly Being Reformed," March 1993, 22.

[135] Wesley Granberg-Michaelson, with Jeffrey Japinga, "Taking a Closer Look," *CH*, July/Aug., 1994, 15-17; Wesley Granberg-Michaelson, "Fleshing out My Faith Journey," Nov. 1994, 12-13.

[136] Phillip Van Dam, Flak and Flattery, *CH*, June 1994, 4.

The Synod of 1994 celebrated Ed Mulder's retirement. It also wrestled with a number of difficult issues in addition to homosexuality. Delegates from the North Grand Rapids and Muskegon classes were not officially seated because the classes had not paid their full assessments. The Christ Community Church in Spring Lake, Michigan, withheld the assessment for the *Church Herald* in what it considered an act of civil disobedience. Christ Community thought of itself as liberal and open minded and did not want to force its congregation to read the denominational magazine. The Seventh Reformed Church in Grand Rapids, Michigan, was a purist church and refused to pay assessments because it had theological and philosophical differences with the denomination. Both churches had resources to pay their assessments, but both refused and their classes chose not to pay for them.[137]

Both Christ Community and Seventh Reformed demonstrated purist tendencies, albeit from different ends of the theological spectrum. Both left the denomination within a few years because they could not remain part of a family that was too liberal (for Seventh) or too narrow (for Christ Community). Both churches had something of a superiority complex. Both lacked patience for the gritty work of belonging to a diverse denomination. Their departures, however, were the exception. Most congregations chose to stay with the Reformed Church, even if they were irritated with certain of its actions. It wasn't perfect, but the denomination did function as a kind of family, and most congregations remained loyal in affiliation if not always in theory and practice.

The family metaphor was becoming more problematic, however. What did family mean, exactly? The Reformed Church clearly welcomed white, middle-class families who lived in homes with two and one-half baths. Were members of other racial/ethnic groups welcome? Did they belong? The Reformed Church claimed to welcome everyone, but its actions did not always match its words, and members of racial/ethnic groups often felt excluded and disempowered. Were moderates welcome? If the majority of the members were more conservative, did moderates still have a voice and a place in the family? How much diversity of opinion could the family tolerate?

The increasing diversity and fragmentation meant that family ties were much more tenuous. Pastors who did not attend a Reformed Church college or seminary did not have the same friendship network that Edwin Mulder did. Purists and moderates were less likely to be good friends despite their differences. During some of the debates of

---

[137] Jeffrey Japinga, "Ten Empty Seats," *CH*, July/Aug., 1994, 9.

the 1990s, a mean-spirited edge frequently appeared, as it had in the late 1940s, 1969, and 1979. A few people threatened schism.

The purist tendency had been very evident during the 1970s in the debate concerning the ordination of women, but it appeared far less frequently during the 1980s. It reappeared in 1990 when the purists were galvanized by the issue of homosexuality, which encompasses a number of challenging questions: biblical interpretation, sexuality, gender roles, purity, qualifications for leadership, and ecumenism. It is an issue that the Reformed Church has not been able to resolve, and it continues as a source of profound anxiety.

There were many reasons for anxiety during the 1980s and 1990s. The denomination continued to lose members. Some members felt the loss of comfortable old patterns of worship when their organ and hymnbooks were replaced with a drum set, guitars, and a screen. Others thought that the church had lost its influence in society. Some Reformed Church members and pastors grieved the loss of what seemed to be traditional and comfortable and meaningful about church life. Others welcomed and encouraged change. In the midst of all this loss and change and growth, denominational identity was unclear. What was absolutely clear, however, was that loyalty to the denomination could no longer be assumed. "You can't tell us what to do" continued to be a powerful theme in the life of the Reformed Church.

Under the leadership of Wesley Granberg-Michaelson, the Reformed Church would again turn to church extension (framed as multiplication and revitalization) as a way to transcend its differences. This strategy would be effective in many ways, but, as in previous decades, it did not resolve the underlying tensions, which continue to erupt. Reformed Church identity has become more evangelical and more shaped by church growth. Ironically, it is now the moderates who appear most committed to Reformed theology, polity, and liturgy, although in a very different way from the purists of the 1940s and 1960s. The identity of the Reformed Church in America is still fragmented and contested.

EPILOGUE

Think back once more to the members of that clean cut, well-dressed family described in the introduction, who typified the Reformed Church in the post World War II years. Then consider what a typical family looks like *now* when it arrives at church. Family members come in two separate cars, because the teenagers want to be dropped off at the mall after church and the younger son has a soccer game. The older son is wearing sagging pants and headphones. The daughter is wearing a mini skirt and a cropped top and is constantly texting on her cell phone. The younger boy is wearing his soccer uniform. They are late, because all three kids had to be "convinced" to get out of bed for church. No one carries a Bible. No one is smiling.

Perhaps this picture is a bit exaggerated. Perhaps all the families in your church do arrive smiling and on time and carrying Bibles. But it is unlikely. American culture has changed dramatically in the last fifty years, and Sunday mornings in particular have been affected. Church services now compete with sports, movies, shopping, and restaurants. Church members (and often their pastors) dress much more casually. If they bring a Bible, it's likely to be found on their phone. Families are

301

busy and fragmented, and the church is not likely to be the center of their lives in the ways it was in 1959.

If families have changed so radically, what about the metaphor of the church *as* a family? Can a congregation—much less an entire denomination—still call itself a family?[1]

The family metaphor may be irrelevant now. Most Reformed Church laypeople did not attend an RCA college, so they do not have ties to members in other areas of the country. They might not know anyone who attends another Reformed church. It is possible that they know little or nothing about the denomination's beliefs, history, and mission, perhaps because their local congregation downplays its denominational connections. The family metaphor also implies a certain degree of congeniality. Does the Reformed Church still possess enough of these good feelings? We all know families fight, but this study suggests that its members fight most of the time! Can the Reformed Church be a family when its members don't seem to like or trust each other? The family metaphor has lost its appeal as the American family—and the Reformed Church—has become more fragmented and problematic.

The family metaphor has also fallen out of favor because it seems exclusive in this age of increased diversity. Can the family include people whose skin is a different color? Who speak a different language? Who live in a different part of town? Who have more or less education? "Family" has often suggested that the Reformed Church was primarily for white, Dutch people. But the denomination is much broader and more welcoming than that. The image of the Reformed Church as family clearly has its limits. But this study also demonstrates that the metaphor has held abiding power for many ministers and some laypeople who have a web of relationships and connections to other people in the Reformed Church. They have close friends from college and seminary. They are related to other members. They served on committees together or attended a General Synod in the same year. Many people with these relationships feel a strong tie to the Reformed Church, and they are often deeply loyal. They care about the church enough that when the denomination betrays or excludes or disappoints, they feel a correspondingly deep sense of personal loss. If they didn't care, it wouldn't matter what the denomination did. But they do care. If someone asks them why they stay in a church that can be so conflicted

---

[1]   In his report to General Synod as president in 2011, the Rev. Donald Poest suggested that the metaphor of the body for the church was better than the family, in part because members of a body could not choose to opt out or leave the body, as they could a family.

and hurtful, they might say, "Because it's *my* church." For these people, the Reformed Church *is* a family. Sometimes a dysfunctional, troubled family, yes. But a family to whom they feel connected. The Reformed Church can be a place where people feel welcomed and valued. It can be a place where people belong.

It can be these things. But often it is not. Conflict has been a painful reality in denominational life. Different segments of the church have very different histories and cultural contexts. They look at the world and the church in very different ways. The reality of conflict within the denomination should not surprise us, and yet it continues to catch us off guard. The immediate response is often to view conflict as evidence that people are sinful, selfish, and stubborn. That may well be true. But the stories told in this book suggest that conflict happened because people cared enough to fight. They loved the church, and they wanted it to live up to its potential. Conflict arose out of loyalty and commitment, not their absence.

Conflict also arises out of loss. Some Reformed Church members think the church is not as meaningful or spiritual or pure as it once was, and they grieve the loss. Their memory may be rosier than the reality, but they still feel that something precious is missing. When they try to get it back...whether "it" be morality or connectedness or inspiration or purity or openness, conflict can ensue.

Conflict also arises out of anxiety and fear. In a time of massive change, can the church be preserved? Can the church survive when it has lost so many members and so much funding? Can the church be culturally relevant without losing the heart of the gospel? If the future of the church depends on human effort, there will be a great deal of debate over what kinds of effort ought to be made.

At its best, I believe the Reformed tradition offers an antidote to this anxiety. It does not give easy answers, but it is substantive, thoughtful, meaningful, and comforting. It is able to deal with ambiguity, doubt, and questions. It is biblical without being literalist. It is personal, but it also values the community of the faithful.

Reformed theology demonstrates a profound sense of human sinfulness and divine grace. Our clever plans and goals, our purity, our intellects, and our good behavior are all compromised by the persistent power of sin, even in the lives of Christians. Salvation is not something we accomplish for ourselves. It is the gift of God, who reaches out to those who, in the words of the baptismal liturgy, "know nothing of it yet." Scripture shows over and over again how much God loves the world and how doggedly loyal God is, even in the face of human sin and brokenness. In love and loyalty, God reaches out, over and over, drawing God's people into God's heart. Salvation is not ultimately about our decisions or our beliefs or our efforts or our purity. Salvation is God's work and God's gift.

This conviction has at times led the Reformed tradition to arrogance and passivity, but it should not. God calls us to show similar grace and loyalty to the world in which we live. If grace could fully shape the life of the church, what would it look like? If God is welcoming, inviting, saving, transforming, and forgiving, how could the church imitate and live out God's work? How could the church be so transformed by the grace and loyalty of God that it could not help but be gracious to others?

This Reformed vision of God as gracious and loyal might help Reformed Church members live with their differences. Disagreement is inevitable in a denomination that encompasses as much diversity as the Reformed Church does. The worst periods of conflict—the most painful and angry moments—have come when people were unable to be gracious to each other. In 1949, in 1969, in 1979, in 1990, and at many other times, people on both sides of the argument have been mean spirited and judgmental. They have questioned the faith and commitment of other church members. They have dismissed one another. They have refused to have difficult conversations with each other. They have assumed they have all the answers. They have been driven by fear. These attitudes have been all too common in the Reformed Church, and they have caused profound damage to individuals, congregations, and the denomination itself.

In the midst of all this, there have also been profound signs of grace. Several practices or attitudes have helped hold the Reformed Church together in the years following World War II.

The first was worship. Some General Synod meetings have been marked by excellent preaching and worship services. Sharing in meaningful worship can lessen the impact of conflict. Communion services have often been particularly transformative, as at the two festivals. The intimacy of eating and drinking together helps break down barriers.

The second was conversation. When synod meetings include time for delegates to talk without debating and deciding, those meetings are often more gracious. The exchange groups of the early 1970s and the more recent discernment groups have shifted the focus from argument to listening.

The third was the *Church Herald*. It was valued by many. It was also criticized at various times, and deservedly so. But despite its failings, it provided a shared space for communication that was invaluable to the well-being of the denomination.

The fourth was a sense of connection. Those who feel that they are known, that they belong, and that they are loved and cared for are not likely to leave. For better or worse, the Reformed Church does function like a family. One of Louis Lotz's most memorable columns in the *Church Herald* told the story of a crusty mountain man in his southern parish who appeared on the doorstep of a young pregnant woman who had been too embarrassed to go to church. The man gave her a fistful of cash and said, "You're family. Don't you forget it, neither." Lotz thought that the best thing he could do as president of the General Synod was to "stand on the doorsteps of people who feel that they don't matter and tell them what they need to hear and must believe: 'You're family. Don't you forget it, neither.'"[2]

The fifth is humility. At their best, Reformed Church members recognize that they are not the only true church, and they do not have all the answers. They cannot be arrogant, but they need not be fearful.

The sixth is that the Reformed Church may be, in Justin Vander Kolk's words, "the most stubborn people on earth." Perhaps congregations have stayed in the Reformed Church primarily because they technically cannot take their property with them if they leave. But there is evidence of a tenacious loyalty among many members—purists, conservatives, and moderates alike. They *belong*, to God and to each other, and that bond is not easily broken. They may be furious with the denomination at times, and yet they stay. It is where they have their roots, and it is where they have found their wings.

The Reformed Church is still one denomination. It has been held together by relationships, by connections, even by the sense that it is a family. It has been held together by mission, in the world and the community. It has been held together by ethnicity and now, it is hoped, by a commitment to welcome people of many different ethnicities. It has been held together by deep loyalty and by a stubborn refusal to give up. It has been held together by worship and by a desire to make a difference in the world. Ultimately, it is held together by trust that the brokenness of humanity is transcended by the grace and loyalty of God.

[2] "You're Family," *CH*, Sept. 1991, 50.

Name Index

Subject Index